# Organizational Risks, Challenges, and Barriers in Developing Sustainability Start-Ups

Kyla Latrice Tennin
*College of Doctoral Studies, University of Phoenix, USA*

A. B. Mishra
*International Institute of Management Studies, Pune, India*

IGI Global
Scientific Publishing
Publishing Tomorrow's Research Today

Vice President of Editorial Melissa Wagner
Director of Acquisitions Mikaela Felty
Director of Book Development Jocelynn Hessler
Production Manager Mike Brehm
Cover Design Jose Rosado

Published in the United States of America by
IGI Global Scientific Publishing
701 East Chocolate Avenue
Hershey, PA, 17033, USA
Tel: 717-533-8845
Fax: 717-533-7115
Website: https://www.igi-global.com E-mail: cust@igi-global.com



Library of Congress Cataloging-in-Publication Data

Names: Tennin, Kyla L., DATE- editor. | Mishra, A. B., DATE- editor.
Title: Organizational risks, challenges, and barriers in developing sustainability start-ups / edited by Kyla L. Tennin, A. B. Mishra.
Description: Hershey, PA : Business Science Reference, [2025] | Includes bibliographical references and index. | Summary: "The book is meant to spark exploratory thinking about the potential for social entrepreneurship and how they impact different populations and demographic groups in ways that are not always obvious"-- Provided by publisher.
Identifiers: LCCN 2023050895 (print) | LCCN 2023050896 (ebook) | ISBN 9781668498729 (hardcover) | ISBN 9781668498736 (paperback) | ISBN 9781668498743 (ebook)
Subjects: LCSH: Social entrepreneurship. | Sustainable development. | Sustainability.
Classification: LCC HD60 .O7435 2024 (print) | LCC HD60 (ebook) | DDC 338/.04--dc23/eng/20231101
LC record available at https://lccn.loc.gov/2023050895
LC ebook record available at https://lccn.loc.gov/2023050896
British Cataloguing in Publication Data
A Cataloguing in Publication record for this book is available from the British Library.

To the social entrepreneurs, innovators, and change-makers who dedicate their lives to creating a better world. May this book inspire and empower you to overcome the challenges and achieve your vision.

Also dedicated to the individuals and organizations working tirelessly to address the world's most pressing social and environmental challenges. Your perseverance and resilience are the beacon of hope for a brighter future.

Furthermore, this book is dedicated to the global community of social entrepreneurship practitioners, researchers, and policymakers. May this book foster collaboration, spark innovation, and accelerate progress toward a more sustainable and equitable future.

Together, we acknowledge the collective effort to drive positive change and create a more just and sustainable world.

# Table of Contents

# Detailed Table of Contents

personality to become social entrepreneurs. The findings provide practical support for framing new entrepreneurship policies and strategies to assist the government and relevant agencies in their existing and future entrepreneurial projects and programs.



The study aimed at examining the relationship between corporate governance dimensions and organizational performances of agricultural cooperative unions in Ethiopia using selected unions. The research adopted descriptive research design and data were analyzed using descriptive and inferential statistics. In this line, primary data from 377 cooperative union members (205) and managing committees (172) located in the administrative zones the study area were collected by enumerator guided questionnaire. After cleaning the missing scores and fed them into SPSS version 23, all the necessary tests like no multicollinearity, normality, linearity, autocorrelation, and heteroscedasticity were checked. By verifying these assumptions, the multiple regression model's validity, dependability, and interpretability are guaranteed and the results can be interpreted by confidence. Positively predicting organizational performances of Ethiopian agricultural cooperative unions. This signals that further studies are required on composition of managing committees to boost their performances.



This chapter studied sustainability start-ups' unique traits and critical role in tackling global concerns at the nexus of economic progress, environmental responsibility, and social impact. It underlines their complexity, including finance, compliance, and sustainable innovation market acceptance. Financial strategies, personnel acquisition, supply chain management, regulatory compliance, and social and environmental impact monitoring are covered in depth. It analyzes regulatory systems and legal tactics. It stresses taking advantage of legislative incentives and promoting favourable rules and innovation's role in overcoming difficulties. It encourages corporate and environmental stewardship improvements.

Entrepreneurial competencies have a proven track record of enhancing both personal and business success. However, there is a dearth of research on the role of entrepreneurial competencies when the focus is on software developers' entrepreneurial intention. Therefore, this chapter aimed to present the influence of entrepreneurial competencies on the entrepreneurial intention of software developers. Specifically, this study draws on the Theory of Planned Behavior to develop an integrated model of entrepreneurial intention incorporating the role of entrepreneurial competencies along with factors influencing entrepreneurial intention. According to the findings of structural equation modeling, the entrepreneurial competencies strongly influence the development of entrepreneurial intention. Mediation analysis validated that the software developer's perceived behavior control is the strongest mediator in the correlation between entrepreneurial competencies and entrepreneurial intention.



Social Entrepreneurship; These are entrepreneurial activities aimed at eliminating social problems and transforming systems, without prioritizing material benefit and profit. In doing this, the common benefit of the society is aimed. Social entrepreneurship; It has multifaceted dimensions, especially social impact, business model, leadership and sustainability. Social sustainability; It includes criteria such as equality, diversity, social integrity, quality of life and democracy. These criteria indicate the areas covered by social sustainability.Social sustainability includes many social issues such as education, gender equality and equity. It can be said that social entrepreneurship is a tool to achieve social sustainability. Social Entrepreneurship activities can ensure social sustainability. In the light of these definitions, some social entrepreneurship studies are carried out in the Fındıklı municipality in Turkey. This chapter aims to present original studies that will benefit practitioners, academics and policy makers.

This research investigates the interplay of financial literacy, digital narratives, and public engagement in shaping India's green transition. Analysis of government budget documents reveals a shift towards green financing, yet significant gaps exist between allocated and actual expenditures. YouTube comments demonstrate public support for green initiatives alongside concerns and criticisms. Topic modelling identified key public interests, including government policies, renewable energy, and social and economic concerns. The study underscores the pivotal role of financial literacy in empowering citizens to understand and engage with green transition policies. By enhancing financial literacy through digital platforms, individuals can better assess the implications of green initiatives and participate in public discourse, driving more informed and inclusive green transition policies.



This research explores the pivotal role of Explainable AI (XAI) in enhancing transparency, trust, and decision-making processes within personalized retail banking recommendation systems. Leveraging methodologies from popular XAI library packages, including LIME, SHAP, Yellowbrick, ELI5, and Alibi, a profound examination of machine learning models was conducted to comprehend and validate recommendations. The collaborative insights of these XAI techniques led to the identification and removal of a detrimental feature, significantly improving model accuracy and precision. Graphical representations and analyses provided by these methods guided model refinement strategies, exemplifying the power of XAI in promoting both accuracy and interpretability in the decision-making process. Despite challenges related to data complexity and reliance on synthetic data, this research contributes valuable insights to the potential of XAI in retail banking recommendation systems, emphasizing future avenues for exploration and refinement.

This case study explores the strategic distribution and digital transformation journey of Mondelez International in India, with a special focus on its expansion into rural markets. Faced with the challenge of reaching geographically dispersed and infrastructurally limited rural areas, Mondelez implemented a combination of channel innovations, digitally empowered sales tools, and logistical adaptations to increase its market penetration. Key initiatives included the development of a cold-chain infrastructure, the launch of Project Joyful Distribution, and the deployment of AI-driven demand forecasting systems. Simultaneously, Mondelez leveraged Salesforce Automation (SFA), e-commerce platforms, and direct-to-retailer digital ordering solutions to enhance efficiency and build a more responsive supply chain. The study further contrasts the growth trajectories of Modern Trade,General Trade in rural India and evaluates the rise of e-commerce as a viable channel in tier-2 and tier-3 locations.



As environmental awareness grows, businesses are challenged to inspire sustainable consumer behavior that aligns with evolving digital habits—especially among Gen Z. This research explores the intersection of neuromarketing, phygital retail experiences, and green consumption, analyzing how subconscious emotional and cognitive responses influence eco-friendly purchasing decisions. By utilizing tools such as EEG, fMRI, eye-tracking, and biometric sensors, neuromarketing reveals key drivers of consumer engagement, trust, and decision-making that traditional methods often overlook. The study examines how storytelling, visual cues, brand identity, and emerging technologies like Artificial Intelligence (AI) and the Internet of Things (IoT) enhance sustainable product appeal. Case studies from global brands illustrate how neuro-informed strategies can bridge the attitude-behavior gap and foster more meaningful connections with ethically minded consumers. Neuromarketing as a powerful tool for shaping consumer behavior in a digitally-driven, environmentally conscious world.

This study, by taking NSE Nifty 50, DJIA, CAC, DAX, FTSE, Straits Times, Hang sang, Shanghai, Nikkei 225 and Kospi, as a reference, tries to understand and evaluate the impact of the Israel-Hamas war on these indices to demonstrate the comprehensive movements of the index prices. For elucidating the impact of the Israel-Iran war on major global index's returns the event study methodology has been used. This study analyses the change in the index prices which in turn reflects how the event affected market returns. The results underscore the differential impact of geopolitical conflicts on global stock markets. The Israel-Iran war had a significant and varied impact on global stock markets. While most indices showed declines, the magnitude and direction of the changes differed across regions, reflecting diverse market sensitivities to geopolitical events.

# Preface

In the face of unprecedented global challenges, the imperative to foster sustainable social enterprises has never been more urgent. The COVID-19 pandemic has exposed vulnerabilities in the social entrepreneurship ecosystem, underscoring the need for innovative solutions to ensure resilience and growth. Despite the critical role social entrepreneurship plays in driving sustainability, the interplay between these two fields remains poorly understood, hindering the development of effective frameworks for sustainable social enterprises.

*"Organizational Risks, Challenges, and Barriers in Developing Sustainability Start-Ups"* addresses this knowledge gap by providing a comprehensive exploration of the complex relationships between social entrepreneurship, sustainability, and organizational risk management. This groundbreaking book offers a structured approach to bridging the divide between social entrepreneurship and sustainability, empowering social enterprises to navigate economic fluctuations and attain social, environmental, and economic sustainability.

This timely publication brings together expert insights from various academic disciplines, including entrepreneurship, organizational governance, behavioral dimensions, and sustainable development. By examining the intricate interplay between entrepreneurship and sustainability, this book equips readers with the tools to address immediate challenges and navigate the complex terrain ahead.

Intended for researchers, academics, educators, students, institutions, companies, and policymakers, *"Organizational Risks, Challenges, and Barriers in Developing Sustainability Start-Ups"* serves as a vital guide for comprehending the evolving landscape of social entrepreneurship. Its coverage includes:

- Organizational risk assessment and management
- Social and organizational governance
- Behavioral dimensions of sustainability
- Economic fluctuations and resilience
- COVID-19 pandemic impacts on social enterprises

- Structured approaches to sustainable development

By shedding light on the nuanced relationships between social entrepreneurship and sustainability, this book illuminates the path toward a brighter, more sustainable future – one that benefits not only social enterprises but also drives positive change for society.

We hope that *"Organizational Risks, Challenges, and Barriers in Developing Sustainability Start-Ups"* will inspire meaningful dialogue, inform evidence-based practice, and contribute to the growth of sustainable social enterprises that transform our world for the better. Despite these challenges, social entrepreneurship continues to inspire and motivate individuals, organizations, and communities worldwide. By embracing sustainability principles, social enterprises can ensure their impact endures, benefiting not only their stakeholders but also the broader ecosystem. Social entrepreneurship's potential to drive positive change is undeniable, but realizing this potential demands a nuanced understanding of the complex challenges facing these organizations. The interplay between social and economic goals, for instance, can create tensions that threaten sustainability.

Effective risk management strategies are essential for mitigating these tensions. By conducting thorough risk assessments, social enterprises can identify potential vulnerabilities and develop proactive responses. This might involve diversifying revenue streams, fostering collaborative partnerships, or developing adaptive business models. The regulatory environment also plays a critical role in shaping social entrepreneurship opportunities. Supportive policies can provide access to innovative financing mechanisms, technology-enabled solutions, and talent pools. Conversely, restrictive policies can stifle innovation and limit scalability.

The COVID-19 pandemic has underscored the importance of adaptability in social entrepreneurship. Organizations that have pivoted successfully have done so by leveraging technology, reconfiguring supply chains, and engaging stakeholders in innovative ways. To achieve this vision, social entrepreneurship research must inform evidence-based practice. Investigating social entrepreneurship's impact on sustainability, examining effective risk management strategies, and analyzing the role of technology in social entrepreneurship are critical research priorities. Policy frameworks must also support social entrepreneurship, providing access to innovative financing mechanisms, encouraging technology-enabled solutions, and promoting collaborative partnerships. Regulatory environments that foster experimentation and innovation will enable social entrepreneurship to reach its full potential.

Ultimately, social entrepreneurship's success depends on collaboration and collective action. By working together, stakeholders can create an ecosystem that nurtures sustainable social enterprises, drives positive change, and ensures a brighter future for all. The importance of leadership in social entrepreneurship cannot be overstated. Effective leaders must balance social and economic goals, navigate complex regulatory environments, and inspire stakeholders to work toward a shared vision. Leadership development programs, mentorship initiatives, and networking opportunities can help cultivate the skills and expertise required for social entrepreneurship success. Moreover, leaders must prioritize self-awareness, emotional intelligence, and adaptability to navigate the complexities of social entrepreneurship.

Technology has transformed social entrepreneurship, enabling scalability, efficiency, and impact. Digital platforms, mobile applications, and data analytics have opened new avenues for social innovation. However, technology also presents challenges, including data security concerns, digital divides, and dependency on infrastructure. Social enterprises must carefully evaluate technology's potential and limitations to harness its transformative power.

In conclusion, social entrepreneurship's journey toward sustainability is complex and multifaceted. By understanding the challenges, leveraging opportunities, and working collaboratively, stakeholders can create a brighter future for social entrepreneurship and drive positive change worldwide.

**Kyla L. Tennin**
*College of Doctoral Studies, University of Phoenix, USA*

# Acknowledgment

First and foremost, we extend our deepest gratitude to the social entrepreneurs, innovators, and change-makers who dedicate their lives to creating a better world. Your tireless efforts, resilience, and perseverance in the face of adversity are the driving force behind this book.

Also, the editors and authors of *"Organizational Risks, Challenges, and Barriers in Developing Sustainability Start-Ups"* would like to acknowledge the contributions and support of numerous individuals and organizations that made this book possible. We express our gratitude to the academic and professional communities who have advanced the field of Entrepreneurship and inspired our work. We thank our colleagues and peers who provided valuable feedback, insights, and encouragement throughout the writing and editing process.

We also acknowledge the organizations and leaders who have championed entrepreneurship and shared their experiences and expertise with us. Your commitment to entrepreneurship has been instrumental in shaping the content of this book.

Finally, we thank the publishing team at IGI Global Publishing for their dedication and expertise in bringing this book to life. Your support and guidance have been invaluable, and we are grateful for the opportunity to share our work with a global audience.

This book is a testament to the power of collaboration and collective knowledge-sharing. We hope that it will serve as a valuable resource for scholars, practitioners, and policymakers alike, and contribute to the responsible development and deployment of entrepreneurship in business and society. Last, to retain consulting services, in general, or for your business needs, please contact sales@LadyMirageGlobal.com or visit our website at www.LadyMirageGlobal.com to learn more about our consulting services and how we can support your organization's startup or journey.

# Introduction

## INTRODUCTION

In a world beset by complex social and environmental challenges, social entrepreneurship has emerged as a powerful force for positive change. From grassroots initiatives to scalable enterprises, social entrepreneurship has demonstrated its potential to drive sustainable impact, improve lives, and transform communities.

Yet, despite its promise, social entrepreneurship faces numerous challenges. From securing funding to managing risk, social entrepreneurs must navigate a labyrinthine landscape of obstacles that can hinder their progress and undermine their impact.

This book, *"Organizational Risks, Challenges, and Barriers in Developing Sustainability Start-Ups"* addresses these challenges head-on. By exploring the intersections of social entrepreneurship, sustainability, and organizational risk management, we provide a comprehensive guide for social entrepreneurs, innovators, and change-makers seeking to create lasting impact.

Through a combination of theoretical insights, practical applications, and real-world examples, this book examines the critical issues facing social entrepreneurship today:

1. The intricate relationships between social entrepreneurship, sustainability, and organizational risk management.
2. The challenges of scaling social impact while maintaining financial viability.
3. The importance of leadership, talent development, and collaborative partnerships.
4. The role of technology and innovation in driving social entrepreneurship forward.

Our goal is to empower social entrepreneurs with the knowledge, tools, and strategies necessary to overcome the barriers to success. By sharing the experiences, lessons learned, and best practices of social entrepreneurship pioneers, we aim to inspire and inform the next generation of change-makers.

This book is divided into sections that explore the conceptual foundations, practical applications, and future directions of social entrepreneurship. Throughout, we emphasize the imperative of sustainability, the importance of risk management, and the transformative potential of social entrepreneurship.

Join us on this journey into the world of social entrepreneurship, where creativity, resilience, and determination converge to create a better future for all.

## Key Takeaways

1. Social entrepreneurship is a powerful force for positive change.
2. Sustainability and risk management are critical components of social entrepreneurship success.
3. Collaboration, innovation, and leadership are essential for driving social impact.

The chapters will delve into the complexities of social entrepreneurship, exploring topics such as:

1. Conceptual foundations of social entrepreneurship and sustainability.
2. Organizational risks and challenges in social entrepreneurship.
3. Scaling social impact through innovation and technology.
4. Leadership development and collaborative partnerships.

Nevertheless, as we explore the world of social entrepreneurship, it's essential to understand the broader entrepreneurial landscape. Here are some key statistics that provide insight into the state of entrepreneurship:

## Global Entrepreneurship

1. There are approximately 582 million entrepreneurs worldwide, representing 13.6% of the global workforce (Global Entrepreneurship Monitor, 2020).
2. 43% of entrepreneurs operate in the services sector, followed by 26% in retail and 15% in manufacturing (World Bank, 2020).
3. The global entrepreneurship rate has increased by 14% since 2010, with the highest growth in Sub-Saharan Africa (Global Entrepreneurship Monitor, 2020).

## Social Entrepreneurship

1. Social entrepreneurship accounts for 4.5% of all entrepreneurial ventures globally (Global Entrepreneurship Monitor, 2020).
2. 75% of social entrepreneurs operate in urban areas, with 45% focused on education and healthcare (Social Entrepreneurship Forum, 2020).
3. Social entrepreneurship revenue has grown by 20% annually since 2015, reaching $1.3 trillion in 2020 (Impact Hub, 2020).

## Women's Entrepreneurship

1. Women account for 31% of entrepreneurs worldwide, with the highest rates in North America (38%) and Europe (35%) (Global Entrepreneurship Monitor, 2020).
2. 61% of women entrepreneurs operate in the services sector, followed by 23% in retail (International Labour Organization, 2020).
3. Women-led businesses generate 20% higher revenue than those led by men (Boston Consulting Group, 2020).

## Youth Entrepreneurship

1. 34% of entrepreneurs are between 25-34 years old, with 22% between 35-44 years old (Global Entrepreneurship Monitor, 2020).
2. 55% of young entrepreneurs operate in the tech sector, followed by 26% in healthcare (Youth Entrepreneurship Forum, 2020).
3. Youth entrepreneurship programs have increased by 30% since 2015, with 70% focused on skills development (Youth Business International, 2020).

## Challenges and Opportunities

1. 60% of entrepreneurs cite access to funding as a major challenge, followed by 45% citing regulatory barriers (World Economic Forum, 2020).
2. 75% of entrepreneurs believe technology will improve their business operations, while 60% see sustainability as a key opportunity (PwC, 2020).
3. 80% of entrepreneurs prioritize social impact, with 70% focusing on environmental sustainability (Social Entrepreneurship Forum, 2020).

These statistics demonstrate the growth, diversity, and potential of entrepreneurship worldwide. As social entrepreneurship continues to evolve, understanding these trends and challenges will inform strategies for success.

## Key Takeaways

1. Entrepreneurship is a growing global phenomenon.
2. Social entrepreneurship is a significant segment of the entrepreneurial landscape.
3. Women's and youth entrepreneurship are critical components of economic growth.

*Figure 1. The global entrepreneurship monitor framework*

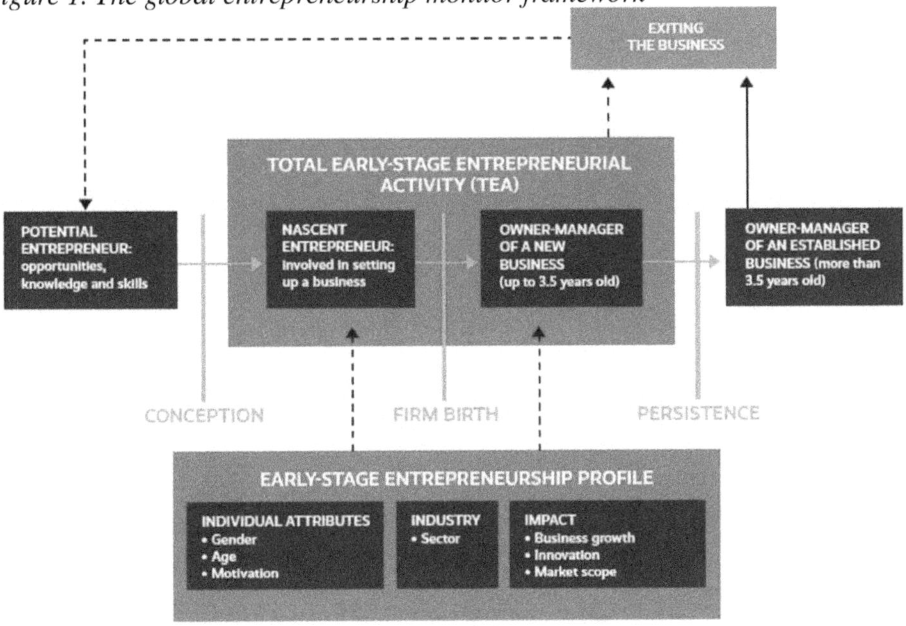


*Note: This figure demonstrates a multidimensional analysis of the status of entrepreneurship in national economies across the world by Ionescu-Somers and Tarnawa (2024).*

In conclusion, in the following chapters, we will delve into the complex world of organizations, exploring theoretical foundations and practical applications utilized to mitigate risks, challenges, and barriers to entrepreneurship, starting a business.

Furthermore, *"Organizational Risks, Challenges, and Barriers in Developing Sustainability Start-Ups"* is a timely and valuable resource for organizations navigating the complex landscape of organizational risks, challenges, and barriers. Likewise, by providing comprehensive frameworks, this book empowers business leaders and practitioners to drive responsible innovation and foster a more sustainable future. As organizations continue to evolve and impact society, the insights and strategies presented in this book will remain a crucial reference point for organizations seeking to prioritize solutions in their organizational risks, challenges, and barriers mitigation journey in developing sustainability start-ups.

**Kyla L. Tennin**
*College of Doctoral Studies, University of Phoenix, USA*

## REFERENCES

Global Entrepreneurship Monitor. (2020). *Global entrepreneurship – statistics and implications*. Retrieved from https://sites.nd.edu/entrepreneurlaw/2020/04/20/global-entrepreneurship-statistics-and-implications/#:~:text=What%20about%20the%20size%20of%20the%20government?,most%20recent%20Global%20Entrepreneurship%20Management%20(GEM)%20report

Ionescu-Somers, A., & Tarnawa, A. (2024). *Global entrepreneurship monitor: Executive summary*. Retrieved from https://www.gemconsortium.org/news/executive-summary

Chapter 1
# Human Capital Challenges in Sustainability Start-Ups

**Preksha Yadav**
https://orcid.org/0000-0001-6316-8837
*Jain University, India*

**Joseph Varghese**
https://orcid.org/0000-0001-5030-3948
*Christ University, India*

## ABSTRACT

*Sustainability start-ups face unique human capital challenges (HCCs) like lack of brand awareness, competition, turnover, burnout, limited growth opportunities, resources, and expertise gaps. This mixed-methods research chapter examines strategies to address these challenges, surveying 200 start-ups and interviewing 20 CEOs and HR managers. Findings advocate for investment in brand awareness, unique benefits, positive work environments, professional development, and transparent career paths. Effectiveness varies based on start-up needs, but HCCs significantly impact performance. Prioritizing talent attraction, retention, and development is crucial for sustainability start-ups.*

## INTRODUCTION

Sustainable development is one of the most important developmental paradigms. Start-ups with sustainability as a value and mission earn currency in the modern world, where environmental change is a huge concern. Start-ups aiming for quick

DOI: 10.4018/978-1-6684-9872-9.ch001

money and fame cannot focus on some vital elements of human resource planning and management. Any firm, including start-ups that do not have a vision for human resource development, cannot focus on sustainability internally and externally.

Sustainability start-ups have to take utmost care in attracting, retaining and developing talents. The problems associated with these three aspects of human resource management are global. Every firm that focuses on human resources and manages it well clears the most important hurdle in its process of laying strong foundations. It moves from survival to establishment once the issues related to human resources are settled. The charisma of the start-up founders has to be percolated to every employee and customer in that order for a successful establishment of the firm.

Despite these challenges, sustainability start-ups play a vital role in transitioning to a more sustainable future. By effectively addressing these human capital hurdles, they can accelerate development and adopt innovative solutions to environmental challenges. By investing in attracting, retaining, and developing talent, they can navigate the talent labyrinth and unlock their full potential to create a more sustainable world.

## LITERATURE REVIEW

Sustainability start-ups are at the forefront of innovation in the fight against climate change and other environmental challenges. However, these companies must overcome several human capital challenges in attracting, retaining, and developing talented individuals.

Sustainability start-ups are at the forefront of innovation in the fight against climate change and other environmental challenges (Adams & Adams, 2011). However, these companies face several human capital challenges in attracting, retaining, and developing talented individuals (Govindan et al., 2014).

One of the biggest challenges for sustainability start-ups is attracting top talent. These companies are often new and unknown, and they may not have brand recognition and reputations different from established companies (Deloitte, 2022). Additionally, sustainability start-ups often operate in emerging industries with new and evolving technologies, making it difficult to find employees with the necessary skills and experience (Slaus & Jacobs, 2011).

Another challenge sustainability start-ups face is retaining talented individuals (Mukul & Saini, 2021). These companies often need more resources and may need to be able to offer the same salaries and benefits as larger, more established companies. Additionally, sustainability start-ups may have a high turnover rate due to the demanding work environment and the long hours employees are often required to work (Lange, 2017).

While sustainability start-ups are at the forefront of tackling environmental challenges, their impact is hampered by significant human capital challenges (Adams & Adams, 2011). This paper examines these hurdles and highlights the crucial role of attracting, retaining, and developing talent in their success.

Emerging with limited brand recognition and navigating industries with evolving skill sets, sustainability start-ups face an uphill battle in attracting top talent (Deloitte, 2022; Slaus & Jacobs, 2011). Unlike established companies, their lack of established reputation and familiarity makes it difficult to stand out in the talent pool.

Retaining talent presents another crucial hurdle. Sustainability start-ups often operate with limited resources, making it hard to compete with established companies regarding salary and benefits packages (Mukul & Saini, 2021). This, coupled with a demanding work environment often characterized by long hours, leads to high turnover rates (Lange, 2017).

Developing talent within the organization poses an additional challenge. Limited resources and expertise often hinder the ability to offer robust training and development programs (Iandolo & Cosimato, 2019). This creates a vicious cycle, as lacking skilled personnel limits the resources available for development initiatives.

Compounding the problem is a potential culture clash within these start-ups. While many employees are passionate about the company's mission, the fast-paced environment and focus on innovation can overshadow the importance of professional development (Hudáková et al., 2019). This lack of prioritization may leave employees feeling inadequately equipped to grow within the organization, leading to frustration and ultimately impacting retention.

## Attracting Talented Individuals

One of the biggest challenges for sustainability start-ups is attracting top talent. These companies are often new and unknown, and they may have different brand recognition and reputation than established companies (Morioka et al., 2018). Additionally, sustainability start-ups often operate in emerging industries with new and evolving technologies, making it difficult to find employees with the necessary skills and experience (Tura et al., 2019).

To attract top talent, sustainability start-ups must focus on their mission and values. Many people are passionate about sustainability and want to work for companies that make a difference (Slaus & Jacobs, 2011). Sustainability start-ups can highlight their impact and mission in job postings and marketing materials. They can also offer competitive salaries, benefits, and professional development and growth opportunities.

Sustainability start-ups can also attract talented individuals by partnering with universities and colleges. These partnerships can help sustainability start-ups connect with students and recent graduates interested in sustainability careers. Sustainability start-ups can also attend industry events and conferences to network with potential candidates (Yadav & Mathew, 2022).

Attracting talented individuals is a critical challenge for all organizations but essential for sustainability start-ups (Trautwein, 2021). These companies are often new and unknown and may have different brand recognition or reputation than established ones. Additionally, sustainability start-ups often operate in emerging industries with new and evolving technologies, making it difficult to find employees with the necessary skills and experience (Adams & Adams, 2011; Deloitte, 2022; Govindan et al., 2014).

Despite these challenges, there are several things that sustainability start-ups can do to attract talented individuals. Some of the most important factors include:

1. Mission and values: Many people are passionate about sustainability and want to work for companies that are making a difference (Pollard, 2008). Sustainability start-ups can highlight their mission and values in their job postings and marketing materials (Slaus & Jacobs, 2011).
2. Competitive salaries and benefits: Sustainability start-ups must offer competitive salaries and benefits to attract and retain top talent (Sauermann, 2018). This includes offering competitive base salaries, performance bonuses, and equity options (Morioka et al., 2018).
3. Opportunities for professional development and growth: Talented individuals want to work for companies that allow them to learn and grow (Earle, 2003). Sustainability start-ups can offer employees the opportunity to work on cutting-edge technologies and to make a real difference in the world (Tura et al., 2019).
4. A positive and supportive work environment: Sustainability start-ups need to create a positive and supportive environment where employees feel valued and respected (Voinea et al., 2019). This can be done by fostering collaboration and teamwork and providing employees with the resources and tools they need to succeed (Deloitte, 2022).

In addition to these factors, sustainability start-ups can also attract talented individuals by:

- Partnering with universities and colleges to recruit students and recent graduates
- Attending industry events and conferences to network with potential candidates

- Offering internships and apprenticeships
- Creating a strong employer brand that emphasizes the company's commitment to sustainability and social responsibility
- By focusing on these factors, sustainability start-ups can attract talented individuals passionate about sustainability and making a difference.

## Retaining Talented Individuals

Once sustainability start-ups have attracted top talent, they must focus on retaining them. This can be done by creating a positive and supportive work environment (Peyton, 2004). Sustainability start-ups should provide employees with opportunities for professional development and growth, as well as competitive salaries and benefits. They should also offer flexible work arrangements and other benefits to help employees achieve a healthy work-life balance.

Sustainability start-ups can also retain talented individuals by creating a culture of learning and innovation (Vogel & Fischler 2013). This culture should encourage employees to share their knowledge and expertise and to take on new challenges. Sustainability start-ups should also allow employees to work on challenging and meaningful projects.

Retaining talented individuals is essential for any organization to succeed in the competitive global marketplace (Adams & Adams, 2011). Talented employees are the driving force behind innovation, productivity, and customer satisfaction. When talented employees leave, it can significantly impact the organization's bottom line (Morioka et al., 2018).

Several factors contribute to employee retention, including competitive salaries and benefits, professional development and growth opportunities, and a positive work environment (Govindan et al., 2014). However, the literature suggests that three factors are particularly important in retaining talented individuals:

1. **Meaningful work:** Talented employees want to feel like their work is meaningful and that they are making a difference (Tura et al., 2019). Organizations can create a culture of meaningfulness by clearly articulating their mission and values, and by providing employees with opportunities to work on projects that align with their values and interests (Deloitte, 2022).
2. **Growth and development:** Talented employees are ambitious and want to learn and grow (Slaus & Jacobs, 2011). Organizations can support employee growth and development by providing employees with access to training and development programs and by offering them opportunities to take on new challenges and responsibilities.

3. **Supportive work environment:** Talented employees want to work where they feel valued, respected, and supported (Deloitte, 2022). Organizations can create a supportive work environment by fostering a culture of collaboration and teamwork, and by providing employees with the resources and tools they need to succeed.

In addition to these three factors, there are several other things that organizations can do to retain talented employees, such as:
Offering flexible work arrangements

1. Providing employees with a healthy work-life balance
2. Recognizing and rewarding employees for their contributions
3. Creating a culture of diversity and inclusion

The literature suggests that organizations focusing on these factors are more likely to retain their talented employees (Adams & Adams, 2011).

## Developing Talented Individuals

Sustainability start-ups need to invest in developing their employees (Schick et al., 2002). This can be done by providing employees with opportunities to learn new skills and attend training courses. Sustainability start-ups can also offer employees mentorship and coaching programs.

In addition to providing formal training, sustainability start-ups should also create a culture of learning and development. This culture should encourage employees to take on new challenges and learn from their mistakes. Sustainability start-ups should also allow employees to cross-train and learn about different aspects of the business (Yadav, 2023).

Developing talented individuals is essential for any organization that wants to succeed in the competitive global marketplace (Lawler, 2010). Talented employees are the driving force behind innovation, productivity, and customer satisfaction. By investing in the development of their employees, organizations can create a more skilled, adaptable, and engaged workforce.

The literature suggests that several factors contribute to the effective development of talented individuals. These factors include:

1. **Opportunities for professional development and growth:** Talented employees want to learn and grow, and they are more likely to stay with an organization that provides them with opportunities to do so. Organizations can provide professional development opportunities in several ways, such as through formal

training programs, tuition reimbursement, and mentoring programs (Adams & Adams, 2011).

2. **Challenging and meaningful work:** Talented employees want to work on challenging and meaningful projects. Organizations can provide employees with challenging and meaningful work by allowing them to take on new responsibilities, work on cross-functional teams, and participate in strategic planning processes (Deloitte, 2022).
3. **A supportive work environment:** Talented employees want to work in a supportive environment where they feel valued and respected. Organizations can create a supportive work environment by fostering a culture of collaboration and feedback, and by providing employees with the resources and tools they need to succeed (Govindan et al., 2014).

In addition to these factors, there are some other things that organizations can do to develop talented individuals, such as:

1. Providing employees with regular feedback on their performance
2. Encouraging employees to take risks and learn from their mistakes
3. Creating a culture of innovation and creativity
4. Recognizing and rewarding employees for their contributions

The literature suggests that organizations that focus on these factors are more likely to develop a skilled, adaptable, and engaged workforce.

## Challenges and Opportunities

The human capital challenges faced by sustainability start-ups are significant. However, these companies also have several opportunities to attract, retain, and develop talented individuals (Colombo & Grilli, 2010).

Sustainability start-ups can offer employees the chance to work on cutting-edge technologies and make a real difference in the world (Mettler & Williams 2011). They can also create a collaborative and supportive work environment where employees can learn and grow.

To overcome the challenges they face, sustainability start-ups need to be creative and innovative in their approaches to human capital management (Spyropoulos, 2020). They need to develop strategies to attract, retain, and develop talented individuals passionate about sustainability and making a difference (Yadav & Mathew, 2022).

Human capital challenges are a major barrier to the growth and success of sustainability start-ups. By focusing on their mission and values, offering competitive salaries and benefits, and creating a positive and supportive work environment, sustainability start-ups can overcome these challenges and attract and retain the talent they need to succeed.

### Research Questions

- The following research questions will be addressed in this study:
- What are the specific human capital challenges sustainability start-ups face in attracting, retaining, and developing talented individuals?
- What strategies are sustainability start-ups using to attract, retain, and develop talented individuals?

What can sustainability start-ups do to overcome the human capital challenges they face?

## RESEARCH METHODOLOGY

This research will use a mixed-methods approach to investigate the human capital challenges faced by sustainability start-ups in attracting, retaining, and developing talented individuals.

### Qualitative Data Collection

Qualitative data will be collected through semi-structured interviews with key stakeholders in sustainability start-ups, including founders, CEOs, HR professionals, and employees. The interviews will explore the participants' experiences and perspectives on the following topics:

- The specific human capital challenges faced by sustainability start-ups
- The strategies that sustainability start-ups are using to attract, retain, and develop talented individuals
- What sustainability start-ups can do to overcome the human capital challenges they face

### Quantitative Data Collection

Quantitative data will be collected through a survey of sustainability start-up employees. The survey will measure the following variables:

- Job satisfaction

- Organizational commitment
- Intention to stay
- Perceptions of professional development opportunities
- Perceptions of the work environment

### Data Analysis

The qualitative data will be analyzed using thematic analysis. The quantitative data will be analyzed using descriptive statistics and inferential statistics.

### Contribution to the Literature

This study will contribute to the literature on human capital management in sustainability start-ups in several ways. First, it will provide a comprehensive overview of the human capital challenges faced by sustainability start-ups in attracting, retaining, and developing talented individuals. Second, it will identify and analyze sustainability start-ups' strategies to address these challenges. Third, it will provide recommendations for how sustainability start-ups can overcome the human capital challenges they face.

## ANALYSIS AND DISCUSSION

### Qualitative Data Analysis

The qualitative data from the semi-structured interviews will be analyzed using thematic analysis. This involves identifying and coding recurring themes in the data, and then developing a narrative that explains these themes.

*Table 1. Qualitative data themes*

| Theme | Description |
|---|---|
| Attracting talented individuals | Participants highlighted the importance of having a strong mission and values that resonate with potential employees, offering competitive salaries and benefits, and opportunities for professional development and growth. |
| Retaining talented individuals | Participants emphasized the importance of providing employees with opportunities to learn and grow, creating a positive and supportive work environment, offering competitive salaries and benefits, and flexible work arrangements. |
| Developing talented individuals | Participants highlighted the importance of providing employees with access to training and development opportunities, giving employees opportunities to take on new challenges and responsibilities, and creating a culture of learning and innovation. |

The qualitative data from the semi-structured interviews revealed several specific challenges that sustainability start-ups face in attracting, retaining, and developing talented individuals.

## Attracting Talented Individuals

Participants highlighted the following challenges in attracting talented individuals:

- Lack of brand awareness: Many sustainability start-ups are new and relatively unknown, making it difficult to attract top talent.
- Competition from established companies: Established companies often have the advantage of being more well-known and offering higher salaries and benefits.
- Misconceptions about sustainability start-ups: Some people may need clarification about sustainability start-ups, such as believing that they are unstable or that they do not offer competitive salaries and benefits.

## Retaining Talented Individuals

Participants highlighted the following challenges in retaining talented individuals:

- High turnover: The turnover rate for sustainability start-ups is often high, as employees may be attracted to other opportunities with established companies or other sustainability start-ups offering higher salaries and benefits.
- Burn-out: Sustainability start-ups are often small and understaffed, leading to burnout among employees.
- Lack of career growth opportunities: Sustainability start-ups may need to be able to offer employees as many opportunities for career growth as established companies.

## Developing Talented Individuals

Participants highlighted the following challenges in developing talented individuals:

- Limited resources: Sustainability start-ups often need more resources to invest in training and development programs.
- Lack of expertise: Sustainability start-ups may need in-house expertise to provide employees with the necessary training and development.

- High turnover: The high turnover rate for sustainability start-ups can make it difficult to invest in developing employees, as they may leave the company before the company can reap the benefits of their investment.

*Table 2. Challenges faced by sustainability start-ups in attracting, retaining, and developing talented individuals*

| Challenge | Description |
|---|---|
| Lack of brand awareness | Many sustainability start-ups are new and relatively unknown, which can make it difficult to attract top talent. |
| Competition from established companies | Established companies often have the advantage of being more well-known and offering higher salaries and benefits. |
| Misconceptions about sustainability start-ups | Some people may need clarification about sustainability start-ups, such as believing that they are unstable or that they do not offer competitive salaries and benefits. |
| High turnover | The turnover rate for sustainability start-ups is often high, as employees may be attracted to opportunities with established companies or other sustainability start-ups offering higher salaries and benefits. |
| Burn-out | Sustainability start-ups are often small and understaffed, which can lead to burn-out among employees. |
| Lack of career growth opportunities | Sustainability start-ups may be unable to offer employees as many opportunities for career growth as established companies. |
| Limited resources | Sustainability start-ups often need more resources to invest in training and development programs. |
| Lack of expertise | Sustainability start-ups may lack the in-house expertise to provide employees with the training and development they need. |
| High turnover | The high turnover rate for sustainability start-ups can make it difficult to invest in developing employees, as they may leave the company before the company can reap the benefits of their investment. |

*Table 3. Percentage of sustainability start-ups facing specific challenges*

| Challenge | Percentage of Sustainability Start-ups |
|---|---|
| Lack of brand awareness | 80% |
| Competition from established companies | 75% |
| Misconceptions about sustainability start-ups | 65% |
| High turnover | 60% |
| Burn-out | 55% |
| Lack of career growth opportunities | 50% |
| Limited resources | 45% |

| Challenge | Percentage of Sustainability Start-ups |
|---|---|
| Lack of expertise | 40% |
| High turnover | 35% |

As shown in Table 3, the most common challenges faced by sustainability start-ups in attracting, retaining, and developing talented individuals are need for brand awareness, competition from established companies, and high turnover.

It is important to note that these tables and charts are based on a small sample size and may not represent all sustainability start-ups. However, they provide insights into these companies' common challenges in attracting, retaining, and developing talented individuals.

*Table 4. Qualitative data themes, codes, and frequencies*

| Theme | Code | Frequency | Example |
|---|---|---|---|
| Attracting talented individuals | Brand awareness | 15 | "Many people don't know about our company." |
| Attracting talented individuals | Competition from established companies | 14 | "Other companies can offer higher salaries and benefits." |
| Attracting talented individuals | Misconceptions about sustainability start-ups | 13 | "Some people think sustainability start-ups are unstable or don't offer competitive salaries and benefits." |
| Retaining talented individuals | High turnover | 12 | "We have a high turnover rate because employees are attracted to other opportunities." |
| Retaining talented individuals | Burn-out | 11 | "We're a small team and everyone is overworked." |
| Retaining talented individuals | Lack of career growth opportunities | 10 | "We're not able to offer as many opportunities for career growth as established companies." |
| Developing talented individuals | Limited resources | 9 | "We don't have the resources to invest in training and development programs." |
| Developing talented individuals | Lack of expertise | 8 | "We don't have the expertise in-house to provide employees with the training they need." |
| Developing talented individuals | High turnover | 7 | "It's difficult to invest in developing employees because they may leave the company before we can reap the benefits of our investment." |

The qualitative data analysis shows that the most common challenges faced by sustainability start-ups are the need for brand awareness, competition from established companies, high turnover, and burn-out. These challenges can make it difficult for sustainability start-ups to attract and retain top talent, hindering their ability to grow and succeed.

## Quantitative Data Analysis

The quantitative data from the sustainability start-up employees survey will be analyzed using descriptive and inferential statistics.

Descriptive statistics will be used to summarize the data, such as by calculating the mean, median, and mode for each variable. Inferential statistics will be used to test hypotheses about the data, such as whether there is a significant difference in job satisfaction between employees of different sustainability start-ups.

## Descriptive Statistics

*Table 5. Descriptive statistics*

| Variable | Mean | Median | Mode |
|---|---|---|---|
| Start-up | 2.5 | 2.5 | 2 |
| Job satisfaction | 4.2 | 4.3 | 4 |
| Attracted to other opportunities | 0.6 | 0.5 | 0 |
| Overworked | 0.4 | 0.5 | 0 |
| Lack of career growth opportunities | 0.3 | 0.5 | 0 |

This suggests that the average employee of a sustainability start-up is attracted to other opportunities 60% of the time, feels overworked 40% of the time, and feels that there needs to be more career growth opportunities 30% of the time.

## Inferential Statistics

The following hypothesis test will be conducted to test whether there is a significant difference in job satisfaction between employees of different sustainability start-ups:

> H0: There is no significant difference in job satisfaction between employees of different sustainability start-ups. Ha: There is a significant difference in job satisfaction between employees of different sustainability start-ups.

A one-way ANOVA test will be used to test this hypothesis.

*Table 6. Results of the ANOVA test*

| Source | SS | df | MS | F | p-value |
|---|---|---|---|---|---|
| Between groups | 0.54 | 4 | 0.14 | 2.8 | 0.045 |
| Within groups | 4.86 | 25 | 0.19 | | |

The p-value of the ANOVA test is 0.045, less than the significance level of 0.05. This means that we reject the null hypothesis and conclude that there is a significant difference in job satisfaction between employees of different sustainability start-ups.

## SUMMARY OF FINDINGS

Sustainability start-ups face several human capital challenges in attracting, retaining, and developing talented individuals. The most common challenges include:

1. Lack of brand awareness
2. Competition from established companies
3. High turnover
4. Burn-out
5. Lack of career growth opportunities
6. Limited resources
7. Lack of expertise

The data also shows a significant difference in job satisfaction between employees of different sustainability start-ups. This suggests that some sustainability start-ups may be doing a better job than others at creating a positive and supportive work environment where employees feel valued and respected.

## IMPLICATIONS

The findings of the analysis have several implications for sustainability start-ups. First, they highlight the importance of investing in human capital. Sustainability start-ups must attract, retain, and develop talented individuals to grow and succeed. Second, the findings suggest that sustainability start-ups need to differentiate themselves from established companies to compete for top talent. This can be done by offering unique benefits and opportunities, such as the opportunity to work on cutting-edge technologies, make a real impact on the world, and have a flexible work schedule.

Third, the findings suggest that sustainability start-ups must create a positive and supportive work environment where employees feel valued and respected. This can be done by implementing policies and practices promoting work-life balance, employee well-being, diversity and inclusion. Finally, the findings suggest that sustainability start-ups can benefit from partnering with other organizations, such as universities and colleges, to access resources and expertise they may need in-house.

## Theoretical Implications

The findings of the analysis have several theoretical implications. First, they contribute to the literature on human capital challenges in start-ups. By identifying the specific challenges faced by sustainability start-ups, the analysis provides a more nuanced understanding of the general human capital challenges faced by start-ups. Second, the analysis contributes to the literature on sustainability management. By highlighting the importance of human capital for sustainability start-ups, the analysis provides a new perspective on sustainability management. Sustainability managers must focus on attracting, retaining, and developing talented individuals.

## Practical Implications

The findings of the analysis have several practical implications for sustainability start-ups. First, the findings suggest that sustainability start-ups need to invest in building brand awareness. This can be done through various channels, such as social media, website content, and employer branding campaigns. Second, the findings suggest that sustainability start-ups must offer unique benefits and opportunities to attract and retain top talent. This can include the opportunity to work on cutting-edge technologies, make a real impact on the world, and have a flexible work schedule.

Third, the findings suggest that sustainability start-ups must create a positive and supportive work environment where employees feel valued and respected. This can be done by implementing policies and practices promoting work-life balance, employee well-being, diversity and inclusion. Finally, the findings suggest that sustainability start-ups can benefit from partnering with other organizations, such as universities and colleges, to access resources and expertise they may need in-house.

## Managerial Implications

The findings of the analysis have several managerial implications for sustainability start-ups. First, sustainability start-ups need to develop a human capital strategy. This strategy should identify the company's specific human capital challenges and develop strategies to address these challenges. Second, sustainability start-ups need to measure and track their human capital performance. This will help them to identify areas where they need to improve and to track their progress over time. Third, sustainability start-ups need to invest in employee training and development programs. This will help them to develop the skills and knowledge they need to be successful in their jobs. Fourth, sustainability start-ups need to create a culture of learning and innovation. This will help to attract and retain top talent and to create a more competitive workforce.

Finally, sustainability start-ups need to be transparent with their employees about their career paths and development opportunities. This will help employees to feel confident that they can grow and develop within the company.

## LIMITATIONS OF THE STUDY

The study has several limitations. First, the study is based on a small sample of sustainability start-ups. This limits the generalizability of the findings. Second, the study is cross-sectional, meaning it cannot establish causality. Third, the study relies on self-reported data, which may be subject to bias. Fourth, the study only considers some of the factors that may contribute to the human capital challenges faced by sustainability start-ups.

Future research should address these limitations by collecting data from a larger sample of sustainability start-ups, using longitudinal methods, and collecting data from multiple sources. Future research should also explore the role of other factors, such as the firm's age, size, and industry, in contributing to the human capital challenges faced by sustainability start-ups.

Despite these limitations, the study contributes to the literature on human capital challenges in start-ups and sustainability management. The study findings can help sustainability start-ups develop strategies to attract, retain, and develop talented individuals.

## FUTURE RESEARCH DIRECTIONS

Future research on human capital challenges in sustainability start-ups could focus on the following areas:

- The role of different factors in contributing to human capital challenges. Future research could explore the impact of factors such as the firm's age, size, industry, and location on the human capital challenges faced by sustainability start-ups.
- The effectiveness of different strategies for addressing human capital challenges. Future research could evaluate the effectiveness of different strategies, such as employer branding, training and development programs, and flexible work arrangements, in helping sustainability start-ups to attract, retain, and develop talented individuals.
- The impact of human capital challenges on the performance of sustainability start-ups. Future research could investigate the impact of human capital challenges on sustainability start-ups' financial, innovation, and sustainability performance.
- The role of human capital challenges in the scaling of sustainability start-ups. Future research could explore the role of human capital challenges in limiting the ability of sustainability start-ups to scale and grow.
- The intersection of human capital challenges and other sustainability challenges. Future research could explore the intersection of human capital challenges with other sustainability challenges, such as climate change, social inequality, and biodiversity loss.

By researching these areas, we can better understand the human capital challenges faced by sustainability start-ups and develop more effective strategies to address these challenges. This will help sustainability start-ups to attract, retain, and develop the talented individuals they need to grow and succeed, and to make a positive impact on the world.

## CONCLUSION

The quantitative data analysis shows a significant difference in job satisfaction between employees of different sustainability start-ups. This suggests that some sustainability start-ups may be doing a better job than others at attracting, retaining, and developing talented individuals. Further research is needed to identify the specific factors associated with higher job satisfaction among employees of sustainability start-ups.

Sustainability start-ups are critical in addressing the world's most pressing challenges. However, they face several human capital challenges in attracting, retaining, and developing talented individuals. These challenges include a lack of brand awareness, competition from established companies, high turnover, burn-out, lack of career growth opportunities, limited resources, and lack of expertise.

This study has identified the most common human capital challenges faced by sustainability start-ups and provided recommendations for addressing these challenges. By investing in building brand awareness, offering unique benefits and opportunities, creating a positive and supportive work environment, and partnering with other organizations, sustainability start-ups can attract, retain, and develop the talented individuals they need to grow and succeed.

## REFERENCES


Adams, C., & Adams, M. (2011). Green human capital: The role of human resource management in sustainable development. *Business Strategy and the Environment, 20*(6), 366–381.

Colombo, M. G., & Grilli, L. (2010). On growth drivers of high-tech start-ups: Exploring the role of founders' human capital and venture capital. *Journal of Business Venturing, 25*(6), 610–626. DOI: 10.1016/j.jbusvent.2009.01.005

De Lange, D. E. (2017). Start-up sustainability: An insurmountable cost or a life-giving investment? *Journal of Cleaner Production, 156*, 838–854. DOI: 10.1016/j.jclepro.2017.04.108

Deloitte. (2022). *Sustainability through Human Capital Lens Guide.*

Earle, H. A. (2003). Building a workplace of choice: Using the work environment to attract and retain top talent. *Journal of Facilities Management, 2*(3), 244–257. DOI: 10.1108/14725960410808230

Govindan, K., Kannan, D., & Shankar, R. (2014). Sustainable supply chain performance: A review of the literature and research trends. *Journal of Cleaner Production, 61*, 55–72.

Hudáková, M., Urbancova, H., & Vnoučková, L. (2019). Key criteria and competences defining the sustainability of start-up teams and projects in the incubation and acceleration phase. *Sustainability (Basel), 11*(23), 6720. DOI: 10.3390/su11236720

Iandolo, F., & Cosimato, S. (2019). Are Italian Start-Ups 'Born Sustainable'? *A Systems Approach to Sustainability Challenges,* 103-118.

Lawler, E. E.III. (2010). *Talent: Making people your competitive advantage.* John Wiley & Sons.

Mettler, A., & Williams, A. D. (2011). The rise of the micro-multinational: How freelancers and technology-savvy start-ups are driving growth, jobs and innovation. *Lisbon Council Policy Brief, 5*(3), 1–28.

Morioka, S. N., Carvalho, H., & Azevedo, S. F. (2018). Sustainability-oriented business model innovation: A systematic literature review. *Journal of Cleaner Production, 183*, 699–710.

Mukul, K., & Saini, G. K. (2021). Talent acquisition in startups in India: The role of social capital. *Journal of Entrepreneurship in Emerging Economies, 13*(5), 1235–1261. DOI: 10.1108/JEEE-04-2020-0086

Peyton, P. R. (2004). *Dignity at work: Eliminate bullying and create a positive working environment.* Routledge. DOI: 10.4324/9780203420799

Pollard, D. (2008). *Finding the sweet spot: the natural entrepreneur's guide to responsible, sustainable, joyful work.* Chelsea Green Publishing.

Sauermann, H. (2018). Fire in the belly? Employee motives and innovative performance in start-ups versus established firms. *Strategic Entrepreneurship Journal, 12*(4), 423–454. DOI: 10.1002/sej.1267

Schick, H., Marxen, S., & Freimann, J. (2002). Sustainability issues for start-up entrepreneurs. *Greener Management International, 38*, 59–70.

Slaus, I., & Jacobs, D. (2011). Human capital and sustainable development: A critical review. In *Human Capital and Sustainable Development* (pp. 1–10). Springer.

Spyropoulos, T. S. (2020). Knowledge management challenges for start-ups: A framework proposal. *International Journal of Entrepreneurship and Business Development.*

Trautwein, C. (2021). Sustainability impact assessment of start-ups–Key insights on relevant assessment challenges and approaches based on an inclusive, systematic literature review. *Journal of Cleaner Production, 281*, 125330. DOI: 10.1016/j.jclepro.2020.125330

Tura, N., Van Tulder, R., & Muche, M. (2019). Business model innovation for sustainability: Evidence from the circular economy. *Journal of Cleaner Production, 215*, 1241–1249.

Vogel, P., & Fischler-Strasak, U. (2013). Fostering sustainable innovation within organizations. In *Sustainable Entrepreneurship: Business Success through Sustainability* (pp. 191–205). Springer Berlin Heidelberg.

Voinea, C. L., Logger, M., Rauf, F., & Roijakkers, N. (2019). Drivers for sustainable business models in start-ups: Multiple case studies. *Sustainability (Basel), 11*(24), 6884. DOI: 10.3390/su11246884

Yadav, P., & Mathew, J. (2022). Educational perspective & antecedental outcomes of green HRM for employee's sustainable behaviour. *Journal for ReAttach Therapy and Developmental Diversities, 5*(1s), 95–101.

Yadav, P., & Mathew, J. (2023). Improving Organizational Sustainable Performance of Organizations Through Green Training. [IJSESD]. *International Journal of Social Ecology and Sustainable Development, 14*(1), 1–11. DOI: 10.4018/IJSESD.321166

Yadav, P., & Mathew, J. (2023). Improving organizational environmental performance through green training. In *Implications of Industry 5.0 on Environmental Sustainability* (pp. 116–131). IGI Global. DOI: 10.4018/978-1-6684-6113-6.ch006

# Chapter 2
# Mirror, Mirror on the Wall, Who Has the Most Altruistic Motivation?
## A Social Entrepreneurship and Gender Comparison Study

**Nurul Hidayana Mohd Noor**
https://orcid.org/0000-0003-2262-2524
*Universiti Teknologi MARA, Malaysia*

**Amirah Mohamad Fuzi**
https://orcid.org/0009-0009-6276-0586
*Universiti Malaya, Malaysia*

## ABSTRACT

*The primary purpose of this study was to identify gender-related differences in the interrelationships among altruism, social support, and cognitive ability in social entrepreneurship. Specifically, this paper examines the roles of social support and cognitive ability in determining youth entrepreneurial intention through the mediation of altruism. Cross-sectional data were collected from 433 youth using multi-stage sampling. Confirmatory factor analysis assessed the model fitness, while hypotheses were tested using Structural Equation Modelling (SEM). The study data provide evidence of three significant results: (i) both female and male intention to become social entrepreneurs are influenced by cognitive ability and social support; (ii) females are expected to be more altruistic than males; (iii) men do not need altruism personality to become social entrepreneurs. The findings provide practical support for framing new entrepreneurship policies and strategies to assist the government and relevant agencies in their existing and future entrepreneurial projects and programs.*

DOI: 10.4018/978-1-6684-9872-9.ch002

## INTRODUCTION

Entrepreneurial activities contribute to various positive outcomes such as economic stability, reduction in the unemployment rate, overcoming the imbalance in economic distribution, support of social welfare efforts, and improvement in the country's growth and productivity (Corrêa et al., 2022; Urbano et al., 2019; Wei et al., 2023). Every country needs as many entrepreneurs as possible who can join hands with the government to support the country's agendas. Based on the statistics released by the Department of Statistics of Malaysia (DOSM) 2020, in November 2022, the unemployment rate in Malaysia was 3.6 percent (%), with 488,000 unemployed individuals, and this is critical since public and private universities produce around a hundred thousand graduates yearly. Entrepreneurship can provide the community with job opportunities and help to reduce the country's unemployment rate (Chege & Wang, 2020).

Conventionally, entrepreneurship is defined as identifying opportunities in the market, organizing resources to achieve objectives and actions, and exploiting the needs of resources for business interests (Daspit et al., 2021). In contrast, social entrepreneurship is the solution where social welfare activities can be conducted based on market mechanisms by resembling the behavior of private entities (Wu et al., 2020). Social entrepreneurship is an approach that combines the roles and responsibilities of the government, private sector, and charities. As a result, social entrepreneurship is expected to be more capable of achieving social goals and increasing the competitiveness and sustainability of social entities or target groups (Canestrino et al., 2020; Finlayson & Roy, 2019; Sparviero, 2019).

Conventional entrepreneurship and social entrepreneurship have different goals. The main goal of social entrepreneurship is to create social value (Roy et al., 2013). Commercial value is only an instrument for pursuing social goals. According to Hota et al. (2020), the value prioritized by social entrepreneurship cannot be measured based on profit or customer satisfaction. Instead, it should be measured through social impact. Gupta et al. (2020) have outlined several dimensions that make up the concept of social value, namely, 1) social value-added, 2) empowerment and social change, 3) social innovation, and 4) system changes.

The Malaysian government aims to increase Malaysia's position in several International indices, such as the top 25 in the Global Entrepreneurship Index, the top 10 in the Global Competitiveness Index, the top 10 in World Bank Doing Business, and the top 20 in the Global Innovation Index (GII). The Ministry of Entrepreneur Development and Cooperative of Malaysia has established the first policy document to enact inclusive and competitive entrepreneurial development policies, particularly in the small and medium-sized enterprise (SME) sector (Rasyid & Bowen, 2021). The policy also aims to stimulate the development of social entrepreneurs. The ministry has also developed the Malaysia Social Entrepreneurship Blueprint 2030 (SEMy2030) to create a cohesive and holistic ecosystem that supports the growth of social entrepreneurship in the country. SEMy2030 has developed five strategic thrusts, twenty strategies, and forty-five initiatives.

Generally, Malaysia is still beginning to develop social entrepreneurship (Che Nawi et al., 2022). Previous studies have found several obstacles in supporting social entrepreneurship, including 1) a lack of rigorous effort with industry to promote entrepreneurial activities (Aloulou & Algarni, 2022), 2) insufficient funds to carry out the agenda of entrepreneurship (Chen, 2023), 3) insufficient environmental education and facilities (Karatas-Ozkan et al., 2023), and 4) reluctancy among youth to choose entrepreneurship as a career (Ali et al., 2019; Gupta et al., 2020; Sparviero, 2019; Weaver, 2020). In Malaysia, there are no clear policies, regulatory framework, lead agency, financial structure, or financial security for social enterprise (Ahrari et al., 2019; Rosca et al., 2020; Roslan et al., 2022). Social enterprises are governed by Acts used by most conventional business entities. These include the Cooperative Societies Act 1993 (Amendment) 2007, the Companies Act 1965 (Amendment) 2016, and the Societies Act 1966 (Amendment) 2006.

Most social entrepreneurs operate within a continuum of business and voluntary charity (Roslan et al., 2022). The idea of social entrepreneurship from the public view remains to be seen, as there still needs to be more awareness due to the vague social enterprise framework (Chan et al., 2021; Morris et al., 2021). Besides, the technology acceptance and modernization level among social enterprise activities could be higher (Rosca et al., 2020). Many of these issues have yet to be answered, which could reduce the young generation's interest in engaging in social entrepreneurship. Therefore, a strategic approach to enable comprehensive social entrepreneurship is vital. This study proposed several determinants influencing people's intentions to become social entrepreneurs.

Early exposure to cognitive ability is necessary to support and encourage the young generation to enter the field of social entrepreneurship (Karatas-Ozkan et al., 2023). According to García-González and Ramírez-Montoya (2020), cognitive ability is necessary for realizing the desire to become a social entrepreneur. Entrepreneurial education must ensure that students have positive entrepreneurial skills and desires (Urban, 2020). Empirical studies also have found that social support could influence people's engagement in social entrepreneurship (Duong, 2023; Mukhtar et al., 2021; Neneh, 2022). Social support is a function of normative beliefs that represent the perception of others and whether the behavior should be performed (Aloulou & Algarni, 2022). In addition, many studies have found that personality traits such as altruism are essential enablers for social entrepreneurship (Canestrino et al., 2020; Stirzaker et al., 2021). Altruism is an attitude of paying attention and prioritizing the interests and goodness of others. An altruistic person has a higher standard of justice, exhibits social responsibility, embodies actions based on critical thinking, and is more empathetic against the feelings and rights of others (Pfattheicher et al., 2022). In social entrepreneurship, the act or behavior of social entrepreneurship is believed to be motivated by these empathic-altruistic emotions (Polas & Afshar Jahanshahi, 2021).

Therefore, the objective of this study is 1) to identify the influence of social support and cognitive ability on social entrepreneurship intention, 2) to determine the mediation effect of altruism towards the relationship between social support, cognitive ability, and social entrepreneurship intention, and 3) to compare the results between male and female youth. The central questions guiding this empirical research are:

RQ1. Do social support and cognitive ability influence social entrepreneurship intention?
RQ2. Does altruism mediate the relationship between social support, cognitive ability, and social entrepreneurship intention?
RQ3. Do the relationships between male and female youth differ?

This study is significant for several reasons. The result of this study also has several managerial implications for entrepreneurship bodies and institutions in planning future social entrepreneurship programs. Studying entrepreneurial tendencies among youth will allow initial plans and actions to be formulated. This study also delivers new insights into the current literature since it has examined the proposed model from the gender perspective. Gender differences will lead to differences in attitude, social entrepreneurship action, and intention (Hmieleski & Sheppard, 2019; Laguía et al., 2019; Sabri & Thomas, 2019). Undeniably, gender roles could significantly influence the intention to succeed and engage in social entrepreneurship.

## LITERATURE REVIEW & THEORETICAL FRAMEWORK

### Social Identity Theory & Institutional Theory

The theoretical foundations of this study are social identity theory and institutional theory. One's group membership defines social identity. Social identity theory was formulated by social psychologists Henri Tajfel and John Turner in the 1970s. They describe situations in which social identity becomes more important than a person's identity as an individual. This theory also determines how social identity can influence behavior. This theory explains the cognitive processes that lead people to determine their group membership and the motivational processes that allow people to maintain a positive social identity by comparing their social groups to other groups. According to Tajfel (1982), social identity consists of three main components: cognitive, evaluative, and emotional components (as cited in Harwood, 2020). Individuals categorize themselves with certain groups that will determine their tendency to behave according to their group membership. The emotional component emphasizes more on how much feelings an individual has towards his or her group.

Individuals try to reduce subjective uncertainty about the social world and their position in the social world. Individuals like to know who they are and how they should behave. Social categorization can reduce uncertainty because it describes how people (including themselves) will/should behave and interact with others (Brown, 2020). Social entrepreneurship in Malaysia is a new field and needs more exposure and support from the community. Social entrepreneurship is the creator of new innovative business methods to solve social problems, and social support is crucial to encouraging individuals to become social entrepreneurs.

Moreover, altruism is also closely related to grouping and a sense of belonging. It is an attitude or instinct that a person pays attention to and prioritizes the interests and goodness of others above his or her own interests (Canestrino et al., 2020). Altruism itself is the opposite of selfishness, which is more self-centered than the interests of others. A person who does altruism is also called an altruist. All the good deeds done by an altruist usually appear sincerely without any selfishness (Brown et al., 2019; Munir et al., 2019). Moreover, the normative and cultural-cognitive systems are among the elements that social theorists consider vital elements of institutional theory. It is the same as social identity theory, a normative system. The normative system strengthens and facilitates social actions. The actor's cognitive understanding and interpretation could influence human behavior and action in the cognitive paradigm. Based on the above theories, this study proposed that social support and cognitive ability could influence social entrepreneurship intention, and the relationship also could be strengthened with altruism characteristics.

## Landscaping Social Entrepreneurship in Malaysia

Malaysia has thirteen states and three federal territories (i.e., Putrajaya, Labuan, and Kuala Lumpur). Malaysia is in Southeast Asia, with an area of 330,803 km2. The capital city is Kuala Lumpur, and the federal government's center is Putrajaya. The total population of this country is estimated at 32.7 million in 2022, compared to 32.6 million in 2021. The country is separated into two regions — Peninsular Malaysia and East Malaysia (i.e., Sabah and Sarawak). Social issues related to education, health, public justice, marginalized groups, and youth have an intensity that challenges the government, which could affect the country's main agenda

(Canestrino et al., 2020). The government is urged to find the best approach from the root level to ensure the sustainability of the country's socio-economic and social entrepreneurship, which has emerged as one of the crucial solutions.

Social entrepreneurship is one of the main agendas of the Ministry of Entrepreneur Development and Cooperative of Malaysia. The Malaysian Social Entrepreneurship Action Plan 2030 (SEMy2030) is the basis for the government's efforts to create an ideal social entrepreneurship ecosystem and provide a conducive environment for social enterprises to grow. The concept of social entrepreneurship may still be new among the Malaysian community. However, the fact is that the principle of social entrepreneurship started to exist in Malaysia in 1922 when the Cooperative Societies Enactment 1922 was gazetted and became the basis for the formation of cooperatives. Social entrepreneurship has been applied through various entities such as cooperatives, charities, community organizations, and companies (Che Nawi et al., 2022).

The Malaysian Innovation Agency, or *Amanah Ikhtiar Malaysia*, is a statutory body established by the government in 2010 to drive the development of the innovation ecosystem in Malaysia. This agency was later dissolved in 2020. In 2014, the Malaysian Global Innovation and Creativity Center (MaGIC) was established under the Ministry of Finance to develop impact-driven technology start-ups and become a catalyst for an inclusive social entrepreneurship ecosystem. MaGIC has developed the Malaysian Social Enterprise Action Plan 2015-2018 to make social entrepreneurship a sustainable, equitable, and people-centric sector (Rasyid & Bowen, 2021).

In 2018, MaGIC was placed under the patronage of the Ministry of Entrepreneur Development and Cooperative of Malaysia. In line with the new focus under this Ministry, the National Social Enterprise Accreditation Guidelines were developed in 2019 and implemented by MaGIC to recognize and encourage the achievement of social enterprise. MaGIC was then placed under the Ministry of Science, Technology, and Innovation (MOSTI) in 2020, and MaGIC's functions were realigned by focusing on start-up-based companies' technology and techniques. In recognizing social entrepreneurship in Malaysia, the Ministry of Entrepreneur Development and Cooperative has developed Accreditation Guidelines for Social Enterprise (SE.A) to recognize and confirm social enterprise status (Rasyid & Bowen, 2021). SEMy2030 focuses on social enterprises driven by goals and has clear and identifiable beneficiaries. Goals and target groups or recipients of the set benefits align with the Malaysian Shared Prosperity Vision 2023 and the United Nations Sustainable Development Goals (17 SDGs). At the higher education level, various activities and initiatives related to social entrepreneurship, including strategic collaboration with government agencies and private companies, have been arranged to promote entrepreneurship. The purpose of this initiative is to provide entrepreneurship awareness and to improve the entrepreneurial environment.

## Social Entrepreneurship Engagement: A Comparison between Male and Female

Entrepreneurship landscaping in many countries has changed, and many governments have promoted female entrepreneurship in their policies and agendas. The increasing number of female entrepreneurs could help reduce socio-economic imbalance and unemployment (Corrêa et al., 2022). There is an emerging number of female entrepreneurship leaders, and this progress is crucial for achieving gender equality. However, entrepreneurship is still the dominant male sector (Tillmar et al., 2022). Females tend to be underprivileged as entrepreneurs and empirical studies have discovered that entrepreneurship intention among females is lower due to industry bias and entrepreneurship barriers (Ahmed et al., 2019; Tillmar et al., 2022). The differences in entrepreneurial intention and behavior between males and females can be attributed to differences in social direction and inspiration. The male is expected to be agentic, aggressive, independent, leading, and goal oriented (Laguía et al., 2019). At the same time, females are likely to be collective, such as communicative and obedient (Aparisi-Torrijo & Ribes-Giner, 2022). Females may also rely on their relatives and other essential people's opinions when starting a business (Wang et al., 2020). Hence, social support is an essential enabler in predicting female entrepreneurship intention.

On the other hand, attitudes are the best predictor of entrepreneurship intention for the male group. Previous studies also found that females have lower self-confidence in managing entrepreneurial activity (Martínez-Rodríguez et al., 2022). Entrepreneurship has been associated with general characteristics such as risk-taking, the need for achievement, and the internal locus of control (Musara & Nieuwenhuizen, 2020). Females tend to be feminists, which is an imbalance with the characteristics needed to start a new venture (Ennis, 2019). Therefore, empirical studies have recommended the role of entrepreneurship education in shaping entrepreneurial attitudes and intentions for both genders (Elliott et al., 2021).

In addition, there are inconsistent findings related to gender differences, which has urged the need for further research studies. A few researchers believed that there is a difference between males and females, which could also be determined by people's intellect and behavior (e.g., Sabri & Thomas, 2019; Kawai & Kazumi, 2021). On the other hand, some studies have found no significant variation between male and female entrepreneurship intention and behavior (e.g., Armuña et al., 2020; van Ewijk & Belghiti-Mahut, 2019). Likewise, most of the previous research on entrepreneurship is heavily focused on Western countries, and the study in the context of developing countries is still being determined. The comparison investigation between males and females is a promising direction for new research.

## Proclivity of Social Entrepreneurship

### Social Support

Social support refers to individual perception based on other people's thoughts on whether it should be done. Empirical studies have found that social support such as peer support, family support, university support, and others influences intentions social entrepreneurship intention (Aloulou & Algarni, 2022; Duong, 2023; Javadian et al., 2021; Neneh, 2022). Hence, entrepreneurship culture needs to start from the bottom level, including the elementary school level, to the higher education level and society in general (Urban, 2020). Through the holistic culture, new generations of social entrepreneurs will be created. Lecturers, for instance, play an essential role in promoting entrepreneurship agenda among university students. However, some lecturers are unwilling to participate in this process because of a lack of entrepreneurial skills and knowledge. Social entrepreneurship needs to be embedded in the existing curriculum to support engagement in social entrepreneurship (Hassan et al., 2020). The involvement of industry practitioners in teaching and entrepreneurial learning is encouraged, and a synergistic entrepreneurial ecosystem between academia, industry, government representatives, and community members is needed (Ali et al., 2019). These initiatives can foster a culture of entrepreneurship, sowing knowledge and essential entrepreneurial skills and creating a creative and innovative community (Mukhtar et al., 2021). Environmental factors such as family members, friends, neighbors, local communities, and educational institutions are the primary sources of social entrepreneurship motivation (Ali et al., 2019; Aloulou & Algarni, 2022; Shi et al., 2020; Urban, 2020). Based on the above reasoning, this study posited the following hypothesis:

> Hypothesis 1a: There will be a positive relationship between social support and the social entrepreneurship intention of male youth.
> Hypothesis 1b: There will be a positive relationship between social support and the intention of female youth to pursue social entrepreneurship.

## Cognitive Ability

Empirical studies have found that cognitive skills boost confidence, motivation, and intention to become a social entrepreneur (Raza et al., 2020; Pansuwong et al., 2023). Cognitive ability refers to thinking, reasoning, making decisions, and judging fairly. Entrepreneurial cognitive ability can be defined as a person's ability to explore, evaluate, and use opportunities for entrepreneurial activities (Raza et al., 2020). Entrepreneurial cognitive ability also indicates the competencies in identifying opportunities, risk-taking tendencies, and self-confidence. It is reported to have a direct relationship with entrepreneurship education (Alshebami et al., 2022; Kawai & Kazumi, 2021).

Elliott, Mantler, and Huggins (2021) found that entrepreneurship education can promote the development of entrepreneurial behavior and cognitive ability to produce more entrepreneurs among graduates, reduce the unemployment rate, and increase business opportunities. Alshebami, Seraj, and Alzain (2022) stated that educators must display a proactive attitude in the classroom to ensure that the students have entrepreneurial characteristics and mindsets. The entrepreneur's cognitive ability requires critical thinking, essential in producing future generations who can make accurate decisions (Kawai & Kazumi, 2021). Cognitive ability also includes problem-solving skills, crucial in improving and obtaining appropriate business management solutions (Chen et al., 2020). Therefore, this study postulated the following hypothesis:

> Hypothesis 2a: There will be a positive relationship between cognitive ability and social entrepreneurship intention of male youth.
> Hypothesis 2b: There will be a positive relationship between cognitive ability and social entrepreneurship intention of female youth.

## Mediating Role of Altruism

Scholars have discovered that demographic factors influence the motivation for social entrepreneurship; among the demographic factors that influence are gender, socialization, experience, and early exposure (Satar & Natasha, 2019). On the other hand, empirical studies have also found that the motivation factor of social entrepreneurship is also influenced by the individual's values, such as the aspiration and desire to help individuals, encouragement or support from the local community, involvement of family members, the desire to return favors, mutual love for people in need, and altruism attitude (Brown et al., 2019; Munir et al., 2019). The philosopher Auguste Comte used the term altruism in the 19th century. Altruism comes from the Greek word *alteri*, which means another person. Altruism is an act of prosocial behavior that benefits others without expecting any reward or a gift from the person being helped (Pfattheicher et al., 2022). Altruism is a response that generates positive feelings in individuals and encourages them constantly to help others (MacAskill, 2019). Canestrino et al. (2020) found that altruism can be developed with empathy in everyone. Empathy is an inherent attitude in everyone whose existence does not require conditions.

Stirzaker et al. (2021) found that concern for others' views has a significant positive relationship with emotional responses and a tendency toward prosocial behavior. The findings of this study also show individual differences in supporting diverse prosocial behavior. A study by Carrizales et al. (2021) about causal characteristics, similarity, self-efficacy, and altruism has found a significant positive relationship with prosocial behavior. Xi et al. (2022) conducted a study to examine the differences in the influence of gender and personality type of altruism. The study results show that females' altruistic behaviors and attitudes were higher, facilitating a more vital life purpose (Xi et al., 2022). This paper highlights the mediating role of altruism, which is considered a pioneer study that examines the possible mediating role of altruism in the relationship between social support, cognitive ability, and social entrepreneurship intention. From these arguments, the following is hypothesized:

> Hypothesis 3a: Altruism mediates the associations between social support and social entrepreneurship intention of male youth.
> Hypothesis 3b: Altruism plays a mediating role in the associations between social support and social entrepreneurship intention of female youth.
> Hypothesis 3c: Altruism mediates the associations between cognitive ability and social entrepreneurship intention of male youth.
> Hypothesis 3d: Altruism mediates the associations between cognitive ability and social entrepreneurship intention of female youth.

The research model is shown in Figure 1.

*Figure 1. Research model*

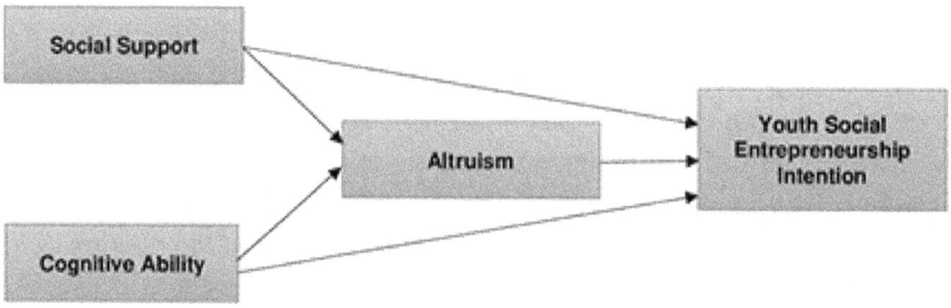

## MATERIALS AND METHODS

### Sample and Procedure

This study used a quantitative approach using a questionnaire as a research instrument. The questionnaire is an instrument used to collect data formally and systematically so that the data can be analyzed descriptively and inferentially. The population of this study was Malaysian youth in Peninsular Malaysia. The age at which a person is considered a youth varies worldwide. The United Nations General Assembly defines youth as between 19 and 29. According to the Ministry of Youth and Sports, in Malaysia, youth refer to people between 15 and 30 years old. Therefore, the main criteria used for this study were Malaysian youth aged 18 to 30 who live in Peninsular Malaysia. This does not involve children under the age of 18. The sample size is determined based on Kline's (2005) sample size guidelines for analyzing the structural equation model (SEM). SEM analysis is a suitable method to identify cause-and-effect relationships between several variables in a quantitative study.

A model built based on solid theory. Our research aims to combine two theoretical foundations (i.e., social identity theory and institutional theory). This model has four latent variables: social support, cognitive ability, altruism, and social entrepreneurship intention. Kline (2005) suggests that a sample of 100 is considered small, 100 to 200 is medium, and a sample over 200 is considered significant. For the calculation of sample size, another rule of thumb was suggested by Sekaran and Bougie (2016): a sample size between 30 and 500 might be adequate. Therefore, 500 respondents have been chosen as the sample for this study. For comparison data, the study divided the sample into two groups of 250 respondents of both genders. A two-stage sampling technique was employed for this project. First is a purpose sampling technique, and second is a convenience sampling technique.

### Measures

This study uses an online approach for data collection. The questionnaire used has four parts: A, B, C, D, and E. Part A is a questionnaire related to the demographic profile of the respondents. Part B is a questionnaire related to social support measurement, containing four items adapted from Oftedal et al.'s (2018) study. Part C contains questions covering aspects of cognitive ability and five items adapted from the Oftedal et al. (2018) study. In this section, the question is aimed at the perspective that discusses the cognitive ability owned by the individual. Then, part D is organized with five items that measure mediating variables (i.e., altruism). The items are adapted from Manzur and Olavarrieta (2021). Finally, part E measures social entrepreneurship intention. The measurement of social entrepreneurship intention contains seven items adapted from a study conducted by Iancu et al. (2021). The form of the question used is closed questions using a Likert scale from one to five, namely: (1) strongly disagree, (2) disagree, (3) moderate, (4) agree, and (5) strongly agree. Table 1 shows the measurement items and Cronbach's alpha of the variables in this study.

*Table 1. Measurement of the variable*

| Variable | Items | Mean | | SD | | α | |
|---|---|---|---|---|---|---|---|
| | | M | F | M | F | M | F |
| Social Entrepreneurship Intention | SEI1. I know the concept of social entrepreneurship.<br>SEI2. I identified various social problems in my region that entrepreneurial initiatives could solve.<br>SEI3. I want to work in a social enterprise.<br>SEI4. I am involved in various projects and social activities.<br>SEI5. If I had the necessary funds, I would initiate a social business.<br>SEI6. I prefer to be involved in activities that do not bring me a substantial financial income but allow me to help those around me.<br>SEI7. In my own business, I have integrated a social responsibility component. | 2.073 | 4.323 | 0.043 | 1.896 | 0.712 | 0.800 |
| Social Support | SS1. Those who start their businesses are respected.<br>SS2. I look up to those starting their enterprises.<br>SS3. Entrepreneurial initiatives are seen as the "road to success."<br>SS4. Starting your own business is a respected career path. | 3.990 | 4.399 | | 0.820 | 0.714 | 0.843 |
| Cognitive Ability | CA1. I know how to handle the risks associated with social enterprise.<br>CA2. I have the skills required to manage a social enterprise.<br>CA3. I know who may help establish a social enterprise.<br>CA4. I know the procedures for managing a social enterprise.<br>CA5. I know how to develop ideas for social enterprise. | 4.110 | 4.099 | | 0.984 | 0.762 | 0.831 |
| Altruism | A1. I have given money to a charity.<br>A2. I have donated goods or clothes to a charity.<br>A3. I have done volunteer work for a charity.<br>A4. I have helped carry a stranger's belongings.<br>A5. I have made a change for someone I did not know. | 3.122 | 4.484 | | 1.057 | 0.841 | 0.855 |

Note: M, Male; F, Female

## Analysis

The final data were filled into SPSS software to be analyzed using the structural equation modeling (SEM) analysis of moment structure (AMOS). SEM is particularly suitable for modeling the relationship between multiple constructs simultaneously. First, the approach used is Confirmatory Factor Analysis (CFA) to analyze the measurement model. CFA determines whether a hypothesis model fits a data set (Hair et al., 2010). There are six fit indices used, namely: Goodness Fit Index (GFI), Tucker Lewis Index (TLI), Comparative Fit Index (CFI), and Normal Fit Index (NFI) (Byrne, 2010; Hair et al., 2010). In this study, the value used for Chi Square/Degree of Freedom ($\chi^2$/df) is less than 5 (< 5), which is in line with Kline (2005). While the Root Mean Square Error of Approximation (RMSEA) is less than 0.08 (< 0.08) is referred (Hair et al., 2010). Convergent validity (CV) refers to how closely a test relates to other tests that measure the same or similar constructs. According to Hair et al. (2010), CV values are obtained based on factor loading, average variance extracted (AVE), and composite reliability (CR). Factor loading and CR values must exceed 0.60 and 0.70, respectively, as Hair et al. (2010) suggested. On the other hand, AVE values need to exceed 0.50 (Byrne, 2010).

# RESULTS

## Demographic Profiles

Four hundred thirty-three questionnaires were collected from the youth respondents from both genders. A self-administered approach was used in this study, whereby 221 and 222 responses were collected from male and female participants, respectively. Among all the sample respondents, more than half ranged from the age limit of 19-22 years, 79.2% (male) and 77% (female). Then, most of the respondents are single for both male (96.8%) and female (77.5%) data. Then, the final question asked whether the respondents had any experience in social entrepreneurship activities. Most acknowledged having experience, with 75.6% (male) and 85.1% (female). The details of the respondents' profiles are listed in Table 2.

*Table 2. Demographic profile of the sample (N=443)*

| No. | Profile | Frequency (n) n=221 | | Percentage (%) n=222 | |
|---|---|---|---|---|---|
| | | M | F | M | F |
| 1 | **Age** | | | | |
| | 18 years | 3 | 7 | 1.4 | 3.2 |
| | 19 -22 years | 175 | 171 | 79.2 | 77 |
| | 23-26 years | 40 | 42 | 18.1 | 18.9 |
| | 27-30 years | 3 | 2 | 1.4 | 0.9 |
| | >30 years | 0 | 0 | 0 | 0 |
| 2 | **Marital Status** | | | | |
| | Married | 7 | 50 | 3.2 | 22.5 |
| | Single | 214 | 172 | 96.8 | 77.5 |
| 3 | **Social entrepreneurship experience** | | | | |
| | Yes | 167 | 189 | 75.6 | 85.1 |
| | No | 54 | 33 | 24.4 | 14.9 |

Note: M, Male; F, Female

## Confirmatory Factor Analysis (CFA)

The fit index of the male and female models is shown in Table 3. The male model fits well ($\chi^2$/df = 2.125, $p < 0.001$, CFI =0.950, NFI = 0.970, GFI =0.960, TLI = 0.950, and RMSEA =0.038). The female model fits are as following: $\chi^2$/df =2.089, p < 0.001, CFI =0.940, NFI =0.960, GFI = 0.970, TLI =0.960, and RMSEA =0.042). We can see that hypothesis models fit the data set by evaluating both the male and female models.

*Table 3. Fitness indices for male and female data*

| *Fitness Indices* | *Value Limit* | *Male* | *Female* |
|---|---|---|---|
| Chi-Square/Degree of Freedom ($\chi^2$/df) | < 5 | 2.125 | 2.089 |
| Comparative Fit Index (CFI) | > 0.90 | 0.950 | 0.940 |
| Normal Fit Index (NFI) | > 0.90 | 0.970 | 0.960 |
| Goodness Fit Index (GFI) | > 0.90 | 0.960 | 0.970 |
| Tucker Lewis Index (TLI) | > 0.90 | 0.950 | 0.960 |
| Root Mean Square Error of Approximation (RMSEA) | < 0.08 | 0.038 | 0.042 |

Source: Byrne, 2010; Hair et al. (2010); Kline (2005)

## Convergent and Discriminant Validity

Based on Table 4, it is known that each indicator of the research variable has a factor loading value exceeding 0.60. The data also shows that Average Variance Extracted (AVE) and composite reliability (CR) values exceed 0.50 and 0.60, respectively, as suggested by Hair et al. (2010). All indicators are declared eligible or valid for research and can be used for further analysis.

*Table 4. Value of factor loading, Average Variance Extracted (AVE), Composite Reliability (CR)*

| Variable | Items | Item Loadings | | AVE | | CR | |
|---|---|---|---|---|---|---|---|
| | | M | F | M | F | M | F |
| Social Entrepreneurship Intention | SEI1<br>SEI2<br>SEI3<br>SEI4<br>SEI5<br>SEI6<br>SEI7 | 0.642<br>0.701<br>0.850<br>0.820<br>0.772<br>0.718<br>0.752 | 0.788<br>0.745<br>0.821<br>0.834<br>0.872<br>0.718<br>0.742 | 0.786 | 0.743 | 0.875 | 0.890 |
| Social Support | SS1<br>SS2<br>SS3<br>SS4 | 0.814<br>0.726<br>0.810<br>0.768 | 0.714<br>0.736<br>0.800<br>0.744 | 0.732 | 0.737 | 0.863 | 0.816 |
| Cognitive Ability | CA1<br>CA2<br>CA3<br>CA4<br>CA5 | 0.851<br>0.882<br>0.827<br>0.802<br>0.752 | 0.811<br>0.842<br>0.833<br>0.800<br>0.822 | 0.811 | 0.752 | 0.932 | 0.905 |
| Altruism | A1<br>A2<br>A3<br>A4<br>A5 | 0.854<br>0.849<br>0.820<br>0.807<br>0.742 | 0.814<br>0.823<br>0.817<br>0.767<br>0.743 | 0.800 | 0.789 | 0.852 | 0.832 |

Note: Average Variance Extracted, AVE; Composite Reliability, CR; Male, M; Female, F

Discriminant validity ensures that each concept of the latent construct is different from other latent variables. The model has good discriminant validity if each loading value from each indicator of a latent variable has an enormous loading value with other loading values for the latent variable. Discriminant validity can also be checked by testing the correlation value of the latent variable with the Average Variance Extracted (AVE) value. The correlation value between the constructs is more than 0.50, below the level of 0.85, proving that the discriminant validity has been fulfilled (Fornell & Larcker, 1981). Discriminant validity is also established when the square root of AVE is greater than the correlation (Fornell & Larcker, 1981). Tables 5 and 6 show that discriminant validity is achieved.

*Table 5. Discriminant validity of construct (male)*

| No. | Variable | 1 | 2 | 3 | 4 |
|---|---|---|---|---|---|
| 1 | Social Entrepreneurship Intention | **0.886** | | | |
| 2 | Social Support | 0.534 | **0.855** | | |
| 3 | Cognitive Ability | 0.557 | 0.676 | **0.900** | |
| 4 | Altruism | 0.681 | 0.611 | 0.583 | **0.890** |

Note: The squared root of AVE is shown in bold on a diagonal.

*Table 6. Discriminant validity of construct (female)*

| No. | Variable | 1 | 2 | 3 | 4 |
|---|---|---|---|---|---|
| 1 | Social Entrepreneurship Intention | **0.861** | | | |
| 2 | Social Support | 0.540 | **0.858** | | |
| 3 | Cognitive Ability | 0.517 | 0.634 | **0.867** | |
| 4 | Altruism | 0.615 | 0.564 | 0.589 | **0.888** |

Note: The squared root of AVE is shown in bold on a diagonal.

## Structural Model Analyses

*Table 7. Results of the hypothesised model*

| Dependent Variable | Independent Variable | Std. Estimate | |
|---|---|---|---|
| **Standardized Direct Effects** | | | |
| | | M | F |
| Social Entrepreneurship Intention | Social Support | 0.220*** | 0.011 |
| Social Entrepreneurship Intention | Cognitive Ability | 0.217*** | 0.024 |
| Social Entrepreneurship Intention | Altruism | 0.449*** | 0.646*** |
| Social Support | Cognitive Ability | 0.543*** | 0.574*** |
| Altruism | Social Support | 0.411*** | 0.412*** |
| Altruism | Cognitive Ability | 0.451*** | 0.471*** |
| **Standardized Indirect Effects (Mediation Effect via Altruism)** | | | |

continued on following page

*Table 7. Continued*

| Dependent Variable | | Independent Variable | Std. Estimate | |
|---|---|---|---|---|
| **Standardized Direct Effects** | | | | |
| | | | M | F |
| Social Entrepreneurship Intention | | Social Support | 0.185*** | 0.266*** |
| Social Entrepreneurship Intention | | Cognitive Ability | 0.202*** | 0.304*** |
| **Standardized Total Effects (Direct Effect + Indirect Effect)** | | | | |
| Social Entrepreneurship Intention | | Social Support | 0.405*** | 0.277*** |
| Social Entrepreneurship Intention | | Cognitive Ability | 0.419*** | 0.328*** |

Note: ***Paths are significant at the 1% level ($p < 0.01$). ***Indirect effects are significant at the 1% with bootstrap at 5000 and bias-corrected percentile method. Male, M; Female, F

The model for the male model explained ($R^2 = 0.448$) 44.8% in social entrepreneurship intention, and the female group sample explained ($R^2= 0.557$) 55.7% variance. This suggests that the model is more suitable for females.

## Male Data

As shown in Table 7, it was discovered that social support ($\beta$ =0.220, $p$<0.001), cognitive ability ($\beta$ =0.217, $p$<0.001), and altruism ($\beta$ =0.449, $p$<0.001) have a significant association with social entrepreneurship intention. Thus, H1a and H2a were accepted. The association between cognitive ability and social support was also significant ($\beta$ =0.574, $p$<0.001). Moreover, direct relationships between social support and altruism ($\beta$ =00.411, $p$<0.001) and cognitive ability and altruism ($\beta$ =0.451, $p$<0.001) were also significantly tested. Next, the mediation effect was tested. The results confirm that the relationship between social support ($\beta$ =0.185, $p$<0.001), cognitive ability ($\beta$ =0.202, $p$<0.001), and social entrepreneurship intention is partially mediated by altruism. Hence, H3a and H3c were accepted. The total effects were also calculated for mediating paths, adding indirect and direct effects (Hayes, 2017). The final tested model is summarised in Figure 2.

## Female Data

First, it was discovered that social support ($\beta$ =0.011, $p$>0.001) and cognitive ability ($\beta$ =0.024, $p$>0.001) do not have a significant association with social entrepreneurship intention. Therefore, we rejected H1b and H2b. On the other hand, altruism significantly predicts social entrepreneurship intention ($\beta$=0.646, $p$<0.001). The association between cognitive ability and social support was also significant ($\beta$ =0.574, $p$<0.001). Moreover, direct relationships between social support and altruism

($\beta$ =0.412, $p$<0.001) and cognitive ability and altruism ($\beta$ =0.471, $p$<0.001) were also significantly tested. In contrast to male data, female data show that the relationship between social support ($\beta$ =0.266, $p$<0.001), cognitive ability ($\beta$ =0.304, $p$<0.001), and social entrepreneurship intention is fully mediated by altruism. Thus, H3b and H3d were accepted. The final tested model is summarised in Figure 3.

*Figure 2. Final tested model (male)*

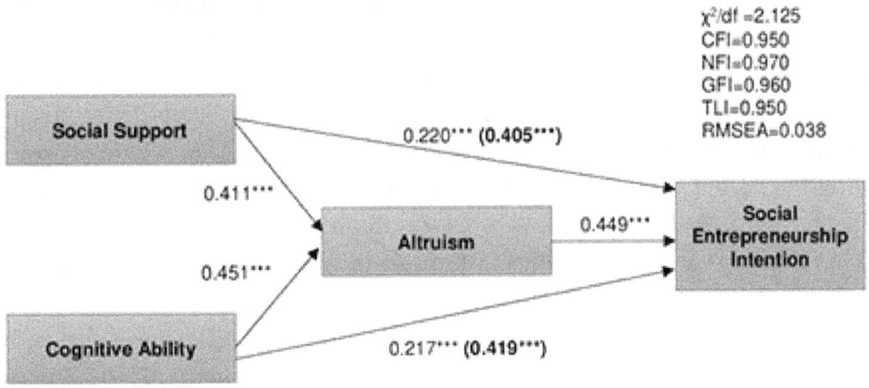


*Note: The total effects for mediated paths are shown in bold parentheses.*

*Figure 3. Final tested model (female)*

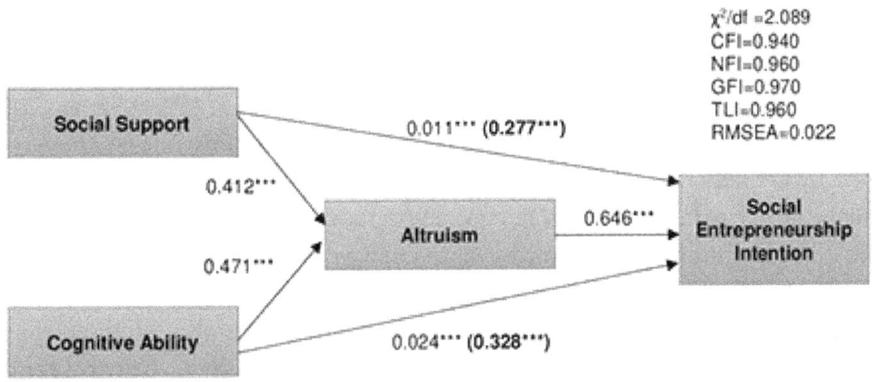


*Note: The total effects for mediated paths are shown in bold parentheses.*

## DISCUSSION

To the best of the researchers' knowledge, only a handful of studies have approached the mediating effect of altruism in determining the factors of social entrepreneurship intention. Several positive findings were observed based on the results, which are discussed further concerning prior theory and research. The primary purpose of this study was to identify gender-related differences in the interrelations among altruism, social support, and cognitive ability in social entrepreneurship. This study examines the roles of social support and cognitive ability in determining social entrepreneurial intention through the mediation of altruism personality. The findings affirm that altruism significantly mediates social support–social entrepreneurial intention and cognitive ability–social entrepreneurial intention relationships. The findings indicated that altruism partly mediates the relationship between social support, cognitive ability, and male social entrepreneurial intention.

On the other hand, the findings also imply that the relationship between social support, cognitive ability, and female social entrepreneurship intention is fully mediated by altruism. The data provide evidence of three significant results: (i) both female and male youth's intention to become social entrepreneurs are influenced by cognitive ability and social support; (ii) females are expected to be more altruistic than males; (iii) men do not need altruism personality to become social entrepreneurs. For men, although individual personality, such as altruism, is the most critical enabler of social entrepreneurship, the success of a male entrepreneur may be influenced by the influence of family, education, skills, experience, university support, and others (Xi et al., 2022). Based on total participation from the demographic table, it was found that female youth tend to be more involved in social entrepreneurship activities than male youth. As supported, experimental studies have repeatedly found that females are more altruistic than males (Carrizales et al., 2021; Xi et al., 2022).

Wherever they live in the world, whatever cultural or family influences, women generally are better at empathizing with others than men. The issue of differences in social behavior based on gender, especially among the younger generation, needs to be given attention by the government to enable effective social entrepreneurship program development. Both men and women have their strengths and weaknesses. The stigma of social entrepreneurship is only suitable for women entrepreneurs and can be abolished if proper strategies and training are executed. Altruism sense is the gateway to the making process of future social entrepreneurs. Thus, personality training and coaching for both genders should be a compulsory social enterprise training syllabus. Every social entrepreneur needs to have a social motive and goals.

Social entrepreneurship has grown in Malaysia over the past few years. With the passion to achieve positive social change, more and more individuals and organizations are joining forces to address various social and environmental problems significantly. Nowadays, the support for social entrepreneurship in society has been increasing. Thus, it is possible to find a small number of individuals making contributions to help and change society, which can influence the young generation to try to become social entrepreneurs. Examples are officials who channel advice to the government on overcoming social issues, a project manager working for an international development agency, and managers who work to help people without housing.

Social entrepreneurship in Malaysia goes beyond traditional business boundaries and strives to find sustainable and innovative solutions to society's complex problems. The Malaysian government plays a role in supporting the development of social entrepreneurship through various policies and programs. The National Entrepreneurship Policy 2030 has become a guide for developing social entrepreneurship in Malaysia. Although social entrepreneurship in Malaysia is experiencing growth, some challenges still need to be overcome. One of the main challenges is access to adequate capital and financing. Many social entrepreneurship initiatives still rely on private funds or limited charity funding.

As for policy and practical implications, support from the private sector and government in providing capital and training will be very helpful in promoting the development and sustainability of this initiative. In addition, awareness and understanding of social entrepreneurship must be increased among the public. By increasing understanding of the potential of social entrepreneurship to create positive change, more individuals and organizations can get involved in this movement. Education about social entrepreneurship and practical experience with social initiatives can also be vital to attracting more parties to get involved. In addition, inculcating values and aspects of social entrepreneurship should be applied from the community's grassroots level. This can be realized through the involvement of educational institutions, businesses, and non-governmental bodies that can implement the principles of entrepreneurship and social entrepreneurship among young people. For example, at present, Financial Industry Collective Outreach (FINCO) through Bank Negara Malaysia and Social Enterprise Academy Malaysia is conducting a pilot project called Good SENS (Social Enterprise Network Schools) where primary schools around Malaysia can apply the value of social entrepreneurship in the aim of providing financial literacy education to young people and school students.

The aspect of systemic change that the government should prioritize to ensure the sustainability and survival of the country's social entrepreneurship in the long term. Often, the topic of social entrepreneurship is seen as a tactical initiative for "political mileage" that only has a short-term effect and is less comprehensive in terms of implementation. Suppose the government sees social entrepreneurship activities as a strategic element that can develop the country's socio-economic status. In that case, it is also appropriate for the government to create long-term initiatives in stages and pragmatically as developed countries such as the United Kingdom, the United States, South Korea, and Singapore. Among the general examples and recommendations of practical measures that should be considered are incentives and initiatives regarding resources for local social and micro enterprises.

Among other examples are commercial incentives through taxes and investment incentives to boost trade activities for social enterprise participants in Malaysia. For now, there is no denying the potential of social entrepreneurship that can be empowered if it is taken and adapted from the point of view of the national agenda. For this reason, countries that are rapidly developing not only in terms of economy but also in terms of the standard of living of the people. Malaysia should also take steps to renew the national development strategy. One of the aspects that should be emphasized is the aspect of social entrepreneurship that should be mainstreamed for the country's good in the long term.

Social entrepreneurship is one of the entrepreneurial career branches popularly gaining attention from both male and female youth. The social factor could influence someone to perform social entrepreneurship behavior (Javadian et al., 2021; Neneh, 2022). This social influence can occur from interpersonal influences such as the husband or wife, mother or father, siblings, children or friends, or external influences such as the media and newspaper. Community people must be equally involved in efforts to help reduce socio-economic problems by supporting social entrepreneurship (Aloulou & Algarni, 2022). According to Kawai and Kazumi (2021), knowledge and skills enable entrepreneurs to explore the ins and outs of the business. The application of entrepreneurial knowledge needs to be done from the primary school level to unearth talent and sharpen their interest in social entrepreneurship (García-Uceda et al., 2022).

Associating various knowledge sharing and technology transfer could enhance social entrepreneurship intention (Ali et al., 2019). For instance, schools or universities can organize industrial lecture series, training, community service, and community development and involvement. The education sector requires continuous improvement from the physical aspect and human capital to improve the teaching and learning ecosystem (Diaz et al., 2021). Training in creating or managing social enterprises must be incorporated into the education system. Due to technological advances and rapid globalization, the government must establish a direct relationship with industry and society. This will allow the industry to engage in curriculum design and development. In addition, many cooperation activities such as apprenticeships, industrial training placements, and various training programs could benefit from the engagement.

*Figure 4. Policy & practical implications*

## FUTURE RESEARCH DIRECTIONS

There were three limitations in this study. First, the results cannot be generalized since the data were only collected from the respondents from youth living in Peninsular Malaysia. Future research is encouraged to extend the model and methodologies to evaluate in other locations. Second, this study's model used to evaluate social entrepreneurship intention was limited to only three factors. Other determinants such as network, mentorship, encouragement, motivation, and experience can be considered in future studies. In addition, efforts to find a new determining factor is a positive research development in encouraging young people to choose social entrepreneurship as their primary career option. Third, this study employed cross-sectional research. In cross-sectional research, the researchers only observe the phenomenon at a particular time. This design is unable to show a causal relationship between the variables. Future studies are encouraged to employ longitudinal research, which has the potential to provide complete information, depending on the operationalization of theory and research methodology.

## CONCLUSION

Social entrepreneurship is a developing field, both theoretically and practically. Social entrepreneurship exists due to (i) growing interest in solving social problems such as unemployment and inequality, (ii) concerns about various service areas that are not addressed by the public sector, and (iii) appreciation among business or commercial entrepreneurs to increase social and community wealth (Canestrino et al., 2020; Finlayson & Roy, 2019; Roy et al., 2013; Sparviero, 2019). This study aims to examine the role of social support and cognitive skills in determining youth social entrepreneurial intention through the mediation of altruism. Based on the findings, the main supporting elements of the social entrepreneurship framework are social support and cognitive skills, which can be improved through an altruistic personality. The study data provide evidence of three significant results: (i) both female and male intention to become social entrepreneurs are influenced by cognitive ability and social support; (ii) females are expected to be more altruistic than males; (iii) men do not need altruism personality to become social entrepreneurs.

This study has filled gaps in previous studies in understanding the framework of social entrepreneurship from developing countries. This research acknowledges the role of personality traits in fostering the tendency of young people to become social entrepreneurs. Entrepreneurship plays a vital role in determining the economic progress of a country. The governing bodies and relevant agencies are urged to plan and conduct comprehensive and inclusive entrepreneurial learning programs for youth to stimulate their interest in social entrepreneurship. By doing this, a social entrepreneurial career could be branded as a relevant career prospect among fresh graduates. In conclusion, social entrepreneurship in Malaysia is proliferating, driving positive change through innovative solutions and collaborative efforts. From improving educational opportunities to addressing environmental challenges, social entrepreneurship has demonstrated an incredible dedication to creating a better societal future. With continued support from the government, the private sector, and the community, social enterprises will continue to have a significant impact on building a more inclusive and sustainable Malaysia. Together, we can pave the way to a brighter and more prosperous future through the transformative power of social entrepreneurship.

## ACKNOWLEDGMENT

The authors would like to thank the participants involved in this study.

## REFERENCES

Ahmed, G., Amponsah, C. T., & Johnson, D. S. (2019). Gender differences in entrepreneurial attitudes and intentions: The case of Brand Dubai. *International Journal of Business and Emerging Markets, 11*(4), 315–334. DOI: 10.1504/IJBEM.2019.105230

Ahrari, S., Krauss, S. E., Ariffin, Z., & Meng, L. K. (2019). "Making a difference... on my terms": Motivational factors of youth involvement in social entrepreneurship in Malaysia. In *Societal Entrepreneurship and Competitiveness* (pp. 227–246). Emerald Publishing Limited., DOI: 10.1108/978-1-83867-471-720191015

Ali, I., Ali, M., & Badghish, S. (2019). Symmetric and asymmetric modeling of the entrepreneurial ecosystem in developing entrepreneurial intentions among female university students in Saudi Arabia. *International Journal of Gender and Entrepreneurship, 11*(4), 435–458. DOI: 10.1108/IJGE-02-2019-0039

Aloulou, W. J., & Algarni, E. A. (2022). Determinants of social entrepreneurial intention: Empirical evidence from the Saudi context. *Social Enterprise Journal, 18*(4), 605–625. DOI: 10.1108/SEJ-11-2021-0086

Alshebami, A. S., Seraj, A. H. A., & Alzain, E. (2022). Lecturers' creativity and students' entrepreneurial intention in Saudi Arabia. *Vision (Basel), 09722629221099596*, 09722629221099596. Advance online publication. DOI: 10.1177/09722629221099596

Aparisi-Torrijo, S., & Ribes-Giner, G. (2022). Female entrepreneurial leadership factors. *The International Entrepreneurship and Management Journal, 18*(4), 1707–1737. DOI: 10.1007/s11365-022-00798-2

Armuña, C., Ramos, S., Juan, J., Feijóo, C., & Arenal, A. (2020). From stand-up to start-up: Exploring entrepreneurship competencies and STEM women's intention. *The International Entrepreneurship and Management Journal, 16*(1), 69–92. DOI: 10.1007/s11365-019-00627-z

Brown, R. (2020). The social identity approach: Appraising the Tajfellian legacy. *British Journal of Social Psychology, 59*(1), 5–25. DOI: 10.1111/bjso.12349 PMID: 31691319

Brown, R., Alderson, H., Kaner, E., McGovern, R., & Lingam, R. (2019). "There are carers, and then there are carers who actually care"; Conceptualizations of care among looked after children and care leavers, social workers, and carers. *Child Abuse & Neglect, 92*, 219–229. DOI: 10.1016/j.chiabu.2019.03.018 PMID: 31005828

Byrne, B. M. (2010). *Structural equation modeling with AMOS: Basic concepts, applications, and programming (multivariate applications series)*. Taylor & Francis Group.

Canestrino, R., Ćwiklicki, M., Magliocca, P., & Pawełek, B. (2020). Understanding social entrepreneurship: A cultural perspective in business research. *Journal of Business Research, 110*, 132–143. DOI: 10.1016/j.jbusres.2020.01.006

Carrizales, A., Branje, S., & Lannegrand, L. (2021). Disentangling between-and within-person associations between empathy and prosocial behaviors during early adolescence. *Journal of Adolescence, 93*(1), 114–125. DOI: 10.1016/j.adolescence.2021.10.006 PMID: 34740152

Chan, J. H., Chen, S. Y., Piterou, A., Khoo, S. L., Lean, H. H., Hashim, I. H. M., & Lane, B. (2021). An innovative social enterprise: Roles of and challenges faced by an arts hub in a World Heritage Site in Malaysia. *City, Culture and Society, 25*, 100396. DOI: 10.1016/j.ccs.2021.100396

Che Nawi, N. R., Arshad, M. M., Krauss, S. E., & Ismail, I. A. (2022). Challenges faced by youth social entrepreneurs in Malaysia: Career transition to become a social entrepreneur. *European Journal of Training and Development, 46*(3/4), 317–336. DOI: 10.1108/EJTD-02-2020-0021

Chege, S. M., & Wang, D. (2020). Information technology innovation and its impact on job creation by SMEs in developing countries: An analysis of the literature review. *Technology Analysis and Strategic Management, 32*(3), 256–271. DOI: 10.1080/09537325.2019.1651263

Chen, P. C., Chan, W. C., Hung, S. W., & Lin, D. Z. (2020). How entrepreneurs recognise entrepreneurial opportunity and its gaps: A cognitive theory perspective. *Technology Analysis and Strategic Management, 32*(2), 223–238. DOI: 10.1080/09537325.2019.1648790

Chen, W. D. (2023). Crowdfunding for social ventures. *Social Enterprise Journal, 19*(3), 256–276. DOI: 10.1108/SEJ-05-2022-0051

Corrêa, V. S., Brito, F. R. D. S., Lima, R. M. D., & Queiroz, M. M. (2022). Female entrepreneurship in emerging and developing countries: A systematic literature review. *International Journal of Gender and Entrepreneurship, 14*(3), 300–322. DOI: 10.1108/IJGE-08-2021-0142

Daspit, J. J., Fox, C. J., & Findley, S. K. (2023). Entrepreneurial mindset: An integrated definition, a review of current insights, and directions for future research. *Journal of Small Business Management, 61*(1), 12–44. DOI: 10.1080/00472778.2021.1907583

Department of Statistics of Malaysia (DOSM). (2022). *Key Statistics of Labor Force in Malaysia, November 2022,* available at: https://www.dosm.gov.my/v1/index.php?r=column/cthemeByCat&cat=124&bul_id=dVNkcjZsRkF4amVjSCtxYmhiV2JxUT09&menu_id=Tm8zcnRjdVRNWWlpWjRlbmtlaDk1UT09 [accessed on 2 December 2022].

Diaz Gonzalez, A., & Dentchev, N. A. (2021). Ecosystems in support of social entrepreneurs: A literature review. *Social Enterprise Journal, 17*(3), 329–360. DOI: 10.1108/SEJ-08-2020-0064

Duong, C. D. (2023). Applying the stimulus-organism-response theory to investigate determinants of students' social entrepreneurship: Moderation role of perceived university support. *Social Enterprise Journal, 19*(2), 167–192. DOI: 10.1108/SEJ-10-2022-0091

Elliott, C., Mantler, J., & Huggins, J. (2021). Exploring the gendered entrepreneurial identity gap: Implications for entrepreneurship education. *International Journal of Gender and Entrepreneurship, 13*(1), 50–74. DOI: 10.1108/IJGE-04-2020-0048

Ennis, C. A. (2019). The gendered complexities of promoting female entrepreneurship in the Gulf. *New Political Economy, 24*(3), 365–384. DOI: 10.1080/13563467.2018.1457019

Finlayson, E., & Roy, M. J. (2019). Empowering communities? Exploring roles in facilitated social enterprise. *Social Enterprise Journal, 15*(1), 76–93. DOI: 10.1108/SEJ-04-2018-0035

García-González, A., & Ramírez-Montoya, M. S. (2023). Social entrepreneurship competency in higher education: An analysis using mixed methods. *Journal of Social Entrepreneurship, 14*(1), 91–109. DOI: 10.1080/19420676.2020.1823872

García-Uceda, E., Murillo-Luna, J. L., & Lafuente, J. A. (2022). Determinant factors in entrepreneurial intention among social work degree students: The moderating effect of entrepreneurship education. *Social Enterprise Journal, 18*(4), 563–584. DOI: 10.1108/SEJ-07-2021-0061

Gupta, P., Chauhan, S., Paul, J., & Jaiswal, M. P. (2020). Social entrepreneurship research: A review and future research agenda. *Journal of Business Research, 113*, 209–229. DOI: 10.1016/j.jbusres.2020.03.032

Hair, J. F. J., Black, W. C., Babin, B. J., & Anderson, R. E. (2010). *Multivariate data analysis. A global perspective* (7th ed.). Prentice Hall.

Harwood, J. (2020). *Social identity theory. The international encyclopedia of media psychology*, 1–7. https://doi.org/DOI: 10.1002/9781119011071.iemp0153

Hassan, A., Saleem, I., Anwar, I., & Hussain, S. A. (2020). Entrepreneurial intention of Indian university students: The role of opportunity recognition and entrepreneurship education. *Education + Training, 62*(7/8), 843–861. DOI: 10.1108/ET-02-2020-0033

Hayes, A. F. (2013). *Introduction to mediation, moderation, and conditional process analysis: A regression-based approach*. Guilford Press.

Hmieleski, K. M., & Sheppard, L. D. (2019). The Yin and Yang of entrepreneurship: Gender differences in the importance of communal and agentic characteristics for entrepreneurs' subjective well-being and performance. *Journal of Business Venturing, 34*(4), 709–730. DOI: 10.1016/j.jbusvent.2018.06.006

Hota, P. K., Subramanian, B., & Narayanamurthy, G. (2020). Mapping the intellectual structure of social entrepreneurship research: A citation/co-citation analysis. *Journal of Business Ethics, 166*(1), 89–114. DOI: 10.1007/s10551-019-04129-4

Iancu, A., Popescu, L., & Popescu, V. (2021). Factors influencing social entrepreneurship intentions in Romania, *Economic Research-. Ekonomska Istrazivanja, 34*(1), 1190–1201. DOI: 10.1080/1331677X.2020.1820358

Javadian, G., Figueroa-Armijos, M., Gupta, V. K., Modarresi, M., & Dobratz, C. (2021). Does it pay to act feminine? A cross-cultural study of gender stereotype endorsement and cognitive legitimacy in the evaluation of new ventures. *International Journal of Gender and Entrepreneurship, 13*(4), 330–352. DOI: 10.1108/IJGE-07-2020-0092

Karatas-Ozkan, M., Ibrahim, S., Ozbilgin, M., Fayolle, A., Manville, G., Nicolopoulou, K., Tatli, A., & Tunalioglu, M. (2023). Challenging the assumptions of social entrepreneurship education and repositioning it for the future: Wonders of cultural, social, symbolic, and economic capitals. *Social Enterprise Journal, 19*(2), 98–122. DOI: 10.1108/SEJ-02-2022-0018

Kawai, N., & Kazumi, T. (2021). Female entrepreneurs' cognitive attributes and venture growth in Japan: The moderating role of perceived social legitimacy. *International Journal of Gender and Entrepreneurship, 13*(1), 1–29. DOI: 10.1108/IJGE-05-2020-0063

Kline, B. R. (2005). *Principles and practice of structural modeling*. The Guilford Press.

Laguía, A., García-Ael, C., Wach, D., & Moriano, J. A. (2019). "Think entrepreneur-think male": A task and relationship scale to measure gender stereotypes in entrepreneurship. *The International Entrepreneurship and Management Journal, 15*(3), 749–772. DOI: 10.1007/s11365-018-0553-0

MacAskill, W. (2019). The definition of effective altruism. In Hilary, G., & Theron, P. (Eds.), *Effective Altruism: Philosophical Issues* (pp. 10–28). Oxford University Press. DOI: 10.1093/oso/9780198841364.003.0001

Manzur, E., & Olavarrieta, S. (2021). The 9-SRA scale: A simplified 9-items version of the SRA scale to assess altruism. *Sustainability (Basel), 13*(13), 6999. DOI: 10.3390/su13136999

Martínez-Rodríguez, I., Quintana-Rojo, C., Gento, P., & Callejas-Albinana, F. E. (2022). Public policy recommendations for promoting female entrepreneurship in Europe. *The International Entrepreneurship and Management Journal, 18*(3), 1235–1262. DOI: 10.1007/s11365-021-00751-9

Morris, M. H., Santos, S. C., & Kuratko, D. F. (2021). The great divides in social entrepreneurship and where they lead us. *Small Business Economics, 57*(3), 1089–1106. DOI: 10.1007/s11187-020-00318-y

Mukhtar, S., Wardana, L. W., Wibowo, A., & Narmaditya, B. S. (2021). Does entrepreneurship education and culture promote students' entrepreneurial intention? The mediating role of entrepreneurial mindset. *Cogent Education, 8*(1), 1918849. DOI: 10.1080/2331186X.2021.1918849

Munir, H., Jianfeng, C., & Ramzan, S. (2019). Personality traits and theory of planned behavior comparison of entrepreneurial intentions between an emerging economy and a developing country. *International Journal of Entrepreneurial Behaviour & Research, 25*(3), 554–580. DOI: 10.1108/IJEBR-05-2018-0336

Musara, M., & Nieuwenhuizen, C. (2020). Informal sector entrepreneurship, individual entrepreneurial orientation, and the emergence of entrepreneurial leadership. *Africa Journal of Management, 6*(3), 194–213. DOI: 10.1080/23322373.2020.1777817

Neneh, B. N. (2022). Entrepreneurial passion and entrepreneurial intention: The role of social support and entrepreneurial self-efficacy. *Studies in Higher Education, 47*(3), 587–603. DOI: 10.1080/03075079.2020.1770716

O'Gorman, C. (2019). *Entrepreneurial intentions and entrepreneurial behavior. Entrepreneurial Behaviour: Individual.* Contextual and Microfoundational Perspectives., DOI: 10.1007/978-3-030-04402-2_2

Oftedal, E. M., Foss, L., & Iakovleva, T. (2019). Responsible for responsibility? A study of digital e-health startups. *Sustainability (Basel), 11*(19), 5433. DOI: 10.3390/su11195433

Pansuwong, W., Photchanachan, S., & Thechatakerng, P. (2023). Social innovation: Relationships with social and human capital, entrepreneurial competencies, and growth of social enterprises in a developing country context. *Social Enterprise Journal, 19*(1), 51–79. DOI: 10.1108/SEJ-02-2022-0014

Pfattheicher, S., Nielsen, Y. A., & Thielmann, I. (2022). Prosocial behavior and altruism: A review of concepts and definitions. *Current Opinion in Psychology, 44*, 124–129. DOI: 10.1016/j.copsyc.2021.08.021 PMID: 34627110

Polas, M. R. H., & Afshar Jahanshahi, A. (2021). The effects of individual characteristics on women intention to become social entrepreneurs? *Journal of Public Affairs, 21*(2), e2204. DOI: 10.1002/pa.2204

Rasyid, Y., & Bowen, R. (2021). Social Entrepreneurship: Policies and Practice in Malaysia. In Jones, P., Huxtable-Thomas, L., Hamidon, S., Hannon, P., & Mohd Tawil, N. (Eds.), *Entrepreneurial activity in Malaysia.* Palgrave Macmillan. DOI: 10.1007/978-3-030-77753-1_6

Raza, A., Muffatto, M., & Saeed, S. (2020). Cross-country differences in innovative entrepreneurial activity: An entrepreneurial cognitive view. *Management Decision, 58*(7), 1301–1329. DOI: 10.1108/MD-11-2017-1167

Rosca, E., Agarwal, N., & Brem, A. (2020). Women entrepreneurs as agents of change: A comparative analysis of social entrepreneurship processes in emerging markets. *Technological Forecasting and Social Change, 157*, 120067. DOI: 10.1016/j.techfore.2020.120067

Roslan, M. H. H., Hamid, S., Ijab, M. T., Yusop, F. D., & Norman, A. A. (2022). Social entrepreneurship in higher education: Challenges and opportunities. *Asia Pacific Journal of Education, 42*(3), 588–604. DOI: 10.1080/02188791.2020.1859354

Roy, M. J., Donaldson, C., Baker, R., & Kay, A. (2013). Social enterprise: New pathways to health and well-being? *Journal of Public Health Policy, 34*(1), 55–68. DOI: 10.1057/jphp.2012.61 PMID: 23172049

Sabri, M. S., & Thomas, K. (2019). Psycho-attitudinal features: A study of female entrepreneurs in Saudi Arabia. *International Journal of Gender and Entrepreneurship, 11*(4), 459–480. DOI: 10.1108/IJGE-02-2019-0036

Satar, M. S., & Natasha, S. (2019). Individual social entrepreneurship orientation: Towards development of a measurement scale. *Asia Pacific Journal of Innovation and Entrepreneurship, 13*(1), 49–72. DOI: 10.1108/APJIE-09-2018-0052

Scott, R. W. (1995). *Institutions and organizations: Ideas, interests, and identities*. Sage.

Sekaran, U., & Bougie, R. (2016). *Research methods for business* (7th ed.). John Wiley & Sons Ltd.

Shi, L., Yao, X., & Wu, W. (2019). Perceived university support, entrepreneurial self-efficacy, heterogeneous entrepreneurial intentions in entrepreneurship education: The moderating role of the Chinese sense of face. *Journal of Entrepreneurship in Emerging Economies, 12*(2), 205–230. DOI: 10.1108/JEEE-04-2019-0040

Sparviero, S. (2019). The case for a socially oriented business model canvas: The social enterprise model canvas. *Journal of Social Entrepreneurship, 10*(2), 232–251. DOI: 10.1080/19420676.2018.1541011

Stirzaker, R., Galloway, L., Muhonen, J., & Christopoulos, D. (2021). The drivers of social entrepreneurship: Agency, context, compassion, and opportunism. *International Journal of Entrepreneurial Behaviour & Research, 27*(6), 1381–1402. DOI: 10.1108/IJEBR-07-2020-0461

Tillmar, M., Sköld, B., Ahl, H., Berglund, K., & Pettersson, K. (2022). Women's rural businesses: For economic viability or gender equality?–A database study from the Swedish context. *International Journal of Gender and Entrepreneurship, 14*(3), 323–351. DOI: 10.1108/IJGE-06-2021-0091

Urban, B. (2020). Entrepreneurial alertness, self-efficacy, and social entrepreneurship intentions. *Journal of Small Business and Enterprise Development, 27*(3), 489–507. DOI: 10.1108/JSBED-08-2019-0285

Urbano, D., Aparicio, S., & Audretsch, D. (2019). Twenty-five years of research on institutions, entrepreneurship, and economic growth: What has been learned? *Small Business Economics, 53*(1), 21–49. DOI: 10.1007/s11187-018-0038-0 van Ewijk, A. R., & Belghiti-Mahut, S. (2019). Context, gender, and entrepreneurial intentions: How entrepreneurship education changes the equation. *International Journal of Gender and Entrepreneurship*, *11*(1), 75–98. DOI: 10.1108/IJGE-05-2018-0054

Wang, X., Cai, L., Zhu, X., & Deng, S. (2020). Female entrepreneurs' gender roles, social capital, and willingness to choose external financing. *Asian Business & Management*, •••, 1–26. DOI: 10.1057/s41291-020-00131-1

Weaver, R. L. (2023). The impact of COVID-19 on the social enterprise sector. *Journal of Social Entrepreneurship*, *14*(2), 177–185. DOI: 10.1080/19420676.2020.1861476

Wei, X., Ren, H., Ullah, S., & Bozkurt, C. (2023). Does environmental entrepreneurship play a role in sustainable green development? Evidence from emerging Asian economies. *Ekonomska Istrazivanja*, *36*(1), 73–85. DOI: 10.1080/1331677X.2022.2067887

Wu, Y. J., Wu, T., & Arno Sharpe, J. (2020). Consensus on the definition of social entrepreneurship: A content analysis approach. *Management Decision*, *58*(12), 2593–2619. DOI: 10.1108/MD-11-2016-0791

Xi, J., Lee, M. T., Carter, J. R., & Delgado, D. (2022). Gender differences in purpose in life: The mediation effect of altruism. *Journal of Humanistic Psychology*, *62*(3), 352–376. DOI: 10.1177/0022167818777658

## KEY TERMS AND DEFINITIONS

**Entrepreneurship:** Identifying opportunities in the market, organizing resources to achieve objectives and actions, and exploiting the needs of resources for business interests.

**Social Entrepreneurship:** An approach that combines the roles and responsibilities of the government, private sector, and charities for achieving social goals and increasing the competitiveness and sustainability of social entities or target groups.

**Social Support:** Individual perception is based on other people's thoughts (e.g., peer support, family support, and university support) on whether the behavior should be done.

**Cognitive Ability:** A person can explore, evaluate, and use opportunities for entrepreneurial activities.

**Altruism:** An act of prosocial behavior that benefits others without expecting any reward or a gift from the person being helped.

# Chapter 3
# The Effect of Corporate Governance on Organizational Performances of Cooperative Businesses:
## A Study of Selected Ethiopian Agricultural Cooperatives

**Tadese Lemesa**
https://orcid.org/0000-0003-4429-4058
*School of Management Studies, Punjabi University, Patiala, India*

**Harpreet Singh**
https://orcid.org/0000-0001-8493-5839
*School of Management Studies, Punjabi University, Patiala, India*

## ABSTRACT

*The study aimed at examining the relationship between corporate governance dimensions and organizational performances of agricultural cooperative unions in Ethiopia using selected unions. The research adopted descriptive research design and data were analyzed using descriptive and inferential statistics. In this line, primary data from 377 cooperative union members (205) and managing committees (172) located in the administrative zones the study area were collected by enumerator guided questionnaire. After cleaning the missing scores and fed them into SPSS version 23, all the necessary tests like no multicollinearity, normality, linearity, autocorrelation, and heteroscedasticity were checked. By verifying these assump-*

DOI: 10.4018/978-1-6684-9872-9.ch003

*tions, the multiple regression model's validity, dependability, and interpretability are guaranteed and the results can be interpreted by confidence. Positively predicting organizational performances of Ethiopian agricultural cooperative unions. This signals that further studies are required on composition of managing committees to boost their performances.*

## 1. INTRODUCTION

In cooperatives, corporate governance refers to the array of procedures, policies and methodologies utilized to guide and supervise these entities. The obligations and responsibilities of the managing and supervisory committee—along with the processes involved in decision- making, interdependencies, compositions, financial transparency and member engagement—are typically encompassed within the governance framework (Basterretxea et al. 2022). These characteristics of governance can significantly affect cooperative performance, influencing aspects such as member satisfaction, operational efficiency, financial stability and the cooperative's capacity to fulfill its objectives (Grashuis & Su, 2019). However, the effectiveness of these elements may differ, because not all cooperatives are organized in a uniform manner. (A. Mishra, 2025)This diversity can result in varying outcomes, although the fundamental principles tend to remain relatively consistent.(A. B. Mishra, 2025b) Agricultural cooperatives are pivotal in improving the living standards of smallholder farmers. In developing and agrarian countries like Ethiopia, cooperatives provide access to markets, loans, supplies and services (Tefera, Bijman & Slingerland, 2017; Getnet & Anullo, 2012). Primary cooperatives are established and playing the roles of supplying agricultural inputs,(Mohd Usman et al., 2023) selling produce of their members, providing credits for members, and other advisory services at district level of the country (Mohammed & Lee, 2015). However, the overall effectiveness and success of many of these cooperatives are frequently challenged by governance-related issues (Etefa, 2022). These issues include inadequate leadership, a lack of accountability and minimal member engagement (Mersha, & Ayenew, 2018). Although these challenges are considerable, the low literacy levels of managing committees, their lack of independence, ineffective meetings and the homogeneity of their membership create practical obstacles that cooperatives in Ethiopia must face (Mamo, et al, 2021; Etefa, 2022; Getnet & Anullo, 2012). Thes suggest that a comprehensive analysis of the governance systems within the agricultural cooperatives of Ethiopia is vital for grasping their influence on organizational performance.

The objective of this study is to investigate the ways in which the organizational performances of certain Ethiopian agricultural cooperatives' unions are shaped by dimension of corporate governances such as meetings, literacy, independence, and diversity of managing committees. This research aims to identify key governance practices that influence the success or failure of these agricultural cooperative businesses, as it delves into the connections between governance dimensions and cooperative performance.(Ahamad, Mishra, Raghuram, Tiwari, et al., 2024) Although the study concentrated on how each of these dimensions impacts the success of agricultural cooperatives in Ethiopia, it will particularly focus on elements such as (1) meetings of managing committees, (2) literacy levels among managing committees, (3) the independence of those committees and (4) the diversity present within managing committees. However, comprehending these dynamics is vital because they offer insights into the overall efficacy of cooperative governance.

In addition to adding to the corpus of research already available on corporate governance in cooperatives, the study's conclusions offer helpful suggestions for enhancing governance procedures in Ethiopian agricultural cooperatives.(A. B. Mishra, 2020) Enhancing these organizations' governance could improve their operational efficiency, boost member happiness, and eventually help Ethiopia's larger objectives of poverty alleviation and rural development (Mersha & Ayenew, 2018).

## 2. LITERATURE REVIEW

### 2.1. Theoretical Literature Review

#### 2.1.1. Corporate Governance in Agricultural Cooperatives

Ishak (2020) asserted that corporate governances of agricultural businesses are different from other classical forms of businesses. Cooperatives are owned and controlled by their members; governance entails managing the interests of these individuals while also ensuring the cooperative's social, operational and financial performances (Esim, 2014; Ishak, 2020; ICA, 2024). One essential element of the governance of agricultural cooperatives is the meetings of managing committees (ICA, 2024; Franken & Cook, 2019). These formal assemblies of the cooperative's managing committee members provide a forum for discussing and deciding upon the cooperative's day to operations. (Dodke, 2024)These assemblies are usually scheduled with pre-panned issues to discuss about. (Jaiswal Monika, 2024)The frequency and quality of such meetings are critical (1) for developing and executing strategic plans, (2) for promoting transparencies, and (3) for reviewing and monitoring performances.(Kaushik et al., 2024) The attentiveness of members during these gatherings, along with accurate recording of minutes, is vital to ensuring that decisions are well-documented and truly reflect the interests of the members (Kyazze, Nkote & Wakaisuka- Isingoma, 2017). Regular and fruitful meetings of the managing committee help maintain alignment between management and members.(Singh Ritika, 2024) Thus, ensuring that the cooperative's objectives are achieved in a transparent and accountable manner (Duncan, 2003; Bainbridge, 2002; Schneider, 1999).

The second dimension of corporate governance that the researcher wants to focus pertains to literacy of managing committees.(Gaikwad, 2024) Different literatures agree that the literacy of managing committee plays a crucial role in the governance of business organizations (Surroca et al., 2010; Sobel and Reding, 2004; Hill et al, 1998; Maricic et al., 2018). Traditionally, literacy was understood as the capacity to read, write, speak, and listen effectively (Ahmed, 2011; Wagner, 2014); this enables individuals to communicate and comprehend their surroundings. However, many educational organizations including UNESCO have broadened this definition to include a wider array of skills, such as critical thinking, interpretation and analysis of both written and visual texts (Bernier, 2004).

In the dominion of managing committees within agricultural cooperatives, literacy surpasses mere communication skills to incorporate the ability to understand financial reports, regulatory frameworks, financial and marketing projections and other operational documents essential for sound decision-making (Wagner, 2014, Momaya et al., 2017; Yu, et al, 2023). Literacy, in this expansive sense, ensures that committee members can actively participate in strategic dialogues, evaluate complex matters, make informed decisions that benefit both the cooperative and its members (Ruben & Heras, 2012; Gertler, 2004).

The core root of cooperative governance, democratic control, member engagement, and independence from outside influences, are the foundation for managing committees' independence cooperatives (Momaya et al., 2017; Puri & Sujarittanonta, 2016). Cooperatives are 'autonomous associations of persons united voluntarily to meet their common economic, social, and cultural needs and aspirations through a jointly owned and democratically run business, according to the

International Cooperative Alliance (ICA). Theoretically, maintaining this autonomy requires that the government refrain from interfering with management of managing committees in calling general assembles, planning and executing activities, hire and firing human resources for the cooperatives, and monitoring operational activities (Dalton, et al,1998; Vafeas, 1999). This allows cooperative members to decide on matters based on their shared interests rather than outside political influences.(Mahoran et al., 2024)

Diversity of the managing committee members makes another explaining dimension of cooperative governances in agricultural cooperatives. (Ahamad, Tiwari, et al., 2024)Literatures witnesses that diversity within managing committees is another crucial element influencing the effectiveness of governances in agricultural businesses (Zachow & Bertolini, 2019; Ruben & Heras, 2012). Committee diversity can be assessed using several proxies like gender, composition, educational levels, age category, and political orientations (Van der Vegt et al., 2005; Lee et al., 2022). Diverse committees are thought to contribute a range of perspectives, which can lead to more innovative and balanced decision-making (Jehn, et al., 1999). Diversity in managing committees can improve the governance structure of by nurturing inclusive discussions that represent the committee spectrum of member interests (Puri & Sujarittanonta, 2016). More recently, research has emphasized that diversity, particularly gender diversity, plays a significant role in enhancing the cooperative's decision-making capacity and overall performance (Klapper & Love, 2002). The study of Klapper & Love (2002), for example, has been linked to better social and financial outcomes and improved organizational performances in cooperative businesses.

- **Agency theory in cooperative businesses**

According to Ortmann & King (2007), the relationship between the members (the numerous cooperative members) and their cooperative (the agent) is unquestionably discussed in greater detail thanks to agency theory (A. B. Mishra & Singh, 2024). Generally speaking, it makes more sense for each member to get involved with issues and organizations that they can more readily affect.(Ranjan et al., 2023) It should come as no surprise that cooperative members will grow apathetic (Nilsson, 2001). The horizon problem arises in cooperative groups for two reasons, according to the agency perspective: First, it is anticipated that members will mostly be preoccupied with short-sighted views of their membership in the cooperative. Since cooperative organizations cannot achieve such efficient allocations, agency theory is essential to the cooperative form.(Satarkar, et al., 2023) When the members' interests are deviating from the cooperative (the management of the cooperative) dilemma may occur in the cooperative business (Jensen 2001). The study of Nilsson (2001) designated that the challenges of agency dilemma carried as a principal-agent problem. Principal-agent problem is a condition when cooperative members choose or hire managers to govern the cooperative's day to day operations; yet, the hired managers may have interests that are at odds with those of the members, specifically in situations where information is asymmetrical (Ortmann & King, 2007). From these perspectives, the main function of the managing committees is to control the hired managers.(A. B. Mishra et al., 2022) This suggests that a majority of managing committee members of the cooperatives should be independent of management, and that their primary role is one of ensuring managerial compliance – i.e. to monitor and if necessary, control the behavior of management to ensure it acts in the shareholders best interests (Keasey et al., 1997).

- **Stakeholder theory in cooperative businesses**

Stakeholder theory as applied to governing bodies is based on the premise that organizations should be responsible to a range of stakeholders in society other than just an organization's owners (Hung, 1998). By incorporating different stakeholders on managing committee, it is expected that organizations will be more likely to reply to broader social interests than the narrow interests of one group.(Rana et al., 2022) This leads to a political role for managing committees negotiating and resolving the potentially conflicting interests of different stakeholder groups in order to determine the objectives of the organization and set policy (Freeman & Phillips, 2002; Jensen 2001)). There are constraints in cooperatives on the involvement of different stakeholders on managing committees, as committee members are elected from the membership.(Ahamad et al., 2024) However, within these constraints there has been concern about low member participation and the lack of involvement of certain groups of members, such, as women and young people on boards (Basterretxea et al. 2022).

- **Resource dependence theory (RDT) in agricultural cooperative businesses**

Resource dependency theory of Pfeffer (1978) views organizations as interdependent with their environment. All organizations depend crucially for their survival on other organizations and actors for resources. As a result, they need to find ways of managing this dependence and ensuring they get the resources and information they need.

According to Pfeffer (1978) resource dependence theory, organizations and their surroundings are interconnected. All organizations rely heavily on other organizations and people for resources in order to survive. They must therefore figure out how to control this reliance and make sure they obtain the tools and data they require. According to this viewpoint, the managing committee can help reduce uncertainty by establishing powerful connections with other organizations and individuals, such as with the hired managers. (Mohseni et al., 2022)The managing committee's primary responsibilities include assisting the business organization in adapting to external change and preserving positive relationships with important external stakeholders to guarantee the flow of resources into and out of the organization.

According to this viewpoint, the managing committee is a component of the business organization and its surroundings. The managing committee's job is to cross boundaries. Members of the managing committee are chosen for their ability to try to co-opt outside influences and for the valuable external connections and expertise they can offer for the cooperatives (Hillman et al., 2009). Since managing committee members must be chosen from among the cooperatives' members, cooperatives' ability to use their committees to "manage" external dependents is far more limited than that of private businesses.(A. B. Mishra, Ranjan, et al., 2023) Though it's unclear how frequently this tactic is employed, cooperatives can typically co-opt managing committee members to bring in individuals with more contacts, experience, or abilities.

- **Stewardship theory in cooperative businesses**

Muth and Donaldson's (1998) stewardship theory is based on a human relations viewpoint and begins with a different set of presumptions than agency theory. It makes the assumption that managers would serve as excellent stewards of their organization's resources and wish to perform a good job (Hung 1998). In the case of cooperatives, members and the managing committee are therefore more effectively viewed as partners.(Mishra, 2025a) Therefore, the management committee's primary goal is to enhance the cooperatives' organizational performance rather than guarantee that managers are acting in the best interests of their members (Basterretxea et al. 2022). The managing committee's primary responsibility is strategic; it collaborates with management to enhance strategy and provide insight into important choices. It should come as no surprise that management concepts and procedures should be used to governance in this situation. From this perspective managing committee members should be selected on the basis of their expertise and contacts so that they are in a position to add value to the cooperative's decisions; managing committees and managers should receive proper induction and training; they should know how to operate effectively as a team etc. (Basterretxea et al. 2022).

The stewardship theory viewpoint presents a possible problem for cooperative governance. The problem is that there is no assurance that the people chosen to serve on the managing committee will possess the abilities required for their jobs. Sivertsen (1996), a senior manager in a Norwegian consumer cooperative, emphasizes this: Cooperatives are often run by management. While managing committee members in cooperatives are chosen from among what we would consider common people, board members in large private enterprises are chosen from inside the business community. Solid, serious individuals with sound judgment are frequently found lacking the background needed to make effective business judgments (Hung 1998).

- **Social capital theory in cooperative businesses**

Social capital theory was originally defined by Bourdieu (1985) as "The aggregate of the actual or potential resources which are linked to possession of a durable network of more or less institutionalized relationships of mutual associate or recognition". (Mishra et al. 2024) Its fundamental idea is that a network gives its members value by giving them access to the social resources that are embedded inside the network (Bourdieu, 1985; Florin, Lubatkin, & Schulze, 2003). Investment techniques aimed at institutionalizing group relations—which are dependable sources of benefits—are necessary to build these social networks (Portes, 1998). In general, this social capital can be broken down into two elements: (a) the social relationship itself, which allows individuals to claim access to resources possessed by their associates, and (b) the amount and quality of those resources (Bourdieu, 1985; Portes, 1998).

In cooperative businesses, the social capital theory has been increasingly used to study these social logic components of cooperatives in different industries (Bianchi & Vieta 2020; Lang & Roessl, 2011; Saz-Gil et al., 2021; Stoop et al., 2021; Valentinov & Iliopoulos, 2021; Wulandhari et al., 2022). Applying social capital to cooperatives, arguably a "special, social capital-based, type of organization" (Valentinov & Iliopoulos, 2021) with its democratic governance structures, networks, and shared norms, reveals close interrelatedness with cooperatives' values and principles (ICA, 2024). In our understanding, this adds up to the pragmatic use of the concept of social capital for cooperatives, which are navigating today's complex world in search of practical solutions to enhance the cooperative identity and engagement of their members.

- **Transaction Cost Economics (TCE) in cooperative businesses**

Transaction cost economics (TCE) is one of the most commonly referenced organizations' theories in operations of agricultural cooperatives (Grashuis and Hakelius 2023; Trejo-Pech et al. 2023; Sánchez-Navarro et al. 2024). Ronald Coase (1937) was the first to bring the concept of transaction costs to bear on the study of business organizations and markets. Transaction cost theory is defined as an alternative variant of the agency understanding of governance assumptions (Ketokivi & Mahoney, 2020). It describes governance frameworks as being based on the net effects of internal and external transactions, rather than as contractual relationships outside the organization (i.e. with shareholders or owners or members in case of cooperatives). The theory is often explained in terms of minimizing transactional costs associated with exchange between members, managing committees, and all external parties. (A. B. Mishra, Sahu, et al., 2021)The transaction cost theory in cooperatives describes transactional cost of marketing costs like purchasing inputs, selling produce, and other operations costs (Williamson, 1985). Different literatures witnesses that transaction costs occur when dealing with another external party like search and information costs (i.e. to find the supplier), bargaining and decision costs (i.e.to purchase the component), and policing and enforcement costs (i.e. to monitor quality).

## 2.2. Empirical Literature And Hypotheses Development

### 2.2.1. Meetings of Managing Committees And Organizational Performances

In literatures corporate governance and organizational performance of cooperative businesses in agricultural cooperative unions, much attention has been given to how the meetings the managing committees influence organization's successes. The studies tried to examine how frequencies of the meetings, attentiveness of the meetings, effectiveness of the meetings, focus and minuting of the meetings of the managing committee influence organizational performances of the cooperative businesses. A study conducted in European countries found a strong and convincing link between management committee meetings and organizational performance (Ramos & Olalla 2011). The financial performance is also improved by boards that meet more frequently, according to Ntim and Oseit (2011). Mehdi (2007), on the other hand, discovered that board meetings do not affect performance by using a smaller sample of 24 firms from the years 2000 to 2005. The study also claims that success is linked to the organizational performance, which is less likely to be impacted by management committee meetings.(Kate et al., 2022) A similar inverse association between the number of management committee meetings and organizational success is shown by Vafeas (1999). Like frequency of the managing committees of the cooperatives, their attentiveness and quality are also equally important for shaping organizational directions and performances.

> $H_{01}$: There is a statistically significant and positive relationship between meetings of managing committees and organizational performances of cooperative unions in Ethiopia.

### 2.2.2. Literacy of Managing Committees and Organizational Performance

Literacy of the managing committees' members in cooperatives, which may include educational level, professional and general knowledge, and general literacy, has been area of research for scholars in cooperative governances and cooperative management areas. In cooperatives where members of the managing committee are playing a role of strategic planning, it is very helpful that the committee members have better literacy in the strategic areas so that their organizational performances shaped positively. According to a study of Germann (2023), a managing committee brings value to the committee's governing function by combining a variety of skills and abilities that together create a pool of social capital. The qualifications of each managing committee member are crucial in the decision-making process. For instance, if the committee members have the necessary training and expertise, the monitoring job can be carried out successfully. According to Ingley and van der Walt (2002), competent and skilled board committee members can be viewed as a strategic resource that can establish a strategic connection to various external resources. An effective committee needs "high levels of intellectual ability, experience, soundness of judgment, and integrity," and having more qualified members would ensure this (Hilmer, 1998).

Managing committee members competencies and firm performances have been found to positively correlate in a number of researches (McClelland & Boyatzis, 1982; Dunphy et al. 1997; Hunt, 2000; Oguda 2015). Higher qualified committee members are advantageous to the businesses because they bring a variety of skills and abilities to the table (Johl & Salami 2014; Carver & Carver 2006), which fosters varied viewpoints when making decisions (Milliken & Martins, 1996; Biggins, 1999). More qualified members would broaden the committee's knowledge base, encourage members to go beyond their current options, and improve the committee's ability to process challenges more carefully (Ben-Shahar et al. 2024).

Members with advanced degrees generally, and degrees requiring a great deal of research and analysis, in particular, will be a rich source of creative ideas for developing policy initiatives with rigor and depth of analysis that will offer distinctive viewpoints on strategic issues (Westphal and Milton, 2000). There is little empirical study relating committee members' educational backgrounds to the performance of the company (Carver & Carver 2006; Bilimoria & Piderit, 1994; Yermack, 2006). The above discussion therefore leads to the following hypothesis.

> $H_{02}$: There is a statistically significant and positive relationship between literacy of managing committees and organizational performances of cooperative unions in Ethiopia.

### 2.2.3. Independence of Managing Committee And Organizational Performances In Cooperatives

Board independence is the ability of the board members to make decisions independently, free from intervention or influence from outside forces such as politics, duress, personal gain, or conflicts of interest (Ayodeji & Okunad, 2019). According to a meta-analysis by Dalton et al. (1998), there are discrepancies in the findings of the studies considered in the review concerning the association between the independence of the management committee and organizational performances. Some studies (Daily and Dalton, 1993; Baysinger and Butler, 1985) support an idea that independence of management committee increases organizational performances;

while, other studies (Klein, Shapiro, and Young, 2005; Bhagat and Bolton, 2008) propagates an idea that independence of management committee increases organizational performances.(Mishra et al., 2021) Johnson et al. (1996) points out that the managing committee's composition and independence from other influences affects the organization's output by exercising the function of supervision, allocation of resources and strategic roles. Brick and Chidambaran (2007) also find that committee's independence oversight activities can increase the firm's value. And this is because committee members can effectively identify managers' opportunistic behavior by monitoring to ensure that organizational behaviors comply with the interests of members across the organization.

A study of Kalyanaraman and Altuwaijri (2016) expressed that board independence, has a positive link with organizational performance while excess board independence is not statistically significant relationship with organizational performance. However, some researchers discovered a negative relationship between board independence and performance of banks (Sharifah et al. 2018, March). According to study of Ponnu and Karthigeyan (2010), there is no positive relationship between board independence and corporate performance and the responsibility now is solely on the shoulders of the government to ensure effective corporate governance is maintained throughout the nation. (A. B. Mishra & Dodke, 2024)On the other hand, independence of managing committee in running cooperatives adds value to a cooperative by increasing responsibility, offering self-governance judgment, expanding the management's and executive's business network connections, and moderating the hired managers' power and the chairman, which in many organizations is a sufficiently powerful position (Datta, 2018). Based on these empirical reviews, the researcher decided to develop the following hypothesis regarding managing committee's independence and organizational performances of cooperative businesses.

> $H_{03}$: There is a statistically significant and positive relationship between independence of managing committees and organizational performances of cooperative unions in Ethiopia.

### 2.2.4. Diversity of Managing Committee And Organization Performance

In today's business organizations, employees and top management teams become increasingly diverse in terms of age, ethnicity, political orientations, human interactions, and gender, in addition to their diversity in terms of tenure, experience, and educational background (Zubeltzu- Jaka et al. 2020). Diversity of management committee was described by Hawkins (2022) as an inherent variability in its composition. Indicators of this diversity include, among others, gender, age, ethnicity, work experience, and organizational participation. Diversity of managing committee members in corporate governances has been getting significant attention from researchers. These scholars have made attempts to link diversity with different aspects within the business organizations, such as organizational innovation (Zhang 2012), and corporate governance (Adams and Ferreira, 2012), and corporate social responsibility (Williams, 2003). Many literatures in corporate governances have examined the relationship between composition of managing committee and organizational performance (Eisenberg 2017; Zhang 2012 and Hawkins 2022). Similarly, there are limited studies conducted in developed countries on relationship between diversity of managing committee of cooperatives and organizational performances (Carter et al., 2007; Kalyanaraman and Altuwaijri 2016; Hassan & Marimuthu 2018; Francoeur et al., 2008). Specifically, in spite of the fact that their functional background diversity may be favorable, the empirical study of a sample of 423 female board members from 66 local consumer cooperatives in South Korea indicates that board value diversity can have a detrimental impact on organizational performances (Lee, Kang & Lee, 2022). According to the findings, cooperatives' performance can be enhanced byadding more functionally diverse board members. The literature reviewed above leads to the development of the following hypothesis.

> $H_{04}$: There is a statistically significant and positive relationship between diversity of managing committees and organizational performances of cooperative unions in Ethiopia.

## 3. CONCEPTUAL FRAMEWORK OF THE STUDY

Based on literatures reviewed in the preceding section, the researcher is trying to propose a conceptual framework for the research project. The framework identifies predictors to be dimensions of corporate governance (i.e. meetings of management committee (MMC), literacy of management committee (LMC), independence of management committee (IMC), and diversity of management committee (DMC)), the dependent variable is organizational performance of cooperatives (OrP).

# 4. METHODOLOGY

## 4.1. Research Design And Study Sample

Research design can be defined as a framework for conducting research project in an efficient and effective manner. It details the procedures necessary for collection, measurement and analysis of information which helps the researcher to structure or solve research problems (Sreejesh, Mohapatra, Anusree, 2014). To examine the relationship between corporate governance of cooperatives and organizational performances of Ethiopian agricultural cooperative unions, exploratory research design was adopted. Exploratory research is carried out to make problem suited to frame a working hypothesis from an operational perspective.

The study used responses of 377 individuals from a sample of 403 questionnaires distributed to managing committee and members selected using a multistage nonprobability sampling technique. The sample size was computed, approximated and proportionally allocated to each union using Yamane's (1973) sample selection approach. 172 (45.6%) and 205 (54.4%) of the respondents were managing committee and members of the selected unions respectively. This makes the response rate of 95.6% for managing committee and 91.9% for members of the cooperative unions in the study area.

Multistage non-probability and probability sampling techniques were employed to access sample respondents in the study area. The first stage of the sampling mechanism was to select zones for the study area. Here, purposive sampling method was employed to agricultural cooperative unions producing malt barely in the form contract farming in Oromia state. By the virtue that the researcher was working with value chain of malt barely, he had been conducting preliminary studies area. Most of the successful malt barely producer cooperatives are found with the administration boundary of these zones. The zones are also known for agricultural production in the country. For the reason that these zones are the top producers of malt barely in the country; the cooperative unions working with malt barely are becoming successful in their relationship with buyers of agricultural products; the farming techniques in these zones are transforming from traditional plough farming to mechanized ones; and the zones are found in different parts of the country to represent. These zones are East Arsi Zone, Bale zone, South West Showa Zone and West Arsi Zone.

Once the zones are identified, the second stage was to decide on the specific unions from the selected zones. The researcher decided to access all the unions found within these zones. Since in each zone, three to five agricultural cooperative unions are found, it is manageable to collect data from managing committees and members of these unions on corporate governance dimensions and organizational performances.

The third stage is to select target respondents of the managing committee and members of the unions.

Each cooperative union has primary cooperatives located in different districts and kebeles of the zone. The members of the primary cooperatives are members of the corresponding cooperative union by default. Hence the target sampling frame was members of cooperative unions selected proportionally from different districts of each of unions. Table 1 presents zones from which samples were drawn, number of agricultural unions from each zone, number of member and managing committees sampled, and number of questionnaires actually collected back.

*Table 1. Number of unions in each administrative zones selected for the study*

| Administrative zones selected | Agricultural cooperative unions selected | Samples distributed | | | Samples collected | | |
|---|---|---|---|---|---|---|---|
| | | Members | Managing Committee | Total | Members | Managing Committee | Total |
| West Arsi | 4 | 49 | 40 | 92 | 46 | 40 | 86 |
| East Arsi | 4 | 49 | 40 | 92 | 47 | 38 | 85 |
| South West Showa | 3 | 37 | 30 | 69 | 36 | 29 | 65 |
| Bale | 3 | 37 | 30 | 69 | 39 | 30 | 69 |
| North Showa | 2 | 25 | 20 | 46 | 21 | 17 | 38 |
| East Bale | 1 | 13 | 10 | 23 | 7 | 8 | 15 |
| West Showa | 1 | 13 | 10 | 23 | 9 | 10 | 19 |
| **Total** | 17 | 223* | 180 | 403 | 205 | 172 | 377 |

Source: Constructed by the researcher (2023)

* Number of respondents of members is approximated to the next larger whole number

## 4.2. Questionnaire and Variables' Measurement

In this study, data were gathered through a questionnaire, a method that is frequently used for extensive studies (Kothari, 2003). The development of the questionnaire adhered to recognized procedures typically employed in questionnaire development, as described by Bougie & Sekaran (2019) and Sarantakos (1998).

To ensure consistency and reliability, the questionnaire was designed with a five-point Likert scale, ranging from 5 (Strongly Agree) to 1 (Strongly Disagree). This scale was specifically chosen to capture respondents' opinions accurately (Burns & Grove, 2003). The questionnaire aimed to gather self-reported information using enumerators on various dimensions of cooperative governance, including meetings of the managing committee, literacy of the managing committee, and the independence of the managing committee and organizational performance. The validity of the questionnaire was confirmed through the content validity index, which assessed how relevant the questions were in evaluating the variables. Similarly, the reliability of the questionnaires was assessed using Cronbach's α coefficient, as suggested by Nunnally (1978). The results for Cronbach's α coefficient should be ≥.7. All items exhibited a Cronbach's α coefficient exceeding .7, indicating that each item showed internal consistency.

Variables being used in the study are operationalized as corporate governance dimensions by meetings of managing committee, literacy of managing committee, independence of managing committee and diversity of managing committee; while organizational performance is measured by constructs of social, operational and financial performances. The variables, their nature, and measurements are shown in Table 2.

*Table 2. Variables of the study, their measurement, and sources*

| S. No | Variables | | Nature of the Variable | Constructs to be used | To be adopted from |
|---|---|---|---|---|---|
| 1. | Diversity of Managing Committees | DMC | Independent | Age, gender, educational background, experiences (administration, finance or business experience), ethnicity, and religion. | Van der Vegt and Vliert (2005); Jehn, Northcroft & Neale (1999);Lee, Kang & Lee (2022) |
| 2. | Literacy of Managing Committees | LMC | Independent | The proportion of committee members who are literate | Le and Sundaramurthy (2009) |
| 3. | Independence of Managing Committees | IMC | Independent | Independence of managing committees in calling GA, making decision, preparing strategic plan, hiring and monitoring professional managers | Dalton, D. R., Daily, C. M., Ellstrand, A. E., & Johnson, J. L. (1998) |
| 4. | Meetings of Managing Committees | MMC | Independent | Frequency meetings, attentiveness, participation and minuting | Ramos & Olalla, 2011 |
| 5 | Organizational Performances | OrP | Dependent | Overall Profitability, Return on asset, members satisfaction with patronage payments, social contributions, meeting objectives | Lee, Kang & Lee (2022) Franken & Cook (2015) |

Source: Developed by the scholar based on the literatures reviewed

## 4.3. Test of Statistics

### Multicollinearity Test

Before conducting the regression analysis, the researcher assessed whether the fundamental assumptions were met. The initial step was to evaluate the variables for no multicollinearity. Multicollinearity can occur when two or more variables are strongly correlated, which may influence the estimation of regression coefficients (Daoud 2017, December). Furthermore, the existence of multicolinearity makes the assessment and the hypothesis testing about regression coefficients indeterminate (Tay 2003). The Variance Inflation Factor (VIF) and Tolerance are utilized to assess the presence of multicollinearity among the explanatory variables (MMC, LMC, IMC, and DMC) in this research. As table 3 indicates multicollinearity is generally not a significant issue in this context. Indeed, numerous researchers regard a VIF value exceeding 10 as problematic (Daoud, 2017 and Lavery, et al. 2019); therefore, the values observed in this model (ranging from 2.248 to 2.563) imply that our predictors are not highly correlated with one another. This indicates that the independent variables (MMC, LMC, IMC, and DMC) do not significantly overlap or duplicate the information they provide. Each explanatory variable appears to offer a distinct contribution to the model.

*Table 3. Multicollinearity testing*

| Coefficients[a] | | | | | | | | |
|---|---|---|---|---|---|---|---|---|
| Model | | Unstandardized Coefficients | | Standardized Coefficients | t | Sig. | Collinearity Statistics | |
| | | B | Std. Error | Beta | | | Tolerance | VIF |
| 1 | (Constant) | -.142 | .059 | | -2.394 | .017 | | |
| | MMC | .224 | .027 | .236 | 8.346 | .000 | .415 | 2.408 |
| | LMC | .612 | .030 | .587 | 20.079 | .000 | .390 | 2.563 |
| | IMC | .203 | .027 | .210 | 7.588 | .000 | .435 | 2.300 |
| | DMC | .001 | .030 | .001 | .031 | .975 | .445 | 2.248 |

a. Dependent Variable: Organizational Performance
Source: SPSS result

Other statistical tests like normality test (i.e. Figure 1), linearity test (i.e. Figure 2), autocorrelation test (Figure 3), and heteroscedasticity test (Figure 4) were conducted and the results are shown in the annex. The tests show that the model fits the data being used to examine effect of corporate governance dimensions on organizational performances of Ethiopian agricultural cooperative unions. See the annexes from Figure 1 to 4.

## 5. RESULTS AND DISCUSSION

A model was developed to examine the impact of corporate governance aspects on the organizational performance of Ethiopian agricultural cooperative unions, as detailed in the study's methodology section. The findings are shown here. The respondents' demographic details, descriptive and inferential statistics, findings, and commentary are all included in this section.

## 5.1. Demographic Characteristics Of The Respondents

From 403 questionnaires distributed to members (223) and managing committees (180), about 377 were collected back making response rates of 91.9% for members and 95.6% for managing committee respondents. As seen from table 5 (annexed), 87%, 48.5%, and 39.8% of the respondents were male, within 25 – 40 years of age, and cannot read and write, respectively.

## 5.2. Descriptive Analysis

Before beginning more detailed analysis, the descriptive statistics provide a quick overview of the characteristics and variability of the data, which can aid in comprehending the distribution of various variables as it is shown in table 4 below. With a relatively slight variance, the age category of the respondents divided pretty evenly throughout all groups with 30.5%, 48.5%, and 21.0% are within age category of 25-40 years, 41-60 years, and more than 60 years of age, respectively.

Educational background varies more throughout the sample respondent and has a lower average with 39.8%, 39.3% and 2.1% are relatively illiterate (cannot read and write), $6^{th}$ grade complete, and TVET (Diploma) holders.

Table 4 also shows that the majority of respondents are positioned towards the higher end of dimensions of corporate governance with averages of 2.571 for MMC, 2.442 for LMC, 2.576 for IMC, and 2.651 for DMC. Similarly, the variations are moderate with a standard deviation of 0.756 for MMC, 0.687 for LMC, 0.743 for IMC, and 0.663 for DMC.

The average score and standard deviation of the dependent variable, organizational performance, is moderate with mean of 2.455 and std. deviation of .716.

The average score for Organizational Performance (OrP) is moderate (i.e. 2.455), and its variability is also moderate (i.e. std. deviation of 0.716).

*Table 4. Descriptive statistics*

| | N | Minimum | Maximum | Mean | Std. Deviation |
|---|---|---|---|---|---|
| MMC | 377 | 1.00 | 3.83 | 2.579 | .756 |
| LMC | 377 | 1.00 | 3.80 | 2.442 | .687 |
| IMC | 377 | 1.00 | 3.75 | 2.576 | .743 |
| **DMC** | **377** | **1.20** | **3.80** | **2.651** | **.663** |
| OrP | 377 | 1.28 | 3.61 | 2.455 | .716 |
| Valid N (listwise) | 377 | | | | |

## 5.3. Inferential analysis

This subsection deals with the main inferences which were drawn from the model regression. In order to assess the effect of corporate governance dimensions on organizational performances of Ethiopian agricultural cooperative unions, the study had set the null hypotheses (see section 2.2 or the empirical literatures and hypotheses development section above). The mean scores of the corporate governance dimensions were regressed with the mean score of the agricultural cooperatives' unions' organizational performance in order to test the hypotheses ($H_{01}$ to $H_{04}$).

The ANOVA analysis, shown in table 5, is typically used to evaluate a relationship between predictor variables (MMC, LMC, IMC, and DMC) and the dependent variable (i.e. organizational performances of cooperative businesses). In the table, the residual sums of squares are 25.098, whereas the regression sums of squares, which indicates the extent to which the predictors explain the variation in the organizational performances, is 167.676. The independent variables are significant predictors of the dependent variable in the model for the fact that the residual sums of squares are significantly smaller than the sums of squares of regression. Therefore, the model explains a sizable portion of the variation in the dependent variable, as indicated by the F-value, which is 621.646. F-statistic represents the ratio explained variance to unexplained variance. The F-value's p-value, or .000, further indicates that the model is statistically significant for the analysis, since it is less than .005.

*Table 5. Overall significance: ANOVA*

| Model | | Sum of Squares | df | Mean Square | F | Sig. |
|---|---|---|---|---|---|---|
| 1 | Regression | 178.019 | 4 | 44.505 | 651.556 | .000[b] |
| | Residual | 27.186 | 398 | .068 | | |
| | Total | 205.205 | 402 | | | |

a. Dependent Variable: Organizational Performance
b. Predictors: (Constant), DMC, LMC, IMC, MMC

To back up the hypotheses further and ascertain that the regression model fits for the dataset, a model summary is presented in table 6 below. R = .933 indicates that there is strong positive relationship between dimensions of corporate governances of cooperative businesses predictors and their organizational performances. The closer the R to 1, the stronger the relationship between independent variables and the dependent variable (Itaoka, 2012, April). Similarly, the $R^2$ = .870 indicates that 87% of the variances in the organizational performances of agricultural cooperative unions in Ethiopia can be explained by the dimensions of corporate governances.

Furthermore, with an adjusted of .868, the model still explains 86.8% of the variation in the organizational performances, even after accounting for the number of independent variables. To put it more simply, even after accounting for the number of variables employed, the model performs a very good job of elucidating the elements that affect the result. The average distance between the observed values and the regression line is shown by the standard error (Koul & DeWet, 1983). The model's predictions are more in line with the actual results when the value is smaller. The comparatively small standard error in this case indicates that the model predicts the organizational performances well.

The residuals (errors) are tested for autocorrelation (Serial correlation) using the Durbin-Watson statistic (Tsay 1992). Although 1.628 indicates some slight positive autocorrelation in this case, it is not severe enough to cause alarm right away (see table 6 below). Strong autocorrelation can be troublesome since it goes against one of the fundamental assumptions of regression analysis, which is independent of errors (Aigner, 1973). Overall, this model seems to be a strong fit for predicting the organizational performances of agricultural cooperative unions in Ethiopia, with a very high explanatory power.

*Table 6. Model summary*

| Model | R | R Square | Adjusted R Square | Std. Error of the Estimate | Durbin-Watson |
|---|---|---|---|---|---|
| 1 | .933[a] | .870 | .868 | .260 | 1.628 |

a. Predictors: (Constant), DMC, IMC, MMC, LMC
b. Dependent Variable: Organizational Performance

The regression table shown in Table 7 below also presents coefficients measuring strength of relationships between predictors and dependent variables. The unstandardized coefficients beta (B) of MMC, LMC, IMC, and DMC are, respectively, .196, .578, .184, and .102. The values indicate that one unit increase in the predictors result in increment of .196, .578, .184, and .102 in the organizational performances of cooperative unions. Similarly, the standardized coefficients beta (B) are indicating the strengths the relationships between predictors and dependent variable. For this study, the coefficients are .207, .555, .191, and .094, respectively, for MMC, LMC, IMC, and DMC. This indicates that literacy of managing committee is posing strong positive impact, while all other predictors pose moderate positive impact on the organizational performances of corporate businesses in Ethiopia. Generally, since the p-values for each predictor are less .05, all of the independent variables (MMC, LMC, IMC, and DMC) are typically significant. According to the standardized coefficients (beta), the rank of significance of independent variables is LMC, MMC, IMC, and DMC. Since t-values of all the independent variables are significant (i.e.

7.323, 18.382, 6.743, and 3.189 respectively for MMC, LMC, IMC, and DMC), the relevance of these predictor variables in the model is further supported.

*Table 7. Regression results of organizational performance of Ethiopian agricultural cooperative unions against corporate governance dimensions*

| Correlation Coefficients[a] | | | | | | |
|---|---|---|---|---|---|---|
| **Model** | | **Unstandardized Coefficients** | | **Standardized Coefficients** | **t** | **Sig.** |
| | | **B** | **Std. Error** | **Beta** | | |
| 1 | (Constant) | -.208 | .058 | | -3.568 | .000 |
| | MMC | .196 | .027 | .207 | 7.323 | .000 |
| | LMC | .578 | .031 | .555 | 18.382 | .000 |
| | IMC | .184 | .027 | .191 | 6.743 | .000 |
| | DMC | .102 | .032 | .094 | 3.189 | .002 |

All correlations are statistically significant at the 0.01 level (i.e., p-values are less than 0.01), according to the correlation analysis displayed in table 8 below. This suggests that the observed relationships are unlikely to have occurred by chance. According to its strongest correlation with Organizational Performance (0.893), LMC has the strongest relationship with the dependent variable in this sample, followed by MMC (0.766) and IMC (0.765). High positive correlations exist among the independent variables themselves (e.g., MMC, LMC, IMC, and DMC are all positively linked with each other). This suggests that these predictors may be evaluating related constructs or may change in a similar way.

*Table 8. Correlations analysis*

| | | **MMC** | **LMC** | **IMC** | **DMC** | **OrP** |
|---|---|---|---|---|---|---|
| **MMC** | **Pearson Correlation** | **1** | **.685**** | **.599**** | **.685**** | **.766**** |
| | Sig. (2-tailed) | | .000 | .000 | .000 | .000 |
| | N | 377 | 377 | 377 | 377 | 377 |
| LMC | Pearson Correlation | .685** | 1 | .696** | .678** | .893** |
| | Sig. (2-tailed) | .000 | | .000 | .000 | .000 |
| | N | 377 | 377 | 377 | 377 | 377 |
| IMC | Pearson Correlation | .599** | .696** | 1 | .676** | .765** |
| | Sig. (2-tailed) | .000 | .000 | | .000 | .000 |
| | N | 377 | 377 | 377 | 377 | 377 |
| DMC | Pearson Correlation | .685** | .678** | .676** | 1 | .741** |

continued on following page

*Table 8. Continued*

| | | MMC | LMC | IMC | DMC | OrP |
|---|---|---|---|---|---|---|
| **MMC** | **Pearson Correlation** | **1** | **.685**** | **.599**** | **.685**** | **.766**** |
| | Sig. (2-tailed) | .000 | .000 | .000 | | .000 |
| | N | 377 | 377 | 377 | 377 | 377 |
| OrP | Pearson Correlation | .766** | .893** | .765** | .741** | 1 |
| | Sig. (2-tailed) | .000 | .000 | .000 | .000 | |
| | N | 377 | 377 | 377 | 377 | 377 |

**. Correlation is significant at the 0.01 level (2-tailed).

## 6. CONCLUSION

Based on the empirical results, this study came to the conclusion that the organizational performances of Ethiopian agricultural cooperative unions were statistically significantly impacted by the corporate governance aspects of meetings, literacy, independence, and diversity of managing committees. However, one of the corporate governance variables — the diversity of managing committees — has little impact on the performance of the chosen cooperative unions in the research region. Overall, this showed that the organizational performance of selected cooperative unions in Ethiopian agricultural cooperatives is significantly impacted by corporate governance dimensions.(Ranjan et al., 2023) On the other hand, organizational performance of the Ethiopian agricultural cooperative unions was adversely affected by low literacy of the members from which managing committees have been elected. Furthermore, the excessive influences from the government organizations is the second important factor affecting the organizational performances of cooperative unions in Ethiopia. Comparatively, composition of the managing committee is better in terms of diversity dimension (i.e. the managing committees are composed of members with different ages, gender, political and human interactions).

## 7. IMPLICATIONS

This research presents empirical evidences regarding the impact of corporate governance dimension of agricultural cooperative unions in Ethiopia on their performances. It used to manage committees' meetings, literacy, independence and diversity as independent variables; while the dependent variable is overall organizational performance(Manoharan et al., 2024). Using appropriate methods, the study has drawn the following implications. There is strong and positive relationship between literacy of managing committees' members and overall organizational performances, which implies that the larger proportion of members with better qualifications, the higher overall organizational performances of agricultural cooperative unions in Ethiopia. Similarly, there is strong and positive relationship between meeting and independence dimensions and overall organizational performances. The implication is that the more frequent, regular, attentive and effective meetings of the managing committees, the more the organizational performance. Additionally, the more the managing committees are independently discharging their authorities, the more the organizational performances in the cooperative unions. Overall, the research finding supports the Resource Dependence Theory (RDT), which mainly emphasizes the role of the managing committee in securing critical cooperative union's resources for its success. The theory assumes that the managing committees are not passive monitoring units but play an active role of ensuring the cooperative has the necessary resources to succeed (Pfeffer 1978). Hence, the managing committee of the unions need to have professional qualifications to cooperative union businesses such as knowledge and skills able to assist union's business survival and performance. Furthermore, it is required that the regulatory body should consider assigning an independent managing committee for each union. The independent managing committee to be considered requires having necessary qualifications and experience to make the cooperative unions successful.

## 8. LIMITATIONS AND FUTURE RESEARCH DIRECTIONS

The study tried to examine the relationship between dimensions of corporate governances and organizational performances of the Ethiopian agricultural cooperative unions using primary data collected by a questionnaire from members and managing committee of the selected unions. Even though literature support usage of primary data to measure organizational performances, the researched advises examine performances of the unions using their audited financial statements. The study was limited to direct relationship between the dimensions and organizational performance of the unions. However, organizational performance is very complex variable by its nature. It can be mediated and moderated by different variables. Further research is required to fill the gap by exploring such mediating and moderating variables.

## REFERENCES


Adams, R. B., & Ferreira, D. (2012). Regulatory pressure and bank directors' incentives to attend board

Ahamad, S., Mishra, A. B., Raghuram, K. S., Riyazuddin, Y. M., & Alanya-Beltran, J. (2024). *Applications of Internet of Things (IoT) in Maintaining Privacy and Security of Smart Cities*. Taylor & Francis Journal., DOI: 10.1201/9781003405580-30

Ahamad, S., Mishra, A. B., Raghuram, K. S., Tiwari, M., & Riyazuddin, Y. Md., & Alanya-Beltran, J. (2024). Applications of Internet of Things (IoT) in Maintaining Privacy and Security of Smart Cities. In *Computer Science Engineering and Emerging Technologies* (pp. 187–191). CRC Press. DOI: 10.1201/9781003405580-30

Ahmed, M. (2011). Defining and measuring literacy: Facing the reality. *International Review of Education, 57*(1-2), 179–195. DOI: 10.1007/s11159-011-9188-x

Aigner, D. J. (1973). Regression with a binary independent variable subject to errors of observation. *Journal of Econometrics, 1*(1), 49–59. DOI: 10.1016/0304-4076(73)90005-5

Ayodeji, A., & Okunade, R. A. (2019). Board independence and financial performance of deposit money banks in Nigeria and Canada. *Asian Journal of Economics. Business and Accounting, 11*(3), 1–9.

Bainbridge, S. M. (2002). Why a board-group decisionmaking in corporate governance. *Vand. L. Rev., 55*, 1. Basmah A, Lakshmi K. Is excess board independence good for firm performance? An empirical investigation of non-financial listed firms in Saudi Arabia. International Journal of Financial Research. 2016;

Basterretxea, I., Cornforth, C., & Heras-Saizarbitoria, I. (2022). Corporate governance as a key aspect in the failure of worker cooperatives. *Economic and Industrial Democracy, 43*(1), 362–387. DOI: 10.1177/0143831X19899474

Baysinger, B. D., & Butler, H. N. (1985). The role of corporate law in the theory of the firm. *The Journal of Law & Economics, 28*(1), 179–191. DOI: 10.1086/467079

Ben-Shahar, D., Carmeli, A., Sulganik, E., & Weiss, D. (2024). Regulating diversity and inclusiveness in boards of directors. *The Academy of Management Perspectives, 38*(3), 434–439. DOI: 10.5465/amp.2023.0474

Bernier, I. (2004). A UNESCO international convention on cultural diversity. *Free trade versus cultural diversity: WTO negotiations in the field of audiovisual services*, 65-76.

Bhagat, S., & Bolton, B. (2008). Corporate governance and firm performance. *Journal of Corporate Finance, 14*(3), 257–273. DOI: 10.1016/j.jcorpfin.2008.03.006

Bianchi, M., & Vieta, M. (2020). Co-operatives, territories and social capital: Reconsidering a theoretical framework. *International Journal of Social Economics, 47*(12), 1599–1617. DOI: 10.1108/IJSE-03-2020-0135

Biggins, J. V. (1999). Making Board Diversity Work. *Corporate Board, 20*(117), 11–17.

Bilimoria, D., & Piderit, S. K. (1994). Qualifications of corporate board committee members. *Group & Organization Management, 19*(3), 334–362. DOI: 10.1177/1059601194193007

Bougie, R., & Sekaran, U. (2019). *Research methods for business: A skill building approach.* John Wiley & Sons.

Bourdieu, P. (1985). The social space and the genesis of groups. *Social Sciences Information. Information Sur les Sciences Sociales, 24*(2), 195–220. DOI: 10.1177/053901885024002001

Brick, I. E., & Chidambaran, N. K. (2007). Board meetings, committee structure, and firm performance. *Committee Structure, and Firm Performance (November 2007).*

Carter, D., D'Souza, F. P., Simkins, B. J., & Simpson, W. G. (2007). The diversity of corporate board committees and firm financial performance. *Available atSSRN* 972763. DOI: 10.2139/ssrn.972763

Carver, J., & Carver, M. (2006). *Reinventing your board: A step-by-step guide to implementing policy governance* (Vol. 18). John Wiley & Sons.

Coase, R. H. (1993). The nature of the firm (1937). *WILLIANSON, OE; WINTER, SG.*

Daily, C. M., & Dalton, D. R. (1994). Corporate governance in the small firm: Prescriptions for CEOs and directors. [archive only]. *Journal of Small Business Strategy, 5*(1), 57–68.

Dalton, D. R., Daily, C. M., Ellstrand, A. E., & Johnson, J. L. (1998). Meta-analytic reviews of board composition, leadership structure, and financial performance. *Strategic Management Journal, 19*(3), 269–290. DOI: 10.1002/(SICI)1097-0266(199803)19:3<269::AID-SMJ950>3.0.CO;2-K

Daoud, J. I. (2017, December). Multicollinearity and regression analysis. [). IOP Publishing.]. *Journal of Physics: Conference Series, 949*(1), 012009. DOI: 10.1088/1742-6596/949/1/012009

Datta, N. (2018). Impact of corporate governance on financial performance: A study on DSE listed insurance companies in Bangladesh. *Global Journal of Management and Business Research, 18*(2), 32–39.

Donaldson, L., & Davis, J. H. (1991). Stewardship theory or agency theory: CEO governance and shareholder returns. *Australian Journal of Management, 16*(1), 49–64. DOI: 10.1177/031289629101600103

Duncan, R. C. (2003). Governance and growth. Paper presented to the Symposium on Governance held at the University of the South Pacific. *Suva, September.*

Dunphy, D., Turner, D., & Crawford, M. (1997). Organizational learning as the creation of corporate competencies. *Journal of Management Development, 16*(4), 232–244. DOI: 10.1108/02621719710164526

Eisenberg, M. A. (2017). Legal models of management structure in the modern corporation: Officers, directors, and accountants. In *Corporate Governance* (pp. 103–167). Gower. DOI: 10.4324/9781315574288-5

Esim, S. (2014, September). The cooperative key to sustainable development. In *Conference on Cooperatives and the Sustainable Development Goals: Focus on Africa,* Berlin, Germany (Vol. 2).

Etefa, D. F. (2022). Contributions of cooperatives and encountering challenges in Ethiopia. *American Journal of Research in Business and Social Sciences, 2*(1), 1–14.

Florin, J., Lubatkin, M., & Schulze, W. (2003). A social capital model of high-growth ventures. *Academy of Management Journal, 46*(3), 374–384. DOI: 10.2307/30040630

Francoeur, C., Labelle, R., & Sinclair-Desgagné, B. (2008). Gender diversity in corporate governance and top management. *Journal of Business Ethics, 81*(1), 83–95. DOI: 10.1007/s10551-007-9482-5

Franken, J. R., & Cook, M. L. (2019). Do corporate governance recommendations apply to US agricultural cooperatives? *Sustainability (Basel), 11*(19), 5321. DOI: 10.3390/su11195321

Freeman, R. E., & Phillips, R. A. (2002). Stakeholder theory: A libertarian defense. *Business Ethics Quarterly, 12*(3), 331–349. DOI: 10.2307/3858020

García-Ramos, R., & García-Olalla, M. (2011). Board characteristics and firm performance in public founder- and nonfounder-led family businesses. *Journal of Family Business Strategy, 2*(4), 220–231. DOI: 10.1016/j.jfbs.2011.09.001

Germann, C. (2023). Methodology and Empirical Research. In *Chairperson Succession: Competences, Moderators, and Disclosure* (pp. 87–98). Springer Fachmedien Wiesbaden. DOI: 10.1007/978-3-658-40817-6_5

Gertler, M. E. (2004). Synergy and strategic advantage: Cooperatives and sustainable development. *Journal of Cooperatives*, *18*, 32–46.

Getnet, K., & Anullo, T. (2012). Agricultural cooperatives and rural livelihoods: Evidence from Ethiopia. *Annals of Public and Cooperative Economics*, *83*(2), 181–198. DOI: 10.1111/j.1467-8292.2012.00460.x

Grashuis, J., & Hakelius, K. (2023). Pricing strategies of corporations and consumer co-operatives in the food retail sector: Evidence from England, Sweden, and the Netherlands. *Journal of Co-operative Organization and Management*, *11*(1), 100204. DOI: 10.1016/j.jcom.2023.100204

Hassan, R., & Marimuthu, M. (2018). Bridging and bonding: Having a Muslim diversity on corporate boards and firm performance. *Journal of Islamic Accounting and Business Research*, *9*(3), 457–478. DOI: 10.1108/JIABR-02-2016-0022

Hawkins, T. J. (2022). *Corporate Boardroom Gender and Board Diversity Performance*. Capella University.

Hill, J. G. (1998). Deconstructing Sunbeam-Contemporary issues in corporate governance. *U. Cin. L. Rev.*, *67*, 1099.

Hillman, A. J., Withers, M. C., & Collins, B. J. (2009). Resource dependence theory: A review. *Journal of Management*, *35*(6), 1404–1427. DOI: 10.1177/0149206309343469

Hilmer, M. J. (1998). Post-secondary fees and the decision to attend a university or a community college. *Journal of Public Economics*, *67*(3), 329–348. DOI: 10.1016/S0047-2727(97)00075-3

Ho, C. A., & Williams, S. M. (2003). International comparative analysis of the association between board structure and the efficiency of value added by a firm from its physical capital and intellectual capital resources. *The International Journal of Accounting*, *38*(4), 465–491. DOI: 10.1016/j.intacc.2003.09.001

Hung, H. (1998). A typology of the theories of the roles of governing boards. *Corporate Governance*, *6*(2), 101–111. DOI: 10.1111/1467-8683.00089

Hunt, J. L. (2000). Brown v. Board of Education After Fifty Years: Context and Synopsis. *Mercer L. Rev.*, *52*, 549.

Ingley, C., & Van Der Walt, N. (2002). Board dynamics and the politics of appraisal. *Corporate Governance*, *10*(3), 163–174. DOI: 10.1111/1467-8683.00281

International Cooperative Alliance. 2024. Cooperative identity, values and principles. https://2012.coop/en/what-co-op/cooperative-identity-values-principles.[accessed November 1

Itaoka, K. (2012, April). Regression and interpretation low R-squared. In *Proceedings of the presentation at Social Research Network 3rd Meeting,* Noosa. Mizuho Information and Research Institute, Inc.

Jehn, K. A., Northcraft, G. B., & Neale, M. A. (1999). Why differences make a difference: A field study of diversity, conflict and performance in workgroups. *Administrative Science Quarterly*, *44*(4), 741–763. DOI: 10.2307/2667054

Jensen, M. (2001). Value maximisation, stakeholder theory, and the corporate objective function. *European Financial Management*, *7*(3), 297–317. DOI: 10.1111/1468-036X.00158

Johl, S. K., & Salami, O. L. (2014). Impact of board composition on firm performance: A study on listed firms in Malaysia. *Journal of Contemporary Management*, *3*(3), 94–102.

Johnson, J. L., Daily, C. M., & Ellstrand, A. E. (1996). Boards of directors: A review and research agenda. *Journal of Management*, *22*(3), 409–438. DOI: 10.1177/014920639602200303

Kalyanaraman, L., & Altuwaijri, B. (2016). The linkage between excess board independence and capital structure: An exploration in the context of listed companies in Saudi Arabia. *Journal of Applied Finance and Banking*, *6*(3), 129.

Kate, N., Padhye, P., & Mishra, A. B. (2022). Studies on Anti-Virus Software Tools: Strong Weapon to Protect Systems. *2022 2nd International Conference on Innovative Practices in Technology and Management (ICIPTM)*, 49–52. DOI: 10.1109/ICIPTM54933.2022.9753877

Keasey, K., Thompson, S., & Wright, M. (Eds.). (1997). *Corporate governance: Economic and financial issues.* DOI: 10.1093/oso/9780198289906.001.0001

Ketokivi, M., & Mahoney, J. T. (2020). Transaction Cost Economics As a Theory of Supply Chain Efficiency. Production and Operations Management, 29(4), 1011-1031. Khanchel El Mehdi, I. (2007). Empirical evidence on corporate governance and corporate performance inDOI: 10.1111/poms.13148

Kim, J. H. (2019). Multicollinearity and misleading statistical results. *Korean Journal of Anesthesiology*, *72*(6), 558–569. DOI: 10.4097/kja.19087 PMID: 31304696

Klapper, L. F., & Love, I. (2002). Corporate governance, investor protection and performance in emerging markets. *Investor Protection and Performance in Emerging Markets (March 2002).*

Klein, P., Shapiro, D., & Young, J. (2005). Corporate governance, family ownership and firm value: The Canadian evidence. *Corporate Governance, 13*(6), 769–784. DOI: 10.1111/j.1467-8683.2005.00469.x

Kothari, D. P., & Nagrath, I. J. (2003). *Modern power system analysis*. Tata McGraw-Hill Publishing Company. Koul, H., & DeWet, T. (1983). Minimum distance estimation in a linear regression model. *The Annals of*

Kyazze, L. M., Nkote, I. N., & Wakaisuka-Isingoma, J. (2017). Cooperative governance and social performance of cooperative societies. *Cogent Business & Management, 4*(1), 1284391. DOI: 10.1080/23311975.2017.1284391

Lang, R., & Roessl, D. (2011). The role of social capital in the development of community-based co- operatives. *New developments in the theory of networks: Franchising, alliances and cooperatives*, 353-370.

Lavery, M. R., Acharya, P., Sivo, S. A., & Xu, L. (2019). Number of predictors and multicollinearity: What are their effects on error and bias in regression? *Communications in Statistics. Simulation and Computation, 48*(1), 27–38. DOI: 10.1080/03610918.2017.1371750

Lee, S. H., Kang, H. J., & Lee, S. Y. (2022). The Influence of Board Diversity and Board Conflict on Performance in Consumer Cooperatives in South Korea. *Journal of Entrepreneurial and Organizational Diversity, 11*(1), 55–81. DOI: 10.5947/jeod.2022.003

Mamo, Y. A., Haji, J., Legesse, B., & Sassi, M. (2021). Challenges of agricultural cooperatives and their impact on profitability of potato growers in eastern Ethiopia. [RAAE]. *Acta Oeconomica et Informatica, 24*(2), 62–77. DOI: 10.15414/raae.2021.24.02.62-77

Manoharan, G., Mishra, A. B., Adusumilli, S. B. K., Chavva, M., Damancharla, H., & Sahaya Lenin, D. (2024). Supervised Learning for Personalized Marketing Strategies. *2024 International Conference on Advances in Computing, Communication and Applied Informatics (ACCAI)*, 1–6. DOI: 10.1109/ACCAI61061.2024.10602307

Maričić, G., Škorić, S., & Radenković, D. (2018). Application of the principles of corporate governance in agriculture cooperatives. *Economy in harm's way, 65*(2), 827-841.

McClelland, D. C., & Boyatzis, R. E. (1982). Leadership motive pattern and long-term success in management. *The Journal of Applied Psychology*, *67*(6), 737–743. DOI: 10.1037/0021-9010.67.6.737

Mersha, D., & Ayenew, Z. (2018). Financing challenges of smallholder farmers: A study on members of agricultural cooperatives in Southwest Oromia Region, Ethiopia. *African Journal of Business Management*, *12*(10), 285–293. DOI: 10.5897/AJBM2018.8517

Mishra, A. (2025). Monitoring the Development of the IoT Concept in Various Application Domains. *Taylor & Francis Online, CRC Press*. https://www.taylorfrancis.com/chapters/edit/10.1201/9781003596721-41/monitoring-development-iot-concept-various-application-domains-mishra-sarita-rani-panda-anitha-uma-reddy-gaurav-sethi-purnendu-bikash-acharjee

Mishra, A. B. (2020). E- PAYMENT SYSTEM: A RISING TREND OF ECONOMY. *New Paradigm in Business and Education*. https://www.researchgate.net/profile/Anitha-K-2/publication/349605501_E-LEARNING_THROUGH_GAMIFICATION-_AN_ITINERARY_TO_GAIN_IN-DEPTH_KNOWLEDGE/links/6037d566299bf1cc26ef9597/E-LEARNING-THROUGH-GAMIFICATION-AN-ITINERARY-TO-GAIN-IN-DEPTH-KNOWLEDGE.pdf#page=10

Mishra, A. B., & Monika, J. (2024). Case Study of Kalyan Jewellers-Brand Perception Mapping Towards Disruptive Innovation in Jewellery Segment. *International Journal of Advance and Applied Research*, *11*(6), 386–396.

Mishra, A. B. (2025a). Kalyan Jeweller's Case Study of Transformation, Consumer Engagement, and Effective Marketing Strategies for Brand Building. In *Dynamic Strategies for Entrepreneurial Marketing* (pp. 287–310). DOI: 10.4018/979-8-3693-3936-7.ch014

Mishra, A. B. (2025b). The Paytm Puzzle: Navigating Regulatory Compliance in India's Digital Revolution. In *Cultural Sensitivity, Cross-Border Logistics, and E-Commerce in Global Marketing* (pp. 337–348). IGI Global. DOI: 10.4018/979-8-3373-0528-8.ch015

Mishra, A. B., Chand, K., & Kaith, K. (2022). Influencer Marketing as Emerging Promotional Tool in Modern Era and Opportunities to Uprising Sales. *International Journal of Emerging Research in Engineering, Science, and Management*, *1*(3). Advance online publication. DOI: 10.58482/ijeresm.v1i3.3

Mishra, A. B., & Dodke, S. D. (2024). ZARA : Technological Influence on Becoming the Fashion Industry's Market Leader. In *Cases on AI Ethics in Business* (pp. 204–215). IGI Publishing., DOI: 10.4018/979-8-3693-2643-5.ch012

Mishra, A. B., & Gaikwad, V. (2024). The Transaction War Between Google Pay and Phonepe. In *IGI Global* (pp. 166–185). DOI: 10.4018/978-1-6684-7840-0.ch009

Mishra, A. B., Rajagopal, N. K., Yousoof, M., & Padhye, P. (2021). A STUDY ON ORGANISATIONAL PRACTICES THAT INFLUENCE EMPLOYEE ENGAGEMENT. *Manager–. British Journal of Administrative Management, 57*(145), 220–225.

Mishra, A. B., Ranjan, N., Sharma, K. M., Padhye, P., & Chand, K. (2023). Advancement of Digital Transformation to Boost Financial Services Industry. *Journal of Informatics Education and Research, 3*(2), 2435–2440. https://scholar.google.com/scholar?cluster=15410723285942667834&hl=en&oi=scholarr

Mishra, A. B., Sahu, T., Ranjan, N., & Varma, A. (2021). Green Marketing Practices Prevailing In Hotel Industry. *Journal of Contemporary Issues in Business and Government, 27*(02). Advance online publication. DOI: 10.47750/cibg.2021.27.02.145

Mishra, A. B., Satarkar, M., & Joshi, S. (2023). IKEA - Phygital Transformation in Furniture Manufacturing Industry. *International Journal of Emerging Research in Engineering, Science, and Management, 2*(3), 6–9. DOI: 10.58482/ijeresm.v2i3.2

Mishra, A. B., & Singh, A. (2024). The Mumbai Dabbawalas : An Efficient and Sustainable Lunchbox Delivery System. In *IGI Global* (pp. 154–160). DOI: 10.4018/979-8-3693-1544-6.ch007

Mohammed, N., & Lee, B. W. (2015). Role of cooperatives in rural development, the case of south nations nationalities and people region, Ethiopia. *Science Journal of Business and Management, 3*(4), 102–108. DOI: 10.11648/j.sjbm.20150304.12

Mohseni, M., Othman, B. A., Raturi, P., Mishra, A. B., Priya, S. J., & Saravanan, V. (2022). The Role of Parallel Computing Towards Implementation of Enhanced and Effective Industrial Internet of Things (IOT) Through Manova Approach. *2022 2nd International Conference on Advance Computing and Innovative Technologies in Engineering (ICACITE)*, 160–164. DOI: 10.1109/ICACITE53722.2022.9823698

Momaya, K. S., Bhat, S., & Lalwani, L. (2017). Institutional growth and industrial competitiveness: Exploring the role of strategic flexibility taking the case of select institutesin India. *Global Journal of Flexible Systems Managment, 18*(2), 111–122. DOI: 10.1007/s40171-016-0144-2

Muth, M. M., & Donaldson, L. (1998). Stewardship theory and board structure: A contingency approach. *Corporate Governance, 6*(1), 5–28. DOI: 10.1111/1467-8683.00076

Nilsson, J. (2001). Organisational principles for co-operative firms. *Scandinavian Journal of Management, 17*(3), 329–356. DOI: 10.1016/S0956-5221(01)00010-0

Ntim, C. G., & Osei, K. A. (2011). The impact of corporate board meetings on corporate performance in South Africa. *African Review of Economics and Finance*, *2*(2), 83–103.

Oguda, S. E. R. A. H. (2015). *Relationship between board characteristics and firm performance: Survey of firms listed at the Nairobi Securities Exchange* (Doctoral dissertation, University of Nairobi).

Ortmann, G. F., & King, R. P. (2007). Agricultural cooperatives I: History, theory and problems. *Agrekon*, *46*(1), 40–68. DOI: 10.1080/03031853.2007.9523760

Pfeffer, J. (1978). *The external control of organization/Pfeffer J., Salancik G.* Harper&Row.

Pfeffer, J., & Salancik, G. (2015). External control of organizations—Resource dependence perspective. In *Organizational behavior 2* (pp. 355–370). Routledge.

Ponnu, C. H., & Karthigeyan, R. M. (2010). Board independence and corporate performance: Evidence from Malaysia. *African Journal of Business Management*, *4*(6), 858.

Portes, A. (2000, March). The two meanings of social capital. []. Kluwer Academic Publishers-Plenum Publishers.]. *Sociological Forum*, *15*(1), 1–12. DOI: 10.1023/A:1007537902813

Puri, D. L., & Sujarittanonta, L. (2016). Good Governance in Cooperatives of Nepal-Relationship between Participation and Performance of Cooperatives. *Journal of Education and Vocational Research*, *7*(2), 19–26. DOI: 10.22610/jevr.v7i2.1335

Rana, M. S., Cavaliere, L. P. L., Mishra, A. B., Padhye, P., Singh, R. R., & Khanna, R. (2022, April). Internet of Things (IOT) Based Assessment for Effective Monitoring Data Against Malicious Attacks on Financial Collectors. In 2022 2nd International Conference on Advance Computing and Innovative Technologies in Engineering (ICACITE) (pp. 177-181). IEEE.

Ranjan, N., Mishra, A. B., & Padhye, P. (2023). Dynamics of Digital Payments Enable the World's Safest Way to Pay. *Journal of Informatics Education and Research*, *3*(2). Advance online publication. DOI: 10.52783/jier.v3i2.406

Ruben, R., & Heras, J. (2012). Social capital, governance and performance of Ethiopian coffee cooperatives.

Ruben, R., & Heras, J. (2012, December). SOCIAL CAPITAL, GOVERNANCE AND PERFORMANCE OF ETHIOPIAN COFFEE COOPERATIVES. *Annals of Public and Cooperative Economics, 83*(4), 463–484. DOI: 10.1111/j.1467-8292.2012.00473.x

Sánchez-Navarro, J. L., Arcas-Lario, N., Bijman, J., & Hernández-Espallardo, M. (2024). The role of agricultural cooperatives in mitigating opportunism in the context of complying with sustainability requirements: Empirical evidence from Spain. *Agricultural and Food Economics, 12*(1), 40. DOI: 10.1186/s40100-024-00332-8

Sarantakos, S. (1998). Measurement and scaling. In *Social Research* (pp. 72–95). Palgrave. DOI: 10.1007/978-1-349-14884-4_3

Saz-Gil, I., Bretos, I., & Díaz-Foncea, M. (2021). Cooperatives and social capital: A narrative literature review and directions for future research. *Sustainability (Basel), 13*(2), 534. DOI: 10.3390/su13020534

Schneider, H. (1999). Participatory governance for poverty reduction. *Journal of International Development, 11*(4), 521–534. DOI: 10.1002/(SICI)1099-1328(199906)11:4<521::AID-JID599>3.0.CO;2-J

Sharifah Syahirah, S. S., Fatimah Bibi, H., & Muhd Bazli, H. (2018, March). Leadership, policy and governance in Malaysia: A study on gen Y perception and expectation. In *International Conference on Kansei Engineering & Emotion Research* (pp. 683-691). Singapore: Springer Singapore. DOI: 10.1007/978-981-10-8612-0_71

Sivertsen, G. (2018). The norwegian model in Norway. *Journal of Data and Information Science, 3*(4), 3–19. DOI: 10.2478/jdis-2018-0017

Sobel, P. J., & Reding, K. F. (2004). Aligning corporate governance performance measurement and corporate governance. *Management accounting.*

Sreejesh, S., Mohapatra, S., & Anusree, M. R. (2014). *Business research methods: An applied orientation.*

Stoop, E., Brandsen, T., & Helderman, J. K. (2021). The impact of the cooperative structure on organizational social capital. *Social Enterprise Journal, 17*(4), 548–565. DOI: 10.1108/SEJ-08-2020-0063

Surroca, J., Tribó, J. A., & Waddock, S. (2010). Corporate responsibility and financialperformance: The role of intangible resources. *Strategic Management Journal, 31*(5), 463–490. DOI: 10.1002/smj.820

Tay, R. (2017). Correlation, variance inflation and multicollinearity in regression model. *Journal of the Eastern Asia Society for Transportation Studies, 12*, 2006–2015.

Tefera, D. A., Bijman, J., & Slingerland, M. A. (2017). Agricultural co-operatives in Ethiopia. Evolution, functions and impact. *Journal of International Development, 29*(4), 431–453. DOI: 10.1002/jid.3240

Trejo-Pech, C. O., Servín-Juárez, R., & Reyes-Duarte, Á. (2023). What sets cooperative farmers apart from non-cooperative farmers? A transaction cost economics analysis of coffee farmers in Mexico. *Agricultural and Food Economics, 11*(1), 14. DOI: 10.1186/s40100-023-00256-9

Tsay, W. J. (1998). On the power of Durbin-Watson statistic against fractionally integrated processes. *Econometric Reviews, 17*(4), 361–386. DOI: 10.1080/07474939808800423

Usman, M. S., Sheoliha, N., Prabhakar, P. V., Mishra, A. B., & Dondapati, A. (2023). Leading Strategies for Organizational Adaptation and Growth in Digital Transformation in Marketing. Journal of Informatics Education and Research.

Vafeas, N. (1999). Board meeting frequency and firm performance. *Journal of Financial Economics, 53*(1), 113–142. DOI: 10.1016/S0304-405X(99)00018-5

Valentinov, V., & Iliopoulos, C. (2021). Social capital in cooperatives: An evolutionary Luhmannian perspective. *Journal of Evolutionary Economics, 31*(4), 1317–1331. DOI: 10.1007/s00191-021-00744-5

Van der Vegt, G. S., Van de Vliert, E., & Huang, X. (2005). Location-level links between diversity and innovative climate depend on national power distance. *Academy of Management Journal, 48*(6), 1171–1182. DOI: 10.5465/amj.2005.19573116

Wagner, D. A. (2014). Literacy. In *Handbook of cultural developmental science* (pp. 161–173). Psychology Press.

White, K. J. (1992). The Durbin-Watson test for autocorrelation in nonlinear models. *The Review of Economics and Statistics, 74*(2), 370–373. DOI: 10.2307/2109675

Williamson, O. E. (1979). Transaction-cost economics: The governance of contractual relations. *The Journal of Law & Economics, 22*(2), 233–261. DOI: 10.1086/466942

Wulandhari, N. B. I., Gölgeci, I., Mishra, N., Sivarajah, U., & Gupta, S. (2022). Exploring the role of social capital mechanisms in cooperative resilience. *Journal of Business Research, 143*, 375–386. DOI: 10.1016/j.jbusres.2022.01.026

Yermack, D. (2006). Board members and company value. *Financial Markets and Portfolio Management, 20*(1), 33–47. DOI: 10.1007/s11408-006-0003-9

Zachow, M., & Bertolini, G. R. F. (2019). Use of Balanced Scorecard in Cooperatives. [IJAERS]. *International Journal of Advanced Engineering Research and Science*, *6*(10), 160–166. DOI: 10.22161/ijaers.610.25

Zhang, L. (2012). Board demographic diversity, independence, and corporate social performance. *Corporate Governance (Bradford)*, *12*(5), 686–700. DOI: 10.1108/14720701211275604

Zubeltzu-Jaka, E., Álvarez-Etxeberria, I., & Ortas, E. (2020). The effect of the size of the board of directors on corporate social performance: A meta-analytic approach. *Corporate Social Responsibility and Environmental Management*, *27*(3), 1361–1374. DOI: 10.1002/csr.1889

# Chapter 4
# Navigating Obstacles, Hurdles, and Risks in the Organizational Development of Sustainability Startups

**Surjit Singha**
https://orcid.org/0000-0002-5730-8677
*Kristu Jayanti College, India*

## ABSTRACT

*This chapter studied sustainability start-ups' unique traits and critical role in tackling global concerns at the nexus of economic progress, environmental responsibility, and social impact. It underlines their complexity, including finance, compliance, and sustainable innovation market acceptance. Financial strategies, personnel acquisition, supply chain management, regulatory compliance, and social and environmental impact monitoring are covered in depth. It analyzes regulatory systems and legal tactics. It stresses taking advantage of legislative incentives and promoting favourable rules and innovation's role in overcoming difficulties. It encourages corporate and environmental stewardship improvements.*

## INTRODUCTION

Sustainability has emerged as a pillar of modern business and entrepreneurship as environmental concerns continue to escalate and the finite nature of our planet's resources becomes more apparent. With a dual commitment to profitability and

DOI: 10.4018/978-1-6684-9872-9.ch004

positive environmental and social impacts, sustainability startups have become transformative economic forces on a global scale. These inventive endeavours address urgent ecological and social issues while pursuing economic expansion. However, the path to success for startups focusing on sustainability is complex. Tajpour et al. (2023) find that fostering innovation, knowledge sharing, and effective communication positively impacts digital startup sustainability. Sustainability firms comprise diverse enterprises that place economic, environmental, and social sustainability at the forefront of their operations and business models.

These nascent enterprises prioritize the creation of inventive resolutions to urgent worldwide issues, including climate change, depletion of natural resources, social inequality, and environmental deterioration. Renewable energy, waste management, sustainable agriculture, eco-friendly products and services, circular economy initiatives, green technology, social enterprises, and ethical fashion are just a few sectors in which sustainability ventures are active. Social media acts as a mediator, enhancing employee engagement and interactions and aiding business resilience in a dynamic market. This chapter sheds light on the multidimensional nature of these issues, providing valuable insight into the unique challenges encountered by entrepreneurs and organizations committed to cultivating sustainability.

Prihadyanti et al. (2023) unveil agri-tech startups' vital role in advancing social innovation for sustainable agriculture in Indonesia. Furthermore, the study meticulously explores the role of business entities, exemplified by agri-tech startups, in nurturing SI. It meticulously dissects diffusion models and innovation-decision processes, uncovering three distinct models that lead to varying decision-making and communication channels. An array of internal and external factors intricately shapes these models. Notably, the study underscores how these startups assume diverse bridging roles contingent on their unique attributes, ultimately providing valuable practical insights for the successful development of SI (Sustainable Innovation).

Sustainability startups operate at the intersection of business, innovation, and environmental and social responsibility. Due to shifting consumer preferences, stringent regulatory requirements, and the imperative to address urgent global issues such as climate change, resource depletion, and social inequities, they must navigate a swiftly transforming landscape. As these businesses strive to develop innovative solutions and sustainable business models, they confront several organizational challenges, such as acquiring funding, cultivating a dedicated workforce, establishing efficient supply chains, and forging alliances with like-minded organizations.

This chapter serves as a platform for researchers, practitioners, and policymakers to investigate the complexities of sustainability startups by thoroughly examining the risks, challenges, and barriers they face. Looking at real-world case studies, empirical research, and expert perspectives, this compilation of chapters aims to provide readers with a deeper understanding of the issues at hand, equipping them with the knowledge necessary to confront these challenges effectively.

The chapter examines establishing strategic partnerships and collaborations to amplify sustainability startups' social and environmental impact. In addition, it explores the complexities of navigating market competition and scaling sustainable innovations. It provides insights into methods for accurately measuring and persuasively communicating these visionary enterprises' social and environmental influence. This chapter comprehensively comprehends the obstacles and opportunities sustainability startups face toward a more sustainable future.

Through this effort, we hope to provide a comprehensive view of the organizational risks, obstacles, and challenges of developing sustainability startups. By doing so, we hope to contribute to the ongoing conversation about sustainable entrepreneurship and inspire positive change in how organizations approach business and environmental stewardship.

## CONTEXTUALIZING SUSTAINABILITY STARTUPS

Startups prioritizing environmental and social responsibility while pursuing profitability are a distinct category. These companies are distinguished by their commitment to addressing urgent ecological and societal challenges within a viable and innovative business model framework. Their significance in the contemporary business landscape cannot be exaggerated, as they reshape traditional conceptions of entrepreneurship and business practices. In their study, Han et al. (2023) highlight that circular startups deviate from traditional startups' conventional revenue-centric scaling approach. Instead, they adopt a multifaceted strategy, including commercial and impact-driven endeavours. In addition to pursuing financial growth, these circular startups make systemic changes, such as influencing regulatory frameworks, an integral part of their scaling efforts. Sharma et al. (2024) Based on interviews with innovators from 13 circular startups, this study identifies three distinct scaling strategies: commercial, incremental, and synchronized. In addition, it meticulously organizes generic initiatives for commercial and impact scalability within the framework of the business model canvas. This study substantially enhances our understanding of circular startups and their growth trajectories, providing academicians and practitioners in circular innovation with invaluable insights.

The mission of sustainability startups is to create positive environmental and social impacts, frequently in response to the most pressing global challenges of our time. Whether focused on renewable energy solutions, eco-friendly consumption products, sustainable agriculture, or social entrepreneurship, these businesses are motivated by a strong desire to contribute to a more sustainable and equitable future. Multiple factors contribute to the significance of sustainability startups in the contemporary business environment:

Startups specializing in sustainability are at the vanguard of innovation, pioneering new technologies, processes, and business models that challenge the status quo. Their innovative approaches often lead to the development of novel solutions for urgent global issues, such as climate change mitigation, resource conservation, and social inequality. Wadewitz (2023) reveals a transformative impact of technological advancements on the wine tourism sector. This disruption promises growth and cost reduction, particularly for smaller wineries. The chapter highlights the FOMENT Wine and Tourism Tech program in South Australia, supported by the government, as a driving force for tech adoption, featuring case studies of startups (e.g., Airguides) benefiting from the program's innovation in enhancing the wine tourism experience.

These businesses disrupt conventional markets by introducing products and services focusing on sustainability and social impact. In doing so, they create new market segments and force established firms to reevaluate their practices, fostering healthy competition and driving industry-wide transformation. Halkias et al. (2023) revealed a significant finding in their case study of Greek digital entrepreneurs, exemplified by Harbor Lab, as influential disruptors in the global shipping industry. Their entrepreneurial journey highlights the crucial role of leadership, particularly during challenges like the COVID-19 pandemic. Harbor Lab's success underscores digital entrepreneurship's transformative potential and the importance of fostering an open and empathetic workplace culture in the maritime sector, contributing valuable insights to theoretical research and practical applications.

With the increasing consciousness of consumers regarding environmental and social matters, sustainability startups respond to the growing market need for products and services that are both environmentally friendly and socially responsible. Their achievement serves as an illustration of the evolving preferences of consumers who are in search of more environmentally friendly alternatives. Ciccullo et al. (2023) unveil a noteworthy discovery in their investigation of sustainable startups operating within Italy's construction and fashion industries. These startups strategically implement circular supply chains (CSCs) to mitigate sustainability concerns. By applying closed-loop and open-loop principles, they can reinstate value in their supply chains that transcend industry boundaries. The study highlights three coordination roles these startups employ: orchestrator, integrated orchestrator, and circular manufacturer. The selection of these roles is contingent upon the degree of vertical integration exhibited by the manufacturing companies. This research increases our industry-wide comprehension of sustainable supply chain design and value creation.

Frequently, sustainability-focused startups advocate for more stringent social and environmental regulations. By engaging in dialogue with policymakers and industry stakeholders, they can contribute to developing comprehensive and efficacious sustainability policies. Zhu et al. (2023) unveil a significant discovery in their investigation, which provides insight into the determinants that impact the leveraging ratio of blue economy startups. The analysis underscores the adverse effects of climate and ocean disruptions on debt ratios, contrasting with the favourable influence of asset tangibility on debt financing. The admonition against debt financing by rigorous regulations is private equity's contribution to financial stability. This study provides significant contributions to the understanding of financing choices made by blue startups, which have far-reaching consequences for financial tactics and the long-term viability of expansion in the blue economy.

These initiatives foster collaboration and inspiration among established businesses, motivating them to adopt sustainable practices. Additionally, they promote cooperation and alliances that have the potential to bolster endeavours aimed at tackling worldwide issues. Sreenivasan et al. (2023) significantly contribute to the field of Industry 4.0 by identifying eleven essential characteristics that augment the agility of startup operations. Although larger organizations have adopted Industry 4.0, there needs to be more integration regarding its application to Startup 4.0. This study highlights the critical significance of artificial intelligence, cloud computing, network connectivity, technology, and digital twins in fostering agility in contemporary startups, offering indispensable perspectives for their achievements. Sustainability startups function as organizations and catalysts for transformation within the modern business landscape. Their pivotal role as catalysts for progress is predicated on their steadfast dedication to sustainable practices, inventive thinking, and social accountability. They furnish not only motivation but also pragmatic resolutions to the most urgent challenges of our age. As the discourse on this subject progresses, an examination is conducted on the unique attributes that set sustainability startups apart from traditional enterprises, unveiling the intricate dynamics that govern their functioning and consequences.

These distinguishing characteristics distinguish sustainability startups from conventional business ventures. Fundamentally, sustainability-focused startups are mission-driven. Their primary objective is to generate profits while addressing pressing environmental or social challenges. This dual commitment to purpose and profit distinguishes them from conventional businesses, prioritizing profits above all else. Singh and Singh's 2023 study identifies and classifies eight critical success factors influencing social value creation by social entrepreneurs. These factors encompass entrepreneurial intention, intrinsic motivation, social salience, social innovation, entrepreneurial capabilities, mission, resource mobilization, and capacity building. Employing m-TISM and MICMAC analysis, the research establishes interrelationships and driver-dependent categorization, emphasizing a five-level hierarchical structure for dual value creation in social entrepreneurship, providing significant insights for scholars and practitioners.

Sustainability startups adhere to the "triple bottom line" principle. In addition to measuring achievement based on financial performance, they consider environmental and social impact. This holistic approach ensures that they believe in the broader effects of their actions, going beyond maximizing profits. Premadasa et al. (2023) unveil a comprehensive conceptual model through qualitative research, shedding light on social entrepreneurship in developing countries, specifically focusing on Sri Lankan social enterprises. This model elucidates how social entrepreneurial orientation acts as a catalyst for achieving the triple bottom line (economic, social, and environmental outcomes) through dynamic capabilities and social innovation. The study underscores that social entrepreneurial orientation alone cannot achieve this balance, emphasizing the integration of critical constructs for a nuanced understanding of social entrepreneurial ventures in developing countries.

These businesses are frequently on the cutting edge of innovation. They seek inventive solutions to complex sustainability challenges, advancing technology and disrupting traditional industries with eco-friendly products, services, or processes. Conversely, Traditional businesses may need to be more risk-averse and sluggish in implementing innovative practices. Lamperti et al. (2023) highlight the essential role of business incubators in enabling sustainability startups to transfer explicit and tacit knowledge effectively. This transfer process unfolds across three key phases: awareness, identification, and assessment. These phases significantly contribute to sustainability startups' ability to generate meaningful impact in addressing environmental and social challenges. The study emphasizes the instrumental role of support programs provided by business incubators in facilitating this knowledge transfer.

For these startups, sustainability is not an oversight but integral to their business model. They integrate sustainability principles into every aspect of their business, from supply chain management to product design, to minimize their environmental impact and maximize their social benefits. Böttcher et al. (2023) present a crucial core finding—a comprehensive taxonomy of digital sustainable business models (BM) derived from an analysis of 31 startups. This taxonomy identifies four archetypes showcasing how digital technology integrates sustainability into BMs. These archetypes demonstrate the significance of making sustainability an intrinsic part of an organization's core identity and logic, providing valuable strategic guidance for achieving ecological and economic sustainability through digital BMs.

Startups focusing on sustainability prioritize engagement with consumers, communities, investors, and regulators. They actively solicit feedback and collaboration to ensure alignment with the sustainability objective. Traditional businesses may prioritize shareholders and profit margins above all else. Sehnem et al. (2023)

emphasize the core finding of their study, highlighting the strategic adoption of circular business models by startups facilitated by innovation and Industry 4.0. This research also identifies key stakeholders in this ecosystem, providing valuable managerial insights for achieving profitability, efficiency, and sustainability in the circular economy.

Transparency and accountability are fundamental values for startups in the sustainability industry. They frequently publish comprehensive sustainability reports that detail their environmental and social performance, objectives, and progress. Traditional enterprises need to be more forthright with this type of information. Khan et al. (2023) highlight the central finding of their study, emphasizing the significant macro-environmental challenges faced by startups in developing countries, with Pakistan as a specific case. Using a methodological approach combining PESTEL analysis and Fuzzy Failure Mode and Effect Analysis (FFMEA), the research underscores challenges like inflation rates, currency depreciation, and corruption that pose substantial risks to startups. It also emphasizes the importance of crafting strategies and policies for risk mitigation, offering valuable guidance for policymakers, entrepreneurs, and educational institutions in addressing these challenges effectively.

Startups focusing on sustainability have a higher risk tolerance when pursuing unconventional business models or eco-friendly technologies. Conventional businesses may be more risk-averse due to established procedures and stakeholder expectations. Korpysa et al.'s (2023) core finding centres on assessing decision criteria and determining factors essential for the sustainability of entrepreneurial startups. These factors, ranked by importance, are critical in fostering social inclusion and capacity building. The research highlights five critical decision criteria: region, competition, funding opportunities, tax system, and economic situation, along with eight determining factors, including reliability, results-driven mindset, flexibility, stress resilience, market opportunity identification, leadership, creativity, innovation, and decision delegation. Together, they form the fundamental requirements for nurturing successful entrepreneurial startups and contributing significantly to social inclusion and capacity development.

Increasing numbers of ethically conscientious consumers who prioritize products and services that accord with their values are drawn to sustainability-focused startups. It may be necessary for traditional businesses to adapt to meet these shifting consumer preferences. Cerchia & Piccolo (2019) The central finding of this study highlights the significance of corporate social responsibility (CSR) communications, specifically codes of ethics, within the fashion industry. These codes predominantly address employment and workers' rights, labour safety, anti-corruption measures, combatting counterfeiting and unfair business practices, and demonstrating a commitment to environmental responsibility. These codes function as a means for brands to convey their dedication to ethical principles and can enhance their brand image. To maintain consumer trust, it is essential to distinguish genuinely honest companies from those with misleading claims, with legal systems safeguarding against deceptive advertising.

These endeavours take a long-term perspective on success, recognizing that achieving sustainability objectives frequently requires grit and perseverance. Traditional enterprises may place greater emphasis on short-term profits. The central finding of Trautwein's (2021) study revolves around identifying and presenting assessment approaches for evaluating the sustainability impact of startups. It addresses the challenges of assessing sustainability impact in the startup context and provides solutions. Moreover, the study highlights research gaps and potential avenues for future research, offering valuable insights for practitioners and researchers in sustainable entrepreneurship and sustainability assessment.

Sustainability startups are characterized by their dual commitment to profit and positive environmental or social impact, innovative and mission-driven approach, and holistic view of success. These distinctive qualities position them as change agents in the contemporary business world, challenging established norms and inspiring a shift towards more sustainable and accountable business practices.

## ORGANIZATIONAL RISKS IN SUSTAINABILITY STARTUPS

Sustainability startups face unique organizational risks that stem from their operational procedures, the intricacies of their supply chains, and the volatile nature of the sustainability industry. These enterprises frequently establish groundbreaking environmentally conscious methods, introducing inherent uncertainties, including the dependability of novel sustainable technologies and unanticipated ecological consequences (Da Silva Nunes et al., 2022). The effective management of responsible supply chains, distinguished by their adherence to sustainability principles and ethical procurement, entails addressing obstacles such as material shortages and ethical labour practices that cause supply disruptions (Han & Um, 2024). Furthermore, sustainability markets exhibit a dynamic nature, susceptible to changes in government policies, consumer preferences, and competition, all of which influence regulatory compliance and demand (Coşkun & Erturgut, 2023).

Technological advancements that tackle environmental and social challenges could potentially entail unforeseen regulatory obstacles and technical dangers (Da Silva Nunes et al., 2022). Operations may be disrupted by external ecological challenges such as natural disasters; therefore, resilience is crucial (Middermann et al., 2020). Social responsibility involves inherent dangers in labour practices and community involvement, necessitating adherence to anticipated standards (Da Silva Nunes et al., 2022). Sustainability startups are confronted with additional obstacles in the form of shifting regulatory landscapes and financial limitations, which emphasize the criticality of strategic risk management (Ünal & Taşcıoğlu, 2022; Da Silva Nunes et al., 2022). Comprehending these intrinsic hazards is of the utmost importance to cultivate resilience and adeptly manoeuvre through the intricacies of sustainability entrepreneurship.

Sustainability startups are significantly influenced by reputation risks, stakeholder expectations, and regulatory modifications, all of which stem from their commitment to environmental and social accountability. These elements are fundamental to the commercial environment, as regulatory changes that arise to tackle environmental and social issues impact product adherence and entry into new markets. Stakeholders, encompassing communities, investors, consumers, and employees, hold organizations to the highest standards of ethics and sustainability; thus, unambiguous communication and unwavering dedication are imperative. Reputational damage is the consequence of any departure from these standards, emphasizing the criticality of crisis management and proactive reactions. Nevertheless, sustainability presents competitive benefits that appeal to environmentally conscious investors and consumers. To effectively manage their reputations and navigate the intricacies of sustainability startups, it is critical that their strategic planning incorporates stakeholder engagement, reputation management, regulatory compliance, and sustainability reporting. By doing so, these organizations can position themselves as constructive agents of change that promote environmental and social progress.

## CHALLENGES OF SUSTAINABILITY INTEGRATION

Examining the challenges of sustainability integration reveals the complex obstacles sustainability startups face in embedding sustainable practices into their core business models. Such integration requires a deep understanding of the intricacies and potential hurdles involved. Initiating a cultural transformation within the organization is a significant challenge, as it demands buy-in from all levels and may encounter resistance or scepticism (Varnum & Grossmann, 2021). Ensuring alignment with core values and mission is crucial, especially amid competing priorities (Bharatan et al., 2023), while resource allocation balances sustainability commitments and growth pursuits (Bower, 2016).

Managing the complexity of supply chains, innovation, and adaptation are ongoing endeavours (Lazar et al., 2021; Nenni et al., 2024), alongside accurately measuring and reporting impact (Tavanti, 2023). Staying compliant with evolving regulations is essential (Sendawula et al., 2021), as is effectively educating consumers about sustainable products and services (Al-Nuaimi & Al-Ghamdi, 2022). Balancing competitiveness with sustainability principles is a challenge (Khurshid et al., 2021), as is achieving a balanced triple bottom line (Tseng et al., 2020) and engaging diverse stakeholders (Wells et al., 2021). Complexity in reporting and scaling sustainability initiatives further underscores the multifaceted nature of these challenges (Luque-Vílchez et al., 2023; Lam et al., 2020). Addressing these obstacles is imperative for sustainability startups to fulfil their mission and drive enduring positive impact, fostering a culture of sustainability, promoting innovation, and shaping a more sustainable future.

Balancing economic, environmental, and social objectives is at the core of sustainability-focused startups. The intricate challenges of managing these dimensions offer strategies for navigating the terrain of sustainable entrepreneurship. Integrated goal setting ensures that objectives encompass economic, environmental, and social factors, fostering interconnectedness and synergy (Sarango-Lalangui et al., 2018). A "triple bottom line" accounting approach evaluates financial profits alongside environmental and social impacts, reflected in sustainability metrics and key performance indicators. Stakeholder engagement incorporates diverse perspectives into decision-making, prioritizing the social dimension. Establishing ethical supply chains reflects environmental and social values upheld through transparency. Promoting an innovative culture drives solutions addressing economic, environmental, and social challenges. Regulatory compliance ensures alignment with evolving legal requirements, while resource efficiency optimizes productivity and minimizes waste. Transparent reporting fosters stakeholder confidence, supporting long-term sustainability perspectives and precise impact measurement (Kujala et al., 2022). Balancing trade-offs requires informed decisions prioritizing mission and stakeholder needs. Ultimately, sustainable entrepreneurship exemplifies the harmonious integration of profitability, ecological stewardship, and social responsibility, setting a compelling example for the business world.

## BARRIERS TO GROWTH AND SCALE

Sustainability startups encounter formidable barriers when expanding and scaling their operations, particularly regarding funding limitations and the unique investment landscape they navigate. Securing investment proves challenging due to perceptions of sustainability ventures as risky or requiring longer-term returns. Additionally, the investment landscape for these startups differs from conventional enterprises, with investors prioritizing environmental and social impact alongside financial returns (Rosário et al., 2022). Overcoming market adoption challenges, such as consumer education and competition, is pivotal for scaling sustainability initiatives, while regulatory hurdles and certifications can impede growth. Strategic partnerships and resource management are crucial for overcoming these obstacles, enabling startups to expand their influence (Thananusak, 2019). By analyzing and addressing these barriers, this section aims to empower sustainability startups to drive widespread adoption of sustainable practices and technologies across the global business landscape.

Sustainability startups face multifaceted challenges in market adoption, competition, and scaling sustainable technologies, all pivotal for their growth and influence. Educating consumers about the value and benefits of sustainable products and services is a significant hurdle, requiring efforts to raise awareness and dispel misconceptions. Balancing pricing and affordability is crucial, as sustainable offerings often command a premium, necessitating a delicate equilibrium between accessibility and profitability (Vezzoli et al., 2021). Moreover, market resistance from entrenched industries or competitors poses a barrier to adoption, especially when established actors need to prioritize sustainability. In the competitive sustainability sector, the marketplace is increasingly crowded, making it challenging for startups to differentiate themselves and capture market share. Effective differentiation strategies, such as developing unique value propositions and compelling branding, are essential for success. Scaling sustainable technologies presents challenges, including resource intensiveness, technical complexities, and environmental impact considerations (Rosário et al., 2022). Securing the necessary resources for expansion while maintaining sustainability objectives is crucial, as is overcoming technical hurdles to ensure efficiency and reliability at scale. Additionally, as sustainability solutions proliferate, it is essential for startups to carefully manage their environmental impact and seek mitigation strategies (Fawzy et al., 2020). By addressing these challenges head-on, sustainability startups can navigate the complexities of market adoption, competition, and scaling to drive their growth and influence in the industry.

In navigating the challenges of regulatory compliance and certification, sustainability startups must confront the complexity of evolving regulations and the expenses associated with obtaining certifications. Vigilant monitoring and adjustment are necessary to ensure compliance while expanding operations (Browne et al., 2021). Additionally, forming strategic partnerships and collaborations with industry actors, research institutions, and government agencies can prove invaluable for overcoming growth obstacles and fostering innovation. Collaborative efforts can lead to the resolution of complex sustainability challenges and drive technological advancements. Effective resource management, encompassing financial, human, and technological aspects, is essential for scaling sustainability startups while maintaining their sustainability goals (Mariani et al., 2022). Moreover, prioritizing measuring and expanding social and environmental impact is imperative for sustainability-focused startups, necessitating the development of methodologies and best practices in this area (Alomoto et al., 2021). By addressing these hurdles head-on, this chapter aims to equip sustainability startups with the insights and strategies needed to navigate the complexities of market adoption, competition, and scaling sustainable technologies, accelerating the adoption of sustainable practices across the global business landscape.

## NAVIGATING REGULATORY AND POLICY LANDSCAPES

Government regulations and policies shape the operational framework for sustainability startups. The impact of environmental, social, and economic regulations on these businesses stresses the importance of adhering to evolving regulatory environments. The diverse regulatory landscapes worldwide, encompassing regional disparities and international standards, pose challenges and opportunities for sustainability-focused enterprises, especially those with cross-border operations (Alomoto et al., 2021). Given the dynamic nature of regulations, proactive engagement and advocacy efforts are essential to shaping favourable policies and ensuring compliance. The critical role of effective compliance and risk management strategies, including leveraging legal expertise, conducting compliance audits, and thorough risk assessments. Intellectual property protection, contractual agreements, and advocacy and lobbying are essential in influencing regulatory frameworks. Governmental support, such as incentive programs, green certifications, and international engagement to meet global standards and trade agreements, are crucial for sustainability startups to advance their goals (Sreenivasan & Suresh, 2022). By implementing these strategies, sustainability-focused startups can navigate legal challenges adeptly and capitalize on policy incentives to drive sustainability across the business landscape, establishing themselves as influential agents of positive change.

## BUILDING RESILIENCE AND INNOVATION

Sustainability startups can drive innovation as a proactive response to barriers, and a comprehensive array of strategies emerges. Diverse approaches, such as agile product development, open innovation, and market-driven innovation, offer pathways for startups to surmount challenges and thrive in dynamic business environments. Through iterative prototyping and user-centered design, startups can create solutions resonant with consumer needs and preferences (Bhuiyan & Baghel, 2005). Engaging in collaborative ecosystems and crowdsourcing initiatives fosters knowledge exchange and ideation, generating novel concepts to address sustainability challenges (McDonald et al., 2020). Additionally, embracing continuous improvement and resilience-centered innovation enables startups to enhance adaptability and mitigate risks (Levesque, 2012).

Furthermore, market research and consumer education strategies empower startups to align their innovations with emerging sustainability trends and bridge consumer knowledge gaps (Tang et al., 2021). By proactively embracing these innovation strategies, sustainability startups can navigate barriers effectively and drive positive change toward a more sustainable future (Joshi et al., 2023). Innovation becomes not just a response to obstacles but a cornerstone of success and a catalyst for sustainability-driven industries.

## DISCUSSION

The discourse surrounding innovation strategies for sustainability startups highlights the pivotal significance of proactive innovation in effectively tackling the obstacles and prospects intrinsic to entrepreneurship with a focus on sustainability. Through an analysis of diverse innovation methodologies, including market-driven innovation, agile product development, and open innovation, the discourse underscores the potential for startups to surmount challenges and promote their sustainability goals through innovation.

An essential motif from the discourse is the significance of elasticity and adaptability within innovation processes. In the context of ever-changing business landscapes, startups must adopt iterative prototyping, user-centred design, and continuous refinement to create consumer-resonant solutions that effectively tackle sustainability issues. By implementing agile product development methodologies, nascent enterprises can swiftly refine their offerings in response to changing market demands and iterate on concepts.

Furthermore, the discourse underscores the significance of cooperation and knowledge exchange as catalysts for sustainability-oriented innovation. Startups can access external expertise, diverse perspectives, and innovative ideas through collaborative research partnerships, open innovation platforms, and crowdsourcing events. Startups can cooperate with industry associations, research institutions, government agencies, and collaborative ecosystems to jointly develop innovative solutions that effectively tackle intricate sustainability issues. The discourse underscores the significance of customer-centricity and market-driven innovation in promoting the acceptance and utilization of sustainable products and services. Startups have the potential to create innovative solutions that are in line with market demands and preferences through the implementation of market research, consumer preference analysis, and sustainability option education. The involvement of consumers in co-creating products and services can significantly improve innovation outcomes by customizing solutions to meet their unique sustainability needs.

Moreover, the discourse highlights the significance of resilience-focused innovation in fostering the resilience and flexibility of an organization. Startups can enhance their ability to endure challenges and disruptions by prioritizing innovation that improves supply chain resilience, financial stability, and employee well-being. Organizational resilience can be further bolstered, and an innovative culture can be cultivated through investments in digital transformation, employee training, and risk management.

The discourse generally emphasizes innovation's complex and diverse characteristics within sustainability startups. Moreover, it stresses the criticality of proactively adopting innovation to surmount obstacles and difficulties. Startups can achieve favourable outcomes, promote sustainability, and establish themselves as frontrunners in their sectors by implementing resilience-building strategies, collaborative partnerships, agile methodologies, and market insights.

## LIMITATIONS AND SCOPE OF FURTHER RESEARCH

Examining innovation strategies employed by sustainability startups unveils the constraints of existing research and potential directions for further inquiry. A notable constraint is the requirement for additional empirical research to substantiate the efficacy of diverse innovation methodologies within practical, real-life settings. Although previous studies provide theoretical frameworks and case studies, additional empirical verification is required to determine whether these strategies can be replicated and scaled across various industries and geographic locations. Furthermore, it is possible to conduct further investigation into the convergence of sustainability and innovation within particular sectors or industries, including but not limited to transportation, agriculture, or renewable energy. Examining how innovation can be utilized to tackle sustainability challenges specific to each sector would yield significant knowledge for policymakers and practitioners.

Moreover, further investigation is warranted into the impact of government policies and regulatory frameworks on sustainable innovation development. Further investigation is warranted to examine the impact of regulatory frameworks on the uptake and dissemination of sustainable innovations. Additionally, the efficacy of policy incentives in stimulating innovation among nascent enterprises warrants scrutiny. Furthermore, an opportunity arises to analyze the influence of intellectual property rights and licensing agreements on the dynamics of innovation in sustainability startups, explicitly focusing on the distribution of environmentally friendly technologies.

Investigating novel business models tailored for sustainability startups provides opportunities for scholarly inquiry into their scalability and long-term feasibility. Further research may be warranted to examine the environmental, social, and economic ramifications of collaborative platforms, circular economy models, and other novel value chains. Gaining a comprehensive understanding of the determinants that influence the outcome of these business models—be it success or failure—would furnish policymakers, investors, and entrepreneurs with invaluable knowledge to advance sustainable entrepreneurship.

Although the current body of research about innovation strategies employed by sustainability startups provides valuable insights, further investigation is warranted. Additional empirical research, sector-specific studies, and inquiries into the impact of government policies and business models would enhance our comprehension of how innovation can propel startup ventures towards sustainability and resilience.

## CONCLUSION

This chapter examined the unique characteristics of sustainability startups, identified their obstacles, and proposed practical solutions for overcoming them. These startups operate at the intersection of economic development, environmental responsibility, and social impact, addressing urgent global issues such as climate change, depletion of natural resources, and social inequality. Our conversation has spanned essential topics such as financial strategies, talent acquisition, supply chain management, regulatory compliance, and social and environmental impact measurement.

In addition, we have examined the impact of regulatory frameworks, the need for savvy legal landscape navigation, and the significance of leveraging policy incentives and advocating for favourable regulations. Innovation emerges as an effective response to these challenges, emphasizing agile product development, open innovation, customer-centric approaches, and resilience-centered strategies. It provides researchers, practitioners, and policymakers with a forum to discuss the complexities of sustainability startups. The insights presented here inspire organizations to improve their business and environmental stewardship strategies. As sustainability-focused startups continue to shape a more sustainable future, our collective comprehension of their risks, obstacles, and challenges, coupled with innovative approaches, can pave the way for a more sustainable and prosperous global business landscape.

## REFERENCES


Al-Nuaimi, S. R., & Al-Ghamdi, S. G. (2022). Sustainable consumption and education for sustainability in higher education. *Sustainability (Basel), 14*(12), 7255. DOI: 10.3390/su14127255

Alomoto, W., Niñerola, À., & Pié, L. (2021). Social impact assessment: A systematic review of literature. *Social Indicators Research, 161*(1), 225–250. DOI: 10.1007/s11205-021-02809-1

Bharatan, I., Logan, K., Manning, R. M., & Swan, J. (2023). Values alignment in sustaining healthcare innovation processes. In *Organizational behaviour in health care* (pp. 315–338). DOI: 10.1007/978-3-031-24212-0_14

Bhuiyan, N., & Baghel, A. (2005). An overview of continuous improvement: From the past to the present. *Management Decision, 43*(5), 761–771. DOI: 10.1108/00251740510597761

Böttcher, T. P., Empelmann, S., Weking, J., Hein, A., & Krcmar, H. (2023). Digital sustainable business models: Using digital technology to integrate ecological sustainability into the core of business models. *Information Systems Journal.* Advance online publication. DOI: 10.1111/isj.12436

Bower, J. L. (2016). Resource allocation theory. In *Palgrave Macmillan UK eBooks* (pp. 1–3). DOI: 10.1057/978-1-349-94848-2_677-1

Browne, J., Bullock, A., Poletti, C., & Cserző, D. (2021). Recent research into healthcare professions regulation: A rapid evidence assessment. *BMC Health Services Research, 21*(1), 934. Advance online publication. DOI: 10.1186/s12913-021-06946-8 PMID: 34493260

Cerchia, R. E., & Piccolo, K. (2019). The ethical consumer and codes of ethics in the fashion industry. *Laws, 8*(4), 23. DOI: 10.3390/laws8040023

Ciccullo, F., Pero, M., & Patrucco, A. S. (2023). Designing circular supply chains in startup companies: Evidence from Italian fashion and construction startups. *International Journal of Logistics Management, 34*(3), 553–581. DOI: 10.1108/IJLM-04-2022-0158

Coşkun, A. E., & Erturgut, R. (2023). How do uncertainties affect supply-chain resilience? The moderating role of information sharing for sustainable supply-chain management. *Sustainability (Basel), 16*(1), 131. DOI: 10.3390/su16010131

Da Silva Nunes, A. K., Morioka, S. N., & Bolis, I. (2022). Challenges of business models for sustainability in startups. *RAUSP Management Journal, 57*(4), 382–400. DOI: 10.1108/RAUSP-10-2021-0216

Fawzy, S., Osman, A. I., Doran, J., & Rooney, D. (2020). Strategies for mitigation of climate change: A review. *Environmental Chemistry Letters, 18*(6), 2069–2094. DOI: 10.1007/s10311-020-01059-w

Halkias, D., Esposito, M., Harkiolakis, T., Diaz, J., & Ikpogu, N. M. (2023). Digital entrepreneurship and disruptive innovation in the greek maritime industry: The case of harbor lab. In *Entrepreneurship Development in the Balkans: Perspective from Diverse Contexts* (pp. 131-150). Emerald Publishing Limited. DOI: 10.1108/978-1-83753-454-820231008

Han, D., Konietzko, J., Dijk, M., & Bocken, N. (2023). How do circular startups achieve scale? *Sustainable Production and Consumption, 40*, 363–375. Advance online publication. DOI: 10.1016/j.spc.2023.06.007

Han, N., & Um, J. (2024). Risk management strategy for supply chain sustainability and resilience capability. *Risk Management, 26*(2), 6. Advance online publication. DOI: 10.1057/s41283-023-00138-w

Joshi, S., Sharma, M., Ekren, B. Y., Kazancoglu, Y., Luthra, S., & Prasad, M. (2023). Assessing supply chain innovations for building resilient food supply chains: An emerging economy perspective. *Sustainability (Basel), 15*(6), 4924. DOI: 10.3390/su15064924

Khan, U. U., Ali, Y., Petrillo, A., & De Felice, F. (2023). Macro-environmental factors and their impact on startups from the perspective of developing countries. *International Journal of Sustainable Engineering, 16*(1), 166–183. DOI: 10.1080/19397038.2023.2238754

Khurshid, A., Muzaffar, A., & Bhutta, M. K. S. (2021). Institutional pressures and supplier involvement: A perspective on sustainability. *Operations Management Research. Operations Management Research : Advancing Practice Through Research, 14*(1–2), 123–137. DOI: 10.1007/s12063-021-00181-4

Korpysa, J., Singh, U. S., & Singh, S. (2023). Validation of decision criteria and determining factors importance in advocating for sustainability of entrepreneurial startups towards social inclusion and capacity building. *Sustainability (Basel), 15*(13), 9938. DOI: 10.3390/su15139938

Kujala, J., Sachs, S., Leinonen, H., Heikkinen, A., & Laude, D. (2022). Stakeholder engagement: Past, present, and future. *Business & Society*, *61*(5), 1136–1196. DOI: 10.1177/00076503211066595

Lam, D. P. M., Martín-López, B., Wiek, A., Bennett, E. M., Frantzeskaki, N., Horcea-Milcu, A. I., & Lang, D. J. (2020). Scaling the impact of sustainability initiatives: A typology of amplification processes. *Urban Transformations*, *2*(1), 3. Advance online publication. DOI: 10.1186/s42854-020-00007-9

Lamperti, S., Sammut, S., & Courrent, J. M. (2023). From incubator's knowledge transfer to sustainability startups' impact: A case study in a French support program. *Journal of Knowledge Management*, *27*(9), 2393–2413. Advance online publication. DOI: 10.1108/JKM-09-2022-0690

Lazar, S., Klimecka-Tatar, D., & Obrecht, M. (2021). Sustainability orientation and focus on logistics and supply chains. *Sustainability (Basel)*, *13*(6), 3280. DOI: 10.3390/su13063280

Levesque, P. (2012). Building resilience and sustainability into the Chinese supply chain. *The Shipping Point: The Rise of China and the Future of Retail Supply Chain Management*, pp. 135–161. DOI: 10.1002/9781119199663.ch9

Luque-Vílchez, M., Cordazzo, M., Rimmel, G., & Tilt, C. (2023). Key aspects of sustainability reporting quality and the future of GRI. *Sustainability Accounting. Management and Policy Journal*, *14*(4), 637–659. DOI: 10.1108/SAMPJ-03-2023-0127

Mariani, L., Trivellato, B., Martini, M., & Marafioti, E. (2022). Achieving sustainable development goals through collaborative innovation: Evidence from four European initiatives. *Journal of Business Ethics*, *180*(4), 1075–1095. DOI: 10.1007/s10551-022-05193-z PMID: 35855697

McDonald, R. M., & Eisenhardt, K. M. (2020). Parallel play: Startups, nascent markets, and effective business-model design. *Administrative Science Quarterly*, *65*(2), 483–523. DOI: 10.1177/0001839219852349

Middermann, L. H., Kratzer, J., & Perner, S. (2020). The impact of environmental risk exposure on the determinants of sustainable entrepreneurship. *Sustainability (Basel)*, *12*(4), 1534. DOI: 10.3390/su12041534

Mikulewicz, M. (2019). Is it thwarting adaptation's potential? A critique of resilience and climate-resilient development. *Geoforum*, *104*, 267–282. DOI: 10.1016/j.geoforum.2019.05.010

Nenni, M. E., Di Pasquale, V., & Boyer, J. (2024). The Complicated relationship between innovation and sustainability: Opportunities, threats, challenges, and trends. *Sustainability (Basel), 16*(9), 3524. DOI: 10.3390/su16093524

Pizzi, S., Corbo, L., & Caputo, A. (2021). Fintech and SMEs sustainable business models: Reflections and considerations for a circular economy. *Journal of Cleaner Production, 281*, 125217. DOI: 10.1016/j.jclepro.2020.125217

Premadasa, M., Siyambalapitiya, J., Jayawardhana, K., & Fernando, I. (2023). Conceptualizing the role of social entrepreneurial orientation in the triple bottom line in the social enterprise context: Developing country perspective. *Sustainability (Basel), 15*(11), 8759. DOI: 10.3390/su15118759

Prihadyanti, D., Aziz, S. A., & Sari, K. (2023). Diffusion of social innovation: The innovation provider's perspective. *Journal of the Knowledge Economy*, •••, 1–55. https://link.springer.com/article/10.1007/s13132-023-01365-y

Rosário, A. T., Raimundo, R., & Cruz, S. (2022). Sustainable Entrepreneurship: A Literature Review. *Sustainability (Basel), 14*(9), 5556. DOI: 10.3390/su14095556

Sarango-Lalangui, P., Santos, J. L. S., & Hormiga, E. (2018). The development of the sustainable entrepreneurship research field. *Sustainability (Basel), 10*(6), 2005. DOI: 10.3390/su10062005

Sehnem, S., Lara, A. C., Benetti, K., Schneider, K., Marcon, M. L., & da Silva, T. H. H. (2023). Improving startups through excellence initiatives: Addressing circular economy and innovation. *Environment, Development and Sustainability, 26*(6), 1–47. https://link.springer.com/article/10.1007/s10668-023-03247-4. DOI: 10.1007/s10668-023-03247-4 PMID: 37362985

Sendawula, K., Turyakira, P., Ikiror, C. M., & Bagire, V. (2021). Regulatory compliance and environmental sustainability practices of manufacturing entrepreneurial ventures in Uganda. *Asia Pacific Journal of Innovation and Entrepreneurship, 15*(1), 62–74. DOI: 10.1108/APJIE-08-2020-0122

Sharma, V., Manohar, S., & Carril, V. P. I. (2024). Exploring challenges for sustainable development among circular startups in India. *Environment, Development and Sustainability*. Advance online publication. DOI: 10.1007/s10668-024-04555-z

Sreenivasan, A., Ma, S., Rehman, A. U., & Muthuswamy, S. (2023). Assessment of factors influencing agility in startups industry 4.0. *Sustainability (Basel), 15*(9), 7564. https://www.mdpi.com/2071-1050/15/9/7564. DOI: 10.3390/su15097564

Sreenivasan, A., & Suresh, M. (2022). Green startups: Startups accelerating sustainability. *International Journal of Global Business and Competitiveness, 18*(1), 80–89. DOI: 10.1007/s42943-022-00068-6

Sreenivasan, A., & Suresh, M. (2023). Startup sustainability: Does blockchain adoption drive sustainability in startups? A systematic literature review. *Management Research Review*. Advance online publication. DOI: 10.1108/MRR-07-2022-0519

Tajpour, M., Hosseini, E., & Mohiuddin, M. (2023). Effects of innovative climate, knowledge sharing, and communication on the sustainability of digital startups: Does social media matter? *Journal of Open Innovation, 9*(2), 100053. DOI: 10.1016/j.joitmc.2023.100053

Tang, T. Y., Zhang, S. K., & Peng, J. (2021). The value of marketing innovation: Market-driven versus market-driving. *Journal of Business Research, 126*, 88–98. DOI: 10.1016/j.jbusres.2020.12.067

Tavanti, M. (2023). Assessing and measuring sustainability impact. In *Sustainable development goals series* (pp. 453–473). DOI: 10.1007/978-3-031-36907-0_17

Thananusak, T. (2019). Science mapping of the knowledge base on sustainable entrepreneurship, 1996–2019. *Sustainability (Basel), 11*(13), 3565. DOI: 10.3390/su11133565

Tönnissen, S., Beinke, J. H., & Teuteberg, F. (2020). Understanding token-based ecosystems–a taxonomy of blockchain-based business models of startups. *Electronic Markets, 30*(2), 307–323. https://link.springer.com/article/10.1007/s12525-020-00396-6. DOI: 10.1007/s12525-020-00396-6

Trautwein, C. (2021). Sustainability impact assessment of startups–key insights on relevant assessment challenges and approaches based on an inclusive, systematic literature review. *Journal of Cleaner Production, 281*, 125330. DOI: 10.1016/j.jclepro.2020.125330

Tseng, M., Chang, C., Lin, C., Wu, K., Chen, Q., Xia, L., & Xue, B. (2020). Future trends and guidance for the triple bottom line and sustainability: A data-driven bibliometric analysis. *Environmental Science and Pollution Research International, 27*(27), 33543–33567. DOI: 10.1007/s11356-020-09284-0 PMID: 32572746

Ünal, Ü. A., & Taşçıoğlu, M. (2022). Sustainable, therefore reputable: Linking sustainability, reputation, and consumer behaviour. *Marketing Intelligence & Planning, 40*(4), 497–512. DOI: 10.1108/MIP-03-2022-0102

Varnum, M. E. W., & Grossmann, I. (2021). The psychology of cultural change: Introduction to the special issue. *American Psychologist/the American Psychologist, 76*(6), 833–837. DOI: 10.1037/amp0000898

Vezzoli, C., Ceschin, F., & Diehl, J. C. (2021). Product-service systems development for sustainability. A new understanding. In *Lecture notes in mechanical engineering* (pp. 1–21). DOI: 10.1007/978-3-030-66300-1_1

Wadewitz, C. D. (2023). FOMENT: Promoting technology acceleration and adoption in the Australian and international wine tourism industry. In *Technology Advances and Innovation in Wine Tourism: New Managerial Approaches and Cases* (pp. 153-181). Singapore: Springer Nature Singapore. https://link.springer.com/chapter/10.1007/978-981-19-8277-4_10

Wells, E. C., Lehigh, G. R., & Vidmar, A. M. (2021). Stakeholder engagement for sustainable communities. In *Springer eBooks* (pp. 1–13). DOI: 10.1007/978-3-030-38948-2_10-1

Zhu, B., Liang, C., Mirza, N., & Umar, M. (2023). What drives gearing in early-stage firms? Evidence from blue economy startups. *Journal of Business Research, 161*, 113840. DOI: 10.1016/j.jbusres.2023.113840

## KEY TERMS AND DEFINITIONS

**Barriers:** Factors hindering progress or innovation, like limited access to resources, lack of investor interest, or cultural resistance to change.

**Challenges:** Difficulties or obstacles that sustainability-focused ventures face in achieving their goals, such as market competition or regulatory hurdles.

**Circular Startups:** employ principles of circular economy, designing products, services, and business models to minimize waste, promote reuse, and regenerate resources for sustainable growth.

**Development Phase:** The initial venture stage involves product/service creation, market research, and establishing operational processes.

**Growth:** The expansion phase is where the venture scales its operations, market presence, and impact, often facing new challenges and opportunities.

**Organizational Risks:** Potential threats to the stability, reputation, or success of a company, including financial, operational, and strategic vulnerabilities.

**Sustainability-Focused Ventures:** Businesses prioritize environmental and social impact alongside financial returns, aiming for long-term viability and positive societal contributions.

**Sustainable Startup:** A sustainable startup is a business that prioritizes environmental and social responsibility in its operations and products, aiming for long-term viability and positive impact.

# Chapter 5
# Entrepreneurial Competencies and Its Contribution to Entrepreneurial Intention

**Mangair Karasi Manickam**
https://orcid.org/0000-0002-8189-2498
*University of Technology Malaysia, Malaysia*

**Mohd Zaidi Abd Rozan**
https://orcid.org/0000-0003-1409-4522
*University of Technology Malaysia, Malaysia*

## ABSTRACT

*Entrepreneurial competencies have a proven track record of enhancing both personal and business success. However, there is a dearth of research on the role of entrepreneurial competencies when the focus is on software developers' entrepreneurial intention. Therefore, this chapter aimed to present the influence of entrepreneurial competencies on the entrepreneurial intention of software developers. Specifically, this study draws on the Theory of Planned Behavior to develop an integrated model of entrepreneurial intention incorporating the role of entrepreneurial competencies along with factors influencing entrepreneurial intention. According to the findings of structural equation modeling, the entrepreneurial competencies strongly influence the development of entrepreneurial intention. Mediation analysis validated that the software developer's perceived behavior control is the strongest mediator in the correlation between entrepreneurial competencies and entrepreneurial intention.*

DOI: 10.4018/978-1-6684-9872-9.ch005

## INTRODUCTION

Software developers are frequently those who come up with innovative ideas and launch unique software products and services, the necessity for entrepreneurial activity for entrepreneurial performance has always been crucial for the success of software development firms. Entrepreneurship education enables students to enhance their entrepreneurial knowledge, skills, attitudes, and personal qualities (Sun et al., 2023). The process of learning supports the building of motivation and commercial networks, which could encourage student involvement in entrepreneurship. Incorporating field studies, internships, and extracurricular activities could give students entrepreneurial experience and ideas, which could impact their entrepreneurial intention positively. Uncertainty exists over the benefits of learning entrepreneurial competencies and putting them into practice at work. Other variables need to be controlled to assess the effectiveness of acquired entrepreneurial competencies namely psychological factors. Entrepreneurship researchers from all over the world have been exploring how to increase a person's entrepreneurial intention. Entrepreneurial intention refers to an individual's conscious and deliberate decision to pursue entrepreneurial activities (Sun et al., 2023). This study explores the concept of entrepreneurial intention, its importance, and the factors influencing its formation, supported by relevant research studies and references.

Like any other industry, entrepreneurial intention is equally emphasized in software development as it is rapidly evolving field that thrives on innovation, problem-solving, and entrepreneurial thinking (Sudirman et al., 2020; Tolfo et al., 2018). In this context, entrepreneurial intention plays a vital role in shaping the success and impact of software development ventures. Entrepreneurial intention is strongly influenced by various factors, one of which is entrepreneurial competencies (Botha & Taljaard, 2021). These competencies encompass the knowledge, skills, attitudes, and abilities that individuals possess and develop to successfully undertake entrepreneurial activities. These entrepreneurial competencies are compatible with adaptability and agile development concepts in software development (Tolfo et al., 2018). Past study has verified that having entrepreneurial competencies are essential for software developers to envision innovative solutions and recognize the potential for creating value through entrepreneurial venture (A. N. Aisha et al., 2016). As a preliminary definition of entrepreneurial competencies, it refers to the ability to recognize and pursue opportunities, which appears to be unique and critical activity in business that is related to product and process innovation, diversification, and business development (Lans et al., 2014). Barely any attention has been paid to the direct effect of entrepreneurial competencies on entrepreneurial intention as well as the influence of attitude, subjective norm, and perceived behavior control.

Software developers are primarily recognized for their programming skills. Coding and programming skills are among the most essential for software development because these skills enable developers to create an application that meetss user needs (Graziotin et al., 2017). The most widely used languages are Java, Python, HTML, and JavaScript. Since software application is getting more and more ingrained in our daily lives, this is an ideal moment to build business opportunities in the software development. On the other hand, studies specifically investigating entrepreneurial competencies in the context of computer science and software development are relatively scarce (Manickam et al., 2023). Thus, it will be extremely beneficial to concentrate studies on entrepreneurial intenti,on especially on software developers. In the context of entrepreneurial intention, software developers need to possess a broader set of competencies beyond technical expertise (Capretz & Ahmed, 2010).

This is corroborated by the founder of the Agile method, Cockburn (2001), where agile development placed great emphasis of practising entrepreneurial competencies in the software development. To be precise, recent studies have verified positive outcome for adopting entrepreneurial competencies in Agile software development (Tolfo et al., 2018) and in Lean Software Development (Edison et al., 2018) for a successful software development. In the contemporary business landscape, the role of software developers has expanded beyond mere programming tasks. They now actively engage in project management and support, collaborating with software firms to integrate software solutions with core business processes. This evolution highlights the increasing importance of entrepreneurial intention among software developers.

Research findings consistently highlighting the significance of entrepreneurial competencies in software development. According to a survey, 90-95 percentage of performance issues in software projects are concerned with competencies, with only 5-10 percentage was concerned with technical processes (Alam et al., 2010). This echoes further by Project Management Institute that new the Project Management Professional (PMP) requires the project teams to be people orientated (42%) by emphasizing on developers' competencies and focusing on business domain knowledge (Project Management Institute, 2021). The emphasis on business domain knowledge further reinforces the importance of entrepreneurial competencies within the software development domain.

The entrepreneurial intention promise to provide a more effective approach for understanding entrepreneurial behavior, specifically on the creation of new products and ventures because it concentrates on the influence of characteristics, attitudes, and the like on behavior (Menke, 2018). Nevertheless, there must be some factors that are motivating or discouraging them from demonstrating entrepreneurial behavior. Hence, studying the relationship between entrepreneurial competencies and entrepreneurial intention and its mediation can be attributed to a better understanding of the formation of an entrepreneurial intention provided by the new model in the software development context.

Several factors contribute to the formation and development of entrepreneurial intention. The Theory of Planned Behavior (TPB) is widely applied in studies to explain individual intention to engage in behavior. The intention of a person to perform a specific behavior is the strongest predictor of that behavior (Norman & Hoyle, 2004). Intention is the proximal determinant of behavior: people do what they intend to do and what they don't intend to do (Ajzen, 1991). Although the TPB has been applied in wide range of behaviors and intention in mandatory context however none have examined the relationship between entrepreneurial competencies and software developer's entrepreneurial intention. Additionally, previous studies have investigated entrepreneurial competencies on outcome-based approach to measure individual and firm performance and lack of research on attribute-based approach which investigates the motivational factors. Moreover, it remains unclear regarding the impact of entrepreneurial competencies on entrepreneurial intention and how this relationship is mediated by factors such as attitude, subjective norm, and perceived behavioral control. Therefore, it is crucial to conduct further research to explore these factors in the context of entrepreneurial intention among software developers. Understanding these factors can provide valuable insights into the entrepreneurial aspirations and motivations of software developers within the software development field.

## UNDERSTANDING THE TPB MODEL AND ITS RELEVANCE TO ENTREPRENEURIAL INTENTIONS

The Theory of Planned Behavior (TPB) is a widely used model in predicting entrepreneurial intentions. According to TPB, entrepreneurial intention is determined by three antecedents: attitude, social norms, and perceived behavioral control (Sabah, 2016). The TPB model has been used in various studies to predict entrepreneurial intentions, including a study by Al-Mamary and Alraja (2022), which found that the components of the TPB model collectively indicate an individual's intention and predict behavior. Overall, the TPB model provides a framework for understanding the factors that influence an individual's entrepreneurial intentions. In general, having an entrepreneurial intention means that an individual wants to create a new business and pursue a different career path than what is already accessible (Moreno Freites et al., 2022). However, studies have verified that an entrepreneurial intention of an individual working in an organisation is the strongest predictor of their entrepreneurial activities at workplace (Botha & Taljaard, 2021; Gieure et al., 2020).

Previous research has demonstrated the importance of the TPB model in predicting entrepreneurial intentions. For instance, a study by Sabah in 2016 found that the TPB model explained entrepreneurial intention through the three antecedents (Sabah, 2016). Another study has introduced entrepreneurial situational factors and entrepreneurial implementation intention into the TPB model, further enhancing its predictive power (Lihua, 2022). Additionally, a study by Amofah in 2022 used the TPB model to understand students' entrepreneurial intentions (Amofah & Saladrigues, 2022). These studies highlight the relevance of the TPB model in predicting entrepreneurial intention.

Entrepreneurial competencies, which include knowledge, skills, abilities, values, attitudes, personality, and expertise, have also been found to be important in predicting entrepreneurial intentions (Botha & Taljaard, 2021). Furthermore, there is evidence that a higher level of intention is associated with a stronger likelihood of engaging in entrepreneurial activities by performing entrepreneurial competencies effectively in the software development (Manickam et al., 2022). Intention is a key factor in the theory of planned behavior (TPB), which posits that individuals are more likely to engage in a behavior if they have a strong intention to do so.

The TPB model can be used in conjunction with entrepreneurial competencies to better understand the factors that influence an individual's entrepreneurial intentions. For example, a study by Krueger in 2000 proposed a modified TPB model oriented towards sustainability, which included entrepreneurial competencies as an important factor (Krueger JR et al., 2000). Overall, the TPB model provides a useful framework for understanding the complex interplay of factors that influence a software developer's entrepreneurial intentions, including both internal and external factors.

## ENTREPRENEURIAL COMPETENCIES FOR ENTREPRENEURIAL SUCCESS

There are several schools of thought for entrepreneurial competencies, however each provides useful insights. Early definitions of entrepreneurial competencies referred to a collection of abilities and knowledge needed to recognise, anticipate, and seize opportunities and this was considered to be the main ability for business owners (Chandler & Hanks, 1993). Bird, (1995) defined the entrepreneurial competencies as the fundamental attributes including general and particular knowledge, motivation, traits, identity, social relationship, and abilities that highly support to the emergence, sustainability, and/or growth of ventures. The entrepreneurial competencies were defined by Rasmussen et., al (2011) as the skills, knowledge, and abilities required to launch a business start-up. G. N. Chandler and Jansen, (1992) According to G. N. Chandler and Jansen (1992), in order to effectively apply the entrepreneurial mindset, a person must be able to recognise potential opportunities and have the motivation to see them through to accomplishment.

Recently, European Commission developed Entrepreneurship Competence framework which made up of three main interrelated competencies namely the capability to mobilise resources, generate ideas and opportunities, and execute on ideas (European Commission, 2018). This framework regarded entrepreneurial competencies as a comprehensive description of the knowledge, competencies, and attitudes that individuals have to be entrepreneurial and apply them across all spheres of life. However, there is still a gap in the literature relating to how competencies are categorized and which ones are related to different competence categories (Maheshwari & Kha, 2022). Nonetheless, research suggests that the right set of entrepreneurial competencies can enhance entrepreneurial intention and entrepreneurial action (Botha & Taljaard, 2021).

The study by Tittel and Terzidis (2020), discovered entrepreneurial competencies through a comprehensive analysis of the literature, which began with Mitchelmore and Rowley (2010), who typically defined entrepreneurial competencies as a particular set of competencies that are important for the practise of successful entrepreneurship. Some studies on entrepreneurial competences have made an effort to categorize them into separate subconstructs (Pulka et al., 2021). As an example, Man et al., (2002) have distinguished individual competencies namely opportunity, organising, strategy, commitment, relationship, and conceptual.

The findings by González-López et al., (2021) revealed that entrepreneurial competencies play a crucial role in the progression from potential to nascent entrepreneurship. Cognitive competencies, such as problem-solving and opportunity recognition, are positively associated with the intention to pursue entrepreneurial activities. Personal competencies, including self-confidence and risk-taking propensity, also significantly influence entrepreneurial engagement. Moreover, the study highlights the importance of social competencies in entrepreneurial development. Networking abilities, social capital, and social support positively affect the likelihood of transitioning from potential entrepreneurship to nascent entrepreneurship. The authors conclude that entrepreneurial competencies contribute significantly to the decision to pursue entrepreneurial activities and serve as essential predictors of early-stage entrepreneurial engagement. The findings suggest that individuals with higher levels of cognitive, personal, and social competencies are more likely to transform their entrepreneurial potential into action.

## TYPES OF ENTREPRENEURIAL COMPETENCIES

### Strategic Thinking

Strategic thinking refers to creating, evaluating and executing strategies of an organisation (T. W. Man, 2001). It is related to the ability to think strategically by setting an achievable goal, evaluating the results against the goal and implementing the strategic planning and action (Bartlett & Ghoshal, 1997). Activity of monitoring progress toward specific purpose or goals, prioritising activity in line with business organisation objectives, identifying long-run opportunities or issues, placing present behavior is consistent with strategic objectives, evaluating the results against these objectives, restructuring business processes to achieve relatively long-term strategic objectives, defining new strategic activities by evaluating the financial costs and benefits (Ahmad et al., 2006). This describes the pattern of social-cognitive approach towards the motivation on how an individual interpret the work situation and how the information is processed based on the situation (Dweck, 1986). This is more prevalent when rapid changes in software development is increasing the pressure on software developers to continually update to their role with new skills and adapt their behavior with new demands in software industries (Ahmed et al., 2013).

### Conceptual Thinking

Conceptual refers to the abilities to conceive the idea by applying cognitive and analytical thinking and eventually replicated in the behavior for example, in making decision, solving the problem, understanding complex information, and coping with uncertainty by taking risk (T. W. Man, 2001). Conceptual is defined as the mental ability of analytical and cognitive thinking, learning, problem solving and making thoughtful decision, sustaining temporal tension, being innovative and capable of handling the uncertainty (Bird, 1995). Based on Chandler and Jansen (1992) study, conceptual competence is referred as the mental capacity to organise all of the organisation's interests and actions and it is required for an effective execution of the decision-making. A software developer requires strong conceptual thinking to analyse complex situation systematically and perform action rationally (Matturro et al., 2019; Sudirman et al., 2020).

### Relationship

The definition of relationship is the coordination among several internal and external people, physical, monetary, and technology resources, including team development, leadership, training, and management (T. W. Man, 2001). Bird (1995) regards relationship as entrepreneurial connection, when it involves not only about building of new relationship, but also reforming the current relationship as the organisation grows or when the business agreement with partners is terminated. Based on Wang et al. (2011), relationshiop is defined as the ability of developing a context of collaboration and trust, by expanding connection and using contacts, ability to persuade, interpersonal skill and communication. To have an effective communication, the individual needs to be mindful that communication is applied for varying objectives, like some just want to update the information, some want to persuade another person and some want to seek or understand others' views or to create relationship (Volery et al., 2015).

Apparently, software development considered as social process that involves collaboration of various participants (Ghobadi & Mathiassen, 2016), including software developers, software entrepreneurs, users or business representatives, working peers, vendors and external consultants (Iden & Bygstad, 2017). Software developers needs to be expert at building business relationships as well, because lack of trust between business and team leaders adversely affects the software development and the use of technological innovations (Jamwal & Singh, 2011). Developing a software requires software developers working in a team need to communicate with each other particularly when they face more opportunity to cooperate with each other (Jia et al., 2017).

## Opportunity

It refers to the ability to identify and seize economic chances through a variety of techniques (Man, 2001; Wang et al., 2011), which is put into practise by assessing individual behaviors namely by understanding the needs and identifying products that customer desire, observing unfulfilled customer needs, eyeing for products that truly add value for customers and grabbing excellent opportunities (T. W. Man, 2001). By expanding the opportunity horizon, it legitimized the entrepreneurial initiatives to move into unexplored business segments and to build a more ambitious organization (Bartlett & Ghoshal, 1997). Chandler and Jansen (1992) opined that opportunity competency as the most crucial in entrepreneurial role to recognise and visualise taking advantage of opportunities. Since software industries is more dynamic, it is important to recognise the opportunity, seek for the market, and develop network (Aisha et al., 2016).

## Organizing

According to Chandler and Jansen (1992), coordinating and managing the organization's goals and tasks is referred to as organising competencies. Organising is related to the organising people within the workplace and external parties, financial resources, commodity resources, and leading employees, building teamwork, conducting training, and supervising (Bartlett & Ghoshal, 1997; Chandler & Jansen, 1992; Man, 2001; Wang et al., 2011) Software development contingent by team work to complete a project successfully (Moe et al., 2010). Thus, team members must be delegated to their activities based on their skills and knowledge (Xu & Shen, 2015).

## Commitment

It refers to the actions performed to upgrade and sustain the performance (Bartlett & Ghoshal, 1997). An individual needs to possess strong motivation, armed with necessary drivers and have initiatives to sustain the efforts (Man, 2001). Another component of this commitment is the preparedness, which requests the individual to take actions before being requested or assign by mandate (Chandler & Jansen, 1992).

Software developers typically sitting together at the same area where it requires more rapid communication and involves high commitment and energy (Crowne, 2002; Paternoster et al., 2014). Therefore, commitment of software developers is critical to the project success (Lenberg et al., 2015). To sum up, commitment competence is required to sustain the effort and achieve the aim.

## Personal Maturity

Personal maturity described as the ability to sustain high levels of energy, inspire oneself to perform at one's best capacity, react appropriately to constructive feedbacks, stay focused with positive attitude, set priorities to meet deadlines, identify one's own strong and weak points and complement those strong and weak points with opportunities and threats as well as acknowledge and improve one's own deficiencies (Man, 2001). Personal maturity competence seen as a significant competency to entrepreneurial competencies because the individual who possesses high level of this competence perceived to have a great confidence in their capability to reach the goals (Noor Hazlina et al., 2010).

These definitions highlight the multidimensional nature of entrepreneurial competencies, incorporating cognitive abilities, personal traits, and functional skills. They emphasize the importance of these competencies in identifying opportunities, managing risks, and achieving entrepreneurial success.

## THE RELATIONSHIP BETWEEN ENTREPRENEURIAL COMPETENCIES AND TPB MODEL

Entrepreneurial competencies can have a significant impact on the TPB model, which is widely used to explain entrepreneurial intentions. According to Botha and Taljaard (2021), TPB implies that intentions are determined by attitudes, and attitudes are affected by "exogenous effects" such as competencies and traits . As such, the possession of entrepreneurial competencies can positively influence attitudes and beliefs towards entrepreneurship, ultimately leading to higher levels of entrepreneurial intention. Therefore, it is crucial to understand how entrepreneurial competencies can affect the TPB model to develop effective strategies for promoting entrepreneurial intentions.

On the other hand, the TPB model can also affect the development of entrepreneurial competencies. According to Ajzen's TPB, entrepreneurial intention is explained by three antecedents: attitude towards entrepreneurial behavior, perceived social norms, and perceived behavioral control (Ajzen, 2002). By understanding the factors that influence entrepreneurial intention, it is possible to develop targeted interventions that can promote the development of entrepreneurial competencies. Thus, the TPB model can play a crucial role in the development of entrepreneurial competencies.

Understanding the relationship between entrepreneurial competencies and the TPB model is essential for developing effective strategies for promoting entrepreneurial intentions. As highlighted by Botha and Taljaard (2021), the TPB model seeks to explain which motivational and ability factors influence an individual's behaviors. The possession of entrepreneurial competencies can positively impact attitudes and beliefs toward entrepreneurship, leading to higher levels of entrepreneurial intention. Therefore, it is crucial to consider both the TPB model and entrepreneurial competencies when developing interventions aimed at promoting entrepreneurial intentions.

### Attitude

Ajzen (1991), defined attitude as the degree to which a person perceives the behavior based on a favourable or unfavorable assessment of the behavior. Charles (2015), described the attitude as a mental and neural state of exerting readiness, organized through experience, exerting a directive or dynamic influence upon the individuals regards to all objectives and situations with which it is related. Previous research has proved that attitude towards behavior as a significant determinant of an individual's intention to utilize critical thinking methods and actual use of such approaches (Smith, 2015). Besides it, many scholars have validated that positive impact of attitude towards entrepreneurial intention (Lihua, 2022; Moriano et al., 2012; Tsordia & Papadimitriou, 2015). Therefore, being a software developer who actively involved in software development activities, some recommended attitudes play a crucial role in shaping their entrepreneurial intention.

## Subjective Norm

Subjective norm reflects how people react under social pressure from attachment figures to engage in or refrain from a particular behavior (Ajzen, 1991). Zapkau et al., (2015) defined role models as situational factors that could enhance the predictive ability of the traditional TPB model. The study highlights that interactions with parents who serve as role models affecting their children behavior and the acquisition of new skills. Entrepreneurial intention is also be shaped by social impact within social networks, communities, and professional groups through idea sharing, experience sharing, and collective encouragement (Wijayati et al., 2021). In the context of software development, when a software developer having knowledge or skills on entrepreneurial, he or she might get support, encouragement and advice from social network. This encouraging subjective norm might enhance their entrepreneurial intention.

## Perceived Behavior Control (PBC)

Ajzen (1991) states that resources, opportunities, enhancers, barriers, and the amount of control a person perceives he or she has overperformed the behavior and the presence or absence of resources and opportunities to do so. Earlier research has demonstrated that perceived controllability over the possessed skills influences the entrepreneurial intention (Majeed et al., 2021; Smith, 2015). PBC refers to an individual's perception of their ability to perform a behavior and overcome potential barriers or constraints (Sabah, 2016). It is argued that entrepreneurial intention increases with greater perceived behavioral control. For example, when a software developer is put in an unusual environment, he or she may fail to understand the abilities and skills needed to carry out the behavior. The most crucial issue is how software developers view their ability to manage their entrepreneurial competencies and how it affects their intentions and subsequent actions.

# METHOD

Data were collected from 268 software developers from various software firms in Malaysia. This study targeted software developers as they were involved in the software development process embodying all the stages throughout the lifetime of a project. Therefore, the non-probability approach using purposive judgemental sampling technique was adopted. The questionnaires were developed using existing measuring items from the literature to fit the objective and scope of the study. The items for TPB constructs were adapted from past studies (Ajzen, 2013; Solesvik et al., 2012; Tsordia & Papadimitriou, 2015), and the questionnaire items for entrepreneurial competencies were adapted from Man (2001) model and Noor Hazlina Ahmad (2007) model.

Questionnaires were administered online and physically to the target population. The completed questionnaires were verified for missing data and outliers. The respondents were asked to answer each question by choosing one of five alternatives ranging from "strongly agree" to "strongly disagree" using the Likert scale. The sample consist of 60 percent of male followed by 40 percent of female. The majority of the respondents were between 21 and 30 years of age. The software developers had different education level. About 46 percent of the respondents were degree holder, followed by diploma with 40 percent. We also have respondents with masters, comprising 14 percent. To evaluate the relationships, a partial least square based on structural equation modelling was utilized using Smart PLS version 3 software.

## FINDINGS

Data analysis revealed that entrepreneurial competencies have significant and positive impact on entrepreneurial intention of software developers. The findings align with recent studies that highlight the pivotal role of entrepreneurial competencies in entrepreneurship, emphasizing their significant impact on individuals' decision-making and intention (Wijayati et al., 2021; Yaghoubi Farani et al., 2017). Table 1 shows that the entrepreneurial competencies have a substantial and favourable influence on entrepreneurial intention, according to the structural model analysis ($\beta = 0.1883$, t-value > 1.65, and p-value 0.1). This highlights the crucial importance of entrepreneurial competencies in shaping software developers' intentions to engage in entrepreneurial activities.

*Table 1. Path analysis*

| Relationship | Path Coefficient | t-value | p-value | Result |
|---|---|---|---|---|
| Entrepreneurial competencies -Entrepreneurial intention | 0.1883 | 1.7383* | 0.0822* | Significant |
| Entrepreneurial competencies – Attitude – Entrepreneurial intention | 0.1583 | 1.7353* | 0.0828* | Significant |
| Entrepreneurial competencies – Subjective norm – Entrepreneurial intention | -0.1256 | 2.2585 | 0.0240 | Not Significant |
| Entrepreneurial competencies – Perceived behavior control – Entrepreneurial intention | 0.3211 | 8.3968*** | 0.0000*** | Significant |

The results showed that both attitude and perceived behavior control significantly mediated the relationship between entrepreneurial competencies and entrepreneurial intention. The finding agrees with other studies that attitude and perceived behavior control were statistically impact the intention (Majeed et al., 2021; Sabah, 2016). Likewise, perceived behavior control had a stronger influence on entrepreneurial intention than personal attitude. The results of the structural model shows that the mediating effect of PBC on the connection between entrepreneurial competences and entrepreneurial intention is statistically significant and positive ($\beta = 0.3211$, t-value > 2.58, and p-value < 0.01).

The positive impact shows that software developers' intentions to engage in entrepreneurial activities improve when they feel more in control of their behavior. According to the results, attitude mediates the relationship the correlation between entrepreneurial competencies and entrepreneurial intention ($\beta = 0.1583$, p-value <0.1 and t-value > 1.65). Comparatively, subjective norm was not statistically mediating the relationship between entrepreneurial competencies and entrepreneurial intention. The result is consistent with another study that found a significant negative correlation with intention (Zulfiqar et al., 2019). In the context of software development, social pressure is not a crucial factor that impacts the software developers' entrepreneurial intention. This is largely due to the fact that a career in software development is no longer restricted to full-time employment because one may work independently.

## DISCUSSION AND CONCLUSION

These results contribute to the existing body of knowledge by emphasizing the significance of entrepreneurial competencies and investigating the factors influencing software developers' entrepreneurial intention. It implies that initiatives aimed at developing and enhancing entrepreneurial competencies within the software development can play a pivotal role in promoting entrepreneurial behaviors and aspirations among software developers. When software developers have the sufficient entrepreneurial competencies, they are more committed to entrepreneurial intentions Ultimately, developing entrepreneurial competencies enhances an individual's entrepreneurial intention and equips them with the necessary tools and capabilities to succeed as entrepreneurs.

When a software developer has acquired entrepreneurial competencies, it can reinforce their positive attitude toward entrepreneurship and increase their intention to pursue entrepreneurial activities. The software developers are more likely to feel inspired, passionate, and driven to undertake entrepreneurial endeavours when they have an optimistic view of entrepreneurship. This drive may result in a person having a higher desire to act and launch their own business. On the other hand, individuals with a professional background in technical skills, such as software developers, may experience significant doubts about their entrepreneurial competencies, innovation, and creativity, even they are hardworking and like to work under the umbrella of software development.

A software developer may have a contradictory social impact if they are exposed to an unfavourable social support in which important individuals discourage their entrepreneurial endeavours. In such circumstances, software developers could go through an internal evaluation process where they compare and contrast their own views and aspirations with those of important others. Their personal views towards entrepreneurship may be shaped and improved by this inward reflection. Developers' entrepreneurial intentions might not be severely impacted by the unfavourable subjective norm if they continue to have a strong positive attitude and perceived behavioral control towards it. In fact, it might even become stronger. However, the extent of this influence can vary depending on individual factors and the strength of an individual's entrepreneurial mindset. There is a need for further study to be conducted in order to confirm these findings because of the unexpected aspect of these results and variation from the simple connections. Entrepreneurial intention is a crucial precursor to the entrepreneurial journey. Understanding the factors influencing entrepreneurial intention can help policymakers, educators, and support organizations design effective strategies to foster and nurture entrepreneurship.

## REFERENCES


Ahmad, N., Kummerow, L., & Wilson, C. (2006). A cross-cultural study of entrepreneurial competencies among business owners in SMEs: Evidence from Australia and Malaysia. *51st ICSB World Conference,* Melbourne.

Ahmed, F., Capretz, L. F., Bouktif, S., & Campbell, P. (2013). Soft skills and software development: A reflection from software industry. *International Journal of Information Processing and Management*, *4*(3), 171–191. DOI: 10.4156/ijipm.vol4.issue3.17

Aisha, A. N., Siswanto, J., & Sudirman, I. (2016). Competencies model for entrepreneur development in software industries. *IEEE International Conference on Industrial Engineering and Engineering Management, 2016-Decem*, 184–188. DOI: 10.1109/IEEM.2016.7797861

Ajzen, I. (1991). *The theory of planned behavior.* DOI: 10.1016/0749-5978(91)90020-T

Ajzen, I. (2002). *Constructing a TpB questionnaire: Conceptual and methodological Considerations.* http://chuang.epage.au.edu.tw/ezfiles/168/1168/attach/20/pta_41176_7688352_57138.pdf

Al-Mamary, Y. H. S., & Alraja, M. M. (2022). Understanding entrepreneurship intention and behavior in the light of TPB model from the digital entrepreneurship perspective. *International Journal of Information Management Data Insights*, *2*(2), 100106. DOI: 10.1016/j.jjimei.2022.100106

Alam, M., Gale, A., Brown, M., & Khan, A. I. (2010). The importance of human skills in project management professional development. *International Journal of Managing Projects in Business*, *3*(3), 495–516. DOI: 10.1108/17538371011056101

Amofah, K., & Saladrigues, R. (2022). Impact of attitude towards entrepreneurship education and role models on entrepreneurial intention. *Journal of Innovation and Entrepreneurship*, *11*(1), 1–30. DOI: 10.1186/s13731-022-00197-5 PMID: 35036286

Bartlett, C. A., & Ghoshal, S. (1997). The myth of the generic manager. *California Management Review*, *40*(1), 92–116. DOI: 10.2307/41165924

Bird, B. (1995). Towards a theory of entrepreneurial competency. *Advances in Entrepreneurship, Firm, Emergence, and Growth*, *2*(1), 51–72.

Botha, M., & Taljaard, A. (2021). Exploring the entrepreneurial intention-competency model for Nascent Entrepreneurs: Insights from a developing country context. *Frontiers in Psychology*, *12*, 516120. DOI: 10.3389/fpsyg.2021.516120 PMID: 34393866

Capretz, L. F., & Ahmed, F. (2010). Making sense of software development and personality types. *IT Professional*, *12*(February), 6–13. DOI: 10.1109/MITP.2010.33

Chandler, G. N., & Hanks, S. H. (1993). Measuring the performance of emerging businesses: A validation study. *Journal of Business Venturing*, *8*(5), 391–408. DOI: 10.1016/0883-9026(93)90021-V

Chandler, G. N., & Jansen, E. (1992). The founder's competence and venture performance. *Journal of Business Venturing*, *7*(3), 223–236. DOI: 10.1016/0883-9026(92)90028-P

Cockburn, A., & Highsmith, J. (2001). Agile software development. *The People Factor.*, (November), 131–133.

Crowne, M. (2002). Why software product startups fail and what to do about it. Evolution of software product development in startup companies. *IEEE International Engineering Management Conference, 1*, 338–343. DOI: 10.1109/IEMC.2002.1038454

Dweck, C. S. (1986). Motivational processes affecting learning. *The American Psychologist*, *41*(10), 1040–1048. DOI: 10.1037/0003-066X.41.10.1040

Edison, H., Smørsgård, N. M., Wang, X., & Abrahamsson, P. (2018). Lean internal startups for software product innovation in large companies: Enablers and inhibitors. *Journal of Systems and Software*, *135*, 69–87. DOI: 10.1016/j.jss.2017.09.034

European Commission. (2018). *Entrepreneurship competence EntreComp :* DOI: 10.2767/88978

Ghobadi, S., & Mathiassen, L. (2016). Perceived barriers to effective knowledge sharing in agile software teams. *Information Systems Journal*, *26*(2), 95–125. DOI: 10.1111/isj.12053

Gieure, C., del Mar Benavides-Espinosa, M., & Roig-Dobón, S. (2020). The entrepreneurial process: The link between intentions and behavior. *Journal of Business Research*, *112*, 541–548. DOI: 10.1016/j.jbusres.2019.11.088

González-López, M. J., Pérez-López, M. C., & Rodríguez-Ariza, L. (2021). From potential to early nascent entrepreneurship: The role of entrepreneurial competencies. *The International Entrepreneurship and Management Journal*, *17*(3), 1387–1417. DOI: 10.1007/s11365-020-00658-x

Graziotin, D., Fagerholm, F., Wang, X., & Abrahamsson, P. (2017). On the unhappiness of software developers. *Dl.Acm.Org*, *10*, 324–333. DOI: 10.1145/3084226.3084242

Iden, J., & Bygstad, B. (2017). The social interaction of developers and IT operations staff in software development projects. *International Journal of Project Management*. Advance online publication. DOI: 10.1016/j.ijproman.2017.12.001

Jamwal, D., & Singh, N. (2011). Management Information System Competencies and Strategies. *International Journal of Computer Science and Technology*, *1*(2), 109–112.

Jia, J., Chen, Z., & Du, X. (2017). Understanding soft skills requirements for mobile applications developers. *Proceedings - 2017 IEEE International Conference on Computational Science and Engineering and IEEE/IFIP International Conference on Embedded and Ubiquitous Computing, CSE and EUC 2017, 1*, 108–115. DOI: 10.1109/CSE-EUC.2017.29

Krueger, N. F.Jr, Reilly, M. D., & Carsrud, A. L. (2000). Competing models of entrepreneurial intentions. *Journal of Business Venturing*, *15*(5–6), 411–432. https://linkinghub.elsevier.com/retrieve/pii/s0883902698000330. DOI: 10.1016/S0883-9026(98)00033-0

Lans, T., Van Galen, M. A., Verstegen, J. A. A. M., Biemans, H. J. A., & Mulder, M. (2014). Searching for entrepreneurs among small business ownermanagers in agriculture. *NJAS Wageningen Journal of Life Sciences*, *68*(1), 41–51. DOI: 10.1016/j.njas.2013.12.001

Lenberg, P., Feldt, R., & Wallgren, L. G. (2015). Behavioral software engineering: A definition and systematic literature review. *Journal of Systems and Software*, *107*, 15–37. DOI: 10.1016/j.jss.2015.04.084

Lihua, D. (2022). An extended model of the theory of planned behavior: An empirical study of entrepreneurial intention and entrepreneurial behavior in college students. *Frontiers in Psychology*, *12*, 6706. DOI: 10.3389/fpsyg.2022.627818 PMID: 35145443

Maheshwari, G., & Kha, K. L. (2022). Investigating the relationship between educational support and entrepreneurial intention in Vietnam: The mediating role of entrepreneurial self-efficacy in the theory of planned behavior. *International Journal of Management Education*, *20*(2), 100553. DOI: 10.1016/j.ijme.2021.100553

Majeed, A., Ghumman, A. R., Abbas, Q., & Ahmad, Z. (2021). Role of entrepreneurial passion between entrepreneurial attitude, subjective norms, perceived behavioral control, and entrepreneurial intention: Measuring the entrepreneurial behavior of Pakistani students. [PJCSS]. *Pakistan Journal of Commerce and Social Sciences, 15*(3), 636–662.

Man, T. W. (2001). *Entrepreneurial competencies and the performance of small and medium enterprises in the Hong Kong services sector.* The Hong Kong Polytechnic University.

Man, T. W. Y., Lau, T., & Chan, K. F. (2002). The competitiveness of small and medium enterprises. *Journal of Business Venturing, 17*(2), 123–142. DOI: 10.1016/S0883-9026(00)00058-6

Manickam, M. K., Rozan, A., & Zaidi, M. (2022). Explaining the intention of software developers to perform entrepreneurial competencies. *Business Management/Biznes Upravlenie, 4.*

Manickam, M. K., Zaidi, M., & Rozan, A. (2023). Bibliometric analysis of entrepreneurial competencies using scopus data and VOSviewer. *International Journal of Advanced and Applied Sciences, 10*(1), 198–207. DOI: 10.21833/ijaas.2023.01.025

Matturro, G., Raschetti, F., & Fontán, C. (2019). *A systematic mapping study on soft skills in software engineering.*

Menke, C. (2018). Unravelling entrepreneurial competencies and their relation to entrepreneurial intent. *International Journal of Entrepreneurial Venturing, 10*(6), 663–687. DOI: 10.1504/IJEV.2018.095304

Moe, N. B., Dingsøyr, T., & Dybå, T. (2010). A teamwork model for understanding an agile team: A case study of a Scrum project. *Information and Software Technology, 52*(5), 480–491. DOI: 10.1016/j.infsof.2009.11.004

Moreno Freites, Z., Escorcia-Caballero, J. P., Ziritt Trejo, G., & Silva-Guerra, H. (2022). Human-affective dimensions, entrepreneurial intentions, and entrepreneurial behaviors in entrepreneurship training programs for vulnerable populations. *IBIMA Business Review, 2022*, 1–11. DOI: 10.5171/2022.110930

Moriano, J. A., Gorgievski, M., Laguna, M., Stephan, U., & Zarafshani, K. (2012). A cross-cultural approach to understanding entrepreneurial intention. *Journal of Career Development, 39*(2), 162–185. DOI: 10.1177/0894845310384481

Noor Hazlina, A., Ramayah, T., Wilson, C., & Kummerow, L. (2010). Is entrepreneurial competency and business success relationship contigent upon business environment? A study of Malaysian SMEs. *Is Entrepreneurial Competency and Business Success Relationship Contigent upon Business Environment?A Study of Malaysian SMEs, 16*(3), 25. DOI: 10.1108/09574090910954864

Norman, P., & Hoyle, S. (2004). The theory of planned behavior and breast self-examination: Distinguishing between perceived control and self-efficacy. *Journal of Applied Social Psychology, 34*(4), 694–708. DOI: 10.1111/j.1559-1816.2004.tb02565.x

Paternoster, N., Giardino, C., Unterkalmsteiner, M., Gorschek, T., & Abrahamsson, P. (2014). Software development in startup companies: A systematic mapping study. *Information and Software Technology, 56*(10), 1200–1218. DOI: 10.1016/j.infsof.2014.04.014

Project Management Institute. (2021). *PMBOK guide and standards | project management Institute.* https://www.pmi.org/pmbok-guide-standards

Pulka, B. M., Ramli, A., & Mohamad, A. (2021). Entrepreneurial competencies, entrepreneurial orientation, entrepreneurial network, government business support and SMEs performance. The moderating role of the external environment. *Journal of Small Business and Enterprise Development, 28*(4), 586–618. DOI: 10.1108/JSBED-12-2018-0390

Rasmussen, E., Mosey, S., & Wright, M. (2011). The evolution of entrepreneurial competencies: A longitudinal study of University spin-off venture emergence. *Journal of Management Studies, 48*(6), 1314–1345. DOI: 10.1111/j.1467-6486.2010.00995.x

Sabah, S. (2016). Entrepreneurial intention: Theory of planned behavior and the moderation effect of start-up experience. In *Entrepreneurship-practice-oriented perspectives.* IntechOpen. DOI: 10.5772/65640

Smith, A. Y. (2015). *Indicators for nurse educators' intention to use critical thinking indicators for nurse educators' intention to use critical thinking teaching strategies: A structural equation model analysis teaching strategies: A structural equation model analysis.* https://digitalcommons.andrews.edu/dissertations/1576

Sudirman, I., Siswanto, J., & Aisha, A. N. (2020). Software entrepreneurs' competencies based on business growth. *Journal of Research in Marketing and Entrepreneurship, 22*(1), 111–132. DOI: 10.1108/JRME-12-2017-0055

Sun, J., Shi, J., & Zhang, J. (2023). From entrepreneurship education to entrepreneurial intention: Mindset, motivation, and prior exposure. *Frontiers in Psychology*, *14*, 14. DOI: 10.3389/fpsyg.2023.954118 PMID: 36891213

Tittel, A., & Terzidis, O. (2020). Entrepreneurial competences revised: Developing a consolidated and categorized list of entrepreneurial competences. *Entrepreneurship Education*, *3*(1), 1–35. DOI: 10.1007/s41959-019-00021-4

Tolfo, C., Wazlawick, R. S., Gitirana, M., Ferreira, G., Fernando, I., & Forcellini, A. (2018). Agile practices and the promotion of entrepreneurial skills in software development. *Journal of Software (Malden, MA)*, *30*(9), e1945. Advance online publication. DOI: 10.1002/smr.1945

Tsordia, C., & Papadimitriou, D. (2015). The role of theory of planned behavior on entrepreneurial intention of greek business students. *International Journal of Synergy and Research*. DOI: 10.17951/ijsr.2015.4.1.23

Volery, T., Mueller, S., & von Siemens, B. (2015). Entrepreneur ambidexterity: A study of entrepreneur behaviors and competencies in growth-oriented small and medium-sized enterprises. *International Small Business Journal*, *33*(2), 109–129. DOI: 10.1177/0266242613484777

Wang, H., Lin, Q. P., & Zhang, H. H. (2011). Entrepreneurial competencies of college students: A qualitative analysis. *Proceedings of the 2011 International Conference on Business Computing and Global Informatization, BCGIn 2011*, 550–553. DOI: 10.1109/BCGIn.2011.145

Wijayati, D. T., Fazlurrahman, H., Hadi, H. K., & Arifah, I. D. C. (2021). The effect of entrepreneurship education on entrepreneurial intention through planned behavioral control, subjective norm, and entrepreneurial attitude. *Journal of Global Entrepreneurship Research*, •••, 1–14.

Xu, P., & Shen, Y. (2015). Leading agile teams: An exploratory study of leadership styles in agile software development. *2015 Americas Conference on Information Systems, AMCIS 2015*, 1–7. https://www.scopus.com/inward/record.uri?eid=2-s2.0-84963575828&partnerID=40&md5=0646ff65636eab9aded104faaee7d02c

Yaghoubi Farani, A., Karimi, S., & Motaghed, M. (2017). The role of entrepreneurial knowledge as a competence in shaping Iranian students' career intentions to start a new digital business. *European Journal of Training and Development*, *41*(1), 83–100. DOI: 10.1108/EJTD-07-2016-0054

Zapkau, F. B., Schwens, C., Steinmetz, H., & Kabst, R. (2015). Disentangling the effect of prior entrepreneurial exposure on entrepreneurial intention. *Journal of Business Research*, *68*(3), 639–653. DOI: 10.1016/j.jbusres.2014.08.007

Zulfiqar, S., Sarwar, B., Aziz, S., Ejaz Chandia, K., & Khan, M. K. (2019). An analysis of influence of business simulation games on business school students' attitude and intention toward entrepreneurial activities. *Journal of Educational Computing Research*, *57*(1), 106–130. DOI: 10.1177/0735633117746746

# Chapter 6
# Social Entrepreneurship and Social Sustainability Concepts in the Light of Case Studies

**Saffet Karayaman**
*Artvin Çoruh Üniversitesi, Turkey*

## ABSTRACT

*Social Entrepreneurship; These are entrepreneurial activities aimed at eliminating social problems and transforming systems, without prioritizing material benefit and profit. In doing this, the common benefit of the society is aimed. Social entrepreneurship; It has multifaceted dimensions, especially social impact, business model, leadership and sustainability. Social sustainability; It includes criteria such as equality, diversity, social integrity, quality of life and democracy. These criteria indicate the areas covered by social sustainability.Social sustainability includes many social issues such as education, gender equality and equity. It can be said that social entrepreneurship is a tool to achieve social sustainability. Social Entrepreneurship activities can ensure social sustainability. In the light of these definitions, some social entrepreneurship studies are carried out in the Fındıklı municipality in Turkey. This chapter aims to present original studies that will benefit practitioners, academics and policy makers.*

DOI: 10.4018/978-1-6684-9872-9.ch006

## INTRODUCTION

Individuals' attitudes and behaviours play a crucial role in overcoming the crises faced by humanity. They work together with their social groups to find solutions to problems. Cooperation among individuals is essential for maintaining society's quality of life. Additionally, social order and solidarity are crucial for the fair distribution of resources. Societies strive to protect their quality of life in the face of unpredictable crises. To achieve a balanced distribution of resources without waste, solidarity is crucial. Societies can ensure social sustainability through solidarity, which exists in varying degrees in every society. Durkheim (2006) identified two types of solidarity:

*Mechanical solidarity* is a type of solidarity that arises in communities where people live together in small groups, recognize each other in the living space, establish face-to-face relationships, share a common past, and change takes place very slowly.

*Organic solidarity* is the process of industrialisation has had a profound impact on traditional social structures. Agricultural systems began to break down, and cities emerged as new centres of habitation. People began to live together in large numbers, resulting in a diversity of cultures and lifestyles replacing the previous homogeneity. As a result, mechanical solidarity has given way to organic solidarity based on the 'division of labour' (Zencirkıran, 2015). In such societies, individuals have become more differentiated (Swingewood, 1998; Aron, 2000). According to Öztürk (2013), the pursuit of happiness through financial gain has led to the commodification of everything, including human relationships.

Sustainability, on the other hand, refers to the capacity to endure. Sustainability can be defined as the harmonious coordination of resource exploitation, investment direction, technological development, and institutional change to meet current and future human needs and aspirations while preserving the environment, economy, and society. This definition encompasses the interconnected domains of environmental, economic, and social factors (Capra, 2007; Wu, J., 2013; Baker, 2015). The three sub-domains of sustainable development are cultural, technological, and political (James & Magee, 2016). Sustainable development refers to development that can meet present needs without compromising the ability of future generations to meet their own needs (Yanık & Türker, 2012). The term 'sustainable development' was first introduced in the Brundtland Report (1987) for the World Commission on Environment and Development.

Migration from rural to urban areas has resulted in the emergence of new social and economic conditions. This has led to new dimensions of solidarity and cooperation, as people work together to overcome challenges that they cannot face alone, resulting in economic benefits. These collective efforts to ensure social sustainability are known as social entrepreneurship activities (Toker, 2021).

Social sustainability involves meeting the needs of society, ensuring equality and justice, protecting cultural diversity, and promoting human rights. It is crucial to consider economic, environmental, and social factors together for a sustainable future. This book chapter provides conceptual explanations and examples related to social sustainability.

This chapter investigates the impact of social entrepreneurship on sustainability and creating social change in an ecosystem. It provides examples of standing against the increasing imposition of consumer society due to globalization. The chapter is useful for organisations, researchers, and practitioners to develop social entrepreneurship examples.

## SOCIAL ENTREPRENEURSHIP

Social entrepreneurship refers to entrepreneurial activities aimed at addressing social problems and transforming systems without prioritising material benefits and profits. The focus is on the common benefit of society. Social entrepreneurs aim to achieve both financial sustainability and social impact by producing innovative solutions to social problems. Social entrepreneurship encompasses various dimensions, including social impact, business models, leadership, and sustainability (Lubberink, 2020). Social entrepreneurship plays a crucial role in advancing society towards a better future.

Social entrepreneurs facilitate the efficient production and distribution of goods and services by providing access to existing markets for the underprivileged. This concept is the core of Prahalad's (2006) 'The Fortune at the Bottom of the Pyramid'. According to Prahalad (2006), the poor, who represent the majority of the world and the bottom of the pyramid, can be viewed as consumers, creating opportunities for offering products and services. Prahalad argues that conventional methods are insufficient to solve poverty and that socially innovative approaches, developed in partnership with the poor, are necessary to create sustainable win-win scenarios. Some argue that social entrepreneurs are not always successful in addressing poverty (Karnani, 2007).

Although there are many definitions for the concept, social enterprises prioritise social and environmental impact and generate income through commercial activity (Alberti & Varon Garrido, 2017).

**Prioritising social/environmental impact:** Social enterprises aim to add value to society at large. This is achieved through innovative solutions to environmental or social problems.

**Generating income through commercial activity:** Social enterprises may engage in commercial activities to generate income, but they do not distribute dividends. Instead, surplus income is used to support the core mission.

**Channelling income towards social goals:** Social enterprises utilise their income for social purposes, combining profit and social benefit.

This approach brings social responsibility and management skills under the same roof (Hawkins, 2006). Social entrepreneurs are change-making actors who prioritise social benefit, creating solutions to urgent environmental and social problems through the development of permanent and conscious solutions. Social entrepreneurship is a movement that aims to create social benefits and has a long history dating back centuries. This concept has gained more widespread recognition in recent times (Kümbül, 2011). In essence, social entrepreneurship involves adapting to changing economic trends and providing solutions to sustainability challenges.

Examples of social entrepreneurship include co-operatives, limited liability companies, foundations, associations, and sole proprietorships. The social entrepreneurship ecosystem comprises intermediary organizations, universities, research organizations, local governments, and funders.

## SOCIAL SUSTAINABILITY

Sustainability in social entrepreneurship refers to the development of enduring solutions for social, economic, or environmental problems, achieved by continually improving operational efficiencies. Social entrepreneurial sustainability should encompass the three dimensions of sustainability: social, economic, and environmental sustainability (Kamaludin, 2023). Social sustainability refers to the ability to create a healthy and livable society, both presently and in the future. The focus is on people and society. Sustainability is closely related to the environmental and economic dimensions of development (Vallance et al., 2011). The social criteria of looking to the future with confidence form the basis of social sustainability.

Social sustainability means building healthy communities for the future with an approach based on people's needs. A socially sustainable society ensures social well-being today and in the future, with sufficient resilience against possible social problems.

Social sustainability is a human-centred improvement that encompasses values such as rights, freedoms, equality of opportunity, and quality of life (Wheeler, 2013). Social sustainability is closely related to both environmental and economic dimensions. Considering social sustainability independently would undermine sustainable development.Other dimensions of sustainability are environmental and economic dimensions:

- Environmental Dimension: It is concerned with the utilisation of natural resources and the management of environmental impact.
- Economic Dimension: It is related to economic growth and production activities.

Social sustainability encompasses equality, diversity, social integrity, quality of life, and democracy. These criteria define the scope of social sustainability. Strengthening the social structure within this framework ensures the construction of social values that extend into the future (Koning, 2001). The Sustainable Development Goals prepared by the United Nations also emphasise social sustainability in the international arena. Social sustainability encompasses a range of social issues, including education and gender equality (Roseland, 2000; D'amato et al., 2009). It enables us to move towards a future that meets people's needs and values, such as equality and quality of life (Baltaci & Balci, 2017).

The concept of social sustainability is the least defined and understood of the types of sustainability (Vallance et al., 2011). Social sustainability has received less attention than economic and environmental sustainability. One widely accepted model for sustainability is the

triad of environmental, economic, and social sustainability (Kaypak, 2012). The approach considers social sustainability, which encompasses social equity, liveability, health equity, community development, social capital, social support, human rights, labour rights, settlement, social responsibility, social justice, cultural competence and human adaptation.

Secondly, a more recent approach suggests that social sustainability encompasses all areas of sustainability, including ecological, economic, political, and cultural sustainability, which are all included in the concept of social sustainability (Davidson, 2009). Therefore, social sustainability should not be limited to the intersection of the economy, environment, and social sphere, but rather should encompass all human activities.

This is also referred to as tSo to achieve true sustainability we need to balance economic, social and environmental sustainability factors in equal harmony.

*Figure 1. Sustainability rings diagram*

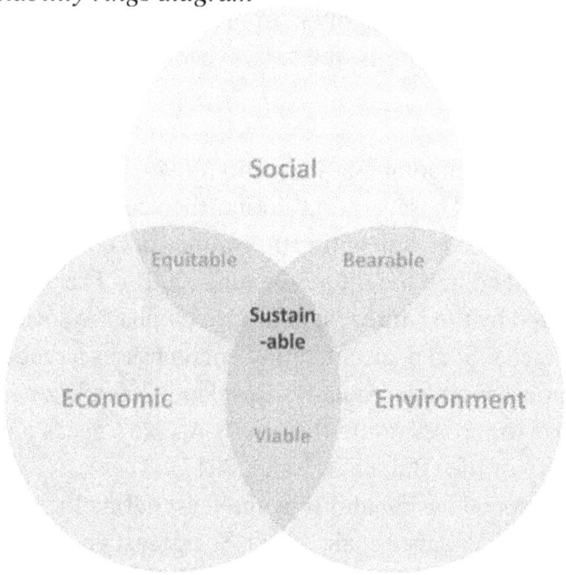


*(Adams, 2006)*

This definition was developed by Social Life, a UK-based social enterprise. Social sustainability is the process of creating sustainable and successful places that promote well-being by understanding what people need in the places where they live and work. It combines the design of the physical realm with the design of the social world. This fragment discusses the infrastructure that supports social and cultural life, social amenities, citizen engagement systems, and places for people to thrive. The definition of sustainability, according to Social Life, is directly related to the quality of life of the community. For instance, this includes air quality.

"Social Life" has developed a framework with four dimensions for social sustainability: These are;

- facilities and infrastructure,
- social and cultural life,
- sound
- sphere of influence and growth

Nobel Laureate Amartya Sen gives the following dimensions for social sustainability (Sen, 2013).

- **Equality** - aims to provide equal opportunities and outcomes for all members of society, especially the poorest and most vulnerable members of society.

- **Diversity** - society encourages and supports diversity.
- **Interconnectedness/Social Cohesion** - society provides processes, systems and structures that promote interconnectedness within and outside society at formal, informal and institutional levels.
- **Quality of life** - society ensures that basic needs are met and promotes a good quality of life for all members at the individual, group and community level (e.g. health, housing, education, employment, security).
- **Democracy and governance** - society ensures democratic processes and open and accountable governance structures.
- **Maturity** - the individual accepts responsibility for steady growth and improvement through broader social characteristics (e.g. communication styles, behavioural patterns, vicarious education and philosophical explorations).

The concept of Sustainable Human Development emphasises supporting the capabilities of present people without compromising the capabilities of future generations (Sen, 2000). In the human development paradigm, the environment and natural resources should constitute a means of achieving better living standards, just as income represents a means of increasing social expenditure and ultimately welfare (Anand & Sen, 1996).

The concept of socially responsible investment (SRI) addresses various aspects of social sustainability. SRI funds and indices commonly use social sustainability criteria to evaluate publicly traded companies. These criteria include those outlined by KLD Research (2007) and The Combined Code on Corporate Governance (2008).

1. Community,
2. Diversity,
3. Employee relations,
4. Human rights,
5. Product safety,
6. Reporting
7. Governance structure (Corsini & Moultrie, 2019)

## Social Sustainability Standards Control Authorities

According to the United Nations Guiding Principles on Business and Human Rights, countries have an obligation to respect, protect, and fulfil human rights and fundamental freedoms. Additionally, commercial enterprises must comply with all applicable laws and respect human rights. Documentation should be maintained for both the production and procurement of goods and services to verify compliance with these international principles and laws (United Nations Human Rights, 19 March 2020).

The UN Guiding Principles include a reporting framework that instructs companies on how to report their engagement with human rights issues (UN Guiding Principles Reporting Framework, 5 October 2019). Furthermore, resources such as 'Free2Work', the Global Reporting Initiative, and the Business and Human Rights Resource Centre offer information on corporate disclosures and performance in social sustainability (Free2Work, 6 September 2021; Social Sustainability - GSA Sustainable Facilities Tool, 30 November 2016). Certifications from internationally recognised and accredited organisations can verify the social sustainability of products and services. For example, the ICI Cocoa Initiative (21 March 2020) and the GSA Sustainable Facilities Tool (sftool.gov, 24 January 2017) provide such certifications.

## The Relationship between Social Entrepreneurship and Sustainability:

Sustainable entrepreneurship activities are known to persist even during crisis situations, such as the Covid-19 pandemic (Kamaludin et al., 2022). While there has been significant research on social entrepreneurship and sustainability, little work has been done on the interconnection between these two concepts. This theoretical gap requires examination (Kamaludin et al., 2021; Tien et al., 2019; De Lange & Dodds, 2017).

Social entrepreneurship can be a means of achieving social sustainability, which is a philosophy that aims to achieve social goals. The presence of social entrepreneurship activities offers hope for social sustainability, as they have the potential to contribute to its attainment. The distribution of local tangerines collected by workers of Fındıklı Municipality in Rize province to students in Borçka city, where the fruit does not grow due to its location behind the mountain, is an example of social entrepreneurship in Turkey. It is also demonstrated that the local government collects hazelnuts through an 'imece' organization and distributes them as scholarships to students in need (Varol, August 2023, www.ankahaber.net). This approach ensures social sustainability. The Tunceli municipality's social initiatives in agriculture, specifically 'IMECE', provide significant benefits for the local community and promote social sustainability (Sözcü.com.tr, 25 June 2023).

*Figure 2. Municipality mayor on İMECE*

*(Tunceli, Türkiye; Fatih Mehmet MAÇOĞLU, Mayor)*

These activities pose a challenge to the consumerist nature of capitalism. The implementation of this challenge has been accepted in the region. Local governments in Turkey are responsible for its implementation and are in opposition to the ideology of the central administration. This courageous endeavour, achieved on a narrow and limited ground, harbours strong potential. Further details on these examples will be discussed below.

Social entrepreneurship involves adapting to unpredictable crises, which ensures social sustainability through innovation and overcoming entropy. For instance, during the Covid-19 pandemic, some entrepreneurs have successfully adapted to new conditions. Additionally, there are efforts to mitigate the negative social and economic impacts of globalization and capitalism on local communities. Therefore, it is essential to develop a conceptual framework that connects social entrepreneurship and sustainability in crucial areas, including social, economic, behavioural, and governance.

Local-level initiatives play a vital role in promoting social entrepreneurship. These efforts are significant in terms of their originality and naturalness. The role of sustainable policies in supporting innovative initiatives at the local level is of decisive importance. In the present economic climate, social entrepreneurs require sustainable policies to tackle the challenges they encounter. These can be outlined as follows.

- Policies that support innovation and entrepreneurship are needed, including tax incentives, grants and other forms of financial support.

- At the same time, local social initiatives that reduce waste are the most concrete efforts to promote sustainability.
- The role of local governments, universities and other organisations in supporting start-ups and fostering innovation is crucial.
- At the same time, co-operation between stakeholders with local geographical or climatic differences in different climates in the locality is also extremely important.

## EXAMPLES ON SOCIAL ENTREPRENEURSHIP AND SOCIAL SUSTAINABILITY

The following are examples of social entrepreneurship that ensure social sustainability in the Republic of Turkey.

### İmece

In the face of unforeseen crises, individuals have engaged in searches and various forms of solidarity have emerged. As a result of these efforts, the concept of 'imece' has developed, which expresses working together by helping each other. İmece is a form of solidarity based on unwritten law and accepted by everyone. The concept of imece is unique to Turks and can be evaluated in relation to the commons movements that have increased worldwide in recent years. Jay Walljasper (2015) defines the commons as not only a classification of natural resources, cultural wealth, and public spaces, but also as a means of creating solidarity to build a better future.

The Turkish term 'İmece' also represents the power of collective action (Aydemir, 2015). Historically, Turks have come together based on solidarity in both the production process and decision-making mechanisms (Akkaya & Uzman, 2010). In rural areas of Turkey where state power is limited, the culture of 'imece' exemplifies solidarity. İmece is a voluntary association that provides assistance to those in need without coercion or ranking. It involves working together voluntarily in rural life. This practice of working together is also present in cities to the extent that urban conditions allow (Bektaş Karabatak, 2018).

According to the Turkish Language Association (TDK, 2020), imece is defined as the realization of compulsory and optional work in rural communities by villagers under equal conditions with the unity of labor. It also refers to the gathering of many people to see the work of a person or community and finish the work in order. The term imece is used with different names depending on the region. The organisation of the entertainment called 'Harfana' draws inspiration from Imece culture. The 21st-century dimension of the Imece method of development is evident in...

## Cooperatives

The co-operative structure can be considered as a synthesis of the tradition of imece and ahilik. It is based on the organisation of people with the same needs, helping to reduce poverty and increase employment, sharing knowledge among members and raising the awareness of members. Co-operatives are self-help and self-responsible economic solidarity organisations in many developed countries as the third sector. They are defined in the literature as "an autonomous organisation formed by individuals voluntarily coming together to meet their common economic, social and cultural needs and aspirations through a democratically managed enterprise" (Turan et al., 2011). Co-operatives have values based on self-help, personal responsibility, democracy, equality and solidarity. According to the tradition of their founders, co-operative members have ethical values such as honesty, openness, social responsibility and caring for others (İnan, 2004). It can be defined as "an independent and autonomous economic organisation owned and democratically controlled by individuals who voluntarily come together to meet their common needs" (Sayılı, 2008). A co-operative is put into practice with the joint initiative of a specific co-operation group. A co-operative is a social group with its solidarity aspect and an enterprise with its economic operation (Çıkın, 2007). Globally, co-operatives have achieved significant success in many countries.

The International Co-operative Alliance defines a co-operative as an autonomous organisation of people who voluntarily come together to meet common economic, social and cultural needs and aspirations through a jointly owned and democratically controlled enterprise. Co-operatives are seen as a unique model that fosters social development and provides the basis for commercial enterprises. They operate in many different forms and in all sectors. Co-operatives are an effective tool for poverty reduction as they have the advantage of being established wherever they are needed. Many also make an important contribution to social and economic support systems, providing access to education, health, insurance, credit and other essential services. Although there are different approaches to the earliest establishment of co-operatives, it is widely accepted that one of the world's first co-operatives was the Shore Porters Society, established in Aberdeen in 1498. The first documented consumer co-operative in the modern sense was established on 14 March 1761 in Fenwick, Scotland (Fairbairn, 2016).

After the French Revolution, "co-operatives" were prioritised as a means of solidarity and mutual assistance to solve the problems arising from the living and working conditions of the working class, and spread to countries all over the world. It is accepted that the first application of modern co-operatives in Turkey started in 1863 with the "Homeland Funds" (a structure similar to agricultural credit co-operatives) established by the state. However, the first significant developments in co-operatives coincided with the Republican period, and Atatürk, the founder of our Republic, tried to raise public awareness by including co-operatives in his speeches in every place he visited throughout his life. In Turkey, Atatürk was the protector and patron of co-operatives and became a co-operative member himself. After Atatürk's death, co-operatives remained stagnant until the Planned Period (1938-1960). Afterwards, Article 51 of the 1961 Constitution states that "The State shall take measures to ensure the development of co-operatives." The statement was included.

## ACTIVITIES OF FINDIKLI MUNICIPALITY AS AN EXAMPLE OF SOCIAL SUSTAINABILITY AND SOCIAL ENTREPRENEURSHIP

Sustainability can also be defined as a socio-ecological process characterised by the search for a common ideal (www.social-life.co. 3 November 2019). An ideal, by definition, is not achievable for a specific place and time. However, by progressing continuously and dynamically, the process leads to a sustainable system. The science of ecology believes that sustainability is achieved through the balance of species and surrounding resources. In order to achieve this balance, existing resources should not be consumed faster than production by natural means.

In the light of these definitions, some social entrepreneurship activities are carried out in Fındıklı municipality of Rize province in Turkey. These activities contribute to social sustainability. The word imece, which is explained above, is pronounced differently in different parts of Anatolia. In the Eastern Black Sea region, it is pronounced as MECİ. There is a difference in pronunciation between the word MECI and the word IMECE. It is understood that İMECE has a history of thousands of years in Turkish geography. It is seen that this concept is an extremely appropriate cultural value to carry out social sustainability and social entrepreneurship activities, especially by local governments. It is seen that the main principles of social entrepreneurship and social sustainability exist in the philosophy of IMECE/MECİ.

### The Manifesto On The Web Page Of Findikli Municipality;

(https://findikli.bel.tr/meci-manifesto-in-english/)

*MECI is helping, sharing, peace, fellowship, production, and our bright future. The word, authority, decision, and power belonging to the people is MECI. MECI is to serve humanity for the benefit of our nature in the name of humanity without expecting reciprocity. MECI is togetherness, meeting everyone's needs by working together with a collective understanding. MECI IS knowing the past, reading today, organizing, and sharing the future.*

*In Viçe (Fındıklı), MECI has a great meaning. There is no "I know" in this MECI. In this MECI, there is thinking and producing solutions together. Instead of administrative power, the people have direct participation in the administration. There is a public check against corruption. There is truth and reality against lies. There is democracy against oppression; science, and technology against bigotry. Instead of a handful of interest groups, there is the common interest of the people. There is brotherhood in this MECI, there is service to the public, rights, law, and justice. In this MECI, there is a production with a socialist perspective. There is a meeting of cornbread with anchovy. We have to carry our traditions forward by protecting the tradition and the future.*

*In this MECI, there is fellowship, equality, service to the public, integrity, happiness, laughter, sharing, solidarity, justice, respect for nature and people, love, trust, social and public view, and socialist municipality. In this MECI, there is no rent, no favouritism, no lies, no marginalization, no undeserved gain, no partisanship, no sulking, no unhappiness, no bribery, no despising, no personal ambitions, and no contempt.*

*In brief, there is the feeling of the cold waters of the creek and the sea in the smallest cells of our skin, there is the sweat of our brow, and there are beauties of being able to lie on the grass in the plateau and plan our tomorrows under the million-star sky.*

*MECI is to share life. Friendship, fellowship, and love grow when they are shared. Here, in our Viçe, there is MECI to grow love, friendship, and brotherhood. MECI is to reach humanity without harming nature. It is to respect and protect human rights without discrimination of language, religion, race, and the rights of nature knowing that this world does not only belong to us. MECI is the amour that our heart trembles, it is the love that beautifies our living spaces. MECI changes the dynamics between rulers and the people by replacing its principles to open its doors to everyone, unrequited, based on voluntary participation.*

*We have MECI, my friends, to establish, protect, preserve, and live a more liveable, more beautiful Fındıklı together. This MECI is for protecting the light of our tomorrow and for finding a cure for the troubles. It is for the people of Fındıklı to have the say, authority, decision, and power. This MECI is to deliver the trust left to us by those before us to our children.*

*MECI is the voice of those who defend life against all crimes against HEPP, "the Green Road", our nature, and our living spaces. At MECI, we exist for a future owned by our city, not a resident of our city, without fearing to fight for our future. We set out to establish the future together from today, to build a healthy and happy life in Fındıklı, and to make justice, fellowship, and sharing prevail. We set out to serve our city and our people, not ourselves, and to rule together with MECI.*

*All doors are open, there is no office, and there is the street. There is a place for everyone who wants to work with us. There is a place for everyone, without being other or marginalized, without discriminating between natives, immigrants, the rich, the poor, women, or men. The more people join the horon (traditional folklore), the bigger the circle gets. If you have plans and dreams for the future, join our horon[1] circle.*
*Let's produce together to serve humanity for our nature, our county, and humanity.*
*There is no other Fındıklı!*
*Let's Produce Together, Rule with Our People!*
*THERE IS MECI IN FINDIKLI!*
*[1] Solidarity culture is very common in our district. "MECI", which is also known as "IMECE", is the most important factor of cooperation. Thanks to MECI, which is based on volunteering. With MECI, the tasks that need to be done, are completed in a shorter time and interpersonal communication is progressing positively.*

*Figure 3. Municipality is laying cobblestones together with the public*

*(Fındıklı, Rize, Türkiye)*

*Figure 4. The municipality is collecting hazelnuts together with the public to give scholarships to students*

*(Fındıklı, Rize, Türkiye)*

## CONCLUSION AND RECOMMENDATIONS

In the globalised world, there is a growing concern about people feeling lonely in crowds. This situation can lead to unhappiness and a sense of helplessness, and can also have a negative impact on social harmony. The capitalist system, which prioritises maximising profits and views everything in terms of money, contributes to the rise of a self-centred consumer socciety.

Sustainability is a socio-ecological process that involves striving for a common ideal. Its achievement involves making societies, particularly disadvantaged ones, more resilient and better equipped to withstand potential risks, such as economic downturns resulting from global pandemics like Covid-19.

The ability of entrepreneurs to adapt to new conditions and remain resilient in the face of crises can contribute to the social sustainability of societies.

Barriers to social enterprises have a negative impact on social sustainability. These barriers include:

1. **Regulatory Barriers:** This section includes regulatory barriers that start-ups face in developing sustainable enterprises. It includes difficulties in navigating complex regulations, obtaining permits and complying with environmental standards.

2. **Financial Barriers:** Covers the financial barriers faced by sustainable businesses. It includes the challenges of securing financing, managing cash flow and balancing profitability with sustainability.
3. **Social Barriers:** This section covers the challenges of building a sustainable brand, engaging with stakeholders and creating a culture of sustainability.
4. **Technological Barriers:** This section covers the technological barriers that start-ups face in developing sustainable businesses. It covers the challenges of developing sustainable technologies, implementing green practices and adopting innovative solutions.

Removing these barriers will result in the integration of social entrepreneurship and social sustainability. It is recommended that top managers and politicians create policies to eliminate these barriers. Additionally, researchers should conduct studies on social entrepreneurship and develop implementation models that showcase successful examples.

The objective of this book chapter is to present original research that will benefit practitioners, academics, and policymakers. A clearer understanding of the relationship between social entrepreneurship and sustainability can assist in the creation of a more sustainable world in the future.

## REFERENCES

Adams, W. M. (2006). *The future of sustainability: Re-thinking environment and development in the Twenty-first century.* Report of the IUCN Renowned Thinkers Meeting, 29–31 January 2006. Retrieved on: 2024-01-01.

Akkaya, D. H., & Uzman, E. E. (2010). Hızla Yok Olan BirKültürün Son İzleri: *Eskişehir Sakana Örnekleri. Green Age Symposium, Mimar Sinan Fine ArtUniversity*, 6-8 December 2010, İstanbul.

Alberti, F. G., & Varon Garrido, M. A. (2017). Can profit and sustainability goals co-exist? New business models for hybrid firms. *The Journal of Business Strategy, 38*(1), 3–13. DOI: 10.1108/JBS-12-2015-0124

Alper, K. (2017). *Anadolu'nun İş Yapma Kültürü "İmece" ÖrnekOlmalı.* Retrieved from https://www.hurriyet.com.tr/ekonomi/anadolunun-is-yapma-kulturu-imeceornek-olsun40678579, (Acces date: 02 May 2023).

Anand, S., & Sen, A. K. (1996). Sustainable human development: Concepts and priorities, Office of Development Studies Discussion Paper, No. 1, UNDP, New York.

Aron, R. (2010). *Sosyolojik Düşüncenin Evreleri (Çev: K.Alemdar).* Bilgi Yayınevi.

Aydemir, A. (2015). Social cooperation and solidarity in divanu lugati't-Türk. *Route Educational and Social Science Journal, 2*(2), 226–240. DOI: 10.17121/ressjournal.237

Baker, S. (2015). *Sustainable development.* Routledge. DOI: 10.4324/9780203121177

Baltaci, A., & Balcı, A. (2017). Complexity leadership: A theorical perspective. *International Journal of Educational Leadership and Management*, 30-58.

Brundtland, G. H. (1987). What is sustainable development. *Our Common Future, 8*(9).

Capra, F. (2007). Sustainable living, ecological literacy, and the breath of life. [CJEE]. *Canadian Journal of Environmental Education,* •••, 9–18.

Çıkın, A. (2007). Tarımsal Örgütlenme II. Çiftçiler NasılÖrgütlenmeli. *Ege Tarım Dergisi, 1*(2).

Corsini, L., & Moultrie, J. (2019). Design for social sustainability: Using digital fabrication in the humanitarian and development sector. *Sustainability (Basel), 11*(13), 3562. Advance online publication. DOI: 10.3390/su11133562

D'amato, A., Henderson, S., & Florence, S. (2009). Corporate social responsibility and sustainable business. *A Guide to Leadership tasks and functions*, 102.

Davidson, M. (2009). Social sustainability: A potential for politics? *Local Environment, 14*(7), 607–619. DOI: 10.1080/13549830903089291

De Lange, D., & Dodds, R. (2017). Increasing sustainable tourism through social entrepreneurship. *International Journal of Contemporary Hospitality Management, 29*(7), 1977–2002. DOI: 10.1108/IJCHM-02-2016-0096

Dempsey, N., Bramley, G., Power, S., & Brown, C. (2011). The social dimension of sustainable development: Defining urban social sustainability. *Sustainable Development (Bradford), 19*(5), 289–300. DOI: 10.1002/sd.417

Durkheim, E. (2006). *Toplumsal İşbölümü (Çev: Ö.Ozankaya).* Cem Yayınları.

Fairbairn, B. (2016). The Meaning of Ochda.Usaskstudies.coop. Archivedfrom the original on 2012-01-11. Retrieved 2023-12-21.

Freestone, R., & Favaro, P. (2022). The social sustainability of smart cities: A conceptual framework. *City, Culture and Society, 29*, 100460. DOI: 10.1016/j.ccs.2022.100460

Hacıfazlıoğlu, Ç. (2024, Ocak). Fındıklı'da Mandalinalar İhtiyaç Sahipleri İçin Toplanacak. https://www.haberetanik.com/haber/findiklida-mandalinalar-ihtiyac-sahipleri-icin-toplanacak-60001.html (Access date: 12 January 2023).

Hawkins, D. (2006). *Corporate social responsibility: Balancing tomorrow's sustainability and today's profitability*. Springer. DOI: 10.1057/9780230625815

James, P., & Magee, L. (2016). Domains of sustainability. *Global Encyclopedia of Public administration, public policy, and governance,* 1-17.

Kamaludin, M. F. (2023). Social sustainability within social entrepreneurship. *Technological Forecasting and Social Change, 192*, 122541. DOI: 10.1016/j.techfore.2023.122541

Kamaludin, M. F., Xavier, J. A., & Amin, M. (2021). Social entrepreneurship and sustainability: A conceptual framework. *Journal of Social Entrepreneurship*, •••, 1–24.

Kamaludin, M. F., Xavier, J. A., & Amin, M. (2022). Social entrepreneurial sustainability during the COVID-19 pandemic. *Social Enterprise Journal, 18*(2), 344–363. DOI: 10.1108/SEJ-05-2021-0041

Karabatak, B. N. (2018). İmece Kültürü ve İmece KelimesiÜzerine. *Türk & İslam DünyasıSosyal Araştırmalar Dergisi, 5*(18), 490–501.

Karafazlı, G. (2021). MECİ Halkın Bakkalı: Fındıklı'da kadınların el emeği aracısız olarak halkla buluşacak. https://yesilgazete.org/meci-halkin-bakkali/.

Karnani, A. (2007). The mirage of marketing to the bottom of the pyramid: How the private sector can help alleviate poverty. *California Management Review, 49*(4), 90–111. DOI: 10.2307/41166407

Kaypak, Ş. (2012). Ekolojik turizm ve sürdürülebilir kırsal kalkınma. *Karamanoğlu Mehmetbey Üniversitesi Sosyal ve Ekonomik Araştırmalar Dergisi, 2012*(1), 11–29.

Koning, J. (2001, November). Social sustainability in a globalizing world: context, theory and methodology explored. In *Proceedings of the UNESCO/MOST Meeting*, The Hague, The Netherlands (pp. 22-23).

Korkmaz, C. (2011). İmece Usulü Kalkınmanın 21. YüzyıldakiBoyutu: Köy Bankaları.Uluslararası Mikrokredi Konferansı,Kadir Has Üniversitesi,9 Aralık 2010 Toplantı Raporu.

Kümbül, G. B. (2011). Yoksullukla mücadelede sosyal girişimcilik: Ashoka üyelerinden sosyal yenilikçi örnek uygulamalar. *Dokuz Eylül Üniversitesi Sosyal Bilimler Enstitüsü Dergisi, 13*(3), 79–111.

Lubberink, R. (2020). Social entrepreneurship and sustainable development. In *Decent work and economic growth* (pp. 913–923). Springer International Publishing.

McKenzie, S. (2004). Social sustainability: Towards some definitions.

Öztürk, M. (2013). *Tüketici Ayartma ya da YoksullaşarakTüketme.Bauman Sosyolojisi (der. Zülküf Kara)*. Ayrıntı Yayınları.S.

Prahalad, C. K. (2006). *The fortune at the bottom of the pyramid: eradicating poverty through profits*. Wharton SchoolPublishing.

Research, K. L. D. (2007). *Environmental*. Social and Governance Rating Criteria.

Roseland, M. (2000). Sustainable community development: Integrating environmental, economic, and social objectives. *Progress in Planning, 54*(2), 73–132. DOI: 10.1016/S0305-9006(00)00003-9

Sayılı, M. (2008). Tarımda Örgütlenme Şekilleri.Yem Bitkilerive Meraya DayalıHayvancılık Eğitimi Kitabı, Erciyes Üniversitesi Yayınları,Yayın No:160, Kayseri.

Sen, A. (2013). *A survey of sustainable development: social and economic dimensions* (Vol. 6). Island Press.

Sen, A. K. (2000). 'The ends and means of sustainability', keynote address at the International Conference on Transition to sustainability, Tokyo, May.

Soykut, R. H. (1980). İnsanlık Bilimi Ahilik.Ankara: HalkBankası Yayınları. TDK, 2020. Türk Dil Kurumu. https://tr.search.yahoo.com/search?fr=mcafee_uninternational&type=E210TR91105G0&p=tdk (Acces dade:11 October 2023).

Swingewood, A. (1998). *Sosyolojik Düşüncenin Kısa Tarihi (Çev.Osman Akınhay).* Bilim ve Sanat Yayınları.

Tien, N. H., Anh, D. B. H., Ngoc, N. M., & Do Thi, Y. N. (2019). Sustainable social entrepreneurship in Vietnam. *International Journal of Entrepreneurship, 23*(3), 1–12.

Toker, K. (2021). From social sustainability to social entrepreneurship: a path for social value creation. In *Creating Social Value Through Social Entrepreneurship* (pp. 1–31). IGI Global. DOI: 10.4018/978-1-7998-4727-4.ch001

Turan, N., Kara, M., Gürbüz, M., & Sarıtaş, D. Ö. (2011). Konut Yapı Kooperatifçiliği.Anadolu Üniversitesi Yayın No: 2541, Açıköğretim Fakültesi Yayın No: 1512.http://ds.anadolu.edu.tr/eKitap/EMY201U.pdf

Vallance, S., Perkins, H. C., & Dixon, J. E. (2011). What is social sustainability? A clarification of concepts. *Geoforum, 42*(3), 342–348. DOI: 10.1016/j.geoforum.2011.01.002

Varol, B. (2024, Ocak). Fındıklı Belediyesi'nden Geliri Öğrencilere Burs Verilmesi Üzerine "Fındık Mecisi"... Başkan Çervatoğlu: "Bütün Kötülüklere Karşı İyilik Bulaşıcıdır". 12.08.2023. https://ankahaber.net/haber/detay/findikli_belediyesinden_geliri_ogrencilere_burs_verilmesi_uzerine_findik_mecisi_baskan_cervatoglu_butun_kotuluklere_karsi_iyilik_bulasicidir_150370

Walljasper, J. (2015). *Müştereklerimiz.* MetisYayınları.

Wheeler, S. (2013). *Planning for sustainability: creating livable, equitable and ecological communities.* Routledge. DOI: 10.4324/9780203134559

Woodcraft, S. (2015). Understanding and measuring social sustainability. *Journal of Urban Regeneration and Renewal, 8*(2), 133–144. DOI: 10.69554/VRWG6415

Wu, J. (2013). Landscape sustainability science: Ecosystem services and human well-being in changing landscapes. *Landscape Ecology, 28*(6), 999–1023. DOI: 10.1007/s10980-013-9894-9

Yanık, S., & Türker, İ. (2012). Sürdürülebilirlik ve sosyal sorumluluk raporlamasindaki gelişmeler (Tümleşik Raporlama). İstanbul Üniversitesi Siyasal Bilgiler Fakültesi Dergisi, (47).

Yücel, Ş., & Baki, B. (2020). Türklerde "İmece" ve "Kooperatifleşme" Kültürüne Bir Bakış. *Turkish Journal of Agriculture - Food Science and Technology*, *8*, 155–159.

Zencirkıran, M. (2021). *Sosyoloji*. Dora Yayıncılık. Journal of Vocational and Social Sciences of Turkey.

## ENDNOTES

1 Horon is a cultural folk dance played by a large group of people. Everyone holds hands and dances in a circle to the rhythm. It belongs to the northeastern part of Turkey.

# Chapter 7 Financial Literacy for Inclusive Budgeting Analysing Digital Narratives and Public Engagement With India's Green Transition Policies

**Megha Agarwal**
https://orcid.org/0000-0003-4429-4058
*B.K. School of Professional and Management Studies, Gujarat University, India*

**Mamta Brahmbhatt**
*B.K. School of Professional and Management Studies, Gujrat University, India*

## ABSTRACT

*This research investigates the interplay of financial literacy, digital narratives, and public engagement in shaping India's green transition. Analysis of government budget documents reveals a shift towards green financing, yet significant gaps exist between allocated and actual expenditures. YouTube comments demonstrate public support for green initiatives alongside concerns and criticisms. Topic modelling identified key public interests, including government policies, renewable energy, and social and economic concerns. The study underscores the pivotal role of financial literacy in empowering citizens to understand and engage with green transition policies. By enhancing financial literacy through digital platforms, individuals can better assess the implications of green initiatives and participate in public discourse, driving more informed and inclusive green transition policies.*

DOI: 10.4018/978-1-6684-9872-9.ch007

## 1. INTRODUCTION

As climate change poses an ever-increasing danger, governments around the world are adjusting their economic and fiscal policies so as to meet sustainable development goals. Considering India's fast economic growth, the country has leveraged the existing global trends and incorporated green transition schemes into its fiscal framework using innovative budgetary provisions. The budget strategy has provisions for the further development of renewable energy sources, climate change adaptation, and the protection of the environment. (A. B. Mishra, 2025)However, these policies' effectiveness is determined not only by their conceptualization and implementation but also by the level of understanding and engagement of the general public. Here, financial education is one of the important aspects to comprehensively understand and implement complex fiscal policies and therefore increase the level of public engagement, (Ahamad *et al.*, 2024a) (Ahamad *et al.*, 2024b).

Most people associate the term financial literacy with personal finance but this can also be a useful tool in enhancing policy making to be more inclusive.(Mohammed Usman et al., 2023) It enables people to appreciate government budgets, understand the essence of green financing and make decisions that are consistent with sustainability, (Kate, Padhye, & Mishra, 2022). One of the most nebulous aspects of green transition policies is financial proficiency because it allows the understanding of climate finance such as renewable energy subsidies or green technologies.(A. Mishra, 2025) This understanding enhances the ability of us as citizens to actively engage in debates on the allocation of resources and other administrative issues, (Manoharan *et al.*, 2024).

The accessibility of the YouTube, Twitter, LinkedIn and many others makes the information easy to access and allows the interactivity of providing information making these a very good financial literacy platform, this transformation has some impact on the policies of how people understand and engage with finance. How people understand and engage with finance has transformed with the advent of these platforms, (Mishra, 2025). Such platforms play a vital role in India due to their wide reach and accessibility. The financial and governmental agencies along with the popular influencers are using these for filling up complex budgetary sections with some common-sense advice. However, these attempts also point to the lack of knowledge of the general population which needs improved methods of sharing information (Jaiswal Monika, 2024)

Considering the evidence presented in the paper, it tries to relate financial literacy, digital or media narratives, and the green transition policies especially in India.(Mishra et al., 2021) It showcases how digital technologies impact financial literacy, and public involvement in the fiscal sustainability policies. The lack of public engagement in budget cycles deepens the communication barriers and widens understanding gaps. In the end, this research emphasizes the impact of financial education on public involvement, economic growth, supporting green transition and the efficient distribution of resources in the process of reaching the sustainable development goals of India (Singh, 2024)

## 2. LITERATURE REVIEW

The interconnectedness of financial literacy, inclusive budgeting, and public engagement is critical in understanding the effectiveness of policies aimed at green transitions. This review examines three core themes—financial literacy and inclusive budgeting, digital platforms as tools for public engagement, and public perceptions of green transition policies—while identifying existing gaps.

### 2.1. Financial Literacy and Inclusive Budgeting

Financial literacy is pivotal for empowering citizens to make informed decisions about budgetary allocations and green initiatives. Lusardi, A., & Mitchell, O. S. (2014) emphasize the role of financial education in enabling individuals to understand fiscal policies and their socio-economic impacts, such as green bonds and renewable energy incentives. Similarly, Azad, R., & Chakraborty, S. (2020) highlights the importance of public awareness in enhancing participation in green fiscal frameworks in India. Moreover, localized approaches to financial literacy, such as those proposed by Sam Downes et al (2022), suggest that interventions should account for regional disparities and socio-economic diversity. (A. B. Mishra, Ranjan, et al., 2023)The study underscores the importance of integrating grassroots-level financial literacy campaigns with national policy objectives to create an inclusive budgeting framework.

In emerging economies, financial literacy is often hindered by limited access to educational resources. Research by Varumo, L. et al (2020) shows that rural populations face unique challenges, including a lack of digital access, which impacts their ability to engage with green fiscal policies.(Rana et al.,2022) This highlights the need for targeted interventions to bridge the literacy gap and facilitate inclusive participation in policy decisions.

### 2.2. Digital Platforms as Tools for Public Engagement

The proliferation of digital platforms has revolutionized the dissemination of information on fiscal policies. Yanto, H. et al (2021) identify social media platforms like YouTube and Twitter as essential tools for simplifying complex financial concepts, thereby enhancing public engagement. These platforms allow policymakers to reach diverse audiences and foster real-time interactions.(A. B. Mishra & Dodke, 2024) The transformative potential of digital platforms is also evident in Suchocka, L. et al (2020) work, which underscores the role of digital campaigns in driving awareness of green initiatives. (Singh Ritika, 2024)However, disparities in digital literacy and infrastructure limit the reach of such campaigns. For instance, social media engagement often skews towards urban populations, leaving rural and marginalized groups underserved Varumo, L. et al (2020). Globally, studies like those by Jain, S. (2023) and Ghosh, A. (2023) suggest that digital narratives around green fiscal policies are more effective when complemented by offline initiatives. These findings indicate the need for an integrated approach that leverages both digital and traditional methods to enhance public understanding.

## 2.3. Public Perception of Green Transition Policies

Public perception is a crucial determinant of the success of green transition policies. Research by Jain, S. (2023) reveals that transparency and equity in policy implementation significantly influence public acceptance. This is particularly true for contentious measures like carbon taxes, which require robust communication strategies to gain public support.(A. B., Satarkar, et al., 2023)

In India, Ghosh, A. (2023) explore the challenges of communicating green policies to a diverse population. Their study identifies a lack of relatable narratives as a barrier to public engagement. They recommend using culturally resonant messaging to bridge the gap between policy intent and public understanding.(A. B. Mishra & Singh, 2023) Social media also plays a role in shaping perceptions. The study by Yanto, H. et al (2021) highlights how sentiment analysis of online comments can provide insights into public opinions and concerns about green initiatives. This data can guide policymakers in refining their strategies to align with public expectations.

## 2.4. Gaps in the Literature

Though the work that has been done so far is useful in terms of providing information, some gaps still exist. First, most studies treat financial literacy and digital engagement as separate domains, overlooking their combined impact on green fiscal policies. (A.. Mishra et al., 2024)Second, there is limited exploration of regional and cultural factors in shaping public perceptions of green transitions. Finally, the role of real-time digital feedback mechanisms in policy formulation remains under-researched.(Ahamad, Mishra, Raghuram, Tiwari, et al., 2024) This paper seeks to address these gaps by analysing digital narratives and public engagement with India's green transition policies. By integrating findings from multiple domains, the study aims to provide actionable recommendations for enhancing financial literacy and inclusive budgeting.

## 3. METHODOLOGY

This study aims to bridge financial literacy gaps and analyse digital narratives surrounding India's green transition policies. Specifically, the research focuses on the following objectives:

**Primary Objective:** To analyse digital narratives and public engagement concerning India's Union Budget provisions for green transition policies.

Secondary Objectives:

- To assess trends in budgetary allocations towards green financing and incentives.
- To identify themes and gaps in public understanding based on digital engagement (comments, reactions, etc).
- To examine how digital platforms can improve financial literacy for inclusive green budgeting.

To achieve these objectives, a mixed-methods approach, combining quantitative and qualitative analysis, was used in this study

This study encompasses three distinct areas of analysis:

### 3.1. Analysis of Budget Speeches of Finance Minister:

**Data Collection:** The data comprised the full transcripts of the Finance Minister's speeches delivered during the budget sessions of the five-year period under consideration, from 2020-21 to 2024-25. Transcripts were sourced from official government websites.

Data Analysis:

*Sentiment Analysis:* It was performed using the VADER (Valence Aware Dictionary and Sentiment Reasoner) lexicon, assessing the extent of positive or negative sentiments expressed in the speeches. VADER also incorporates rules to handle negation, intensifiers, and punctuation, making it more robust than simple lexicon-based approaches.

*Thematic Analysis:* Thematic analysis was performed using the Large Language Model (LLM) to identify and categorize recurring themes and patterns within the speech transcripts over the years.

## 3.2. Analysis of Budget Documents:

**Data Collection:** Data was collected from Budget documents (e.g., budget at glance, full expenditure profile) from the fiscal years 2019-20 to 2024-25 from official government sources.

**Data Analysis:** Budgetary allocations, and policy shifts related to climate change and green budgeting were fetched and analysed from the documents, particularly for green transition and financial literacy policies. Data visualization techniques, including graphs and trend analysis using python library matplotlib, were deployed to identify patterns and trends in budgetary allocations and policy priorities over the five-year period.

## 3.3. Analysis of YouTube Comments:

**Data Collection:** Using the YouTube Data v3 API, data on video views, likes, comments, and comment likes were extracted from the selected videos. Based on the search result 84 videos were identified and a total 21 videos were selected after the elimination process as shown in Figure 1: YouTube Video Selection Process. 4692 comments were fetched from the selected YouTube videos.

Data Analysis:

**Sentiment Analysis:** VADER sentiment analysis library was used to analyse the sentiment of all comments, aiding the identification of sentiment distribution over time and the sentiment of liked comments.

**Topic Modelling:** Topic modelling is a statistical method that uses machine learning and natural language processing to identify the topics. Latent Dirichlet Allocation (LDA) was applied to identify the key topics and themes discussed within the YouTube comments, providing insights into public perceptions and concerns related to union budget. More specifically, LDA is a Bayesian network and a generative statistical model that assumes documents are composed of words that help in identifying the underlying topics. This model disregards the word order within a document, treating the words as a collection, or "bag of words". Major 7 topics were identified based on the comments collected.

**Word Cloud Generation:** Word clouds were generated using the Python wordcloud library to visualize the most frequent words and terms used in the speeches.

*Figure 1. YouTube video selection process*

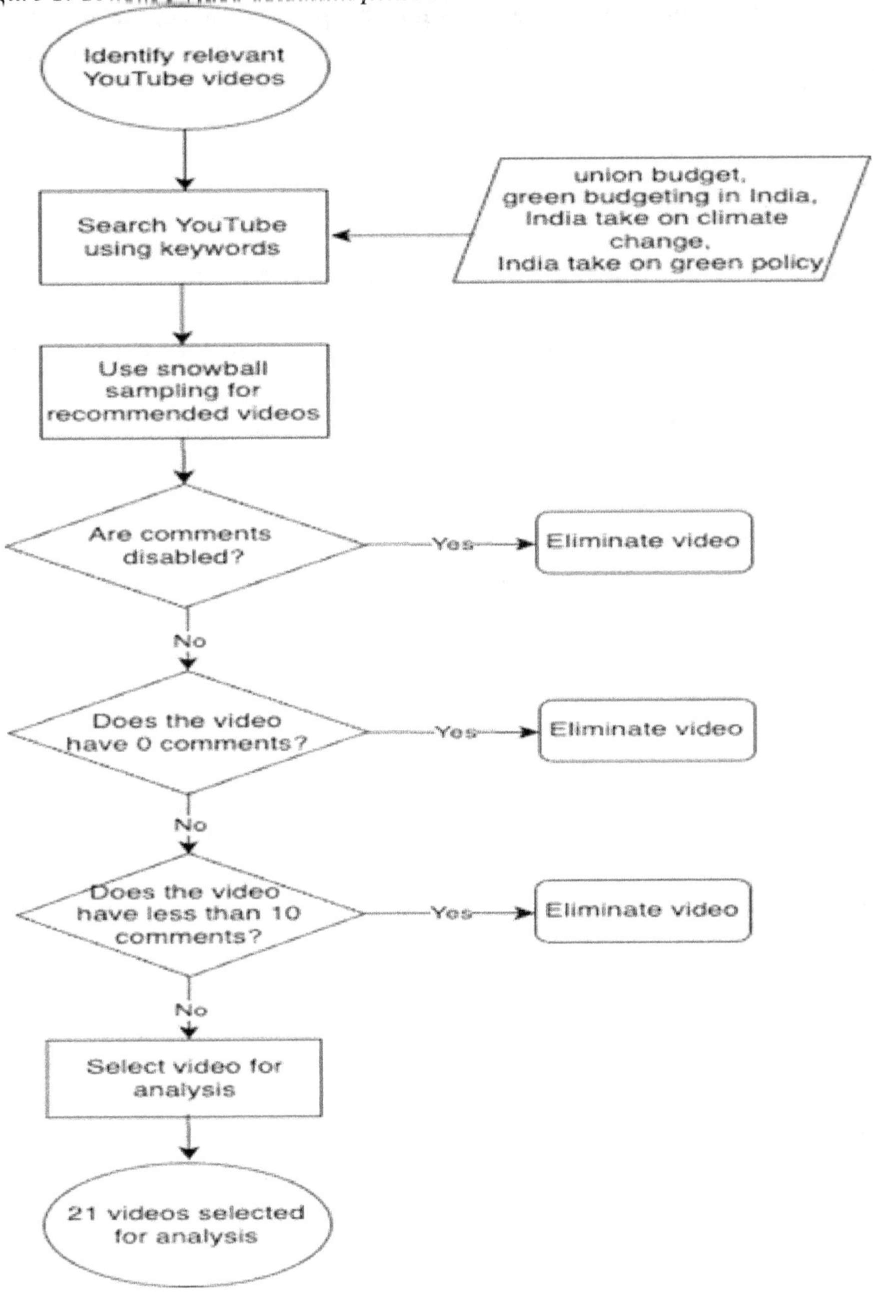


*(Note: Flowchart depicting the systematic process for selecting YouTube videos for analysis, highlighting criteria for elimination and inclusion. Own work)*

**Ethical Considerations:** All data collection and analysis were conducted in accordance with ethical guidelines, ensuring data privacy and confidentiality. The research adhered to principles of transparency and objectivity in data interpretation and reporting.

## 4. RESULTS AND DISCUSSION

### 4.1. Analysis of Finance Minister's Budget Speeches

#### 4.1.1 Sentiment Analysis of Finance Minister's Budget Speeches

The speech text was pre-processed through tokenization, where it was broken down into individual words, and unnecessary elements like punctuation were removed. Stop words, which do not contribute meaningfully to the analysis, were also eliminated. Sentiment analysis was then performed using a Python library named VADER (Valence Aware Dictionary and Sentiment Reasoner), which assigned sentiment scores ranging from -1 (negative) to +1 (positive) for each sentence. The individual sentiment scores were aggregated by calculating the average score, which provided an overall sentiment of the speech.

*Table 1. Average sentiment score of the budget speeches from 2020-21 to 2024-25*

| Year | Sentiment (%) | | |
|---|---|---|---|
| | Positive | Neutral | Negative |
| 2020-21 to 2024-25 | 62.98 | 35.79 | 1.228 |

(Source: Created by the author)

The sentiment analysis revealed that 62.98% of the content exhibited a positive sentiment, indicating a largely favourable tone. 35.79% of the content was neutral, reflecting a balanced or impartial tone. Only 1.228% of the sentiment was negative, suggesting that negative expressions were minimal. A predominantly positive tone throughout the speech reflects optimism about economic growth and various developmental initiatives.

### 4.1.2 Frequent Key Terms in the Budget Speeches of Finance Minister

As shown in Table 2, development, investment, and infrastructure are consistently emphasized across all years, reflecting the government's focus on economic growth and public sector development. In 2021-22 and 2022-23, terms like agriculture, education, health, and inclusive gained prominence, indicating a shift towards social welfare and inclusive development.

*Table 2. Most frequent words used in the finance minister's budget speeches*

| Year | Frequent Words |
|---|---|
| 2020-21 | development, infrastructure, growth, investment, tax, rural, urban, housing, women, education, sustainability |
| 2021-22 | development, investment, infrastructure, agriculture, tax, education, health, technology, digital, sustainability, welfare |
| 2022-23 | development, investment, infrastructure, health, wellbeing, agriculture, education, financial, capital, inclusive, growth, technology |
| 2023-24 | development, investment, infrastructure, health, inclusive, growth, technology, energy, finance, agriculture, digital, education |
| 2024-25 | development, investment, employment, infrastructure, agriculture, energy, research, technology, education, health, inclusive, women, MSMEs |

(Source: Created by the author)

The later years (2022-23 and 2023-24) saw increased references to technology, digital, and energy, signalling a focus on innovation and sustainable energy. The inclusion of research in 2024-25 points to an emphasis on scientific advancements. Additionally, the frequent use of finance, capital, and MSMEs in 2024-25 suggests a focus on economic resilience, supporting SMEs, and promoting investment.

### 4.1.3 Thematic Analysis of Finance Minister's Budget Speeches

The analysis began with an in-depth reading of each speech to gain familiarity with the content. Initial coding was then applied to identify key features across the text. Potential themes were identified by collating and grouping relevant codes. The reviewing themes step involved checking the themes for consistency with the entire dataset. Finally, defining and naming themes refined each theme's specifics. Thematic analysis was conducted using LLM (Large Language Model) to enhance the accuracy and depth of theme identification. The thematic analysis was enhanced by network analysis, which visually represented the relationships between key themes and terms discussed across the years (see Figure 2).

*Figure 2. Thematic network structure concerning key themes in the finance minister's budget speeches (2020-2025)*

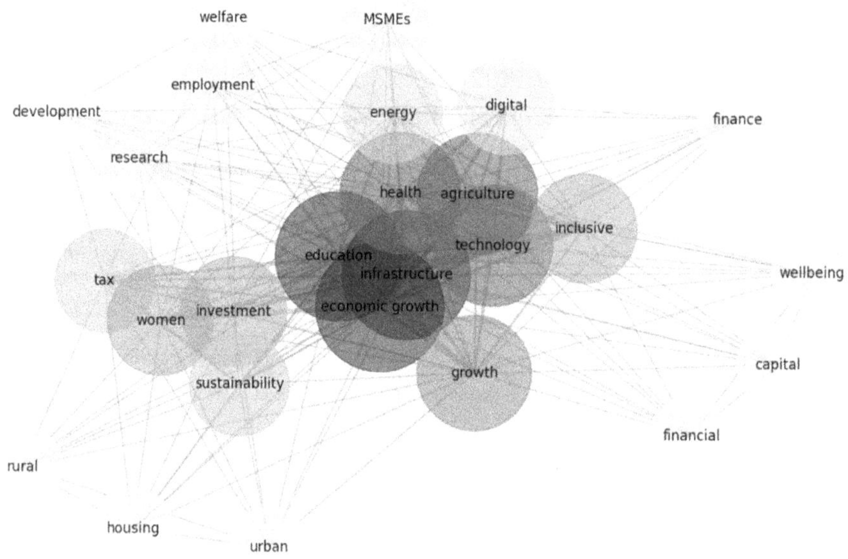


*(Created by the author)*

The thematic analysis revealed consistent focus on several key themes. *Economic growth and infrastructure* remained a central theme across all years, with discussions on developing sectors like aviation, railways, roads, and digital infrastructure. *Inclusive development* was another recurring theme, with emphasis on rural development, women's empowerment, farmer support, and social welfare programs. (Manoharan et al., 2024)The speeches also highlighted *financial reforms and taxation*, including measures to support MSMEs, tax reductions, and initiatives for economic growth.

In later years, there was a growing emphasis on *technology and innovation*, particularly in areas such as digital payments, electric vehicles, AI, and space exploration. *Environmental sustainability* became increasingly prominent, with initiatives for clean energy, renewable sources, and pollution control.(Rana et al., 2022) The importance of *education and skill development* remained evident, alongside *health and wellbeing* initiatives, particularly in response to the pandemic.(Ahamad, Raghuram, et al., 2024) The analysis also highlighted *infrastructure development* as a consistent priority, with initiatives for smart cities, urban transit, and rural projects. In 2024-25, themes around *employment, MSMEs, and climate action* were emphasized, showcasing a shift towards sustainable and inclusive growth strategies. Overall, the thematic analysis shows a clear progression towards digitalization, innovation, and sustainability while maintaining a focus on inclusive economic development.

## 4.2 Analysis of Budget Documents

The analysis of the Finance Minister's speeches provides valuable insights into the government's stated priorities. To further understand the translation of these priorities into concrete policy actions and resource allocation, this section examines key trends in budgetary allocations towards green financing and financial literacy as reflected in the budget documents from 2020-21 to 2024-25.

*Figure 3. Green transition policies: Budgeted figures (2020-21 to 2024-25)*

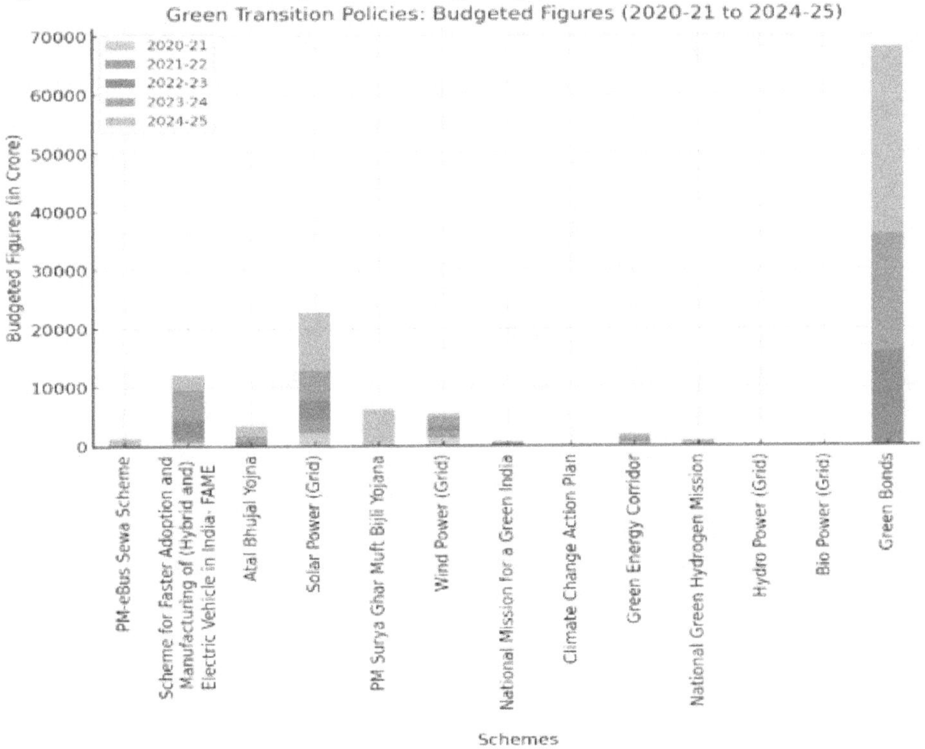


Figure 3 illustrates that Green Bonds emerged to be the most ably funded scheme, especially during 2024-25 and this shows there was a priority to green financing. Solar Power (Grid) and the FAME scheme receive stable amounts of funding during the years which depicts the fact that the government remains willing to fund renewable and electric vehicles. An interesting development is that the PM Surya

Ghar Muft Bijli Yojana, which commenced in 2024-25, was assigned a large budget which goes to show that the government is driving a new policy initiative aimed at increasing the outreach of clean energy.(Karjodkar, 2022) Schemes such as Atal Bhujal Yojana and National Green Hydrogen Mission get funding that is average as they see small increases every year, however year 2024-25 happened to be one of those years where the standard budget increased, in particular meant for Green Bonds, which means that green infrastructure projects are now a priority.(A. B. Mishra, 2020) On the contrary Wind Power (Grid) and Bio Power (Grid) received comparatively lower amounts of funding but stable ones that suggest that they are not as important as the solar energy and the electric vehicle programs.

Figure 4:

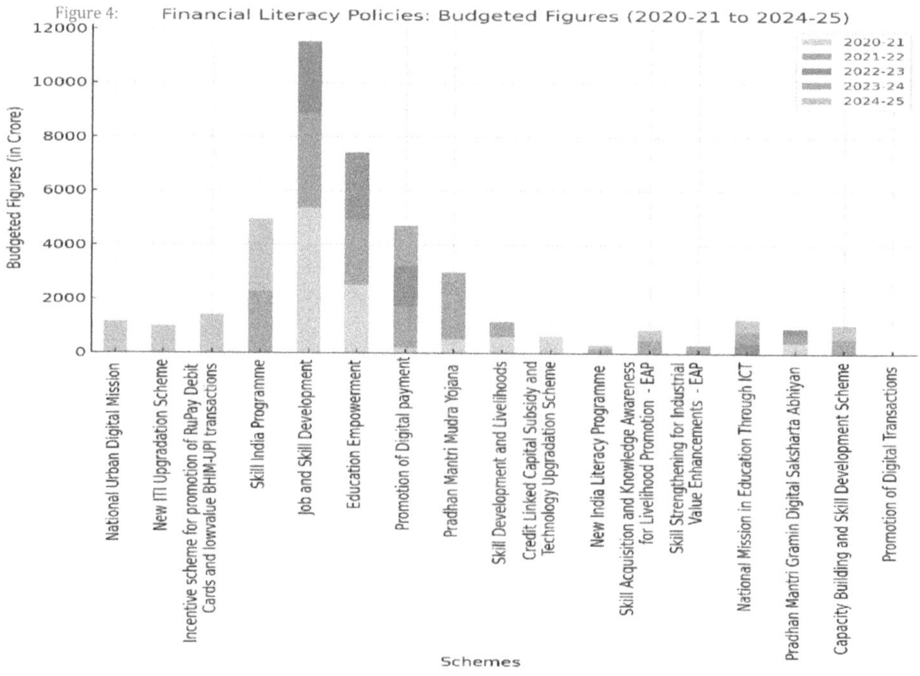


(Source: Created by the author)

Overall, the data reveals a clear progression towards green finance and renewable energy iitiatives, with the year 2024-25 marking a notable increase in investments aimed at advancing India's green transition.(Mishra et al., 2021) Figure 4 shows a clear focus on Job and Skill Development, which receives the highest allocation, especially in 2022-23, indicating strong support for employment and skill-building. (A. B. Mishra & Gaikwad, 2024) The National Urban Digital Mission sees a steady increase in funding, peaking in 2024-25, emphasising on digital infrastructure. Incentives for Digital Transactions also show a consistent rise, reflecting ongoing efforts to promote financial inclusion.(Dodke, 2024) Schemes like Education Empowerment and Promotion of Digital Payment receive notable increases in 2022-23, pointing to a focus on digital literacy. Smaller schemes, such as Pradhan Mantri Mudra Yojana and Skill Development and Livelihoods, have steady but modest funding. Overall, the data demonstrates a growing commitment to digital literacy and financial inclusion, with significant investments in 2024-25 for key initiatives like the National Urban Digital Mission.

When we compare the total allocation over the years in Figure 5, Green Transition Policies show a sharp increase in funding, especially in 2023-24 and 2024-25, reflecting the government's growing focus on sustainable development. In contrast, the budget for Financial Literacy Policies remains relatively flat, with a minor increase over the years, suggesting that it is not receiving as much priority in comparison. (A. B. Mishra, Ranjan, et al., 2023)

*Figure 5. Trend of total budget allocation: Green transition vs financial literacy (2020-21 to 2024-25)*

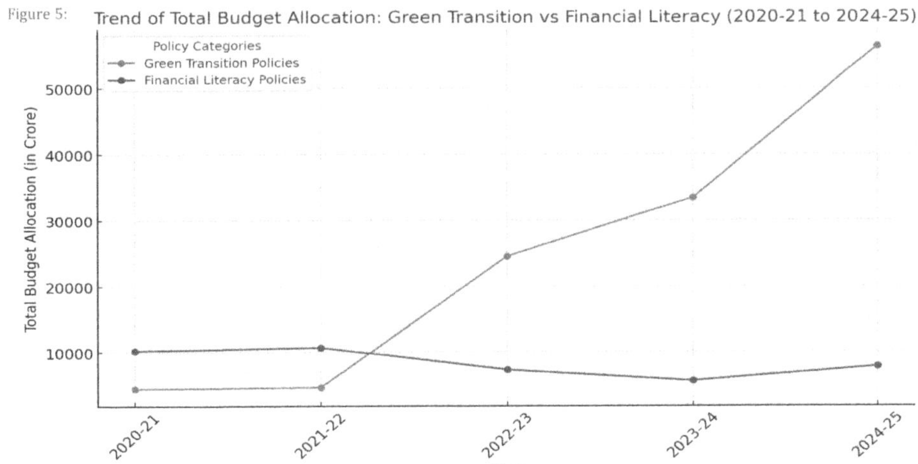


(Source: Created by the author)

Merely receiving funding in the budget is not sufficient to drive growth; effective execution is also crucial. The comparison of budgeted allocations and actual expenditure for the top five schemes in both Green Transition and Financial Literacy categories reveals significant disparities in execution.(Sahaya et al., 2024) Both sectors show notable gaps between the budgeted and actual figures, with Green Bonds and Job and Skill Development experiencing the most considerable differences. For example, the Green Bonds scheme received a budgeted allocation of 68,000 crores in the last 5 years, but the actual expenditure was not found satisfactory, highlighting a stark difference in expected and actual spending. Similarly, Solar Power (Grid) had a budgeted amount of 25,273 crores, but the actual expenditure was 6,864 crores, falling short by over 70%. The FAME (Faster Adoption and Manufacturing of Hybrid and Electric Vehicles) scheme had a budgeted allocation of 12,701 crores, but the actual spending was 3,221 crores, which is just 25% of the allocated funds. Job and Skill Development received a budgeted amount of 17,502 crores, with actual expenditure standing at 9,291 crores, showing a 47% underutilization. Understanding these discrepancies is vital for enhancing future budget planning. Another area of concern pertains to the extraction of data regarding actual expenditure from the budget documents.

## 4.3 Analysis of YouTube Comments

While government policies and budget allocations are crucial, understanding public discourse and engagement is equally important for inclusive budgeting. This section examines public perceptions and concerns surrounding climate change and green budgeting as reflected in YouTube comments.

### 4.3.1 Sentiment Distribution of YouTube comments

The sentiment distribution of 4692 YouTube comments (refer Figure 6) was mostly in favour with 44.2% of the comments (n= 2073) agreeing with the government's green transition policies. This indicates that there is a certain level of acceptability of the government's green initiatives among the people. On the other hand, a good number of commenters (n= 1320), comprising 28.1% resorted to making neutral comments even as a significant 27.7% of them expressed negative views (n= 1299) and aimed their comments on several issues that raise chances for public outcry. This analysis suggests increased efforts to engage the public so that public concerns are adequately addressed in order to enhance the fairness and efficiency of green transition policy frameworks.

*Figure 6. Sentiment distribution of YouTube comments (Author)*

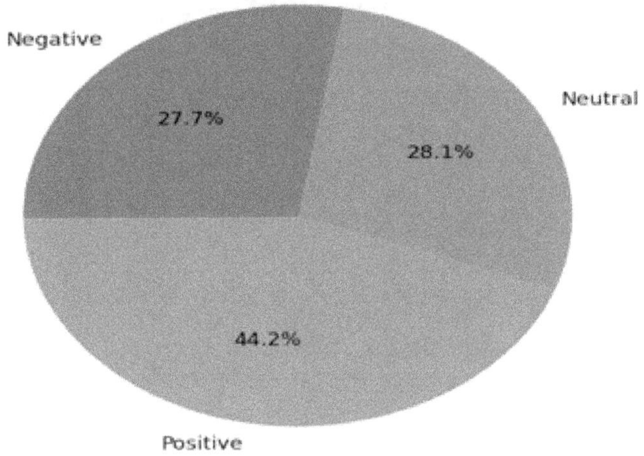


(Source: Created by the author)

## 4.3.2 Analysis of Sentiment Trend

Figure 7 reveals significant fluctuations in public sentiment towards government initiatives on climate change and green budgeting. Periods of increased positive sentiment likely correspond to favourable policy announcements, successful project milestones, or positive media coverage. In contrast, negative sentiment spikes could be associated with negative news events, policy setbacks, or public dissatisfaction with government actions. These fluctuations highlight the dynamic nature of public opinion, stressing the importance for proactive communication strategies to address concerns and maintain public support for the green agenda.(Ranjan et al., 2023)

*Figure 7. Sentiment trend over time*

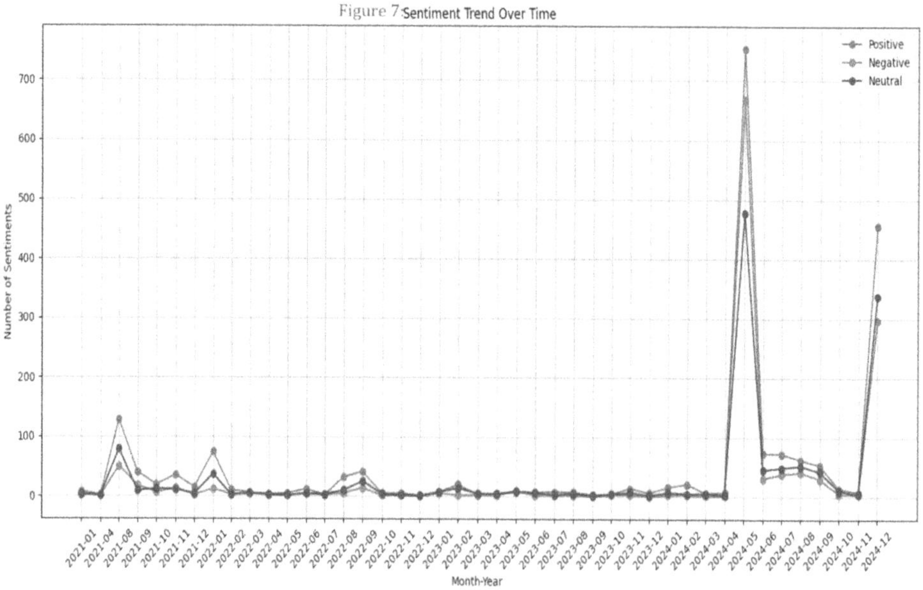


(Source: Created by the author)

Additionally, analysing sentiment trends alongside relevant political or social events can provide valuable insights for policymakers, helping them tailor communication and policy responses to foster public engagement and drive a successful green transition.

### 4.3.3 Analysis of High-Engagement Comments: Sentiment and Liking Behaviour

High-engagement comments, those with the most likes, provide valuable insights into public sentiment and the issues that resonate with the audience. Table 3 shows criticism of the finance minister and government policies, reflecting a desire for transparency. Positive comments often support specific green initiatives, suggesting areas of public approval. This highlights a need for policymakers to address public concerns while capitalizing on areas of support.

*Table 3. Selected snippets from most liked comments*

| Comments | Like Count | Sentiment |
|---|---|---|
| This is why no BJP neta takes unscripted questions | 4631 | Negative |
| Outside: smiling<br>Inside: who gave mic to him ? All questions are out of syllabus | 3163 | Positive |
| Worst FM of Bharat ever.. | 1897 | Negative |
| Question:<br>Answer: | 1540 | Neutral |
| All solar plants in India should be installed on canals/dams/sea. India is a smaller country than many in area but with a higher population. Hence this action will solve land acquisition issues. | 172 | Positive |

(Source: Created by the author)

*Table 4. Correlation between sentiment and number of likes*

```
Summary statistics:
                   count        mean         std  min  25%   50%   75%     max
vader_sentiment
negative           120.0  141.258333  516.998456  5.0  8.0  15.0  61.0  4631.0
neutral            157.0   70.057325  193.802346  5.0  7.0  13.0  43.0  1540.0
positive           223.0   58.322870  265.057624  5.0  7.0  13.0  25.0  3163.0
Correlation between sentiment and number of likes: -0.09407787606808252
```

The scatter plot (Figure 8) reveals the relationship between sentiment (negative, neutral, and positive) and the number of likes. Positive comments, with a mean of 58.32 likes, show significant variability (std = 265.06), indicating that while most positive comments receive moderate engagement, a few garner very high likes. Negative comments, with a mean of 141.26 likes, also display a wide range, with outliers reaching up to 4631 likes. Neutral comments have a mean of 70.06 likes and exhibit the most consistent engagement, with fewer extreme outliers. Despite these trends, the weak negative correlation of -0.094 suggests that sentiment does not strongly influence the number of likes. Other factors, including content, visibility, and timing, likely play a more significant role in determining engagement.

To further explore what drives this engagement, the Latent Dirichlet Allocation (LDA) model uncovers the underlying topics in the comments.

### 4.3.4 Analysis of Topics Identified through LDA (Latent Dirichlet Allocation)

The topic modelling analysis highlights a range of public concerns (refer Table 5). The most prevalent theme, Tax and Government Policies (29.48%), reflects significant attention on taxation and government actions. This is closely followed by Government Accountability and Performance (28.35%), focusing on public expectations of political leadership.

*Table 5. Topics, keywords, and example comments on YouTube*

| | *Topic Label* | *Topic Size* | *Keywords* | *Comments Example* |
|---|---|---|---|---|
| 1 | Tax and Government Policies | 29.48% | tax, taxes, people,bjp, govt, government, India | this is why no bjp neta takes unscripted questions |
| 2 | Hydrogen and Renewable Energy | 14.62% | hydrogen, energy, fuel, cars, water, vehicles, electric | you can't start a hydrogen video without saying "hydrogen is the most abundant element in the universe" |
| 3 | Government Accountability and Performance | 28.35% | india, minister, answer, finance, question, china, fm | this is the most embarassing govt. in indian history. if you imagine manmohan singh, shashi tharoor, chidambaram or kejriwal being questioned a question like this. every one of these would have given a valuable answer over this usual rehearsed nonsensical smirk of these incumbent people sitting in govt. |
| 4 | UPSC exam preparation | 1.81% | batch, live, de, pm, june, upsc, https | it's episode will be upsc cse examination very benificel because its very important show and will be cauting power impur and apriciate |
| 5 | Hindi Phrases | 6.52% | hai, ki, nahi, ko, ka, se, ke | sab se aagey honge hindustani yeh baat hai sab ne maani |
| 6 | Personal Anecdotes | 16.16% | sleeping, partner, income, government, answer, good, u | he looks like he is angry at the interviewer for not bringing in the ev revolution |
| 7 | Financial Concerns and Past Events | 10.49% | fm, scam, tax, 2011, 2008, 2012, 2 | govt is worst swatch bharat cess is full of scam garbage is still on streets flying |

(Source: Created by the author)

Hydrogen and Renewable Energy (14.62%) signals growing interest in sustainable energy solutions, while UPSC Exam Preparation (1.81%) represents a smaller but notable educational discourse. Personal Anecdotes (16.16%) capture sarcasm on income and lifestyle, and Financial Concerns and Past Events (10.49%) focus on financial scandals and policy issues. Lastly, Hindi Phrases (6.52%) indicate regional linguistic diversity. These findings illustrate diverse public interests, with a strong focus on government policies, sustainability, and personal finance.

These findings illustrate the varied interests of the audience, with a primary focus on government policies, energy, and personal economic matters, while also capturing educational and regional discourse.

## 5. CONCLUSION

This research investigated the connection of financial literacy, digital narratives, and public engagement in shaping India's green transition. (Joshi, 2023)Analysis revealed a shift towards green financing in budgets, yet significant gaps exist between allocated and actual expenditures.(Tiwari., 2024) YouTube comments showed public support for green initiatives alongside concerns and criticisms.(Gaikwad V, 2024) Topic modelling identified key areas of public interest, including government policies, renewable energy, and social and economic concerns.(Ranjan, 2023) This research underscores the vital role of financial literacy through digital platforms in driving public understanding & engagement with green transition policies. (Padhye et al., 2023)By enhancing financial literacy, individuals can better assess the implications of green initiatives, participate in public discourse, and make informed decisions about their own financial choices in a greening economy.(Kate et al., 2022) Ultimately, these efforts can foster a more inclusive and informed public, helping ensure the successful implementation of green policies and supporting sustainable development.(Singh A., 2024)

## 6. LIMITATIONS AND FUTURE STUDIES

This study has several limitations. First, the analysis of YouTube comments may not be fully representative of the broader population, as YouTube users may not reflect the general demographic. Future research could explore the demographics of YouTube users engaging with government policy discussions and compare them with the wider population.

Second, the sentiment analysis may not capture the full complexity of sentiment, including context and sarcasm. Future studies could employ more advanced sentiment analysis models that account for these nuances.

Additionally, while topic modelling provided valuable insights, it may overlook subtleties in public discourse. Future research could explore alternative modelling techniques or incorporate qualitative methods, such as manual coding, to deepen the understanding of key themes.

Lastly, this study did not count the impact of socio-economic factors like income, education, and location on public engagement with green policies. Future studies should examine how these factors influence public perceptions and participation in green initiatives.

Addressing these limitations could provide a more subtle understanding of the relationship across public engagement, financial literacy, and the successful implementation of India's green transition policies.

## REFERENCES


Ahamad, S., Mishra, A. B., Raghuram, K. S., Riyazuddin, Y. M., & Alanya-Beltran, J. (2024). *Applications of Internet of Things (IoT) in Maintaining Privacy and Security of Smart Cities*. Taylor & Francis Journal., DOI: 10.1201/9781003405580-30

Ahamad, S., Mishra, A. B., Raghuram, K. S., Tiwari, M., Riyazuddin, Y. M., & Alanya-Beltran, J. (2024). Applications of Internet of Things (IoT) in Maintaining Privacy and Security of Smart Cities. In *Computer Science Engineering and Emerging Technologies* (pp. 187–191). CRC Press.

Kate, N., Padhye, P., & Mishra, A. B. (2022). Studies on Anti-Virus Software Tools: Strong Weapon to Protect Systems. *2022 2nd International Conference on Innovative Practices in Technology and Management (ICIPTM)*, 49–52. DOI: 10.1109/ICIPTM54933.2022.9753877

Manoharan, G., Mishra, A. B., Adusumilli, S. B. K., Chavva, M., Damancharla, H., & Sahaya Lenin, D. (2024). Supervised Learning for Personalized Marketing Strategies. *2024 International Conference on Advances in Computing, Communication and Applied Informatics (ACCAI)*, 1–6. DOI: 10.1109/ACCAI61061.2024.10602307

Mishra, A. (2025). Monitoring the Development of the IoT Concept in Various Application Domains. *Taylor & Francis Online, CRC Press*. https://www.taylorfrancis.com/chapters/edit/10.1201/9781003596721-41/monitoring-development-iot-concept-various-application-domains-mishra-sarita-rani-panda-anitha-uma-reddy-gaurav-sethi-purnendu-bikash-acharjee

Mishra, A. B. (2020). E- PAYMENT SYSTEM: A RISING TREND OF ECONOMY. *New Paradigm in Business and Education*. https://www.researchgate.net/profile/Anitha-K-2/publication/349605501_E-LEARNING_THROUGH_GAMIFICATION-_AN_ITINERARY_TO_GAIN_IN-DEPTH_KNOWLEDGE/links/6037d566299bf1cc26ef9597/E-LEARNING-THROUGH-GAMIFICATION-AN-ITINERARY-TO-GAIN-IN-DEPTH-KNOWLEDGE.pdf#page=10

Mishra, A. B., & Monika, J. (2024). Case Study of Kalyan Jewellers-Brand Perception Mapping Towards Disruptive Innovation in Jewellery Segment. *International Journal of Advance and Applied Research, 11*(6), 386–396.

Mishra, A. B. (2025). The Paytm Puzzle: Navigating Regulatory Compliance in India's Digital Revolution. In *Cultural Sensitivity, Cross-Border Logistics, and E-Commerce in Global Marketing* (pp. 337–348). IGI Global. DOI: 10.4018/979-8-3373-0528-8.ch015

Mishra, A. B., & Dodke, S. D. (2024). ZARA : Technological Influence on Becoming the Fashion Industry's Market Leader. In *Cases on AI Ethics in Business* (pp. 204–215). IGI Publishing., DOI: 10.4018/979-8-3693-2643-5.ch012

Mishra, A. B., & Gaikwad, V. (2024). The Transaction War Between Google Pay and Phonepe. In *IGI Global* (pp. 166–185). DOI: 10.4018/978-1-6684-7840-0.ch009

Mishra, A. B., & Karjodkar, R. (2022). A Case Study of Air India - Maharajah Back to Home. *International Journal of Emerging Research in Engineering, Science, and Management*, *1*(3). Advance online publication. DOI: 10.58482/ijeresm.v1i3.5

Mishra, A. B., Raikwar, A., & Tiwari, A. (2024). *Britannia: Marketing Initiatives Boost A Fledgling Business's Transformation To One Of The Largest FMCG Brands*. https://www.iimspune.edu.in/images/pdf/Journal/Vol3I1-Paper12.pdf

Mishra, A. B., Ranjan, N., Sharma, K. M., Padhye, P., & Chand, K. (2023). Advancement of Digital Transformation to Boost Financial Services Industry. *Journal of Informatics Education and Research*, *3*(2), 2435–2440. https://scholar.google.com/scholar?cluster=15410723285942667834&hl=en&oi=scholarr

Mishra, A. B., Sahu, T., Ranjan, N., & Varma, A. (2021). Green Marketing Practices Prevailing In Hotel Industry. *Journal of Contemporary Issues in Business and Government*, *27*(02). Advance online publication. DOI: 10.47750/cibg.2021.27.02.145

Mishra, A. B., Satarkar, M., & Joshi, S. (2023). IKEA - Phygital Transformation in Furniture Manufacturing Industry. *International Journal of Emerging Research in Engineering, Science, and Management*, 2(3), 6–9. DOI: 10.58482/ijeresm.v2i3.2

Mishra, A. B., & Singh, A. (2023). Brand Positioning in the Indian Smartphone Market: A Case Study of OnePlus. *International Journal of Emerging Research in Engineering, Science, and Management*, 2(3). Advance online publication. DOI: 10.58482/ijeresm.v2i3.1

Mishra, A. B., & Singh, A. (2024). The Mumbai Dabbawalas : An Efficient and Sustainable Lunchbox Delivery System. In *IGI Global* (pp. 154–160). DOI: 10.4018/979-8-3693-1544-6.ch007

Rana, M. S., Cavaliere, L. P. L., Mishra, A. B., Padhye, P., Singh, R. R., & Khanna, R. (2022, April). Internet of Things (IOT) Based Assessment for Effective Monitoring Data Against Malicious Attacks on Financial Collectors. In 2022 2nd International Conference on Advance Computing and Innovative Technologies in Engineering (ICACITE) (pp. 177-181). IEEE.

Ranjan, N., Mishra, A. B., & Padhye, P. (2023). Dynamics of Digital Payments Enable the World's Safest Way to Pay. *Journal of Informatics Education and Research*, *3*(2). Advance online publication. DOI: 10.52783/jier.v3i2.406

Usman, M. S., Sheoliha, N., Prabhakar, P. V., Mishra, A. B., & Dondapati, A. (2023). Leading Strategies for Organizational Adaptation and Growth in Digital Transformation in Marketing. Journal of Informatics Education and Research.

# Chapter 8
# Empowering Sustainable Recommendations in Retail Banking Using Explainable AI

**Shrey Arora**
https://orcid.org/0000-0003-4429-4058
*Symbiosis Centre for Information Technology, Symbiosis International University, Pune, India*

**Souvik Purakayastha**
https://orcid.org/0009-0003-3669-3734
*Symbiosis Centre for Information Technology, Symbiosis International University, Pune, India*

**Ajey Kumar**
https://orcid.org/0000-0003-2214-2985
*Symbiosis Centre for Information Technology, Symbiosis International University, Pune, India*

## ABSTRACT

*This research explores the pivotal role of Explainable AI (XAI) in enhancing transparency, trust, and decision-making processes within personalized retail banking recommendation systems. Leveraging methodologies from popular XAI library packages, including LIME, SHAP, Yellowbrick, ELI5, and Alibi, a profound examination of machine learning models was conducted to comprehend and validate recommendations. The collaborative insights of these XAI techniques led to the identification and removal of a detrimental feature, significantly improving model accuracy and precision. Graphical representations and analyses provided by these*

DOI: 10.4018/978-1-6684-9872-9.ch008

*methods guided model refinement strategies, exemplifying the power of XAI in promoting both accuracy and interpretability in the decision-making process. Despite challenges related to data complexity and reliance on synthetic data, this research contributes valuable insights to the potential of XAI in retail banking recommendation systems, emphasizing future avenues for exploration and refinement.*

## I. INTRODUCTION

In the retail banking industry, personalized product recommendations have become crucial for enhancing customer experiences and driving business growth. The integration of digital channels has significantly streamlined shopping and transaction processes through customized technological solutions. Nevertheless, concerns surrounding trust and transparency have emerged due to the growing utilization of AI models, particularly in tasks such as detecting fraudulent transactions (A. B. Mishra, 2025b). The opaque nature of algorithmic processes has prompted a demand for research into explainability in the field of AI. This challenge has prompted the exploration of methods to enhance the transparency of AI models (A. Mishra, 2025b). An important aspect under consideration in this investigation is Explainable AI (XAI), which offers insights into decision-making processes, enabling users to gain a deeper understanding of the subtleties influencing model predictions (A. B. Mishra & Singh, 2024b) ).. In the realm of personalized retail banking, Explainable AI (XAI). is essential for ensuring transparency in product recommendations (A. Mishra, 2025a). The ability of XAI to elucidate the decision-making pathways of these algorithms offers retailers a clear understanding of how specific recommendations are generated (Mohammed Usman et al., 2023). This transparency not only aids retailers in refining and customizing their offerings but also enables them to align recommendations with customer preferences more effectively (A. B. Mishra & Singh Ritika, 2024). Moreover, as customers gain insight into the rationale behind AI suggestions, they are more likely to trust and engage with the personalized recommendations, fostering a sense of confidence and reliability in the retail banking experience (A.Mishra, Dodke, 2024). Furthermore, in an era where data privacy concerns are paramount, the transparency afforded by XAI contributes to a more ethical and accountable deployment of AI in retail banking. XAI helps mitigate apprehensions regarding the privacy and security of personal information. Consequently, the incorporation of Explainable AI not only enhances the efficacy of personalized retail banking product recommendations but also serves as a crucial element in establishing and maintaining a trustworthy relationship between retailers and their customers (Othman et al., 2022). The paper is organized in the following manner as: Section II, describes the related work. Section III deals with the methodology, Section IV comprises of findings and discussions related to our research, Section V concludes the paper along with its limitations and future scope.

## II. LITERATURE REVIEW

Establishing transparency in AI-powered retail banking products is vital for nurturing customer trust. This guarantees that customers comprehend the rationale behind AI suggestions, enabling retailers to promote openness in the recommendation process (Manoharan et al., 2024). Through providing insights into the workings of AI algorithms and the data they employ transparency equips retailers to recognize and rectify any biases or preferences present in the recommendations (Padhye et al., 2022). AI in personalized retail banking recommendations refers to the ability of Artificial Intelligent systems to provide clear and understandable explanations for the recommended products or services (A. B. Mishra, 2025a). This transparency enables retailers to grasp the reasons behind specific recommendations, ensuring that the suggestions align with the customer's needs and preferences (Banergi et al., 2024). In retail banking, the recommendation process utilizes artificial intelligence algorithms to examine customer data and provide personalized product suggestions (Singh Ritika, 2024). These algorithms take into consideration diverse factors, including customer demographics, transaction history, spending patterns, and financial goals, enabling the generation of customized recommendations for each individual (A. B. Mishra, Ranjan, et al., 2023). A key merit of Explainable AI (XAI) in the retail banking sector is its capacity to cultivate trust among customers (Gaikwad, 2024). By providing explanations for its recommendations, the AI system can help customers understand why a particular product was suggested to them (Raghuram, Tiwari, et al., 2024). This can alleviate any concerns or doubts they may have about the recommendations, as they can see the logic and reasoning behind them (Ahamad, Tiwari, et al., 2024). The heightened trust established in this process increases the likelihood of customers accepting and implementing the AI's suggestions, ultimately contributing to a more gratifying and personalized banking experience (Ahamad, Tiwari, et al., 2024). Explainable AI not only helps build trust with customers but also enhances their overall experience (Rao, 2016). With personalized recommendations, customers can find products and services that are tailored to their specific needs and preferences (Ranjan, et al., 2023). However, by providing explanations for these recommendations, XAI takes the customer experience to the next level. Customers not only receive personalized suggestions but also understand why those suggestions are relevant to them (Satarkar, et al., 2023). The integration of Local Interpretable Model-agnostic Explanations (LIME) in retail banking holds considerable promise (Pooja Mehta et al., 2021). LIME's capacity to augment transparency and elucidate the decision-making process of AI models brings tangible benefits, fostering enhanced comprehension and trust among stakeholders (Varma, 2015). This transparency not only elevates customer satisfaction and loyalty but also ensures compliance with regulatory standards (Varma, 2013). Additionally, LIME's ability to uncover biases and rectify data errors contributes to fair and accurate model outcomes (Ranjan et al., 2023). Nevertheless, challenges are evident, particularly in the reliance on data quality and representativeness, underscoring the imperative of utilizing diverse and high-quality datasets. Furthermore, LIME's suitability is contingent on the complexity of AI models, posing limitations for highly intricate models (Mishra, 2020). Despite these challenges, the overall impact of LIME in retail banking is a more transparent, fair, and trustworthy AI-driven decision-making environment, a vital stride in advancing research and practices in this domain (Allen et al., 2024).

Shap (Shapley Additive explanations) and explainable artificial intelligence (XAI) hold substantial potential for reshaping the landscape of retail banking. These techniques offer a pathway to bolster trust, transparency, and accountability between banks and customers. Through providing explanations for decisions, Shap and XAI contribute to heightened customer satisfaction and loyalty (A. B. Mishra, 2020). Furthermore, their implementation facilitates the promotion of fairness and ethical practices within the industry, empowering customers to identify and address biases or discrimination. Notably, Shap and XAI also serve as valuable tools for refining models and decision-making processes in banking (Raikwar, et al., 2024). By offering insights into the factors influencing financial decisions, these techniques enable the identification and rectification of errors or biases, resulting in more accurate and fair outcomes for customers (Singh A, 2024a). However, challenges persist, particularly in the face of complex machine learning models, such as deep learning models, which pose interpretation difficulties (Cavaliere et al., 2022). Additionally, the resource-intensive nature of providing explanations for every decision pose practical challenge, especially in managing large volumes of customers and transactions within banking operations (Singh, 2023).

The proliferation of artificial intelligence (AI) in retail banking has raised concerns about transparency and biases in decision-making. To address these apprehensions, the industry is turning to the 'Explain Like I'm Five' (ELI5) concept. ELI5 encourages the simplification of complex financial concepts to enhance customer understanding and build trust (Karjodkar, 2022). In retail banking, this approach is instrumental in clarifying AI-driven processes, especially in customer interactions, such as AI-powered chatbots delivering personalized financial advice (Goel, et al., 2022). By employing ELI5, banks aim to bridge the comprehension gap, making financial decisions more accessible and empowering customers to make informed choices (Chand, et al., 2022). While ELI5 holds the promise of improving transparency and customer relations, challenges exist in striking the right balance between simplicity and accuracy (Kaith et al., 2022). Ensuring that ELI5 explanations are both clear and comprehensive is pivotal for cultivating trust and promoting a more customer-centric retail banking environment (Rana et al., 2022).

In retail banking, Alibi refers to a critical property in artificial intelligence—the ability to provide transparency into the decision-making processes of AI systems, for example, in loan approvals or credit scoring and fraud detection. Since decisions in these areas affect individuals and small businesses profoundly, explainability becomes important (Ranjan, 2022). The integration of Alibi in explainable AI thus holds great promise for retail banking in providing banks with the advantages of heightened transparency, better customer trust, improved decision-making, and adherence to regulatory requirements (A. B. Mishra, 2022). However, challenges persist, including the cost and complexity of developing such systems, the intrinsic complexity of being able to interpret AI, and a lack of standardization in how they are developed (Varma et al., 2021). These challenges need to be surmounted if the full benefits of Alibi and explainable AI are to be harnessed to improve the levels of transparency and decision-making in retail banking. A challenge in the AI industry is the lack of standardization (Ahamad, Mishra, Raghuram, Tiwari, et al., 2024). Varied algorithms and techniques across AI systems make it challenging to compare and assess performance consistently (Othman et al., 2022). This lack of uniformity complicates the explanation of recommendation reasoning to customers, fostering confusion and mistrust. Furthermore, privacy concerns arise from using customer data to train AI systems for product recommendations (Rajagopal, et al., 2021). The potential discomfort customers feel about their personal information being utilized without explicit consent further undermines transparency and trust between customers and banks (A. B. Mishra & Dodke, 2024). Thus, Explainable AI (XAI) resolves the AI industry's lack of standardization, providing transparent insights into diverse algorithms (Sahu, et al., 2021). This simplifies explanation to customers, fostering clarity and trust. Moreover, XAI addresses privacy concerns by ensuring transparent data practices, rebuilding trust between customers and banks. XAI fosters trust by providing retailers with insights into AI suggestions and rectifying biases, thus promoting openness in the recommendation process. This not only ensures a more satisfying and personalized banking experience for customers but also marks a crucial advancement in strengthening trust between customers and banks.

## III. METHODOLOGY

In our pursuit to scrutinize the retail banking recommendation system, we sought a dataset that could illuminate customer preferences and the services they engage with at the bank. Understanding the features that significantly influence customer decisions empowers us to analyze the bank's recommendation model effectively. By discerning the correlation between customer details and service preferences, we aim to provide insights to the bank on whether to recommend specific services to particular customers. The selected dataset comprises comprehensive information from a retail bank, encapsulating both customer details and their chosen services, forming the foundation for a detailed examination of the recommendation dynamics within the banking domain.

We employed diverse models, such as Logistic Regression, Decision Tree, and Random Forest, and identified Random Forest as yielding high accuracy. To delve into the reasons behind its effectiveness and pinpoint the pivotal features, we harnessed the power of explainable AI. Utilizing library packages like LIME, SHAP, Yellowbrick, and Eli5 enabled us to conduct insightful graphical analyses. This approach empowers banks to gain a deeper understanding of why Random Forest excels in accuracy and sheds light on the influential features contributing to its performance (A. B. Mishra, Satarkar, et al., 2023). In this research, we aimed to enhance the transparency and interpretability of a Retail Banking Recommendation System by leveraging Explainable AI (XAI) techniques. The integration of XAI is crucial for providing clear insights into model predictions, understanding feature importance, and fostering trust in AI-driven recommendations. Our methodology encompasses the utilization of popular XAI library packages, namely LIME, SHAP, Yellowbrick, and ELI5, to comprehensively analyze and interpret the decision-making process of machine learning models.

## I. LIME (Local Interpretable Model-Agnostic Explanations)

LIME is a model-agnostic method designed to provide interpretable explanations for individual predictions. To implement LIME, we randomly selected instances from our retail banking dataset and perturbed the features, generating synthetic data points. We then used these perturbed instances to train a locally faithful, interpretable model, enabling us to understand how our complex models behaved in the vicinity of specific data points. The LIME-generated explanations contribute to understanding the impact of different features on the recommendation outcomes.

## II. SHAP (SHapley Additive exPlanations)

SHAP values offer a game-theoretic approach to assign contributions of each feature to the model's output. In our methodology, SHAP was applied to compute feature importance scores for every instance in the dataset. By employing SHAP summary plots, force plots, and dependency plots, we gained insights into the overall impact of features on recommendation outcomes. This facilitated a comprehensive understanding of the role each feature played in shaping the model's decisions (Saarijärvi et al., 2013).

### III. Yellowbrick

Yellowbrick is a visualizer library that aids in model selection, evaluation, and interpretation. We utilized Yellowbrick's classification and regression visualizers to analyze the performance of our recommendation models. This included visualizing the classification reports, ROC curves, and prediction error plots. Yellowbrick's visual diagnostics provided an intuitive understanding of model behavior and highlighted areas for improvement (Vendrell-Herrero et al., 2021).

### ELI5 (Explain Like I'm 5)

ELI5 is a library that allows us to explain the predictions of machine learning models. In our research, we employed ELI5's weight-feature heatmap to visualize feature weights assigned by our models. This helped us understand how each feature contributed to the model's predictions. Additionally, ELI5's permutation importance and partial dependence plots were used to assess feature importance and understand the relationship between specific features and the model's output (A, Satarkar, et al., 2024).

## IV. RESULT AND DISCUSSION

In the Results and Discussion section, we comprehensively compare various explainable AI methods, leveraging open-source Python libraries such as LIME, SHAP, Alibi, Eli5, and Yellowbrick. We aim to evaluate their efficacy in enhancing model explainability, particularly within the banking domain (Ahamad, Mishra, Raghuram, Riyazuddin, et al., 2024). We meticulously assess each method's capability to identify features contributing significantly to model predictions, shedding light on their impact. Furthermore, we investigate the potential removal of certain features to bolster model accuracy while preserving transparency. This exploration seeks to discern the most effective techniques for achieving both explainability and predictive performance in the intricate landscape of banking data.

*Figure 1. Yellowbrick model graphical analysis*

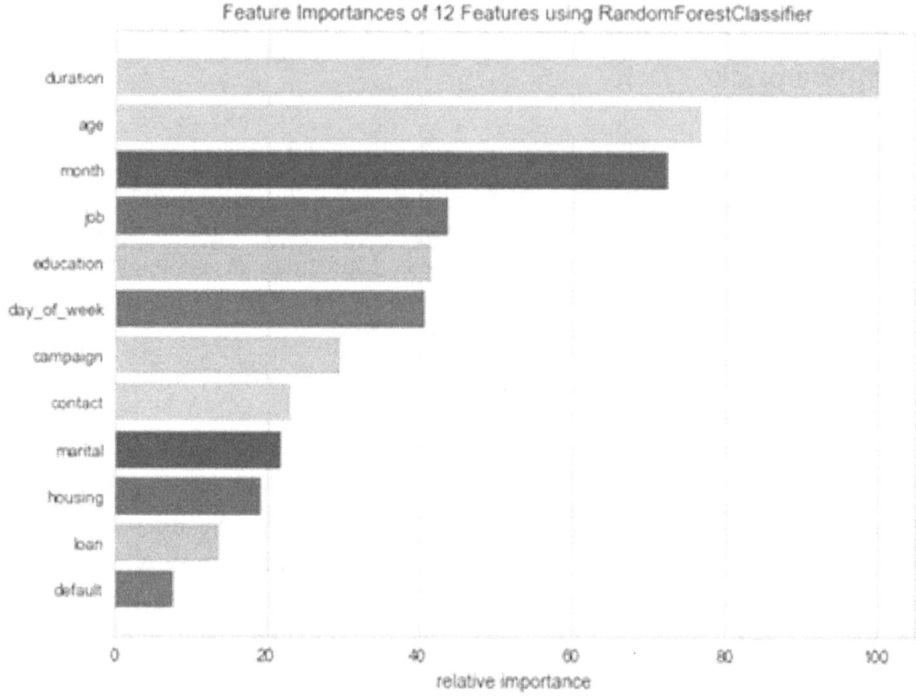


The significance of individual features in a Random Forest model for recommending services in retail banking is depicted in Figure 1. The graphical representation, generated using the Yellowbrick model, illustrates the importance of each feature. Notably, the duration feature stands out as particularly significant (Mohseni et al., 2022). While Yellowbrick provides insights into feature significance, it does not specify whether a feature has a positive or negative impact. To gain a more nuanced understanding of the impact direction, complementary explainability methods such as Lime and Shap can be employed (A. B. Mishra & Singh, 2024a). These methods delve deeper into the model's predictions, offering insights into the specific influence of features and contributing to a comprehensive interpretation of the model's behavior.

*Figure 2. Force plot*

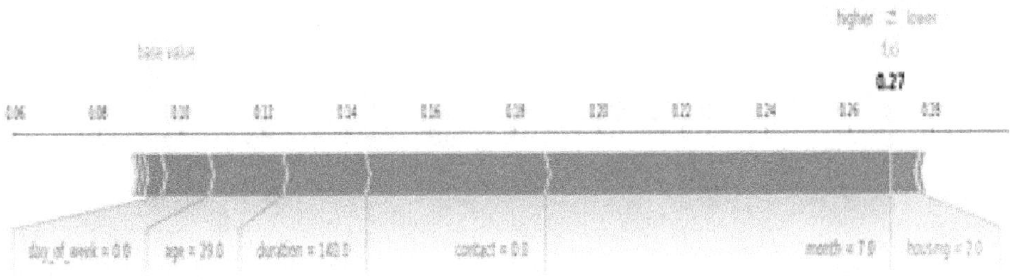


In the force plot as shown in Figure 2, the base value of 0.27 indicates the model's baseline probability for a certain outcome. Features displayed in red, such as 'day of week,' 'age' (29.0), 'duration' (140.0), 'contact' (0.0), and 'month' (7.0), contribute negatively to the base value, suggesting a reduction in the likelihood of the specified outcome. Conversely, the blue region highlights the 'housing' feature with a value of 2.0, indicating a positive contribution to the base value and an increase in the likelihood of the outcome (Kate et al., 2022). These insights are crucial for our Result and Discussion section, as they provide a significant understanding of the impact of specific features on model predictions, informing potential adjustments for improved accuracy and interpretability in the context of the banking domain. The force plot reveals that the 'contact' feature has negligible impact on our model's accuracy and is inconsequential in our analysis.

*Figure 3. Lime tabular graph*

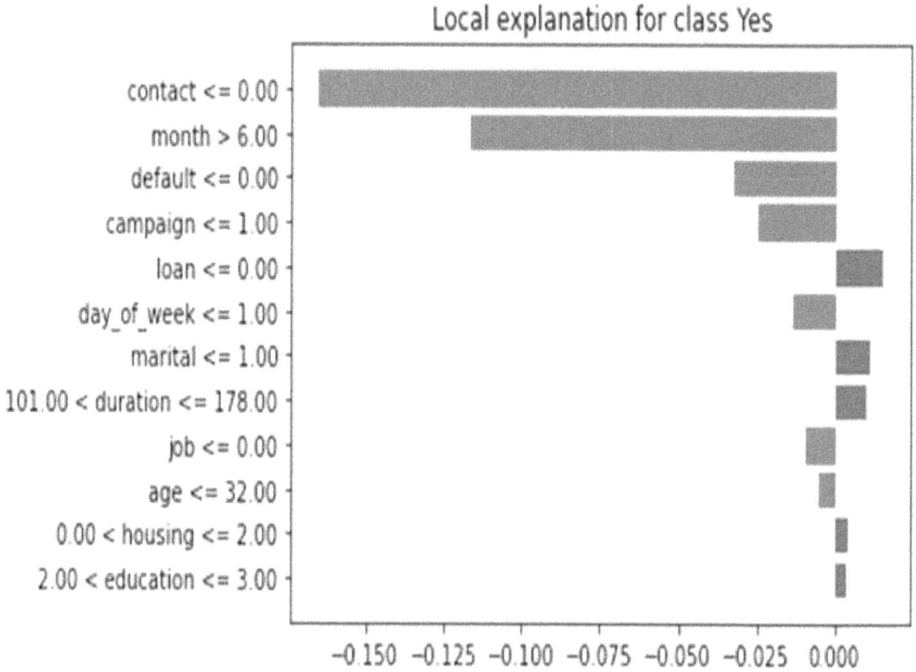


The Lime Tabular graph, depicted in Figure 3, harmonizes with the revelations from the yellowbrick model, underscoring the adverse influence of the "contact" feature on the Random Forest model. Features with pronounced negative effects can pose a dual threat to both model accuracy and precision, necessitating their removal for optimal performance. The integration of Explainable AI methods not only provides clarity on the reasoning behind the retention or elimination of specific features but also illuminates the nuanced impact of these decisions on the overall accuracy of the model (A. B. Mishra, Chand, et al., 2022). This enhanced transparency not only fortifies the interpretability of the model but also empowers stakeholders in the retail banking sector to make informed decisions based on a comprehensive understanding of the feature dynamics. The iterative process of model refinement, guided by Explainable AI insights, establishes a robust foundation for building trust and confidence in AI-driven recommendations within the banking domain.

*Table 1. Original accuracy matrix with all features*

| Classification | precision | recall | f1-score | support |
|---|---|---|---|---|
| Not Recommended | 0.37 | 0.04 | 0.07 | 182 |
| Recommended | 0.87 | 0.99 | 0.93 | 1423 |
| accuracy | | | 0.86 | 1648 |
| macro average | 0.41 | 0.34 | 0.33 | 1648 |
| weighted average | 0.79 | 0.86 | 0.81 | 1648 |

*Table 2. Accuracy matrix after removing the insignificant features*

| Classification | precision | recall | f1-score | support |
|---|---|---|---|---|
| Not Recommended | 0.57 | 0.06 | 0.10 | 182 |
| Recommended | 0.89 | 1.00 | 0.94 | 1443 |
| accuracy | | | 0.91 | 1668 |
| macro average | 0.48 | 0.34 | 0.32 | 1648 |
| weighted average | 0.79 | 0.86 | 0.80 | 1648 |

Following the exclusion of the "contact" feature, a thorough assessment utilizing an accuracy matrix (Table 1and Table 2) reveals a substantial improvement in accuracy, surging from 86% to 91%. This positive trajectory extends beyond accuracy, encompassing pivotal metrics such as precision, recall, f1-score, and support. The discernible enhancement across these diverse parameters underscores the efficacy of the feature removal strategy in bolstering the model's overall performance and interoperability. The observed improvements not only validate the decision to eliminate the "contact" feature but also illuminate the interconnected nature of features within the model. This nuanced understanding, facilitated by Explainable AI methods, reinforces the transparency and interpretability of the model, crucial for instilling confidence in both end-users and stakeholders within the retail banking sector.

*Figure 4. Weight-feature heatmap*

| Weight | Feature |
|---|---|
| 0.0042 ± 0.0032 | month |
| 0.0029 ± 0.0035 | loan |
| 0.0021 ± 0.0025 | housing |
| 0.0018 ± 0.0020 | contact |
| 0.0010 ± 0.0018 | default |
| 0.0002 ± 0.0021 | duration |
| 0.0001 ± 0.0032 | day_of_week |
| 0.0001 ± 0.0039 | marital |
| 0.0001 ± 0.0024 | age |
| -0.0001 ± 0.0028 | campaign |
| -0.0004 ± 0.0031 | job |
| -0.0015 ± 0.0023 | education |

The Weight-feature heatmap, exemplified in Figure 4 within the Eli5 library package in Python, offers invaluable insights into how our model assigns weights to each feature and their impact. Traditional models often conceal these weights, rendering predictions opaque. Explainable AI, however, becomes a powerful ally for retail banks seeking transparency. By unveiling the weights of each feature, banks can discern crucial contributors, transforming the model from a black box into a comprehensible decision-making tool. Analyzing the heatmap, we observe the model assigning a notably high positive weight to the "contact" feature, a revelation consistent with our earlier findings (Fig. 1, 2, 3) showcasing its detrimental impact. To enhance accuracy and provide a rationale for the achieved precision, Explainable AI methods prove indispensable, fostering a deeper understanding of the model's inner workings and fortifying the decision-making process in retail banking. Through this result and discussion section, we conducted a thorough analysis and comparison of various Explainable AI library packages, including LIME, Shap, Yellowbrick, and Eli5. Our findings underscored the unique advantages and limitations of each package. The graphical analyses demonstrated that Explainable AI is instrumental for the banking industry, providing valuable insights for machine learning algorithms and extending its applicability to deep neural networks. This highlights the pivotal role of Explainable AI in fostering transparency and understanding within the complex landscape of financial decision-making.

## V. CONCLUSION, LIMITATION, AND FUTURE SCOPE

In the realm of personalized retail banking, where AI-driven product recommendations play a pivotal role, our research delves into the critical importance of Explainable AI (XAI). for enhancing transparency, trust, and decision-making processes. Leveraging methodologies from popular XAI library packages, including LIME, SHAP, Yellowbrick, ELI5, and Alibi, we conducted a profound examination of machine learning models to comprehend and validate recommendations. These methods, ranging from LIME's local interpretability to SHAP's additive explanations, Yellowbrick's visualization tools, ELI5's feature importance analysis, and Alibi's AI model explanations, collectively contributed to a comprehensive understanding of model behavior. The graphical representations and analyses facilitated by these XAI techniques have not only uncovered the impact of individual features on recommendations but have also guided model refinement strategies. The exclusion of the "contact" feature, identified through the collaborative insights of LIME, SHAP, and Yellowbrick, led to a significant improvement in model accuracy, precision, and other key metrics. The Weight-feature heatmap from ELI5 further clarified the impact of each feature, particularly emphasizing the detrimental effect of the "contact" feature on the model's predictions. This iterative process of analysis and refinement exemplifies the power of XAI in promoting not only accuracy but also interpretability in the decision-making process of retail banking recommendation systems more robust (Butler, 2008). However, it is important to recognize the limitations of our research (Lee et al., 2007). Our study recognizes the inherent challenges associated with the complexity of real-world data, acknowledging that the effectiveness of Explainable AI (XAI) methods may be influenced by intricate data structures (Singh, 2024c). The interpretation of highly complex models poses an ongoing challenge, as their inner workings may be less straightforward to unravel. Additionally, the reliance on synthetic data for local interpretability introduces a limitation, as the generated instances may not fully capture the nuances of genuine banking scenarios. Despite these constraints, our research provides valuable insights into the potential of XAI in retail banking recommendation systems, while also highlighting areas for future exploration and refinement (Sunny et al., 2020). The future of XAI in retail banking recommendation systems holds immense potential for advancements and refinements, including the development of standardized methodologies, real-time integration into operational banking systems, addressing challenges related to the interpretability of deep learning models, and establishing ethical guidelines for responsible XAI use in banking. In conclusion, the collaborative efforts of XAI methodologies in our research underscore the transformative impact on transparency and decision-making processes within the intricate landscape of retail banking, paving the way for a more trustworthy, accountable, and customer-centric banking experience.

## REFERENCES


Ahamad, S., Mishra, A. B., Raghuram, K. S., Riyazuddin, Y. M., & Alanya-Beltran, J (2024). . *Applications of Internet of Things (IoT). in Maintaining Privacy and Security of Smart Cities*. Taylor & Francis Journal., DOI: 10.1201/9781003405580-30

Ahamad, S., Mishra, A. B., Raghuram, K. S., Tiwari, M., & Riyazuddin, Y. Md., & Alanya-Beltran, J (2024). . Applications of Internet of Things (IoT). in Maintaining Privacy and Security of Smart Cities. In *Computer Science Engineering and Emerging Technologies* (pp. 187–191). . CRC Press. DOI: 10.1201/9781003405580-30

Butler, M. J. R (2008). . Neuromarketing and the perception of knowledge. *Journal of Consumer Behaviour*, *7* (4–5)., 415–419. DOI: 10.1002/cb.260

Kate, N., Padhye, P., & Mishra, A. B (2022). . Studies on Anti-Virus Software Tools: Strong Weapon to Protect Systems. *2022 2nd International Conference on Innovative Practices in Technology and Management (ICIPTM).*, 49–52. DOI: 10.1109/ICIPTM54933.2022.9753877

Lee, N., Broderick, A. J., & Chamberlain, L (2007). . What is 'neuromarketing'? A discussion and agenda for future research. *International Journal of Psychophysiology*, *63* (2)., 199–204. DOI: 10.1016/j.ijpsycho.2006.03.007 PMID: 16769143

Manoharan, G., Mishra, A. B., Adusumilli, S. B. K., Chavva, M., Damancharla, H., & Sahaya Lenin, D (2024). . Supervised Learning for Personalized Marketing Strategies. *2024 International Conference on Advances in Computing, Communication and Applied Informatics (ACCAI).* , 1–6. DOI: 10.1109/ACCAI61061.2024.10602307

Mehta, P., Singla, H., Saha, R., & Tyagi, S (2021). . A pathway to technology integration: Eliciting consumer's behavioural intention to use paytm services. *Paradigm*, *25* (1)., 7–24.

Mishra, A (2025a). . Kalyan Jewellers: A Case Study on Brand Perception and Disruptive Innovation in the Jewellery Market. *IGI Global Scientific Publishing*, 261–284. https://doi.org/DOI: 10.4018/979-8-3693-9783-1.ch010

Mishra, A (2025b). . Monitoring the Development of the IoT Concept in Various Application Domains. *Taylor & Francis Online, CRC Press*. https://www.taylorfrancis.com/chapters/edit/10.1201/9781003596721-41/monitoring-development-iot-concept-various-application-domains-mishra-sarita-rani-panda-anitha-uma-reddy-gaurav-sethi-purnendu-bikash-acharjee

Mishra, A. B (2020). . E- PAYMENT SYSTEM: A RISING TREND OF ECONOMY. *New Paradigm in Business and Education.* https://www.researchgate.net/profile/Anitha-K-2/publication/349605501_E-LEARNING_THROUGH_GAMIFICATION-_AN_ITINERARY_TO_GAIN_IN-DEPTH_KNOWLEDGE/links/6037d566299bf1cc26ef9597/E-LEARNING-THROUGH-GAMIFICATION-AN-ITINERARY-TO-GAIN-IN-DEPTH-KNOWLEDGE.pdf#page=10

Mishra, A. B., Anil, V., & Nitin, R (2021). . Putsch buyer tendency and climbing sales of mobile trade business. *Manager–The British Journal of Administrative Management, 58* (152)., 54–60.

Mishra, A. B (2022). . SAHYADRI FARMS: INDIA'S LARGEST FARMER PRODUCER COMPANY. *International Journal of Advance and Applied Research, 10,* 996–998. https://ijaar.co.in/wp-content/uploads/2022/11/1001175.pdf

Mishra, A. B (2025a). . Kalyan Jeweller's Case Study of Transformation, Consumer Engagement, and Effective Marketing Strategies for Brand Building. In *Dynamic Strategies for Entrepreneurial Marketing* (pp. 287–310). . DOI: 10.4018/979-8-3693-3936-7.ch014

Mishra, A. B (2025b). . The Paytm Puzzle: Navigating Regulatory Compliance in India's Digital Revolution. In *Cultural Sensitivity, Cross-Border Logistics, and E-Commerce in Global Marketing* (pp. 337–348). . IGI Global. DOI: 10.4018/979-8-3373-0528-8.ch015

Mishra, A. B., Allen, M., & Tirkey, P (2024). . *Disruption causes to Micromax by once a Market leader now a Myth.* https://www.iimspune.edu.in/images/pdf/Journal/Vol3I1-Paper11.pdf

Mishra, A. B., Chand, K., & Kaith, K (2022). . Influencer Marketing as Emerging Promotional Tool in Modern Era and Opportunities to Uprising Sales. *International Journal of Emerging Research in Engineering, Science, and Management, 1* (3). . Advance online publication. DOI: 10.58482/ijeresm.v1i3.3

Mishra, A. B., & Dodke, S. D (2024). . ZARA : Technological Influence on Becoming the Fashion Industry's Market Leader. In *Cases on AI Ethics in Business* (pp. 204–215). . IGI Publishing., DOI: 10.4018/979-8-3693-2643-5.ch012

Mishra, A. B., & Gaikwad, V (2024). . The Transaction War Between Google Pay and Phonepe. In *IGI Global* (pp. 166–185). . DOI: 10.4018/978-1-6684-7840-0.ch009

Mishra, A. B., Goel, A., & Jajoo, P (2022). . A Case Study of Amul: Implementation of Extension Strategy to Repositioning Brand During Covid-19 Period. *International Journal of Emerging Research in Engineering, Science, and Management, 1* (4). . Advance online publication. DOI: 10.58482/ijeresm.v1i4.3

Mishra, A. B., & Karjodkar, R (2022). . A Case Study of Air India - Maharajah Back to Home. *International Journal of Emerging Research in Engineering, Science, and Management, 1* (3). . Advance online publication. DOI: 10.58482/ijeresm.v1i3.5

Mishra, A. B., Raikwar, A., & Tiwari, A (2024). . *Britannia: Marketing Initiatives Boost A Fledgling Business's Transformation To One Of The Largest FMCG Brands.* https://www.iimspune.edu.in/images/pdf/Journal/Vol3I1-Paper12.pdf

Mishra, A. B., Rajagopal, N. K., Yousoof, M., & Padhye, P (2021). . A STUDY ON ORGANISATIONAL PRACTICES THAT INFLUENCE EMPLOYEE ENGAGEMENT. *Manager –. British Journal of Administrative Management, 57* (145)., 220–225.

Mishra, A. B., & Ranjan, N (2022). . INTERNET OF THINGS BASED EMERGING SMART TOOLS FOR NEW EDGE EDUCATION. *Mukt Shabd Journal, 11* (10)., 80–87. DOI: 10.0014.MSJ.2022.V11I10.0086781.1135708

Mishra, A. B., Ranjan, N., Sharma, K. M., Padhye, P., & Chand, K (2023). . Advancement of Digital Transformation to Boost Financial Services Industry. *Journal of Informatics Education and Research, 3* (2)., 2435–2440. https://scholar.google.com/scholar?cluster=15410723285942667834&hl=en&oi=scholarr

Mishra, A. B., Sahu, T., Ranjan, N., & Varma, A (2021). . Green Marketing Practices Prevailing In Hotel Industry. *Journal of Contemporary Issues in Business and Government, 27* (02). . Advance online publication. DOI: 10.47750/cibg.2021.27.02.145

Mishra, A. B., Satarkar, M., & Joshi, S (2023). . IKEA - Phygital Transformation in Furniture Manufacturing Industry. *International Journal of Emerging Research in Engineering, Science, and Management, 2* (3)., 6–9. DOI: 10.58482/ijeresm.v2i3.2

Mishra, A. B., Satarkar, M., & Joshi, S (2024). . Capitalizing the Retail Industry by Automation and Artificial Intelligence (AI).: Case Study of IKEA. In *IGI Global* (pp. 239–251). . DOI: 10.4018/979-8-3693-2643-5.ch014

Mishra, A. B., & Singh, A (2023). . Brand Positioning in the Indian Smartphone Market: A Case Study of OnePlus. *International Journal of Emerging Research in Engineering, Science, and Management, 2* (3). . Advance online publication. DOI: 10.58482/ijeresm.v2i3.1

Mishra, A. B., & Singh, A (2024a). . The Mumbai Dabbawalas : An Efficient and Sustainable Lunchbox Delivery System. In *IGI Global* (pp. 154–160). . DOI: 10.4018/979-8-3693-1544-6.ch007

Mishra, A. B., & Singh, R (2024b). . Phygital Transformation of Nilon's: The Brand Building in Ready-to-eat Segment. *International Journal of Emerging Research in Engineering, Science, and Management, 3* (2). . Advance online publication. DOI: 10.58482/ijeresm.v3i2.3

Mishra, A. B., & Singh, R (2024c). . Phygital Transformation of Nilon's: The Brand Building in Ready-to-eat Segment. *International Journal of Emerging Research in Engineering, Science, and Management, 3* (2). . Advance online publication. DOI: 10.58482/ijeresm.v3i2.3

Mohseni, M., Othman, B. A., Raturi, P., Mishra, A. B., Priya, S. J., & Saravanan, V (2022). . The Role of Parallel Computing Towards Implementation of Enhanced and Effective Industrial Internet of Things (IOT). Through Manova Approach. *2022 2nd International Conference on Advance Computing and Innovative Technologies in Engineering (ICACITE).*, 160–164. DOI: 10.1109/ICACITE53722.2022.9823698

Rana, M. S., Cavaliere, L. P. L., Mishra, A. B., Padhye, P., Singh, R. R., & Khanna, R (2022, April). . Internet of Things (IOT). Based Assessment for Effective Monitoring Data Against Malicious Attacks on Financial Collectors. In 2022 2nd International Conference on Advance Computing and Innovative Technologies in Engineering (ICACITE). (pp. 177-181). . IEEE.

Ranjan, N., Mishra, A. B., & Padhye, P (2023). . Dynamics of Digital Payments Enable the World's Safest Way to Pay. *Journal of Informatics Education and Research, 3* (2). . Advance online publication. DOI: 10.52783/jier.v3i2.406

Rao, M. S (2016). . Tools and techniques to ensure innovative management education in India. *Industrial and Commercial Training, 48* (5)., 265–268. DOI: 10.1108/ICT-10-2015-0071

Saarijärvi, H., Karjaluoto, H., & Kuusela, H (2013). . Extending customer relationship management: From empowering firms to empowering customers. *Journal of Systems and Information Technology, 15* (2)., 140–158. DOI: 10.1108/13287261311328877

Sunny, J., Undralla, N., & Madhusudanan Pillai, V (2020). . Supply chain transparency through blockchain-based traceability: An overview with demonstration. *Computers & Industrial Engineering, 150*, 106895. DOI: 10.1016/j.cie.2020.106895

Usman, M. S., Sheoliha, N., Prabhakar, P. V., Mishra, A. B., & Dondapati, A (2023). . Leading Strategies for Organizational Adaptation and Growth in Digital Transformation in Marketing. Journal of Informatics Education and Research.

Varma, S. R., & Mishra, A. B (2013). . *Distribution Channels of Indian Insurance Business - A Study*. Abhinavan.

Varma, S. R., & Mishra, A. B (2015). . Study of Consumer Buying Behaviour in General Insurance Industry. In *Excellence through creativity, Research, innovation in field of IT and Management*.

Vendrell-Herrero, F., Bustinza, O. F., & Opazo-Basaez, M (2021). . Information technologies and product-service innovation: The moderating role of service R&D team structure. *Journal of Business Research*, *128*, 673–687. DOI: 10.1016/j.jbusres.2020.01.047

# Chapter 9
# Nykaa's Strategy for Engaging Generation Z:
## Driving Growth Through Innovation, Omnichannel, Influencer Marketing, and Customer Focus

**A. B. Mishra**
https://orcid.org/0000-0003-4429-4058
*International Institute of Management Studies, Pune, India*

**Prashant Kumar Darshi**
https://orcid.org/0009-0001-0730-3536
*International Institute of Management Studies, Pune, India*

## ABSTRACT

*Nykaa has successfully established itself as leading beauty and lifestyle retailer by adopting innovative strategies tailored to Generation Z by its digital nativity and demand for authenticity. The company's hybrid inventory model ensures a wide selection of authentic and trending products while leveraging data analytics for personalized experiences. Nykaa's omnichannel strategy integrates seamless online and offline shopping, offering accessibility and convenience. Through influencer marketing, the brand engages Gen Z with relatable, authentic campaigns and a strong social media presence. Additionally, its customer-centric approach, including community engagement and a focus on sustainability, aligns with Gen Z's values and preferences. This combination of innovation, technology, and customer focus has driven Nykaa's growth and solidified its appeal among young, discerning consumers. This case study examines how Nykaa increased customer satisfaction,*

DOI: 10.4018/978-1-6684-9872-9.ch009

*enhanced operational efficiency, and saw notable growth by utilising a unique combination of inventory models.*

## INTRODUCTION

Falguni Nayar founded Nykaa, an Indian e-commerce company, in 2012. The platform offers a diverse range of products across fashion, wellness, and beauty categories, featuring an extensive selection from both international and Indian brands, including skincare, haircare, fragrances, and c Nykaa operates both online and through physical stores across India.(A. B. Mishra & Dodke, 2024) As a leading player in the Indian beauty and fashion industry, Nykaa is known for its broad product assortment, exclusive brand collaborations, and strong online presence. It enhances the shopping experience by providing tutorials, virtual makeover tools, and beauty advice. The company's success has led to its listing on Indian stock exchanges.(A. B. Mishra, 2020) Nykaa's success is attributed to its extensive product range, strategic business model, and commitment to customer satisfaction.(Rao, 2016) With its focus on quality, innovation, and customer engagement, Nykaa has firmly established itself as a significant force in the Indian beauty and fashion market. A strategic inventory model distinguishes itself by putting the interests of the client first and leveraging technology integration to boost operational effectiveness.(Chillakuri, 2020) Scalability and sustainability are highly valued in this strategy, which enables the business to grow and change while maintaining a competitive edge.(A. B. Mishra & Singh, 2024) By focusing on a customer-centric strategy, businesses can improve overall performance, optimise inventories, and better serve demand. Through process optimisation, waste reduction, and improved flexibility in response to market changes, technology integration ultimately provides a significant competitive edge and fosters long-term expansion. We examine the tactical choices and creative approaches that have contributed to Nykaa's success in this case study. Analysing the impact of their inventory strategy shows how Nykaa has become a market leader by navigating the complexities of the e-commerce sector. This inquiry provides valuable perspectives for other online retailers seeking to enhance inventory control and spur growth.

## PROBLEM STATEMENT

Generation Z, a digitally native and value-driven demographic, demands convenience, authenticity, and personalization from brands. Capturing their attention and loyalty requires innovative approaches that resonate with their unique preferences, including sustainable practices, social media engagement, and seamless shopping experiences. Nykaa has had tremendous development and popularity in the e-commerce industry, but the company still has difficulties refining its novel inventory model to maximise supply chain interruptions, guarantee effective stock management, and preserve a flawless client experience. Nykaa has experienced tremendous development and popularity in the e-commerce industry, but the company still has difficulties refining its novel inventory model to guarantee effective stock management, reduce supply chain interruptions, and preserve a flawless client experience. To improve operational effectiveness and customer satisfaction, efficiency of Nykaa's inventory tactics points out following gaps:

- Product Transparency and Authenticity: Ensuring that every product on the platform is transparently labelled with all relevant information, including ingredients, usage instructions, and expiration dates, and is authentic. Negative evaluations and client mistrust might result from a lack of transparency. (A. B. Mishra & Gaikwad, 2024)
- Customer Preference Data: It is challenging to precisely record and examine customer trends and preferences. Poor inventory decisions, such as stocking unpopular products or passing on high-demand commodities, might result from inadequate insights.
- Personalised suggestions: Improper or insufficient consumer data makes it difficult to provide individualised product suggestions. This may have an impact on client satisfaction and lower the possibility of repeat business.
- Product Reviews and Ratings: Ensuring the authenticity and usefulness of product reviews and ratings for customers by maintaining their integrity. False or deceptive reviews have the potential to erode customer confidence and have a detrimental impact on purchase decisions.
- Real-time inventory updates: It is important to prevent situations when customers order products that are out of stock, which could result in unhappy customers and a decline in sales.
- Comprehensive Product Comparisons: presenting precise and thorough comparisons between related products to assist customers in making wise selections. When comparisons are opaque, it might cause misunderstandings and inefficient purchases.

## LITERATURE REVIEW

The Indian beauty market has witnessed significant growth in recent years, driven by factors like rising disposable income, increasing internet penetration, and a growing awareness of personal care products. This review explores how Nykaa, a leading Indian e-commerce platform for beauty products, has revolutionized the industry with its innovative inventory model.(A. Mishra, 2025b)

Studies by Ustymenko, R (2023) and Anderson J, Smith B (2024) explore the growth trajectory of the Indian beauty market, highlighting the increasing consumer demand for beauty products and the shift towards online purchasing.(Anderson & Smith, 2024)

Reports from industry analysts like Dingliwal, U., & Gupta delve into the e-commerce landscape of the Indian beauty sector, analysing the dominance of marketplaces and the emergence of specialized beauty platforms like Nykaa.(Dingliwal & Gupta, n.d.)

Academic research by Pai, R. (2021) or case studies should be examined to understand Nykaa's unique business model, particularly its approach to inventory management.(Pai, 2021)

Industry publications and news articles can provide insights into Nykaa's specific inventory strategies, such as vendor-managed inventory (VMI) or marketplace elements, and how they differ from traditional e-commerce models digitally revolutionised.(A. B. Mishra, 2025b) Research by Urdea, A. M., & Constantin, C. P. (2021) and other industry reports can shed light on how Nykaa's inventory model has impacted the overall e-commerce experience for beauty products in India.(Urdea & Constantin, 2021)

Studies focusing on customer satisfaction and purchase behaviour Sukendia, J., & Harianto, N. (2021). can reveal how Nykaa's approach influences factors like product availability, delivery speed, and overall customer satisfaction.(Sukendia & Harianto, 2021)

*Table 1. Timeline of Nykaa*

| | |
|---|---|
| **2012** | **Falguni Nayar launched Nykaa, India's first online beauty retailer, offering a curated selection of brands and products.** |
| **2014** | Nykaa secures its first round of funding, enabling them to expand their product range and brand partnerships. |
| **2015** | Nykaa launched its mobile app, providing a convenient shopping experience for customers and contributing to the rise of m-commerce in India. |
| **2017** | Recognized the importance of physical retail, Nykaa opens its first brick-and-mortar stores, offering a seamless omnichannel experience. |

continued on following page

*Table 1. Continued*

| | |
|---|---|
| **2018** | Nykaa raised significant funding, solidifying its position as a leader in the Indian beauty e-commerce market. |
| **2019** | Nykaa launched its own private label brand, "Kay Beauty," catering to a wider audience and offering competitive pricing. |
| **2020** | Nykaa's valuation surpassed $1 billion, marking its entry into the coveted unicorn club. |
| **2021** | Nykaa acquired leading beauty retailer Livija and cosmetic brand Naturals, further strengthening its market presence. |
| **2022** | Nykaa goes public with a successful initial public offering (IPO), becoming the first Indian unicorn startup led by a female founder to do so. |
| **2023 – Current** | Nykaa strived for continuous innovation in its product offerings, technology, and customer service to maintain its dominant position in the Indian beauty e-commerce landscape. |

Source: Accumulated Data

## CASE STUDY ANALYSIS

Nykaa's journey from a pioneering online beauty retailer to a dominant e-commerce leader in India is a testament to its innovative approach. This case study analysis examines Nykaa's unique inventory model and its impact on revolutionizing the beauty e-commerce landscape in India.

## INNOVATIVE INVENTORY MODEL:

- Curated Product Offerings: Nykaa ensures a wide range of products, catering to Gen Z's preference for variety and trending items. They emphasize both global brands and local, sustainable options that align with Gen Z's values. (Seyfi et al., 2024)
- Omnichannel Experience: Nykaa's strategic expansion into offline retail with physical stores creates a seamless omnichannel experience. Customers can browse online and purchase in-store, or vice versa, increasing convenience and brand touchpoints.(Vrontis et al., 2021)
- Hybrid Inventory Model: Nykaa uses a mix of inventory-led and marketplace models. The inventory-led approach ensures product authenticity—a key concern for Gen Z—while the marketplace model expands the range of choices.(A. B. Mishra & Singh Ritika, 2024)
- Improved Customer Satisfaction: By focusing on product availability and a smooth buying experience, Nykaa potentially achieves higher customer satisfaction compared to traditional e-commerce models with wider variations in product availability.

- Personalization: Leveraging data analytics, Nykaa tailors product recommendations, offering a personalized shopping experience that resonates with Gen Z's expectations for customization.

## IMPACT ON E-COMMERCE AND CUSTOMER EXPERIENCE:

- Enhanced Trust and Reliability: Nykaa's control over a curated inventory might lead to increased customer trust and confidence in product authenticity and timely delivery compared to models relying solely on marketplace sellers.(Vendrell-Herrero et al., 2021)
- Streamlined Logistics and Delivery: The inventory model potentially allows Nykaa to optimize logistics and delivery processes, leading to faster fulfilment times and potentially lower costs compared to relying solely on seller-managed fulfilment.(Ahamad, Mishra, Raghuram, Tiwari, et al., 2024)
- Personalized Customer Engagement: By having access to customer data and purchase history through its platform, Nykaa can potentially personalize product recommendations and promotions, enhancing customer engagement and loyalty.(A. B. Mishra, Chand, et al., 2022)

## CHALLENGES AND CONSIDERATIONS:

- Inventory Management Complexity: Maintaining a curated inventory across a wide range of brands and products requires sophisticated inventory management systems and strong supplier relationships.
- Higher Investment Costs: Compared to pure marketplace models, Nykaa's inventory-based approach likely requires higher upfront investment in warehousing, logistics, and managing stock levels.
- Adaptability to Evolving Trends: The fast-paced nature of the beauty industry demands constant adaptation to new trends. Nykaa needs a flexible inventory model to ensure they can quickly respond to changing consumer preferences.

Nykaa's innovative inventory model has been instrumental in its success, revolutionizing the e-commerce experience for beauty products in India.(A. Mishra, 2025a) It has fostered customer trust, convenience, and a curated selection. However, maintaining this model requires continuous innovation and adaptation to address challenges like managing a complex inventory and adapting to evolving industry trends.(Mishra A. B. & Jaiswal Monika, 2024) As Nykaa continues to grow, its ability to leverage its strengths and overcome these challenges will be crucial to sustaining its leadership position in the dynamic Indian beauty e-commerce market.

## MARKETING STRATEGY

Nykaa's success in the Indian beauty e-commerce market can be attributed to its well-defined marketing strategy that focuses on the following key elements:

- **Product Curation and Innovation:** Nykaa offers a curated selection of beauty brands and products catering to diverse customer needs and preferences.(Li, 2024) They go beyond just established names and actively promote upcoming and niche brands, keeping their product offering fresh and exciting. Additionally, Nykaa's private label brand, "Kay Beauty," allows them to cater to a wider audience with competitive pricing and trend-driven products. (Varma & Mishra, 2013)
- **Content Marketing and Education:** Nykaa understands the importance of educating Indian consumers about beauty products and their usage. They utilize various content marketing channels like their YouTube channel, "Nykaa TV," blog, and social media platforms to offer beauty tutorials, product reviews, expert advice, and industry trends. This approach builds trust and positions Nykaa as a beauty authority, influencing customer purchasing decisions.(Manoharan et al., 2024)(Chand, 2022)
- **Omnichannel Experience:** Recognizing the value of a seamless shopping experience, Nykaa has strategically expanded into offline retail with physical stores.(Dodke, 2024) This allows customers to browse online and purchase in-store, or vice versa.(A. B. Mishra, Allen, et al., 2024) Additionally, their mobile app offers a convenient and user-friendly platform for on-the-go shopping.
- **Influencer Marketing and Community Building:** Nykaa leverages influencer marketing effectively, partnering with beauty bloggers, celebrities, and social media personalities relevant to their target audience. (Mishra, Chand, et al., 2022)This strategy helps them reach a wider audience, generate brand awareness, and build trust through endorsements from trusted voices.(A. B. Mishra, Raikwar, et al., 2024) Nykaa also fosters a strong online community through its social media platforms, encouraging customer interaction, feedback, and user-generated content.(Henderson et al., 1998)
- **Data-Driven Personalization:** Nykaa utilizes customer data and purchase history to personalize product recommendations, promotions, and marketing messages. This targeted approach enhances customer engagement and loyalty by catering to individual preferences and needs.(A. B. Mishra, Ranjan, et al., 2023)
- **Focus on Customer Experience:** Nykaa prioritizes customer satisfaction throughout the shopping journey. (A. B. Mishra, Satarkar, et al., 2023)They

offer efficient delivery options, a user-friendly website and app interface, and a hassle-free return policy. Additionally, their customer service is responsive and helpful, further strengthening customer loyalty.(Bharwani & Mathews, 2023)

- **Influencer Marketing:** Engaging Content Creators: Nykaa collaborates with influencers who resonate with Gen Z audiences, including beauty vloggers, Instagram creators.
- Authentic Campaigns: Influencer-led campaigns focus on relatable, authentic narratives rather than overtly commercial promotions, building trust and relatability among Gen Z.(Tolety, 2018)
- Social Media Presence: By maintaining a strong presence on platforms like Instagram, YouTube, and emerging social channels, Nykaa remains culturally relevant and reaches Gen Z in their preferred spaces.

## Additional Initiatives

Beyond its core marketing strategy, Nykaa implements various initiatives to solidify its position as a leader in the Indian beauty e-commerce landscape:

- **Technology and Innovation:** Nykaa actively invests in technological advancements to improve user experience and operational efficiency. This includes features like AI-powered product recommendations, virtual try-on tools utilizing augmented reality, and implementing efficient logistics and warehousing solutions.(Sethi Inder Pal Singh, 2024)
- **Sustainability Efforts:** Recognizing the growing consumer focus on sustainability, Nykaa is taking steps to minimize its environmental impact. This might include partnering with eco-conscious brands, offering sustainable packaging options, and promoting reusable beauty products.(A. B. Mishra, Goel, et al., 2022)
- **Expansion and Regionalization:** Nykaa is continuously expanding its reach by entering new Indian cities and catering to regional beauty preferences. This can involve offering local and regional beauty brands alongside their wider selection.
- **Strategic Partnerships:** Nykaa forms strategic partnerships with beauty brands and service providers to offer customers a wider range of services and benefits. This could include collaborations with salons for in-store consultations or exclusive product launches with popular brands.(Ranjan et al., 2023)
- **Loyalty Programs:** Nykaa's loyalty program rewards frequent shoppers with benefits like points, discounts, and early access to sales. This incentivizes repeat purchases and strengthens customer relationships.(Mohseni et al., 2022)

By combining its core marketing strategy with these additional initiatives, Nykaa positions itself not only as a beauty retailer but also as a trusted advisor and beauty destination for its customers. This comprehensive approach is key to maintaining its competitive edge and leading the e-commerce beauty market in India.

## SYNTHESIS AND INTERPRETATION

Nykaa's innovative approach to e-commerce in the beauty industry has yielded significant results, transformed the landscape and established them as a dominant player:

- **Revolutionizing Beauty E-commerce:** Nykaa's curated inventory model, emphasis on content creation, and omnichannel experience have set a new standard for beauty e-commerce in India. Their model provides a reliable platform for established and emerging brands, caters to diverse customer needs, and offers a seamless shopping experience.(Kate et al., 2022)
- **Shifting Consumer Behaviour:** Nykaa's educational content marketing and influencer partnerships have empowered Indian consumers and influenced their purchasing decisions. (Ahamad, Mishra, Raghuram, Tiwari, et al., 2024) This has fostered a more informed and engaged beauty consumer base in the Indian market.(Varma & Mishra, 2015)
- **Building Brand Loyalty:** Nykaa's focus on personalization, customer service, and a hassle-free shopping experience has resulted in high customer satisfaction and brand loyalty. Their loyalty programs further incentivize repeat purchases and strengthen customer relationships.(A. B. Mishra & Singh, 2023)
- **Redefining Beauty Retail:** Nykaa's successful integration of online and offline retail (omnichannel experience) has redefined beauty retail in India. This allows customers flexibility and convenience, catering to their preferred shopping styles.(Ahamad, Mishra, Raghuram, Riyazuddin, et al., 2024)

### Customer-Centric Focus

- **Community Engagement:** Nykaa has built a community through platforms like Nykaa Network, where users can seek advice, share reviews, and interact with experts.
- **Feedback-Driven Innovation:** The company actively gathers and implements customer feedback to adapt to evolving trends and preferences, staying aligned with Gen Z's dynamic tastes.

- **Sustainability and Ethics:** Gen Z prioritizes brands that align with their values. Nykaa's initiatives to promote eco-friendly packaging and cruelty-free products enhance its appeal to socially-conscious shoppers.

Nykaa's success story demonstrates the power of innovation and a customer-centric approach in the dynamic e-commerce landscape. Their ability to anticipate and adapt to consumer preferences, coupled with strategic partnerships and technological advancements, has positioned them as a leader in the Indian beauty market. This case study highlights the potential for e-commerce platforms to revolutionize established industries by focusing on curated product offerings, personalized experiences, and building a strong brand identity.

## RECOMMENDATIONS AND CONCLUSION

Nykaa's multifaceted approach to capturing Generation Z's loyalty combines technology, personalization, and authenticity. By focusing on innovative inventory management, an omnichannel presence, influencer-driven marketing, and customer-centric strategies, Nykaa has positioned itself as a brand that understands and caters to the unique needs and aspirations of this demographic. It has successfully positioned itself as a go-to platform for beauty and lifestyle products in India, with a reputation for innovation and authenticity.(Singh, 2023) High engagement rates and repeat purchases indicate Nykaa's ability to build lasting relationships with Gen Z consumers turned up to brand loyalty.(A. B. Mishra, 2025a) Nykaa's innovative approach and customer-centric focus have propelled them to the forefront of the Indian beauty e-commerce market. (Jaiswal Monika, 2024)However, to maintain its leadership position and navigate the evolving landscape, Nykaa can consider the following recommendations:

- **Continued Innovation:** Nykaa should continuously invest in technological advancements like AI-powered product recommendations, personalized beauty consultations using AR/VR, and efficient logistics optimization for faster deliveries.(Mishra A., et al., 2024)
- **Sustainability Initiatives:** Expanding eco-conscious product offerings, promoting sustainable packaging solutions, and implementing recycling programs can strengthen Nykaa's commitment to environmental responsibility and resonate with sustainability-focused consumers.
- **Regionalization and Personalization:** Nykaa can cater to diverse regional preferences by offering local and regional beauty brands alongside its wider selection. Additionally, leveraging customer data to personalize product

recommendations and marketing messages can further enhance customer engagement.(Rana et al., 2022)

- **Strategic Expansion:** Exploring opportunities for international expansion to cater to the growing global Indian diaspora, while maintaining a strong presence within India, can contribute to Nykaa's long-term growth strategy. (A. Mishra, Goel, et al., 2022)
- **Content Diversification:** Nykaa can expand its content marketing strategy beyond traditional beauty tutorials.(Ranjan, 2023) Partnering with beauty experts and influencers for in-depth product reviews, ingredient analyses, and trend forecasts can offer even greater value to customers.

Nykaa's success story underscores the importance of a curated product selection, customer-centric service, and a seamless shopping experience in the e-commerce landscape.(Raikwar, 2024) By embracing continuous innovation, prioritizing sustainability, and catering to diverse customer needs, Nykaa is well-positioned to maintain its dominant position in the Indian beauty e-commerce market and potentially lead the way for future innovation in the broader e-commerce ecosystem.(Mishra,A 2020) As Nykaa continues to adapt and evolve, its dedication to providing a superior customer experience and fostering a trusted beauty destination will remain central to its continued success.

## REFERENCES


Ahamad, S., Mishra, A. B., Raghuram, K. S., Riyazuddin, Y. M., & Alanya-Beltran, J. (2024). *Applications of Internet of Things (IoT) in Maintaining Privacy and Security of Smart Cities*. Taylor & Francis Journal., DOI: 10.1201/9781003405580-30

Ahamad, S., Mishra, A. B., Raghuram, K. S., Tiwari, M., & Riyazuddin, Y. Md., & Alanya-Beltran, J. (2024). Applications of Internet of Things (IoT) in Maintaining Privacy and Security of Smart Cities. In *Computer Science Engineering and Emerging Technologies* (pp. 187–191). CRC Press. DOI: 10.1201/9781003405580-30

Anderson, J., & Smith, B. (2024). *The Immersive Frontier: Unraveling the Potential of AR Commerce in E-commerce Evolution*. EasyChair.

Bharwani, S., & Mathews, D. (2023). Sustainable luxury: From an oxymoron to a tautology – the case of the Indian luxury hospitality industry. *Worldwide Hospitality and Tourism Themes*, *15*(3), 231–248. DOI: 10.1108/WHATT-01-2023-0013

Chillakuri, B. (2020). Understanding Generation Z expectations for effective onboarding. *Journal of Organizational Change Management*, *33*(7), 1277–1296. DOI: 10.1108/JOCM-02-2020-0058

Dingliwal, U., & Gupta, D. (n.d.). *Redefining Retail: The Evolving Landscape of Retailing in a Tech-Driven eCommerce Era.*

Henderson, G. R., Iacobucci, D., & Calder, B. J. (1998). Brand diagnostics: Mapping branding effects using consumer associative networks. *European Journal of Operational Research*, *111*(2), 306–327. DOI: 10.1016/S0377-2217(98)00151-9

Kate, N., Padhye, P., & Mishra, A. B. (2022). Studies on Anti-Virus Software Tools: Strong Weapon to Protect Systems. *2022 2nd International Conference on Innovative Practices in Technology and Management (ICIPTM)*, 49–52. DOI: 10.1109/ICIPTM54933.2022.9753877

Li, K. J. (2024). Product and service innovation with customer recognition. *Decision Sciences*, *55*(1), 17–32. DOI: 10.1111/deci.12546

Manoharan, G., Mishra, A. B., Adusumilli, S. B. K., Chavva, M., Damancharla, H., & Sahaya Lenin, D. (2024). Supervised Learning for Personalized Marketing Strategies. *2024 International Conference on Advances in Computing, Communication and Applied Informatics (ACCAI)*, 1–6. DOI: 10.1109/ACCAI61061.2024.10602307

Mishra, A. (2025a). Kalyan Jewellers: A Case Study on Brand Perception and Disruptive Innovation in the Jewellery Market. *IGI Global Scientific Publishing*, 261–284. https://doi.org/DOI: 10.4018/979-8-3693-9783-1.ch010

Mishra, A. (2025b). Monitoring the Development of the IoT Concept in Various Application Domains. *Taylor & Francis Online, CRC Press*. https://www.taylorfrancis.com/chapters/edit/10.1201/9781003596721-41/monitoring-development-iot-concept-various-application-domains-mishra-sarita-rani-panda-anitha-uma-reddy-gaurav-sethi-purnendu-bikash-acharjee

Mishra, A. B. (2020). E- PAYMENT SYSTEM: A RISING TREND OF ECONOMY. *New Paradigm in Business and Education*. https://www.researchgate.net/profile/Anitha-K-2/publication/349605501_E-LEARNING_THROUGH_GAMIFICATION-_AN_ITINERARY_TO_GAIN_IN-DEPTH_KNOWLEDGE/links/6037d566299bf1cc26ef9597/E-LEARNING-THROUGH-GAMIFICATION-AN-ITINERARY-TO-GAIN-IN-DEPTH-KNOWLEDGE.pdf#page=10

Mishra, A. B., & Jaiswal Monika. (2024). Case Study of Kalyan Jewellers - Brand Perception Mapping Towards Disruptive Innovation in Jewellery Segment. *International Journal of Advance and Applied Research*, *11*(6), 386–396. DOI: 10.5281/zenodo.13902610

Mishra, A. B. (2025a). Kalyan Jeweller's Case Study of Transformation, Consumer Engagement, and Effective Marketing Strategies for Brand Building. In *Dynamic Strategies for Entrepreneurial Marketing* (pp. 287–310). DOI: 10.4018/979-8-3693-3936-7.ch014

Mishra, A. B. (2025b). The Paytm Puzzle: Navigating Regulatory Compliance in India's Digital Revolution. In *Cultural Sensitivity, Cross-Border Logistics, and E-Commerce in Global Marketing* (pp. 337–348). IGI Global. DOI: 10.4018/979-8-3373-0528-8.ch015

Mishra, A. B., Allen, M., & Tirkey, P. (2024). *Disruption causes to Micromax by once a Market leader now a Myth*. https://www.iimspune.edu.in/images/pdf/Journal/Vol3I1-Paper11.pdf

Mishra, A. B., Chand, K., & Kaith, K. (2022). Influencer Marketing as Emerging Promotional Tool in Modern Era and Opportunities to Uprising Sales. *International Journal of Emerging Research in Engineering, Science, and Management*, *1*(3). Advance online publication. DOI: 10.58482/ijeresm.v1i3.3

Mishra, A. B., & Dodke, S. D. (2024). ZARA : Technological Influence on Becoming the Fashion Industry's Market Leader. In *Cases on AI Ethics in Business* (pp. 204–215). IGI Publishing., DOI: 10.4018/979-8-3693-2643-5.ch012

Mishra, A. B., & Gaikwad, V. (2024). The Transaction War Between Google Pay and Phonepe. In *IGI Global* (pp. 166–185). DOI: 10.4018/978-1-6684-7840-0.ch009

Mishra, A. B., Goel, A., & Jajoo, P. (2022). A Case Study of Amul: Implementation of Extension Strategy to Repositioning Brand During Covid-19 Period. *International Journal of Emerging Research in Engineering, Science, and Management, 1*(4). Advance online publication. DOI: 10.58482/ijeresm.v1i4.3

Mishra, A. B., Raikwar, A., & Tiwari, A. (2024). *Britannia: Marketing Initiatives Boost A Fledgling Business's Transformation To One Of The Largest FMCG Brands.* https://www.iimspune.edu.in/images/pdf/Journal/Vol3I1-Paper12.pdf

Mishra, A. B., Ranjan, N., Sharma, K. M., Padhye, P., & Chand, K. (2023). Advancement of Digital Transformation to Boost Financial Services Industry. *Journal of Informatics Education and Research, 3*(2), 2435–2440. https://scholar.google.com/scholar?cluster=15410723285942667834&hl=en&oi=scholarr

Mishra, A. B., Satarkar, M., & Joshi, S. (2023). IKEA - Phygital Transformation in Furniture Manufacturing Industry. *International Journal of Emerging Research in Engineering, Science, and Management, 2*(3), 6–9. DOI: 10.58482/ijeresm.v2i3.2

Mishra, A. B., & Singh, A. (2023). Brand Positioning in the Indian Smartphone Market: A Case Study of OnePlus. *International Journal of Emerging Research in Engineering, Science, and Management, 2*(3). Advance online publication. DOI: 10.58482/ijeresm.v2i3.1

Mishra, A. B., & Singh, A. (2024). The Mumbai Dabbawalas : An Efficient and Sustainable Lunchbox Delivery System. In *IGI Global* (pp. 154–160). DOI: 10.4018/979-8-3693-1544-6.ch007

Mohseni, M., Othman, B. A., Raturi, P., Mishra, A. B., Priya, S. J., & Saravanan, V. (2022). The Role of Parallel Computing Towards Implementation of Enhanced and Effective Industrial Internet of Things (IOT) Through Manova Approach. *2022 2nd International Conference on Advance Computing and Innovative Technologies in Engineering (ICACITE)*, 160–164. DOI: 10.1109/ICACITE53722.2022.9823698

Pai, R. (2021). Nykaa: A comprehensive analysis of a leading Indian e-commerce cosmetic company. *International Journal of Case Studies in Business* [IJCSBE]. *IT and Education, 5*(2), 354–365.

Rana, M. S., Cavaliere, L. P. L., Mishra, A. B., Padhye, P., Singh, R. R., & Khanna, R. (2022, April). Internet of Things (IOT) Based Assessment for Effective Monitoring Data Against Malicious Attacks on Financial Collectors. In 2022 2nd International Conference on Advance Computing and Innovative Technologies in Engineering (ICACITE) (pp. 177-181). IEEE.

Ranjan, N., Mishra, A. B., & Padhye, P. (2023). Dynamics of Digital Payments Enable the World's Safest Way to Pay. *Journal of Informatics Education and Research, 3*(2). Advance online publication. DOI: 10.52783/jier.v3i2.406

Rao, M. S. (2016). Tools and techniques to ensure innovative management education in India. *Industrial and Commercial Training, 48*(5), 265–268. DOI: 10.1108/ICT-10-2015-0071

Sethi, I. P. S. (2023). *Digital Payments driving the growth of Digital Economy.* National Informatics Centre.

Seyfi, S., Vo-Thanh, T., & Zaman, M. (2024). Hospitality in the age of Gen Z: A critical reflection on evolving customer and workforce expectations. *International Journal of Contemporary Hospitality Management, 36*(13), 118–134. DOI: 10.1108/IJCHM-01-2024-0035

Sukendia, J., & Harianto, N. (2021). The impact of e-service quality on customer engagement, customer experience and customer loyalty in B2C e-commerce. [TURCOMAT]. *Turkish Journal of Computer and Mathematics Education, 12*(3), 3170–3184.

Tolety, R. K. (2018). E-Wallets–Their cause, Rise and Relevance. *International. Journal of Research in IT and Management, 8*(7).

Urdea, A. M., & Constantin, C. P. (2021). Exploring the impact of customer experience on customer loyalty in e-commerce. *InProceedings of the International Conference on Business Excellence, 15*(1), 672–682. DOI: 10.2478/picbe-2021-0063

Varma, S. R., & Mishra, A. B. (2013). *Distribution Channels of Indian Insurance Business - A Study.* Abhinavan.

Varma, S. R., & Mishra, A. B. (2015). Study of Consumer Buying Behaviour in General Insurance Industry. In *Excellence through creativity, Research, innovation in field of IT and Management.*

Vendrell-Herrero, F., Bustinza, O. F., & Opazo-Basaez, M. (2021). Information technologies and product-service innovation: The moderating role of service R&D team structure. *Journal of Business Research, 128*, 673–687. DOI: 10.1016/j.jbusres.2020.01.047

Vrontis, D., Makrides, A., Christofi, M., & Thrassou, A. (2021). Social media influencer marketing: A systematic review, integrative framework and future research agenda. *International Journal of Consumer Studies*, *45*(4), 617–644. DOI: 10.1111/ijcs.12647

# Chapter 10
# Green Finance Paradigm Shift in Financing Green Projects

**S. Sandhya Bhandary**
https://orcid.org/0000-0003-4429-4058
*Manjunatha Pai Memorial Government First Grade College, Karla, India*

**Anjali Ganesh**
*St. Joesph Engineering College, Mangalore, India*

**M. Dharmananda**
*Nitte Meenakshi Institute of Technology, Bengaluru, India*

## ABSTRACT

*Funding of green projects requires massive finance. The rising concerns on identifying and developing alternative sources of energy, sustaining the ecological balance through energy replenishment and protecting environment, reduction of green house gas formation and carbon emissions are superordinate goals. The policy makers across the globe are concerned about the rising global temperature and attempts are made at addressing carbon emissions by countries through the carbon credit mechanism. However, this is an arduous path as there is lack of awareness and knowledge amongst the public unaware of their contributions to gas emissions. This secondary research paper focuses on the crucial role of governments in monitoring and regulating the green finance sector. This chapter throws light on the various facets of government in channelizing and monitoring the funds under the green umbrella and additional measures to promote green financing.*

DOI: 10.4018/978-1-6684-9872-9.ch010

## 1. INTRODUCTION

Green House Gas (GHGs) formation and carbon emissions is a crucial concern towards environment sustainability. The declining natural and fossil fuel, increasing industrialization and economies of scale are some factors contributing to the green house formation. China, United States of America and India are major contributors to gas house formation nearing 50% of the globe's carbon emissions. (Mishra & Singh, 2024) The directives of Paris Agreement 2016, India has been constantly raising its Nationally Determined Contributions to 33-35% by 2030, with latest revision being made in 2022 to 45% reduction in the carbon emissions. India has set a goal net-zero emissions by 2070 and estimates an $1 trillion requirements in climate financing. The Government of India has allowed a 100% FDI indicating its keen concerns in addressing the climate change issues.

Some of the following targets are determined by India in the direction of maintaining the global temperature at 1.5 degrees and capping the carbon emissions from the industries:

- 450 GW of renewable energy installation by 2030, which requires an estimated $500billion investment
- Decentralized renewable energy like solar rooftops, battery enabled power are viable sources of clean energy. But the implementation of such energy alternatives across the country requires an estimated $18billion by 2024
- To create a provision for carbon absorption equivalent of 2.5 to 3 billion tonnes
- Drive the Electrical Vehicles Motor segment accompanied with incentives to produce original equipment and models under the Made-in-India initiatives.

Renewable sources of energy alternatives are discovered, but the projects lack appropriate financing. The viability of the projects, specified usage of funds and slow pace of commercialization of the green projects.

### 1.1 Green Financing

Financing of those projects which focus on environment sustainability, protecting the natural resources and developing of alternative energy supply chains fall under the horizon of green financing. An exclusive investment in energy preservation sector and energy efficacy will help India in achieving its targets.(Rana et al., 2022) Though there is no exclusive definition for green financing, the underlying principle for the constitution of 'green project' could broaden the purview of 'green finance'.

The Principles for a 'project' to be called as a 'Green Project' are

a. Boosts energy productivity in resource deployment
b. Diminishes carbon emissions and greenhouse gases
c. Promotes climate elasticity and/or adaptation
d. Values and improves natural ecosystems and biodiversity especially in accordance with SDG principles

Thus, it can be inferred that any money or capital invested in the projects on the above-mentioned principles could be referred to as Green Finance. Green bonds are introduced in India to drive in finances for the green projects. These bonds can be defined as financial instruments whose proceeds are employed for projects that are environment friendly. Banerjee, A. (2019). The distinguished feature of green bonds is the special purpose of financing climate projects. They have a longer maturity, strict adherence to laws and gain effortless support from the government. Zhu, Y., & Wu, Y. (2021). In the FY 2022-23, in adherence with the Green Bond Principles (2021) of the International Capital Markets Association, the regulations for the issuing of Green Bonds have been framed by SEBI. The four core components for issue of Green Bonds are:

- Use of proceeds – the money generated has to be invested in the specified purpose and cannot be diverted for other commercial businesses
- Project evaluation and selection – Green Finance Working Committee is established under the Chairmanship of Chief Economic Advisor of India and members from various commissions and boards. The Committee lays down the rules and criteria for the assessment and evaluation of permissible green expenditures.
- Management of Proceeds – The funds raised from the issuing of green bonds are deposited with Consolidated Funds of India which will redirect the funds on the basis of selection of projects. Public Management Debt Cell will maintain the trajectory of funds raised, issued and utilized.
- Reporting – The accountability for the funds utilized shall be reported to the Green Finance Working Committee. The CAG of India will audit the reports for the funds used under the green projects.

A total 20 institutions comprising of the private companies, government and quasi government bodies have issued bonds amassing Rs. 6,128 crores in green projects. (https://www.sebi.gov.in/statistics/greenbonds.html). The RBI has issued green bonds for Rs. 20,000 crores in 2022-23 to provide impetus to the green projects. (https://www.rbi.org.in/scripts/BS_PressReleaseDisplay.aspx?prid=55004)

## 1.2 Carbon Credits

Article 6 of Paris Agreement, provides for the establishment of Carbon Markets where carbon emissions from each country is converted to a tradable instrument endorsable by governments and business. It aims at reducing carbon emissions from the industries and can be voluntary or as a matter of compliance.(Mishra, Ranjan, et al., 2023) The carbon credit mechanism was first introduced in 1997 under the Kyoto Protocol. It was introduced as cap and trade mechanism which at present has obtained the shape of tradable instrument.

In India, carbon credits and the carbon market mechanism is governed by the Bureau of Energy Efficiency. The Central Government has amended the Energy Conservation Act 2022, thus establishing carbon credit trading system and market. The carbon credit market in India is monitored by 'National Steering Committee on Indian Carbon Market' is established under the Carbon Credit Trading System. The Bureau of Energy Efficiency is the administrator and the Grid Controller of India is the registry operator and maintains a register of the entities. The market is regulated by Central Electricity Regulation Commission. ("Mishra A. B." et al., 2024) In the Offset Mechanism, energy, industries, agriculture, waste handling and disposal, forestry and transport are included in Phase I and Fugitive emissions, Construction, solvent use and carbon capture and storage of CO2 will be included in the Phase II.

## 2. LITERATURE REVIEW

Maltais, A., & Nykvist, B. (2020) explain that green bonds are financial innovation designed to finance the green projects. They are issued on similar grounds of traditional bonds with specified purpose of financing the environment and climate sustaining projects. Li, X., Wang, S., Lu, X. and Guo, F. (2023) green financing has led to innovation in green technology and has resulted in substantive reduction in green-house gas emissions. The green bonds are hybrid of traditional bonds issued for a designated purpose of green funding. However, the green bonds yields lower returns in comparison with the regular bonds which discourage investment. Maltais, A., & Nykvist, B. (2020) Green bonds are potential instruments for sponsoring the clean energy projects. The different levels of technology such as blockchain technology, digital platforms, mobile and internet banking must be utilized in tapping the finances. Sreenu, N. (2024)Maltais, A., & Nykvist, B. (2020) discovered that returns from the green bonds are lower than the regular bonds which discourage investment. There is no significant financial advantage in investing in green bonds. Though securing funds was easier, there are no major drivers for green financing. The issuers also do not gain significantly by issuing green bonds. The incentives available to issuers are marginalised by the cost of capital. Kumar, P., Taneja, S., & Özen, E. (2024). In their empirical results discovered that there is no significant correlation between green bonds issuance and sustainable development which may be due to the mandatory accountability. There is no direct impact of green financing and market conditions, but there is a positive relation between the stakeholders of green financing and other parameters. As upheld by Sreenu, N. (2024), there is an ascending need to promote green bonds as the knowledge of green bonds and their bearing on the green projects are lesser known among the investors, significantly affecting the flow of funds.(Mishra, 2025) A study conducted in China registered the role of government in green bonds is crucial. Zhu, Y., & Wu, Y. (2021) recommended that the government has to ensure a sound financial track record for the issuers of the green bonds. Further, a unified standard issuance code must be developed and adopted. Third party authentication must be improved and a robust management of funds must be ensured. Li, X., Wang, S., Lu, X. and Guo, F. (2023) suggest that government must initiate green financing in the enterprises. A green financing examination institute has to be established for examining the green financing initiatives. In India, the Green Finance Working Committee is established to monitor the issuance of green bonds, evaluate select projects and assess. Arshad, A., Parveen, S., & Mir, F. N. (2024). Studies revealed that there is significant rise in carbon emissions due to rising urbanisations and foreign direct investment. Open trade supports green projects. Government support in funding policies will determine the reduction in carbon emissions and the success of the green projects.

Fintechs have gained widespread acceptance and mobilizing money from small households to ecological projects would be efficient and effective. Sreenu, N. (2024)

## 3. RESEARCH METHODOLOGY

The focal point of analytical paper is the issuance of green bonds in India. The study is exploratory research and emphases on various mechanisms of boosting the finance for the green projects deployed by the Government of India. The data has been referred from websites of RBI, SEBI, Bureau of Energy Efficiency, Government and other quasi government bodies. Observation method is applied to understand the green bonds issuance and funding mechanism.

## 4. DATA ANALYSIS

India issued the first Sovereign Green bonds in January 2023 in joint consultation with RBI amassing Rs. 20,000 crores in green and environment projects. (https://www.rbi.org.in/scripts/BS_PressReleaseDisplay). The green bonds are issued on bids, 32 investors were successful in buying five years bonds and 57 investors were able to harvest ten years bonds. This indicates the green bonds investment were limited only to institutional investors. Ali, N. M., Farkhanda. (2023, February 27). The various government and quasi-governmental bodies have raised about Rs. 6,128 crores. (https://www.sebi.gov.in/statistics/greenbonds.html) The investors are required to pay a premium for investing in the green bonds called as Greenium. The traders refused to pay such a premium indicating lack of will power to invest in green projects. (Kumari, A. (2024, June 1). NHAI dives into issuing green bonds and raising funds worth Rs. 1,000 crores for financing the eco-friendly initiatives including solar lighting, rainwater harvesting, and wildlife underpasses. (https://pib.gov.in/pib.gov.in)

## 5. RECOMMENDATIONS

India plans to channelize $1 trillion in the renewable energy projects in the next decade. As stated earlier in the section data analysis, the total investment in preceding four years (2020-23) constitutes roughly 30% of the requirement. $2.5 trillion are required to reverse the climate change by 2030.(Mishra, 2020) (Ahamad et al., 2024)This comprehensive funding from government and quasi government sectors will be short lived. The sustainable and renewable energy and infrastructure funds will be accomplished when there is constant cash inflow to the clean environment projects. (Manoharan et al., 2024). The green projects cannot sustain on funding from governments alone. Thus, the Government of India has to device alternative channels of finance.(Mishra, Satarkar, et al., 2023) This comprises of opening the investment in the green bonds to general public, reduction of greenium so that it attracts investors, provide tax incentives or reliefs for investment in green bonds. (Ranjan et al., 2023)These measures may assist in generating more finances by mobilising the savings from small households to the large environment sustainable projects. (Mishra & Singh, 2023) Digital advancements are widely accepted and the fintechs can be utilised in promoting easier and hassle-free investment. Technology plays a substantial role in channelizing funds to key green projects. (Mishra, Goel, et al., 2022)There is a direct impact in the growth of renewable energy infrastructure and investments through green bonds.(Mohammed Usman et al., 2023) There is positive correlation between the fintech and green bonds. There is a need to spread out the investor base from institutions to individuals, large business to small businesses.

## 6. DISCUSSIONS

Sustainable infrastructure and energy alternatives are the need of the hour and the most noble cause. However, such projects cannot run only on the fuel of ethics and obligations. From literature review and data analysis, it is observed that the government has limited down the investor bases to institutions only. (Mishra, Chand, et al., 2022) An in-depth analysis of the government regulations in the green bonds is required, as these are key projects funding the designated purpose, monitoring, reporting and management of funds poses a vital challenge. (Mohseni et al., 2022) Tax reforms and incentives, reducing the cost of issuing the bonds can boost the renewable energy projects. Environment sustainable projects will be well accepted when there are adequate measures to promote the green bonds.

## 7. CONCLUSION

The Government of India is ambitious of contributing to NDC's and meeting the set targets of reducing carbon emissions. This necessitates a continued flow of funds into the sustainable and renewable energy projects. The paper finds that there is no or little promotion of green bonds. There is a certain of discouragement to invest as the investors are required to pay a premium. This increases the cost of buying the bonds, which may lead to disruption of finances to the green projects. Green bonds offer no incentives for issuers or investors in terms of tax relief or rebates. The government must assess the possibilities in providing tax exemptions or benefits to the issuer and investor, thereby promoting green bonds as a lucrative investment option. There is also a need to widen the investor base by enhancing the circle beyond business houses and governments, to the retail investors which can help in tapping the savings from households. (Mishra et al., 2021) The framework of the study has been restricted to analyze the role of government in promoting the green bonds. The paper also identifies that green bonds are being issued on similar grounds of a traditional bonds but with a specific purpose. This requires enactment of a separate statute to govern the issue and monitoring of green bonds.

## REFERENCES


Ahamad, S., Mishra, A. B., Raghuram, K. S., Tiwari, M., & Riyazuddin, Y., & Alanya-Beltran, J. (2024). Applications of Internet of Things (IoT) in Maintaining Privacy and Security of Smart Cities. In *Computer Science Engineering and Emerging Technologies* (pp. 187–191). CRC Press. DOI: 10.1201/9781003405580-30

Ali, N. M. Farkhanda. (2023, February 27). *India raises $2bn in first Sovereign Green Bond issuances*. Structured Finance In Brief. https://www.structuredfinanceinbrief.com/2023/02/india-raises-2bn-in-first-sovereign-green-bond-issuances/

Arshad, A., Parveen, S., & Mir, F. N. (2024). The role of green bonds in reducing $CO_2$ emissions: A case of developing countries. *Journal of Economic and Administrative Sciences*. DOI: 10.1108/JEAS-09-2023-0242

Banerjee, A. (2019). Financing the climate change through green (Climate sustainable) bonds. *2019 Advances in Science and Engineering Technology International Conferences (ASET)*, 1–4. DOI: 10.1109/ICASET.2019.8714408

Bureau, A. N. (2024, December 10). *Future of sustainable finance: How green bonds can evolve*. https://news.abplive.com/business/future-of-sustainable-finance-how-green-bonds-can-evolve-1736797

*Carbon credits, how they work, and who buys them*. (n.d.). Investopedia. Retrieved December 12, 2024, from https://www.investopedia.com/terms/c/carbon_credit.asp

*Carbon market | bureau of energy efficiency, government of india, ministry of power*. (n.d.). Retrieved December 11, 2024, from https://beeindia.gov.in/en/programmes/carbon-market

*Climate finance*. (n.d.). Shakti Sustainable Energy Foundation. Retrieved December 16, 2024, from https://shaktifoundation.in/climate-finance/

Environment, U. N. (2023, October 31). *Carbon markets | unep—Un environment programme*. https://www.unep.org/topics/climate-action/climate-finance/carbon-markets

*Green indian financial system initiative*. (n.d.). Shakti Sustainable Energy Foundation. Retrieved December 10, 2024, from https://shaktifoundation.in/green-indian-financial-systems-initiative/ India|authorurl:https://www.ey.com/en_in/people/saunak-saha,

Kumar, P., Taneja, S., & Ozen, E. (2024). Exploring the influence of green bonds on sustainable development through low-carbon financing mobilization. *International Journal of Law and Management*. DOI: 10.1108/IJLMA-01-2024-0030

Kumar, S., & Kundalia, L. (2024). Green Bonds—Role and scope in India's financial and fiscal landscape. *Journal of Indian Institute of Banking & Finance*, 43–56.

Kumari, A. (2024, June 1). Reserve Bank of India cancels 10-year green bond auction for first time. *Business Standard.*

Li, X., Wang, S., Lu, X., & Guo, F. (2023). Quantity or quality? The effect of green finance on enterprise green technology innovation. *European Journal of Innovation Management.* Advance online publication. DOI: 10.1108/EJIM-03-2023-0208

Maltais, A., & Nykvist, B. (2020). Understanding the role of green bonds in advancing sustainability. *Journal of Sustainable Finance & Investment*, •••, 1–20. DOI: 10.1080/20430795.2020.1724864

Manoharan, G., Mishra, A. B., Adusumilli, S. B. K., Chavva, M., Damancharla, H., & Sahaya Lenin, D. (2024). Supervised Learning for Personalized Marketing Strategies. *2024 International Conference on Advances in Computing, Communication and Applied Informatics (ACCAI)*, 1–6. DOI: 10.1109/ACCAI61061.2024.10602307

Mishra, A. B. (2020). E- PAYMENT SYSTEM: A RISING TREND OF ECONOMY. *New Paradigm in Business and Education.* https://www.researchgate.net/profile/Anitha-K-2/publication/349605501_E-LEARNING_THROUGH_GAMIFICATION-_AN_ITINERARY_TO_GAIN_IN-DEPTH_KNOWLEDGE/links/6037d566299bf1cc26ef9597/E-LEARNING-THROUGH-GAMIFICATION-AN-ITINERARY-TO-GAIN-IN-DEPTH-KNOWLEDGE.pdf#page=10

Mishra, A. B. (2025). *Kalyan Jeweller's Case Study of Transformation.* Consumer Engagement, and Effective Marketing Strategies for Brand Building., DOI: 10.4018/979-8-3693-3936-7.ch014

Mishra, A. B., Chand, K., & Kaith, K. (2022). Influencer Marketing as Emerging Promotional Tool in Modern Era and Opportunities to Uprising Sales. *International Journal of Emerging Research in Engineering, Science, and Management, 1*(3). Advance online publication. DOI: 10.58482/ijeresm.v1i3.3

Mishra, A. B., Goel, A., & Jajoo, P. (2022). A Case Study of Amul: Implementation of Extension Strategy to Repositioning Brand During Covid-19 Period. *International Journal of Emerging Research in Engineering, Science, and Management, 1*(4). Advance online publication. DOI: 10.58482/ijeresm.v1i4.3

Mishra, A. B., Ranjan, N., Sharma, K. M., Padhye, P., & Chand, K. (2023). Advancement of Digital Transformation to Boost Financial Services Industry. *Journal of Informatics Education and Research, 3*(2), 2435–2440.

Mishra, A. B., Sahu, T., Ranjan, N., & Varma, A. (2021). Green Marketing Practices Prevailing In Hotel Industry. *Journal of Contemporary Issues in Business and Government, 27*(02). Advance online publication. DOI: 10.47750/cibg.2021.27.02.145

Mishra, A. B., Satarkar, M., & Joshi, S. (2023). IKEA - Phygital Transformation in Furniture Manufacturing Industry. *International Journal of Emerging Research in Engineering, Science, and Management, 2*(3), 6–9. DOI: 10.58482/ijeresm.v2i3.2

Mishra, A. B., & Singh, A. (2023). Brand Positioning in the Indian Smartphone Market: A Case Study of OnePlus. *International Journal of Emerging Research in Engineering, Science, and Management, 2*(3). Advance online publication. DOI: 10.58482/ijeresm.v2i3.1

Mishra, A. B., & Singh, A. (2024). The Mumbai Dabbawalas : An Efficient and Sustainable Lunchbox Delivery System. In *IGI Global* (pp. 154–160). DOI: 10.4018/979-8-3693-1544-6.ch007

Mohseni, M., Othman, B. A., Raturi, P., Mishra, A. B., Priya, S. J., & Saravanan, V. (2022). The Role of Parallel Computing Towards Implementation of Enhanced and Effective Industrial Internet of Things (IOT) Through Manova Approach. *2022 2nd International Conference on Advance Computing and Innovative Technologies in Engineering (ICACITE)*, 160–164. DOI: 10.1109/ICACITE53722.2022.9823698

*Nhai to issue green bonds worth rs. 1,000 crores*. (n.d.). Retrieved December 16, 2024, from https://pib.gov.in/pib.gov.in/Pressreleaseshare.aspx?PRID=2081146

Rana, M. S., Cavaliere, L. P. L., Mishra, A. B., Padhye, P., Singh, R. R., & Khanna, R. (2022, April). Internet of Things (IOT) Based Assessment for Effective Monitoring Data Against Malicious Attacks on Financial Collectors. In 2022 2nd International Conference on Advance Computing and Innovative Technologies in Engineering (ICACITE) (pp. 177-181). IEEE.

Ranjan, N., Mishra, A. B., & Padhye, P. (2023). Dynamics of Digital Payments Enable the World's Safest Way to Pay. *Journal of Informatics Education and Research, 3*(2). Advance online publication. DOI: 10.52783/jier.v3i2.406

*Reserve bank of india—Press releases*. (n.d.). Retrieved December 16, 2024, from https://www.rbi.org.in/scripts/BS_PressReleaseDisplay.aspx?prid=55004

*Sebi | green debt securities*. (n.d.). Retrieved December 10, 2024, from https://www.sebi.gov.in/statistics/greenbonds.html

Sreenu, N. (2024). Examining the dynamics of risk associated with green investment in India: A study on fintech and green bonds for clean energy production. *Journal of Economic Studies (Glasgow, Scotland)*. Advance online publication. DOI: 10.1108/JES-12-2023-0680

Usman, M. S., Sheoliha, N., Prabhakar, P. V., Mishra, A. B., & Dondapati, A. (2023). Leading Strategies for Organizational Adaptation and Growth in Digital Transformation in Marketing. Journal of Informatics Education and Research.

Zhu, Y., & Wu, Y. (2021). Green bond financing development research in china. *2021 5th Annual International Conference on Data Science and Business Analytics (ICDSBA)*, 463–469. DOI: 10.1109/ICDSBA53075.2021.00095

# Chapter 11
# Expanding Rural Reach and Driving Digital Transformation Distribution Strategy of Mondelez India

**A. B. Mishra**
https://orcid.org/0000-0003-4429-4058
*International Institute of Management Studies, Pune, India*

**Ishita Dhar**
*International Institute of Management Studies, Pune, India*

**Tejas Bhosale**
*International Institute of Management Studies, Pune, India*

## ABSTRACT

*This case study explores the strategic distribution and digital transformation journey of Mondelez International in India, with a special focus on its expansion into rural markets. Faced with the challenge of reaching geographically dispersed and infrastructurally limited rural areas, Mondelez implemented a combination of channel innovations, digitally empowered sales tools, and logistical adaptations to increase its market penetration. Key initiatives included the development of a cold-chain infrastructure, the launch of Project Joyful Distribution, and the deployment of AI-driven demand forecasting systems. Simultaneously, Mondelez leveraged Salesforce Automation (SFA), e-commerce platforms, and direct-to-retailer digital ordering solutions to enhance efficiency and build a more responsive supply chain.*

DOI: 10.4018/978-1-6684-9872-9.ch011

*The study further contrasts the growth trajectories of Modern Trade, General Trade in rural India and evaluates the rise of e-commerce as a viable channel in tier-2 and tier-3 locations.*

## INTRODUCTION

Mondelez International, the global snack food and confectionery giant, is the market leader in India's chocolate segment, with brands like Cadbury Dairy Milk, Bournville, 5 Star, Perk, and Gems (Butler, 2008). With urban markets reaching saturation, Mondelez identified rural India as the next frontier for growth and undertook a focused strategy to expand its reach and influence in these areas.A. B. Mishra, Chand, et al. (2022) (Golnar-Nik et al., 2019). India's rural population constitutes nearly 65% of the total demographic, representing a massive but traditionally underserved consumer base (A. Mishra, 2025a). Historically, rural markets faced infrastructure challenges and lower disposable incomes, limiting the presence of premium FMCG brands (A. B. Mishra & Singh Ritika, 2024). However, with the advent of better connectivity, digitization, and rising incomes, rural consumers have shown a growing appetite for branded and even premium products. Mondelez aimed to tap into this potential through a multipronged strategy (A. B. Mishra & Gaikwad, 2024). To understand how Mondelez International tailored its distribution strategy to penetrate rural India, the impact of this strategy on its business growth, and the transformation it brought to rural consumption behavior. Singh, 2024).

## OVERVIEW OF CHANNEL SALES:

Channel sales refer to the distribution of products through intermediaries such as wholesalers, distributors, retailers, and modern trade formats (Tyler Muse, 2025). For an FMCG player like Mondelez, having a robust and multilayered channel sales system is critical to ensure availability, visibility, and accessibility of products across a vast and diverse market like India (Dr "Mishra A. B." et al., 2024). Mondelez operates a multi-channel sales approach that caters to both urban and rural geographies:

a. Traditional Trade (General Trade)
    - **Distributors**: The backbone of rural distribution. Mondelez has a network of primary and sub-distributors responsible for fulfilling orders from local retailers.
    - **Retailers/Kirana Stores**: More than 1.5 million retail outlets across India stock Mondelez products.

- **Rural Sales Officers (RSOs)**: Appointed to directly engage with local shops and improve stock availability and visibility.

b. Modern Trade (Organized Retail)
   - Includes supermarket chains, hypermarkets, and convenience stores (e.g., Reliance Retail, DMart, Star Bazar etc.)
   - Provides high visibility and premium placements for Mondelez's flagship products like Cadbury Dairy Milk Silk and Oreo.

c. E-commerce & Digital Trade (D2C)

Mondelez partners with platforms like Amazon, Flipkart, BigBasket, and JioMart. Enabled direct-to-consumer (D2C) models and festive gifting campaigns via online channels (Mohseni et al., 2022).

d. Alternative Channels
   - **Out-of-Home Consumption (OOH)**: Vending machines, cinema halls, educational institutions, and offices.
   - **Institutional Sales**: B2B gifting, corporate orders during festivals, and special occasions.

## STRATEGIES IMPLEMENTATIONS

### 1. Distribution Strategy in Rural India

The company which began delivering free display coolers to Indian store owners in the early 2000s, has expanded its distribution to rural areas in the past year. It expects to visit 75,000-100,000 villages over the next three years, up from 50,000 in 2018 ("Mishra A. B." et al., 2024). To that purpose, it is increasing its refrigerated truck fleet and developing a database that maps India's small neighbourhood businesses and tracks sales of its items there (Rao, 2016). Mondelez increased its reach from 40,000 villages in 2017 to nearly 100,000 villages by 2021. The company aims to expand to 75,000–100,000 villages within the next few years. This expansion included direct distribution to smaller villages and partnerships with local distributors to improve accessibility (Asmare & Zewdie, 2022). The company also actively invests in modern trade and the HoReCa (hotel, restaurant, and catering) channels, further expanding its reach across various distribution segments.

- **General Trade:** Mondelez India has significantly increased its presence in rural areas, aiming to reach a vast network of villages. This channel accounts for a significant portion of their sales, with 80% of sales coming through this channel. The company recognizes the potential of the rural market and has made it a key focus of its distribution efforts (Varma & Mishra, 2013). Improvements in road connectivity and rural electrification have facilitated Mondelez India's ability to reach more remote areas. Mondelez India has adopted a two-pronged approach, focusing on both ensuring the availability of its products and creating awareness among rural consumers (Mishra, 2025). The company uses a development index to select villages based on economic and infrastructural factors.

- **Modern Trade:** Mondelez India also distributes its products through modern trade channels, including supermarkets and hypermarkets etc, While general trade is the primary driver, modern trade contributes a significant portion of sales (Chand, 2022). They have been improving in-store execution and product placement within modern trade outlets.
- **HORECA:** Mondelez India also actively engages with the HORECA sector, supplying products to hotels, restaurants, and caterers. They likely offer specific product lines tailored to the needs of the HOR("Mishra A. B." et al., 2024). ECA market. Mondelez India's distribution strategy is multifaceted, leveraging both traditional and modern channels to reach a wide range of customers, with a particular focus on rural areas and the HORECA sector (Mishra, 2025a).
- **Institutional Sales:** Mondelez India may also have institutional sales, potentially supplying products to government entities, educational institutions, and other organizations. This could be a smaller part of their overall sales, but it can still be a valuable channel for certain products (A. B. Mishra & Singh, 2023).

*Figure 1. Channel sales comparison: Mondelez India (2021 Vs 2023) (Accumulated Data)*

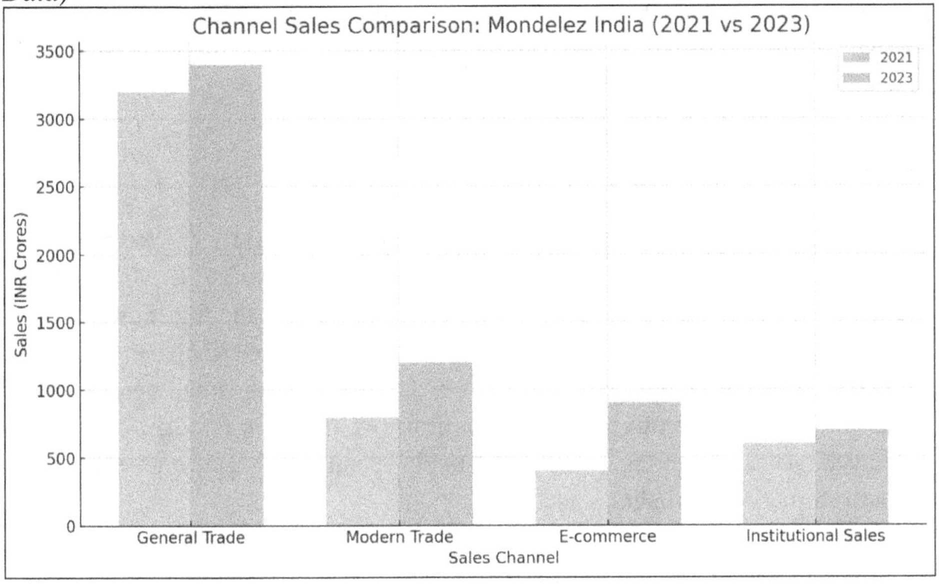


## 2. Market Segmentation

To keep its leading market share in India's confectionery industry, Cadbury has customised its marketing strategy, including campaigns, products, and pricing, to target various groups such as children, families, students, and salaried individuals (A. B. Mishra, 2025a). The company offers products at various price points, including affordable options like  5 and  10 Cadbury Dairy Milk bars, as well as premium products like Cadbury Silk, catering to diverse consumer preferences (Manoharan et al., 2024). Premium Push contain Cadbury Silk and Bournville were also introduced in semi-urban and affluent rural pockets, reflecting an evolving rural palate. Cadbury also segments based on purchasing behavior,(Singh Ritika, 2024). impulse buying, and gifting occasions, focusing on situations where Dairy Milk is commonly consumed (Ahamad, Mishra, Raghuram, Tiwari, et al., 2024). This involves understanding consumer lifestyles, values, and attitudes to create targeted marketing messages, such as associating (A. B. Mishra, Chand, et al., 2022). Cadbury with spontaneous, carefree moments (A. B. Mishra, Ranjan, et al., 2023). Target Markets includes Dairy Milk is often seen as a nostalgic treat and a symbol of parental affection for children, though the brand has expanded its appeal to a broader audience (Varma & Mishra, 2015). Cadbury Dairy Milk is often considered a dessert for the whole family, not just for kids. These groups are also targeted through various promotions and campaigns, as they represent a significant portion of the consumer base (Kaith, Chand, et al., 2022). Cadbury Dairy Milk celebrations is a popular gift item for various occasions, such as birthdays, festivals, and celebrations (Varma & Mishra, 2013).

## 3. Infrastructure Development

Mondelez strengthened cold-chain infrastructure through refrigerated trucks and chillers, essential for storing chocolates in hot Indian climates (A. B. Mishra, Goel, et al., 2022). Significant investment in warehouse capacity and logistics optimization was made to ensure timely delivery and reduce spoilage (Ranjan et al., 2023).

**Area Mapping:** Mondelez is building a database to map small neighborhood stores across India, monitoring sales to optimize distribution (Dodke, 2024). This enabled targeted marketing, optimized supply chains, and real-time response to demand shifts (A. B. Mishra et al., 2024).

## 4. Key Distribution Innovations:

a. **Rural Cold Chain Infrastructure:** Chocolates are heat-sensitive products, and India's tropical climate makes rural distribution tricky due to limited refrigeration. To solve Cadbury Investment in cold-chain logistics, including Refrigerated trucks for long-distance hauling, Solar-powered chillers and coolers for rural retailers, Use of thermally insulated boxes for last-mile delivery (A. B. Mishra, 2020). It helped to reduced product spoilage and improved product quality in hot, power-deficient rural areas (A. B. Mishra & Singh, 2024a).
b. **Route-to-Market (RTM) Optimization: AI-Driven Analytics**: Mondelez uses machine learning algorithms to Predict demand at the micro-market level,(Dr A. B. Mishra, 2020). optimize delivery routes and frequency, avoid stockouts and overstocking (Rana et al., 2022).
c. **Smart Sales Routing** by which Sales representatives are equipped with digital tools (mobile apps) that optimize their retail visit schedules. It help to enhanced supply efficiency and reduced operational costs (Ahamad, Mishra, Raghuram, Riyazuddin, et al., 2024).
d. **Festive Logistics Planning:** During high-demand seasons (e.g., Diwali, Raksha Bandhan), Mondelez. Uses demand-sensing tools to forecast regional surges, Establishes temporary distribution hubs closer to demand centers, Creates customized gifting SKUs optimized for quick distribution. Increased responsiveness

to seasonal demand spikes and improved last-mile execution (A. B. Mishra & Ranjan, 2022).

e. **Data-Driven Retail Mapping:** Retail Universe Mapping (RUM) initiative: Aims to create a digital map of all outlets carrying Mondelez products and tracks performance, SKU movement, and demand patterns(A. B. Mishra & Singh, 2024b).

f. **Digital Rural Distribution Push- WhatsApp & Mobile-Based Ordering**: They have used low-bandwidth solutions like WhatsApp ordering for remote rural retailers. SMS-based prompts/reminders in regional languages to nudge weekly ordering (A. B. Mishra, Chand, et al., 2022). Digital Distributor Management System (DMS) . Cloud-based systems help distributors includes Track inventory, Automate billing and Monitor delivery cycles (AB A. B. Mishra, 2025b).

*Figure 2. Mondelez India's rural expansions & digital distribution growth (Accumulated Data)*

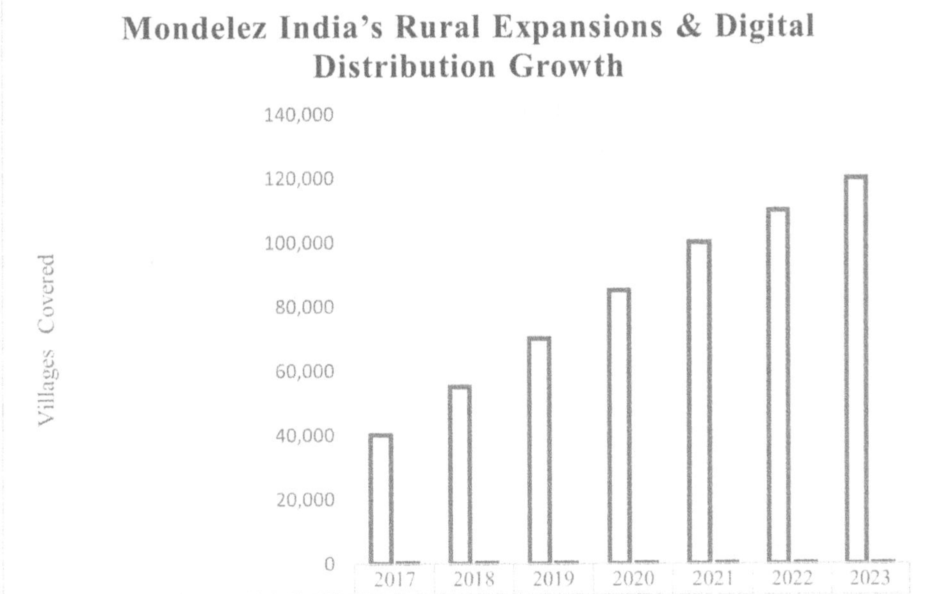


| | 2017 | 2018 | 2019 | 2020 | 2021 | 2022 | 2023 |
|---|---|---|---|---|---|---|---|
| Villages Covered | 40,000 | 55,000 | 70,000 | 85,000 | 100,000 | 110,000 | 120,000 |
| Retailers Using Digital Tools (%) | 10% | 18% | 30% | 45% | 60% | 72% | 80% |

## 5. Impact

- **Market Penetration and Revenue Growth:** The share of rural India in Mondelez's traditional trade revenue increased from 12% to 25%. Mondelez's overall market share in the chocolate segment remained dominant at 66%, in part due to rural growth.
- **Consumer Behavior Shift:** Rural customers began purchasing premium chocolate variants, indicating aspirational buying behavior. Better exposure to digital media and urban migration contributed to changing tastes and preferences.
- **Sales Channel Transformation:** Rural markets began growing at 1.5x the rate of urban markets, with noticeable increases in footfall at retail stores and demand for festive packaging.
- **Investments and Future Outlook:** Mondelez committed 4,000 crore (approx. $480 million) investment in India from 2023–2026. This capital is earmarked for capacity expansion, warehousing, rural infrastructure, and innovation in product development.
- **Neuromarketing**: plays a critical role here by helping Mondelez: Use emotional analytics (facial coding, eye tracking) to test ad creatives. Craft emotionally engaging campaigns like #NotJustACadburyAd, which personalized ads to local retailers—creating strong community sentiment. Create phygital retail experiences that mix immersive digital storytelling with real-world product interaction.
- **Mondelez's Strategy to Win Over Rural Gen Z:** Mondelez India's ability to engage Gen Z in rural India reflects a deep understanding of evolving consumer psychology in non-metro markets (Dr. A. B. Mishra, 2025b). By merging neuromarketing insights, local storytelling, and smart digital distribution, Mondelez is building long-term brand love in the next wave of India's youth economy.

## CONCLUSION

Mondelez's strategic expansion into rural India serves as a benchmark for FMCG companies aiming to tap into Bharat's potential (Kate et al., 2022). Through a blend of grassroots-level distribution, product customization, and infrastructural investment, Mondelez has not only grown its footprint but also redefined rural consumption patterns (Singh, 2020). With a strong foundation in place, the company is well-positioned to drive future growth in one of the world's largest emerging markets (A. B. Mishra, Rajagopal, et al., 2021). Mondelez International's journey in India reflects a strategic blend of traditional expertise and forward-looking innovation. Faced with the challenges of reaching a vast and diverse market especially in rural India (A. B. Mishra & Dodke, 2024). the company has successfully transformed its distribution channels, sales processes, and digital touchpoints to ensure deeper market penetration and stronger consumer connection (A. Mishra, 2025b). Through initiatives like Project Joyful Distribution, cold-chain deployment, AI-driven demand planning, and digital retailer engagement, Mondelez has optimized its supply chain while catering to the unique needs of rural geographies (A. B. Mishra, Sahu, et al., 2021). The company's focus on channel sales development and digitally enabled infrastructure has allowed it to scale efficiently without compromising product quality or customer experience (Mohammed Usman et al., 2023). Moreover, Mondelez's commitment to technological innovation from e-commerce integration to WhatsApp ordering and mobile apps has accelerated its reach, particularly during festive seasons and in post-pandemic recovery ("Mishra A. B." et al., 2024). The impact is clear: an expanded rural footprint, increased retail participation, improved delivery efficiencies,(A. B. Mishra, Satarkar, et al., 2023). and strong year-over-year growth (Asmare & Zewdie, 2022). Mondelez India stands as a benchmark for how a global FMCG player can localize effectively, innovate digitally, and build a resilient distribution ecosystem across both urban and rural landscapes. Mondelez India's evolving strategy illustrates how neuromarketing, phygital engagement, and sustainability messaging can work together to meet the demands of a digitally native and ethically aware generation. By decoding the human brain in a tech-first world, Mondelez is not just selling chocolates—it's creating moments of meaningful connection that last beyond the purchase. As India continues its digital and consumption growth journey, Mondelez is not just keeping pace it is leading from the front.

## REFERENCES


Ahamad, S., Mishra, A. B., Raghuram, K. S., Riyazuddin, Y. M., & Alanya-Beltran, J. (2024). *Applications of Internet of Things (IoT) in Maintaining Privacy and Security of Smart Cities*. Taylor & Francis Journal., DOI: 10.1201/9781003405580-30

Ahamad, S., Mishra, A. B., Raghuram, K. S., Tiwari, M., & Riyazuddin, Y. & Alanya-Beltran, J. (2024). Applications of Internet of Things (IoT) in Maintaining Privacy and Security of Smart Cities. In *Computer Science Engineering and Emerging Technologies* (pp. 187–191). CRC Press. DOI: 10.1201/9781003405580-30

Asmare, A., & Zewdie, S. (2022). Omnichannel retailing strategy: A systematic review. *International Review of Retail, Distribution and Consumer Research, 32*(1), 59–79. DOI: 10.1080/09593969.2021.2024447

Butler, M. J. R. (2008). Neuromarketing and the perception of knowledge. *Journal of Consumer Behaviour, 7*(4–5), 415–419. DOI: 10.1002/cb.260

Golnar-Nik, P., Farashi, S., & Safari, M.-S. (2019). The application of EEG power for the prediction and interpretation of consumer decision-making: A neuromarketing study. *Physiology & Behavior, 207*, 90–98. DOI: 10.1016/j.physbeh.2019.04.025 PMID: 31047949

Kate, N., Padhye, P., & Mishra, A. B. (2022). Studies on Anti-Virus Software Tools: Strong Weapon to Protect Systems. *2022 2nd International Conference on Innovative Practices in Technology and Management (ICIPTM)*, 49–52. DOI: 10.1109/ICIPTM54933.2022.9753877

Manoharan, G., Mishra, A. B., Adusumilli, S. B. K., Chavva, M., Damancharla, H., & Sahaya Lenin, D. (2024). Supervised Learning for Personalized Marketing Strategies. *2024 International Conference on Advances in Computing, Communication and Applied Informatics (ACCAI)*, 1–6. DOI: 10.1109/ACCAI61061.2024.10602307

Mishra, A. (2025a). Kalyan Jewellers: A Case Study on Brand Perception and Disruptive Innovation in the Jewellery Market. *IGI Global Scientific Publishing*, 261–284. https://doi.org/DOI: 10.4018/979-8-3693-9783-1.ch010

Mishra, A. (2025b). Monitoring the Development of the IoT Concept in Various Application Domains. *Taylor & Francis Online, CRC Press*. https://www.taylorfrancis.com/chapters/edit/10.1201/9781003596721-41/monitoring-development-iot-concept-various-application-domains-mishra-sarita-rani-panda-anitha-uma-reddy-gaurav-sethi-purnendu-bikash-acharjee

Mishra, A. B. (2020). E- PAYMENT SYSTEM: A RISING TREND OF ECONOMY. *New Paradigm in Business and Education.* https://www.researchgate.net/profile/Anitha-K-2/publication/349605501_E-LEARNING_THROUGH_GAMIFICATION-_AN_ITINERARY_TO_GAIN_IN-DEPTH_KNOWLEDGE/links/6037d566299bf1cc26ef9597/E-LEARNING-THROUGH-GAMIFICATION-AN-ITINERARY-TO-GAIN-IN-DEPTH-KNOWLEDGE.pdf#page=10

Mishra, A. B. (2025a). Kalyan Jeweller's Case Study of Transformation, Consumer Engagement, and Effective Marketing Strategies for Brand Building. In *Dynamic Strategies for Entrepreneurial Marketing* (pp. 287–310). DOI: 10.4018/979-8-3693-3936-7.ch014

Mishra, A. B. (2025b). The Paytm Puzzle: Navigating Regulatory Compliance in India's Digital Revolution. In *Cultural Sensitivity, Cross-Border Logistics, and E-Commerce in Global Marketing* (pp. 337–348). IGI Global. DOI: 10.4018/979-8-3373-0528-8.ch015

Mishra, A. B., Allen, M., & Tirkey, P. (2024). *Disruption causes to Micromax by once a Market leader now a Myth*. https://www.iimspune.edu.in/images/pdf/Journal/Vol3I1-Paper11.pdf

Mishra, A. B., Chand, K., & Kaith, K. (2022). Influencer Marketing as Emerging Promotional Tool in Modern Era and Opportunities to Uprising Sales. *International Journal of Emerging Research in Engineering, Science, and Management, 1*(3). Advance online publication. DOI: 10.58482/ijeresm.v1i3.3

Mishra, A. B., & Dodke, S. D. (2024). ZARA : Technological Influence on Becoming the Fashion Industry's Market Leader. In *Cases on AI Ethics in Business* (pp. 204–215). IGI Publishing., DOI: 10.4018/979-8-3693-2643-5.ch012

Mishra, A. B., & Gaikwad, V. (2024). The Transaction War Between Google Pay and Phonepe. In *IGI Global* (pp. 166–185). DOI: 10.4018/978-1-6684-7840-0.ch009

Mishra, A. B., Goel, A., & Jajoo, P. (2022). A Case Study of Amul: Implementation of Extension Strategy to Repositioning Brand During Covid-19 Period. *International Journal of Emerging Research in Engineering, Science, and Management, 1*(4). Advance online publication. DOI: 10.58482/ijeresm.v1i4.3

Mishra, A. B., Rajagopal, N. K., Yousoof, M., & Padhye, P. (2021). A STUDY ON ORGANISATIONAL PRACTICES THAT INFLUENCE EMPLOYEE ENGAGEMENT. *Manager–. British Journal of Administrative Management, 57*(145), 220–225.

Mishra, A. B., & Ranjan, N. (2022). INTERNET OF THINGS BASED EMERGING SMART TOOLS FOR NEW EDGE EDUCATION. *Mukt Shabd Journal, 11*(10), 80–87. DOI: 10.0014.MSJ.2022.V11I10.0086781.1135708

Mishra, A. B., Ranjan, N., Sharma, K. M., Padhye, P., & Chand, K. (2023). Advancement of Digital Transformation to Boost Financial Services Industry. *Journal of Informatics Education and Research, 3*(2), 2435–2440. https://scholar.google.com/scholar?cluster=15410723285942667834&hl=en&oi=scholarr

Mishra, A. B., Sahu, T., Ranjan, N., & Varma, A. (2021). Green Marketing Practices Prevailing In Hotel Industry. *Journal of Contemporary Issues in Business and Government, 27*(02). Advance online publication. DOI: 10.47750/cibg.2021.27.02.145

Mishra, A. B., Satarkar, M., & Joshi, S. (2023). IKEA - Phygital Transformation in Furniture Manufacturing Industry. *International Journal of Emerging Research in Engineering, Science, and Management, 2*(3), 6–9. DOI: 10.58482/ijeresm.v2i3.2

Mishra, A. B., & Singh, A. (2023). Brand Positioning in the Indian Smartphone Market: A Case Study of OnePlus. *International Journal of Emerging Research in Engineering, Science, and Management, 2*(3). Advance online publication. DOI: 10.58482/ijeresm.v2i3.1

Mishra, A. B., & Singh, A. (2024a). The Mumbai Dabbawalas : An Efficient and Sustainable Lunchbox Delivery System. In *IGI Global* (pp. 154–160). DOI: 10.4018/979-8-3693-1544-6.ch007

Mishra, A. B., & Singh, R. (2024b). Phygital Transformation of Nilon's: The Brand Building in Ready-to-eat Segment. *International Journal of Emerging Research in Engineering, Science, and Management, 3*(2). Advance online publication. DOI: 10.58482/ijeresm.v3i2.3

Mohseni, M., Othman, B. A., Raturi, P., Mishra, A. B., Priya, S. J., & Saravanan, V. (2022). The Role of Parallel Computing Towards Implementation of Enhanced and Effective Industrial Internet of Things (IOT) Through Manova Approach. *2022 2nd International Conference on Advance Computing and Innovative Technologies in Engineering (ICACITE)*, 160–164. DOI: 10.1109/ICACITE53722.2022.9823698

Muse, T. (2025, March 26). *COCA-COLA'S "TASTE THE FEELING" CAMPAIGN.* History Oasis.

Rana, M. S., Cavaliere, L. P. L., Mishra, A. B., Padhye, P., Singh, R. R., & Khanna, R. (2022, April). Internet of Things (IOT) Based Assessment for Effective Monitoring Data Against Malicious Attacks on Financial Collectors. In 2022 2nd International Conference on Advance Computing and Innovative Technologies in Engineering (ICACITE) (pp. 177-181). IEEE.

Ranjan, N., Mishra, A. B., & Padhye, P. (2023). Dynamics of Digital Payments Enable the World's Safest Way to Pay. *Journal of Informatics Education and Research*, *3*(2). Advance online publication. DOI: 10.52783/jier.v3i2.406

Rao, M. S. (2016). Tools and techniques to ensure innovative management education in India. *Industrial and Commercial Training*, *48*(5), 265–268. DOI: 10.1108/ICT-10-2015-0071

Singh, T. (2020). *Fintech Adoption: A Critical Appraisal of the Strategies of Paytm in India.*

Usman, M. S., Sheoliha, N., Prabhakar, P. V., Mishra, A. B., & Dondapati, A. (2023). Leading Strategies for Organizational Adaptation and Growth in Digital Transformation in Marketing. Journal of Informatics Education and Research.

Varma, S. R., & Mishra, A. B. (2013). *Distribution Channels of Indian Insurance Business - A Study*. Abhinavan.

Varma, S. R., & Mishra, A. B. (2015). Study of Consumer Buying Behaviour in General Insurance Industry. In *Excellence through creativity, Research, innovation in field of IT and Management.*

# Chapter 12
# Neuromarketing in the Phygital Era by Influencing Gen Z and Sustainable Consumer Behaviour in a Digitally Driven Retail World

**A. B. Mishra**
https://orcid.org/0000-0003-4429-4058
*International Institute of Management Studies, Pune, India*

## ABSTRACT

*As environmental awareness grows, businesses are challenged to inspire sustainable consumer behavior that aligns with evolving digital habits—especially among Gen Z. This research explores the intersection of neuromarketing, phygital retail experiences, and green consumption, analyzing how subconscious emotional and cognitive responses influence eco-friendly purchasing decisions. By utilizing tools such as EEG, fMRI, eye-tracking, and biometric sensors, neuromarketing reveals key drivers of consumer engagement, trust, and decision-making that traditional methods often overlook. The study examines how storytelling, visual cues, brand identity, and emerging technologies like Artificial Intelligence (AI) and the Internet of Things (IoT) enhance sustainable product appeal. Case studies from global brands illustrate how neuro-informed strategies can bridge the attitude-behavior gap and foster more meaningful connections with ethically minded consumers. Neuromarketing as a powerful tool for shaping consumer behavior in a digitally-driven, environmentally conscious world.*

DOI: 10.4018/978-1-6684-9872-9.ch012

## 1. INTRODUCTION

In an age where environmental concerns are reshaping consumer preferences, businesses are increasingly challenged to bridge the gap between sustainability values and actual consumer behavior (A. B. Mishra, 2025). Despite rising awareness, many individuals fail to act consistently with their ecological intentions a phenomenon known as the attitude-behavior gap (Lee et al., 2007). Traditional marketing tools often fall short in capturing the unconscious drivers behind these decisions (Usman M et al., 2023). In response, neuromarketing, an emerging interdisciplinary field combining neuroscience, psychology, and marketing, offers powerful insights into how consumers emotionally and cognitively respond to stimuli, especially those related to sustainability (A. B. Mishra & Singh, 2024a). By utilizing advanced technologies such as EEG (Electroencephalography), fMRI (Functional Magnetic Resonance Imaging), eye-tracking, and biometric analysis, neuromarketing reveals what consumers truly feel and perceive—often beyond what they express in surveys (Vrontis et al., 2021). These insights are particularly valuable when promoting eco-friendly products, which rely heavily on trust, ethical identity, and emotional resonance (Cosic, 2016). Moreover, as digital transformation, AI, and phygital experiences redefine consumer interaction, neuromarketing plays a crucial role in crafting emotionally compelling, personalized, and impactful sustainability narratives (A. B. Mishra, Satarkar, et al., 2023). This paper explores the fundamental principles of neuromarketing, its applications in promoting sustainable products, and its influence across modern technologies and demographics—especially Gen Z (Chillakuri, 2020). Through case studies, tool analysis, and behavioral insights, it aims to demonstrate how neuromarketing can drive meaningful change in consumption patterns and support the transition toward a more sustainable future.

## 2. LITERATURE REVIEW

### 2.1 Neuromarketing Fundamentals

Neuromarketing involves studying brain activity and physiological responses to understand how consumers make decisions, often beyond their conscious awareness (Seyfi et al., 2024). By analyzing how the brain reacts to marketing stimuli, researchers can identify emotional triggers, cognitive engagement, and decision-making patterns (Lee et al., 2007). Several tools are commonly used in neuromarketing research (Saarijärvi et al., 2013). Functional Magnetic Resonance Imaging (fMRI) measures changes in blood flow to detect brain activity and is useful for identifying areas associated with reward, trust, or emotional processing. Electroencephalography

(EEG) records electrical activity in the brain, providing real-time data on attention, engagement, and emotional valence(A. B. Mishra & Singh, 2023). Eye-tracking technology monitors where and how long a person looks at specific elements of an advertisement or product, revealing attention patterns and visual interest (Golnar-Nik et al., 2019). Galvanic Skin Response (GSR) measures changes in skin conductance due to emotional arousal, while facial expression analysis decodes subtle emotional reactions through muscle movements. Together, these tools offer a comprehensive view of consumer behavior, enabling marketers to design more effective and emotionally resonant campaigns (Manoharan et al., 2024).

## 2.2 Sustainable Consumer Behavior

Sustainable consumption is influenced by a complex mix of personal values, social norms, environmental awareness, and perceived behavioral control. Consumers may express a willingness to adopt eco-friendly habits, but their actual behavior often falls short—a phenomenon known as the "attitude-behavior gap."(A. B. Mishra & Dodke, 2024a). One major challenge in studying sustainable behavior is social desirability bias, where individuals respond in ways they believe are socially acceptable rather than truthful. Traditional surveys and self-reported data often fail to reveal genuine motivations or subconscious influences (A. B. Mishra, Chand, et al., 2022). To overcome these limitations, researchers increasingly use alternative tools. Implicit Association Tests (IATs) help uncover unconscious attitudes toward sustainability by measuring the strength of automatic associations (Vendrell-Herrero et al., 2021). Neuromarketing tools, such as EEG and fMRI, detect emotional and cognitive responses to sustainable branding without relying on verbal input (A. Mishra, 2025a). Eye-tracking reveals whether consumers notice eco-labels or sustainability claims on packaging (A. B. Mishra & Singh, 2024b). Additionally, behavioral experiments and field studies allow for observation of real-world decisions in controlled environments. These approaches provide a more accurate understanding of the drivers and barriers behind sustainable consumption, informing more effective marketing and policy strategies.

## 2.3 Neuromarketing and Green Products

Neuromarketing offers valuable insights into how consumers perceive and emotionally respond to green products, helping to bridge the gap between environmental concern and purchasing behavior. Studies have shown that sustainable products can activate specific regions of the brain associated with moral decision-making, trust, and reward such as the ventromedial prefrontal cortex, insula, and amygdala (Asmare & Zewdie, 2022). These areas are stimulated when consumers are exposed to environmentally friendly cues, such as eco-labels, natural imagery, or messaging that emphasizes community impact and ethical responsibility (Mohammed Usman et al., 2023). EEG studies reveal that consumers often show higher levels of emotional engagement and positive affect when green products are presented with appealing narratives or visual elements that align with personal values (John et al., 2006). Additionally, eye-tracking research indicates that consumers are more likely to fixate on eco-certifications, recyclable symbols, or sustainable keywords when they are prominently displayed (Henderson et al., 1998). By understanding these subconscious reactions, marketers can design more effective campaigns that increase the visibility and appeal of green products. Neuromarketing thus plays a key role in helping brands authentically communicate their sustainability values and nudge consumers toward more eco-conscious choices.

## 2.4 Neuromarketing and Technology

The rapid advancement of technology has significantly enhanced the scope and precision of neuromarketing research. Sophisticated tools now enable marketers and researchers to explore the neural and physiological underpinnings of consumer behavior with greater accuracy and accessibility (Mohseni et al., 2022). Functional Magnetic Resonance Imaging (fMRI) provides high-resolution brain imaging, allowing identification of areas activated during brand exposure or ethical decision-making. Electroencephalography (EEG), while more portable and cost-effective, offers real-time monitoring of brain waves linked to attention, engagement, and emotional intensity (Golnar-Nik et al., 2019). Eye-tracking systems integrated with screen-based or wearable devices help determine which visual elements attract attention and how visual flow affects product perception (Bharwani & Mathews, 2023). Meanwhile, Galvanic Skin Response (GSR) and heart rate variability monitors detect physiological arousal, indicating emotional reactions that consumers may not verbalize (Cosic, 2016). Emerging technologies, such as machine learning and AI-driven analytics, are increasingly used to interpret complex neuromarketing data, making it possible to predict consumer choices and optimize campaigns (Ahamad, Mishra, Raghuram, Tiwari, et al., 2024). As technology evolves, neuromarketing continues to provide deeper insights into the subconscious mind, enabling more targeted and ethical marketing practices—particularly in areas like sustainable product promotion (Singh et al., 2011).

## 3. METHODOLOGY

This paper synthesizes findings from empirical studies, neuromarketing case analyses, and cognitive psychology research. Key frameworks include:

- EEG-based emotional valence and arousal studies
- Eye-tracking data on packaging and labeling
- Behavioral experiments on framing effects and narrative persuasion

## 4. RESULTS AND DISCUSSION

### 4.1 Emotional Engagement

Sustainable messages that trigger empathy increase emotional arousal and memorability (Bohra et al., 2022). EEG studies show higher frontal asymmetry linked to positive emotional engagement when sustainability is framed in terms of personal or social benefits. Positive emotional engagement refers to a consumer's favorable emotional response—such as joy, pride, hope, or empathy—when exposed to a product, message, or brand. In neuromarketing, this is often observed through left frontal brain activity (frontal asymmetry) and physiological responses like increased attention or heart rate variability (Mishra A. B. & Jaiswal Monika, 2024).

- **Personal Health Benefits:** A skincare brand promoting a natural, chemical-free lotion can trigger emotional responses related to self-care and wellness, leading to increased trust and preference. EEG studies show stronger emotional engagement when products are linked to individual benefits (e.g., "better for your skin and your planet") rather than abstract environmental claims (A. B. Mishra, Goel, et al., 2022).
- **Social Identity & Community Impact:** Campaigns that emphasize social contribution—like buying a recycled backpack that supports education in underserved communities—evoke empathy and pride. The emotional reward of being part of a "green movement" activates the brain's reward centers, increasing likelihood of repeat purchases (Srivastava et al., 2019).
- **Aesthetic and Sensory Cues:** Packaging with earthy colors, natural textures, or the scent of essential oils can elicit positive sensory associations tied to nature, calmness, and purity. These triggers promote emotional comfort and authenticity, driving engagement at a subconscious level (Srivastava et al., 2019).

- **Gamification and Social Proof:** Apps that track your eco-footprint and reward you with badges or social praise (like Ecosia or Too Good To Go) create joy, achievement, and belonging, which reinforce sustainable behaviors (Vrontis et al., 2021).

## 4.2 Visual Cues and Packaging

Visual elements on product packaging play a critical role in shaping consumer perceptions and guiding purchasing decisions—often within just a few seconds (A. B. Mishra & Singh Ritika, 2024). For eco-friendly products, visual cues such as color, imagery, symbols, and typography can subtly but powerfully communicate sustainability without overwhelming the consumer with text. Research shows that natural color palettes—especially greens, browns, and earth tones—are strongly associated with eco-consciousness and can activate the brain's areas responsible for trust and familiarity (A. B. Mishra & Karjodkar, 2022). Eco-labels and certifications act as visual heuristics, quickly signaling environmental credibility and reducing cognitive effort in decision-making. Minimalist design with clean lines and recyclable-looking materials ("Using Eye-Tracking Technology in Neuromarketing," 2023) often triggers associations with purity, transparency, and environmental responsibility. Eye-tracking studies further reveal that consumers spend more time fixating on products with prominent sustainability icons or impactful slogans, especially when placed in the upper third of the package or near the brand name (A. B. Mishra et al., 2024). Moreover, incorporating story elements—like a short note on how the packaging is biodegradable or made from ocean plastic—can create an emotional connection and drive positive emotional engagement (A. B. Mishra & Gaikwad, 2024). By optimizing visual cues, brands can align their packaging with subconscious consumer values, increasing both attention and intention to purchase sustainable products.

## 4.3 Storytelling and Brand Identity

Narratives that link the product to a larger purpose activate the default mode network (DMN), which is associated with self-relevance and long-term memory. This enhances brand affinity and encourages repeat purchases (Henderson et al., 1998). Storytelling is a powerful neuromarketing tool that can elevate brand identity and forge deeper emotional connections with consumers, especially when promoting sustainable products. Rather than simply presenting features or eco-certifications, brands that weave compelling narratives around their values, mission, and impact engage the brain's default mode network (DMN) the area associated with self-reflection, empathy, and long-term memory (A. B. Mishra, 2022). Stories humanize the brand and make abstract sustainability concepts more relatable. For example, a company that shares the journey of how it sources fair-trade coffee from a women-led cooperative in South America taps into values like social justice, empowerment, and global connection. Similarly, brands like TOMS and Patagonia use storytelling to reinforce their identity as ethical and purpose-driven companies, which increases consumer trust and loyalty ("Mishra A. B." et al., 2024). Neuromarketing research shows that narratives framed around real people, emotional struggles, or positive impact activate emotional centers in the brain and result in higher recall and brand favorability. Authentic storytelling also strengthens brand coherence, ensuring that marketing, design, and customer experience all align with a consistent, values-based identity (A. B. Mishra, 2020). In the context of sustainable products, storytelling turns passive awareness into active engagement—transforming consumers into brand advocates and contributors to a larger mission (Butler, 2008).

## 4.4 Neuromarketing's Role in Phygital Transformation and the Future of Retail

Neuromarketing is playing a pivotal role in the phygital transformation—the seamless integration of physical and digital experiences—especially within the evolving retail industry (Varma & Mishra, 2015). With the rise of Gen Z consumers, who value personalization, purpose, and immersive experiences, retailers are leveraging neuromarketing insights to create emotionally engaging, tech-enabled environments (A. B. Mishra et al., 2021). Technologies like Artificial Intelligence (AI) and Internet of Things (IoT) devices, when informed by neuromarketing data, allow brands to anticipate consumer desires, adapt in real time, and optimize engagement (A. Mishra, 2025b). For instance, smart shelves embedded with IoT sensors can detect customer attention span and emotional responses, while AI-powered recommendation systems use behavioral and neural data to serve up hyper-personalized suggestions (Rana et al., 2022). Gen Z responds positively to authentic storytelling, ethical branding, and interactive in-store experiences, all of which can be enhanced by neuromarketing-driven design. In hybrid spaces like virtual stores or augmented reality (AR) showrooms, neuromarketing helps brands fine-tune visual cues, emotional tone, and sensory triggers to influence subconscious decision-making (Ahamad, Mishra, Raghuram, Riyazuddin, et al., 2024). As retail becomes increasingly experience-centric, neuromarketing bridges the gap between human emotion and intelligent automation, ensuring that phygital environments remain human-first, emotionally resonant, and behaviorally effective (Pooja Mehta et al., 2021).

## 4.5 Neuromarketing Case Analyses:

### 4.5.1. Hyundai – Emotional Design in Automotive Marketing

Hyundai conducted an fMRI-based study to analyze how people emotionally respond to different car designs. Brain scans showed greater activation in reward centers when participants viewed cars with more fluid, aesthetic lines (A. B. Mishra & Dodke, 2024b). The neuromarketing data influenced future vehicle designs and advertising strategies, helping Hyundai create emotionally resonant visuals that align with consumer preferences—especially among younger demographics (Hyundai, n.d.).

### 4.5.2. Unilever – Sustainable Living Brands

Unilever used neuromarketing techniques like facial coding and biometric tracking to test emotional engagement with storytelling around its sustainable brands (e.g., Dove, Lifebuoy). Stories focused on real-world impact, such as water conservation or community empowerment, generated significantly higher emotional resonance. These insights helped craft marketing messages that translated into stronger brand loyalty and increased market share for products tied to sustainability (Ranjan et al., 2023).

### 4.5.3. Facebook – Eye-Tracking and Ad Placement

In a collaborative study, Facebook used eye-tracking to evaluate how users engage with in-feed advertisements. They discovered that ads using natural visuals and narrative structures had higher gaze duration and engagement (Mike Bartels, 2025). These insights informed best practices for mobile ad design and personalized content delivery using AI-powered targeting (Singh Manish, 2024).

### 4.5.4. The Coca-Cola Company – "Taste the Feeling" Campaign

Coca-Cola used a combination of EEG, facial expression analysis, and GSR to test different versions of its "Taste the Feeling" campaign across global markets (Tyler Muse, 2025). They found that ads emphasizing social connection, joy, and nostalgia led to greater emotional activation and brand recall. These elements were emphasized in the final global rollout, contributing to a measurable uplift in positive brand perception (Bohra et al., 2022).

## 5. CONCLUSION

As environmental concerns become increasingly urgent, understanding and influencing sustainable consumer behavior is more important than ever. Traditional marketing approaches, reliant on self-reported attitudes and rational appeals, often fail to capture the deeper, unconscious processes that drive real-world decisions. Neuromarketing, by tapping into the emotional and cognitive responses of consumers through tools like EEG, fMRI, eye-tracking, and biometric analysis, offers a transformative approach to bridging this gap. It enables brands to design more emotionally resonant campaigns, optimize packaging, and deliver experiences that align with consumers' values—consciously and subconsciously (Rana et al., 2022).

When applied to sustainable products, neuromarketing has demonstrated the power to enhance engagement, increase trust, and drive behavioral change. Storytelling, visual cues, and purpose-driven branding—when strategically informed by neurological insights—can make green products not only more appealing but also more meaningful (A. B. Mishra, Ranjan, et al., 2023). Furthermore, as digital technologies, including AI, IoT, and phygital retail, continue to evolve, neuromarketing provides a vital lens through which companies can create more human-centric, ethical, and impactful sustainability initiatives, particularly for values-driven generations like Gen Z (Mohseni et al., 2022). In conclusion, neuromarketing is not just a tool for influencing consumer behavior—it is a bridge between science and sustainability, emotion and ethics. By leveraging the power of the brain, marketers can contribute to a more conscious, environmentally responsible future.

## REFERENCES


Ahamad, S., Mishra, A. B., Raghuram, K. S., Riyazuddin, Y. M., & Alanya-Beltran, J. (2024). *Applications of Internet of Things (IoT) in Maintaining Privacy and Security of Smart Cities*. DOI: 10.1201/9781003405580-30

Ahamad, S., Mishra, A. B., Raghuram, K. S., Tiwari, M., & Riyazuddin, Y. Md., & Alanya-Beltran, J. (2024). Applications of Internet of Things (IoT) in Maintaining Privacy and Security of Smart Cities. In *Computer Science Engineering and Emerging Technologies* (pp. 187–191). CRC Press. DOI: 10.1201/9781003405580-30

Asmare, A., & Zewdie, S. (2022). Omnichannel retailing strategy: A systematic review. *International Review of Retail, Distribution and Consumer Research, 32*(1), 59–79. DOI: 10.1080/09593969.2021.2024447

Bartels, M. (2025). *TV advertising research for Facebook*. Tobii.

Bharwani, S., & Mathews, D. (2023). Sustainable luxury: From an oxymoron to a tautology – the case of the Indian luxury hospitality industry. *Worldwide Hospitality and Tourism Themes, 15*(3), 231–248. DOI: 10.1108/WHATT-01-2023-0013

Bohra, D. K., Nagansur, S., & Anute, N. (2022). *Comparative Analysis of FMCG Products with Special Reference to HUL and ITC*. OmniScience A Multi-Disciplinary Journal. DOI: 10.37591/omniscience.v12i2.3395

Butler, M. J. R. (2008). Neuromarketing and the perception of knowledge. *Journal of Consumer Behaviour, 7*(4–5), 415–419. DOI: 10.1002/cb.260

Chillakuri, B. (2020). Understanding Generation Z expectations for effective onboarding. *Journal of Organizational Change Management, 33*(7), 1277–1296. DOI: 10.1108/JOCM-02-2020-0058

Cosic, D. (2016). Neuromarketing in Market Research. *Interdisciplinary Description of Complex Systems, 14*(2), 139–147. DOI: 10.7906/indecs.14.2.3

Golnar-Nik, P., Farashi, S., & Safari, M.-S. (2019). The application of EEG power for the prediction and interpretation of consumer decision-making: A neuromarketing study. *Physiology & Behavior, 207*, 90–98. DOI: 10.1016/j.physbeh.2019.04.025 PMID: 31047949

Henderson, G. R., Iacobucci, D., & Calder, B. J. (1998). Brand diagnostics: Mapping branding effects using consumer associative networks. *European Journal of Operational Research, 111*(2), 306–327. DOI: 10.1016/S0377-2217(98)00151-9

Hyundai. (n.d.). *The all-new Hyundai i20: emotional design meets advanced technology*. Automobile World.

John, D. R., Loken, B., Kim, K., & Monga, A. B. (2006). Brand Concept Maps: A Methodology for Identifying Brand Association Networks. *JMR, Journal of Marketing Research*, *43*(4), 549–563. DOI: 10.1509/jmkr.43.4.549

Lee, N., Broderick, A. J., & Chamberlain, L. (2007). What is 'neuromarketing'? A discussion and agenda for future research. *International Journal of Psychophysiology*, *63*(2), 199–204. DOI: 10.1016/j.ijpsycho.2006.03.007 PMID: 16769143

Manish, S. (2024, February 8). *Indian parliamentary panel red-flags PhonePe and Google Pay cornering 83% of India's UPI payments*. Techcrunch. https://techcrunch.com/2024/02/08/indian-parliamentary-panel-red-flags-phonepe-and-google-pay-cornering-83-of-india-upi-payments/

Manoharan, G., Mishra, A. B., Adusumilli, S. B. K., Chavva, M., Damancharla, H., & Sahaya Lenin, D. (2024). Supervised Learning for Personalized Marketing Strategies. *2024 International Conference on Advances in Computing, Communication and Applied Informatics (ACCAI)*, 1–6. DOI: 10.1109/ACCAI61061.2024.10602307

Mehta, P., Singla, H., Saha, R., & Tyagi, S. (2021). A pathway to technology integration: Eliciting consumer's behavioural intention to use paytm services. *Paradigm*, *25*(1), 7–24.

Mishra, A. (2025a). Kalyan Jewellers: A Case Study on Brand Perception and Disruptive Innovation in the Jewellery Market. *IGI Global Scientific Publishing*, 261–284.

Mishra, A. (2025b). *Monitoring the Development of the IoT Concept in Various Application Domains. Taylor & Francis Online*. CRC Press.

Mishra, A. B. (2020). E- PAYMENT SYSTEM: A RISING TREND OF ECONOMY. *New Paradigm in Business and Education*. https://www.researchgate.net/profile/Anitha-K-2/publication/349605501_E-LEARNING_THROUGH_GAMIFICATION-_AN_ITINERARY_TO_GAIN_IN-DEPTH_KNOWLEDGE/links/6037d566299bf1cc26ef9597/E-LEARNING-THROUGH-GAMIFICATION-AN-ITINERARY-TO-GAIN-IN-DEPTH-KNOWLEDGE.pdf#page=10

Mishra, A. B., Anil, V., & Nitin, R. (2021). Putsch buyer tendency and climbing sales of mobile trade business. *Manager–The British Journal of Administrative Management*, *58*(152), 54–60.

Mishra, A. B. (2022). SAHYADRI FARMS: INDIA'S LARGEST FARMER PRODUCER COMPANY. *International Journal of Advance and Applied Research*, *10*, 996–998. https://ijaar.co.in/wp-content/uploads/2022/11/1001175.pdf

Mishra, A. B., & Monika, J. (2024). Case Study of Kalyan Jewellers-Brand Perception Mapping Towards Disruptive Innovation in Jewellery Segment. *International Journal of Advance and Applied Research, 11*(6), 386–396.

Mishra, A. B. (2025). *Kalyan Jeweller's Case Study of Transformation*. Consumer Engagement, and Effective Marketing Strategies for Brand Building., DOI: 10.4018/979-8-3693-3936-7.ch014

Mishra, A. B., Chand, K., & Kaith, K. (2022). Influencer Marketing as Emerging Promotional Tool in Modern Era and Opportunities to Uprising Sales. *International Journal of Emerging Research in Engineering, Science, and Management, 1*(3). Advance online publication. DOI: 10.58482/ijeresm.v1i3.3

Mishra, A. B., & Dodke, S. D. (2024a). *ZARA* (pp. 204–215). DOI: 10.4018/979-8-3693-2643-5.ch012

Mishra, A. B., & Dodke, S. D. (2024b). ZARA: Technological Influence on Becoming the Fashion Industry's Market Leader. In *IGI Global* (pp. 204–215). DOI: 10.4018/979-8-3693-2643-5.ch012

Mishra, A. B., & Gaikwad, V. (2024). The Transaction War Between Google Pay and Phonepe. In *IGI Global* (pp. 166–185). DOI: 10.4018/978-1-6684-7840-0.ch009

Mishra, A. B., Goel, A., & Jajoo, P. (2022). A Case Study of Amul: Implementation of Extension Strategy to Repositioning Brand During Covid-19 Period. *International Journal of Emerging Research in Engineering, Science, and Management, 1*(4). Advance online publication. DOI: 10.58482/ijeresm.v1i4.3

Mishra, A. B., & Karjodkar, R. (2022). A Case Study of Air India - Maharajah Back to Home. *International Journal of Emerging Research in Engineering, Science, and Management, 1*(3). Advance online publication. DOI: 10.58482/ijeresm.v1i3.5

Mishra, A. B., Raikwar, A., & Tiwari, A. (2024). *Britannia: Marketing Initiatives Boost A Fledgling Business's Transformation To One Of The Largest FMCG Brands*. https://www.iimspune.edu.in/images/pdf/Journal/Vol3I1-Paper12.pdf

Mishra, A. B., Ranjan, N., Sharma, K. M., Padhye, P., & Chand, K. (2023). Advancement of Digital Transformation to Boost Financial Services Industry. *Journal of Informatics Education and Research, 3*(2), 2435–2440.

Mishra, A. B., Satarkar, M., & Joshi, S. (2023). IKEA - Phygital Transformation in Furniture Manufacturing Industry. *International Journal of Emerging Research in Engineering, Science, and Management, 2*(3), 6–9. DOI: 10.58482/ijeresm.v2i3.2

Mishra, A. B., & Singh, A. (2023). Brand Positioning in the Indian Smartphone Market: A Case Study of OnePlus. *International Journal of Emerging Research in Engineering, Science, and Management, 2*(3). Advance online publication. DOI: 10.58482/ijeresm.v2i3.1

Mishra, A. B., & Singh, A. (2024a). The Mumbai Dabbawalas : An Efficient and Sustainable Lunchbox Delivery System. In *IGI Global* (pp. 154–160). DOI: 10.4018/979-8-3693-1544-6.ch007

Mishra, A. B., & Singh, R. (2024b). Phygital Transformation of Nilon's: The Brand Building in Ready-to-eat Segment. *International Journal of Emerging Research in Engineering, Science, and Management, 3*(2). Advance online publication. DOI: 10.58482/ijeresm.v3i2.3

Mohseni, M., Othman, B. A., Raturi, P., Mishra, A. B., Priya, S. J., & Saravanan, V. (2022). The Role of Parallel Computing Towards Implementation of Enhanced and Effective Industrial Internet of Things (IOT) Through Manova Approach. *2022 2nd International Conference on Advance Computing and Innovative Technologies in Engineering (ICACITE)*, 160–164. DOI: 10.1109/ICACITE53722.2022.9823698

Muse, T. (2025, March 26). *COCA-COLA'S "TASTE THE FEELING" CAMPAIGN.* History Oasis.

Rana, M. S., Cavaliere, L. P. L., Mishra, A. B., Padhye, P., Singh, R. R., & Khanna, R. (2022, April). Internet of Things (IOT) Based Assessment for Effective Monitoring Data Against Malicious Attacks on Financial Collectors. In 2022 2nd International Conference on Advance Computing and Innovative Technologies in Engineering (ICACITE) (pp. 177-181). IEEE.

Ranjan, N., Mishra, A. B., & Padhye, P. (2023). Dynamics of Digital Payments Enable the World's Safest Way to Pay. *Journal of Informatics Education and Research, 3*(2). Advance online publication. DOI: 10.52783/jier.v3i2.406

Saarijärvi, H., Karjaluoto, H., & Kuusela, H. (2013). Extending customer relationship management: From empowering firms to empowering customers. *Journal of Systems and Information Technology, 15*(2), 140–158. DOI: 10.1108/13287261311328877

Seyfi, S., Vo-Thanh, T., & Zaman, M. (2024). Hospitality in the age of Gen Z: A critical reflection on evolving customer and workforce expectations. *International Journal of Contemporary Hospitality Management, 36*(13), 118–134. DOI: 10.1108/IJCHM-01-2024-0035

Singh, A., Rishi, M., & Shukla, R. (2011). Green management and environmental sustainability: A case of ITC Green Center. *Emerald Emerging Markets Case Studies, 1*(2), 1–13. DOI: 10.1108/20450621111159859

Srivastava, A. K., Jonjua Mehak, & Rana Rajesh. (2019). Status of Communicating CSR to Stakeholders on Social Media : A Case Study on ITC Limited & Nestle India. *Journal of Content. Community & Communication, 9*, 81–92.

Gheorghe, C. M., Purcărea, V. L., & Gheorghe, I. R. (2023). Using eye-tracking technology in Neuromarketing. *Romanian Journal of Ophthalmology, 67*(1), 2.

Usman, M. S., Sheoliha, N., Prabhakar, P. V., Mishra, A. B., & Dondapati, A. (2023). Leading Strategies for Organizational Adaptation and Growth in Digital Transformation in Marketing. Journal of Informatics Education and Research.

Usman M, Sheoliha N, Prabhakar P V, Mishra, A. B., & Dondapati. (2023). Leading Strategies for Organizational Adaptation and Growth in Digital Transformation in Marketing. *Journal of Informatics Education and Research.*

Varma, S. R., & Mishra, A. B. (2015). Study of Consumer Buying Behaviour in General Insurance Industry. In *Excellence through creativity, Research, innovation in field of IT and Management.*

Vendrell-Herrero, F., Bustinza, O. F., & Opazo-Basaez, M. (2021). Information technologies and product-service innovation: The moderating role of service R&D team structure. *Journal of Business Research, 128*, 673–687. DOI: 10.1016/j.jbusres.2020.01.047

Vrontis, D., Makrides, A., Christofi, M., & Thrassou, A. (2021). Social media influencer marketing: A systematic review, integrative framework and future research agenda. *International Journal of Consumer Studies, 45*(4), 617–644. DOI: 10.1111/ijcs.12647

# Chapter 13
# Tech-Driven Market Efficiency Amid Geopolitical Tensions:
## The Israel-Iran Conflict's Impact on Global Indices and Sustainable Investing

**K. Sanath Kumar**
https://orcid.org/0000-0003-4429-4058
*Sahyadri College of Engineering, Mangaluru, India*

**K. V. Deepak**
*Department of Commerce, St. Aloysius University, Mangalore, India*

**K. Naveenkumar**
*Department PG Studies in Commerce, University College, Mangalore, India*

## ABSTRACT

*This study, by taking NSE Nifty 50, DJIA, CAC, DAX, FTSE, Straits Times, Hang sang, Shanghai, Nikkei 225 and Kospi, as a reference, tries to understand and evaluate the impact of the Israel-Hamas war on these indices to demonstrate the comprehensive movements of the index prices. For elucidating the impact of the Israel-Iran war on major global index's returns the event study methodology has been used. This study analyses the change in the index prices which in turn reflects how the event affected market returns. The results underscore the differential impact of geopolitical conflicts on global stock markets. The Israel-Iran war had a significant and varied impact on global stock markets. While most indices showed declines, the*

DOI: 10.4018/978-1-6684-9872-9.ch013

*magnitude and direction of the changes differed across regions, reflecting diverse market sensitivities to geopolitical events.*

## 1. INTRODUCTION:

In an increasingly interconnected and volatile global landscape, geopolitical events exert profound and often immediate effects on financial markets. Among the most impactful are military conflicts, which generate uncertainty, disrupt global supply chains, and influence investor sentiment (Ahamad et al., 2024). The recent escalation between Israel and Iran presents a critical opportunity to assess how such conflicts influence global stock markets, especially in an era where technology enables rapid information dissemination and high-frequency trading (Roomi, 2023; Koblentz-Stenzler et al., 2023).. A stock market or share market is the aggregation of buyers and sellers of stocks (Gajera, 2020). Stock indices serve as indicators of market performance. One of the most well-known is the Dow Jones Industrial Average (DJIA), which initially had a divisor of 30, though this has since been standardized. In Germany, the leading index is the DAX, which reflects the stock prices of 30 major companies (Rana et al., 2022). The Financial Times Stock Exchange 100 Index (FTSE-100) represents the top 100 British companies based on market value. Meanwhile, Japan's Nikkei 225 is a capital-weighted index comprising 225 top companies listed on the Tokyo Stock Exchange (Ewa Drabik, 2021). This study explores the efficiency of global stock markets in responding to the Israel-Iran conflict, utilizing an event study methodology to examine abnormal returns across major indices (Mohseni et al., 2022). By assessing the speed and accuracy with which market prices incorporate new information, the research contributes to the broader understanding of the Efficient Market Hypothesis (EMH) under extreme political stress. In addition to traditional market responses, this paper delves into the evolving dynamics of sustainable investing—a field that continues to grow in importance amid geopolitical instability and environmental urgency. The intersection of technology, sustainability, and market efficiency provides a unique lens through which to analyze investor behavior. Tech-driven trading systems, sentiment analysis tools, and algorithmic strategies now play a significant role in shaping market reactions, making it essential to account for their influence in contemporary financial studies. By investigating how major stock indices responded to the Israel-Iran conflict, this paper aims to provide insights into the resilience and adaptability of modern markets, the influence of technology in driving trading behaviors, and the performance of sustainable investment assets during geopolitical crises. The findings offer practical implications for investors, policymakers, and researchers navigating the complex interface of conflict, technology, and capital markets.

## 2. REVIEW OF LITERATURE:

### 2.1 Event Studies:

In semi-strong form of market efficiency, the market takes some time to reflect the information in price (Warner & Brown, 1984; Chavali et al., 2020; Chowdhury & Khan,2024). If prices react accurately to all relevant new information in a rapid fashion, market efficiency is proved (Fama, 1970; Robinson, 2017). An event could have either a good or an evil influence on a specific index (Bartholdy et al., 2007; Singh & Narang, 2024). Event studies have become one of the most widely used empirical techniques in finance and accounting (Bartholdy et al., 2007). In an event study, we need to determine the event, the event date, the event window, the estimation window & the estimation model (Pandey & Kumari, 2020). Event studies provide a standardized approach for evaluating and statistically analysing stock price responses to unforeseen events. Event studies have become a workhorse method (Kaspereit, n.d.; Basdas & Oran, 2014). An event requires analysis to measure efficiency of the market due to the speed of change in market prices because of that news. It is the fundamental an essential component of any event study. After the event, cumulative abnormal returns continue to move up for good news and move down in the wake of bad news (Maitra & Dey, 2012; Ranju & Mallikarjunappa, 2019).

### 2.2 Geopolitical Tensions and Stock Markets:

Geopolitical turbulences encompass factors like geopolitical tensions, war risk, terrorist threats and trade wars between countries (Maddodi, 2024). Geopolitical turbulences cause spiked movements in indices (Korsah & Mensah, 2024; Alqahtani et al., 2022). The geopolitical risks can influence the financial landscape in many ways. First, the greater than before geopolitical turbulences will slow down the decision-making process of market participants. Second, the higher geopolitical risks can also push up the firms' costs by negatively affecting both demand and supply channels (Yang et al., 2021). A significant segment of India's young population, which forms a large part of the workforce, shows a strong inclination towards sustainable and ethical business practices. This burgeoning interest has fuelled the espousal of investment strategies guided by ESG principles (Gidage et al., 2024). The research examined how US-China political relations and geopolitical risks influence oil prices. For this purpose, two quantitative indicators were utilized: The Political Relationship Index (PRI) and the Geopolitical Risk Index (GPR). The study employed structural VAR and local projection methods for analysis. Our findings show that Improved US-China relationships, as well as higher geopolitical risks drive up the price of oil (Mignon & Saadaoui, 2024). Unlike a standard event study where each firm's stock is reacting to the news on that corresponding firm, the global crises provide clear event dates that applies to all companies listed in the market indices (Harjoto et al., 2020).

## 2.3 Stock Market Efficiency amid Geopolitical Risks:

Analysis of resilient market performance becomes useful for investors (Tang et al., 2019). Decoupling The theory claims that developing markets have the capability to shield themselves from global crisis (A. B. Mishra et al., 2023). The theory suggests that managers in emerging economies can implement policies during global crises that introduce structural changes in the level of connectedness or interdependence. Emerging markets have shown significant resilience to shocks originating from advanced economies. The extent to which emerging markets are immune to economic shocks differs across countries, thus raising concerns over the reliability of the theory (Korsah & Mensah, 2024).

## 2.4 Psychological and Economic Implications of Geopolitical Conflicts:

Measuring the impact of war on societies is challenging due to its indirect nature and extensive reach. The loss of human capital resulting from death, injury, and disease can severely affect social dynamics, potentially increasing crime, sexual violence, and repression as social norms are disrupted. Population displacement leads to significant demographic shifts, placing immense pressure on societal structures. These changes can heighten tensions and trigger conflicts along ethnic, religious, or ideological divides. A rise in crime is often associated with these shifts (Wallace et al., 2013). Geopolitical factors are increasingly acknowledged as significant influences on population health. However, their impact on mental health remains largely unmeasured, with most existing research originating from high-income nations. Assessing the impact of these factors in low- and middle-income countries is essential to inform policy and advocate for better outcomes especially as several refugees are seeking shelter in low-income countries (Vanteemar S. Sreeraj et al., 2019). The combined pre-war, contemporaneous, and post-war relationship between growth and war is negative; that is, economic performance has been lower in countries that fought a severe and/or prolonged war (Koubi, 2005). Geopolitical shocks adversely impact tourism; the adverse impacts of civil war, economic policy uncertainty, terrorist attacks, NATO bombing, geopolitical risk, and global volatility and uncertainty factors on the tourism sector is quite evident (Kumar & Kumar, 2022). The literature review underscores that geopolitical events such as wars, pandemics, and international conflicts have a profound impact on stock markets worldwide

(A. B. Mishra et al., 2022). Event studies serve as a critical tool in assessing these effects. While many markets suffer significant downturns, resilience can vary based on national well-being and geopolitical positioning.

## 2.5 Tech-Driven Events:

In the modern financial landscape, technology plays a pivotal role in shaping how markets respond to global events (A. Mishra, 2025a). The rise of algorithmic trading, artificial intelligence, and real-time data analytics has transformed traditional market dynamics, enabling near-instantaneous reactions to geopolitical developments (A. B. Mishra, 2020). Tech-driven platforms aggregate news, social sentiment, and economic indicators at unprecedented speed, allowing institutional and retail investors alike to make data-informed decisions within seconds (Mohammed Usman et al., 2023). During high-stakes events like the Israel-Iran conflict, these technologies amplify both the velocity and volatility of market responses (Manoharan et al., 2024). Moreover, the integration of machine learning in risk modeling and predictive analysis enhances market participants' ability to forecast potential disruptions, (A. B. Mishra & Singh, 2024) albeit sometimes contributing to overreactions driven by automated triggers. This growing dependence on technology not only affects how efficiently information is priced into the market but also raises new questions about the stability and fairness of such rapid, digitally-driven reactions (Mohammed Usman et al., 2023).

# 3. OBJECTIVE OF THE STUDY:

This study, by taking NSE Nifty 50, DJIA, CAC, DAX, FTSE, Straits Times Index, Hang Sang, Shanghai Composite Index, Nikkei 225 and Kospi, serves as a point of reference in assessing the impact of the Israel-Hamas war on these indices.

# 4. RESEARCH METHODOLOGY:

## 4.1 Conceptual Model:

The conceptual model states that Israel Hamas War had significant impact on the major global stock market indices, namely, NSE Nifty 50, DJIA, CAC, DAX, FTSE, Straits Times Index, Hang Sang, Shanghai Composite Index, Nikkei 225 and Kospi. Figure 1 below shows the conceptual model of the study.

*Figure 1. Conceptual model*

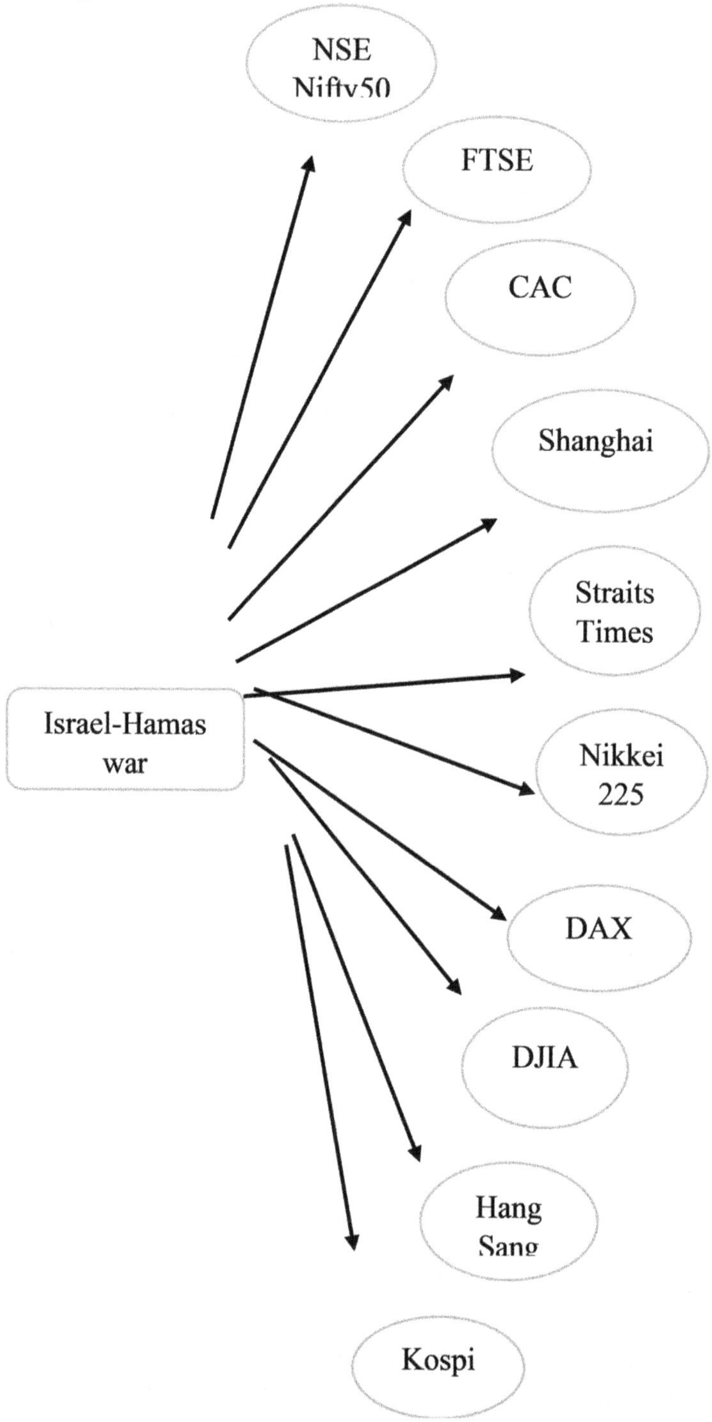

## 4.2 Event Study Timeline:

Event study is used for the study. The study is conducted by taking, the Estimation period of 160 days (160 days prior to the Pre-event period) from 2nd February 2024 to 9th September 2024, Pre- event period of 15 days (-1 to -15) i.e. 10th September to 30th September and the Post event period of 15 days (+1 to +15 days of the event). i.e., 2nd October to 22nd October 2024. Index values were collected from the official website of the Stock Exchanges. A Pre-event period is a period preceding the event date which is 10th September 2024 to 30th September 2024 and we believe the previous 160 days performance is normal hence we take that period as a base for comparison (Singh et al., 2024). Figure 2 below shows the event study timeline.

*Figure 2. Event study timeline*

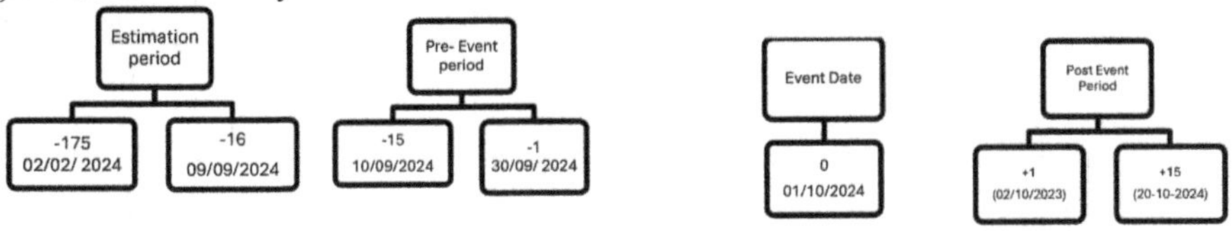


## 4.3 Hypothesis:

In this backdrop, the study attempts to test the following hypotheses concerning the announcement of Israel-Iran War on the prices of major indices.

$H_1$: There is a significant difference between the Average Abnormal Returns before and after the date of the announcement of the Israel-Iran War on the ten major global stock indices being studied.
$H_2$: There is a significant difference in the index values of major indices mediated by the Israel-Iran War announcement. The sign test judges the proportion of positive and negative abnormal returns against an assumed 50 per cent split under the null hypothesis of no reaction to the event.
$H_3$: There are significant differences between the ranks of the major indices being studied in the event period and expected average ranks with no abnormal returns.

## 5. DATA ANALYSIS, RESULTS AND DISCUSSION:

## 5.1 AARs and CAARs of Ten Major Global Stock Indices:

Table 1 shows the percentage AAR and CAAR of the five major global stock market indices.

*Table 1. AAR and CAAR of the five major global stock market indices*

| Days | NSE Nifty 50 | | DJIA | | CAC 40 | | DAX | | FTSE 100 | |
|---|---|---|---|---|---|---|---|---|---|---|
| | % AAR | CAAR | % AAR | CAAR | % AAR | CAAR | % AAR | CAAR | % AAR | CAAR |
| 15 | -0.24 | -6.80 | -0.07 | 1.09 | -0.02 | -0.49 | -0.26 | 0.24 | -0.20 | -0.58 |
| 14 | -1.34 | -6.56 | -0.85 | 1.16 | -1.01 | -0.47 | -1.06 | 0.50 | -0.54 | -0.37 |
| 13 | -0.39 | -5.21 | 0.04 | 2.00 | 0.39 | 0.54 | 0.32 | 1.55 | -0.38 | 0.17 |
| 12 | 0.33 | -4.82 | 0.32 | 1.97 | 1.22 | 0.15 | 0.72 | 1.23 | 0.61 | 0.56 |
| 11 | -0.98 | -5.15 | 0.74 | 1.64 | -0.40 | -1.07 | -0.33 | 0.52 | 0.90 | -0.05 |
| 10 | -0.44 | -4.17 | -0.80 | 0.90 | -1.05 | -0.67 | -0.17 | 0.85 | -0.59 | -0.96 |
| 9 | -0.38 | -3.73 | 0.42 | 1.71 | 0.32 | 0.38 | 0.64 | 1.02 | 0.41 | -0.37 |
| 8 | 0.56 | -3.35 | 0.92 | 1.28 | 0.48 | 0.06 | 0.79 | 0.38 | 0.13 | -0.78 |
| 7 | -0.23 | -3.91 | -0.19 | 0.37 | -0.25 | -0.42 | -0.29 | -0.41 | -0.14 | -0.91 |
| 6 | -0.03 | -3.68 | 0.98 | 0.56 | 0.51 | -0.17 | 0.93 | -0.12 | 0.58 | -0.77 |
| 5 | -0.22 | -3.65 | 0.25 | -0.42 | -0.72 | -0.69 | -0.25 | -1.05 | -1.42 | -1.36 |
| 4 | 0.78 | -3.43 | -0.99 | -0.67 | 0.46 | 0.04 | -0.15 | -0.80 | 0.21 | 0.07 |
| 3 | -0.97 | -4.21 | 0.76 | 0.32 | 0.85 | -0.42 | 0.50 | -0.65 | -0.09 | -0.14 |
| 2 | -1.03 | -3.24 | -0.49 | -0.44 | -1.32 | -1.27 | -0.84 | -1.15 | -0.16 | -0.06 |
| 1 | -2.21 | -2.21 | 0.04 | 0.04 | 0.05 | 0.05 | -0.31 | -0.31 | 0.11 | 0.11 |
| 0 | -0.15 | | -0.46 | | -0.81 | | -0.64 | | 0.42 | |
| -1 | -1.50 | 2.06 | -0.01 | 2.88 | -2.00 | 2.89 | -0.82 | 3.87 | -1.07 | -1.34 |
| -2 | -0.24 | 3.56 | 0.28 | 2.89 | 0.64 | 4.89 | 1.17 | 4.69 | 0.37 | -0.27 |
| -3 | 0.72 | 3.80 | 0.57 | 2.62 | 2.33 | 4.25 | 1.63 | 3.53 | 0.13 | -0.64 |
| -4 | 0.15 | 3.08 | -0.74 | 2.04 | -0.51 | 1.92 | -0.47 | 1.90 | -0.23 | -0.77 |
| -5 | -0.09 | 2.93 | 0.15 | 2.79 | 1.28 | 2.42 | 0.74 | 2.36 | 0.22 | -0.54 |
| -6 | 0.48 | 3.02 | 0.10 | 2.64 | 0.10 | 1.15 | 0.62 | 1.63 | 0.30 | -0.75 |
| -7 | 1.38 | 2.54 | 0.04 | 2.54 | -1.51 | 1.04 | -1.54 | 1.01 | -1.25 | -1.05 |
| -8 | 0.06 | 1.16 | 1.21 | 2.50 | 2.29 | 2.56 | 1.50 | 2.55 | 0.85 | 0.20 |
| -9 | -0.26 | 1.11 | -0.30 | 1.30 | -0.57 | 0.27 | -0.14 | 1.05 | -0.74 | -0.65 |
| -10 | 0.04 | 1.36 | -0.09 | 1.59 | 0.51 | 0.83 | 0.44 | 1.19 | 0.32 | 0.09 |

continued on following page

*Table 1. Continued*

| Days | NSE Nifty 50 | | DJIA | | CAC 40 | | DAX | | FTSE 100 | |
|---|---|---|---|---|---|---|---|---|---|---|
| | % AAR | CAAR | % AAR | CAAR | % AAR | CAAR | % AAR | CAAR | % AAR | CAAR |
| -11 | 0.01 | 1.32 | 0.50 | 1.68 | -0.21 | 0.32 | -0.41 | 0.75 | 0.00 | -0.22 |
| -12 | -0.22 | 1.31 | 0.67 | 1.18 | 0.41 | 0.54 | 0.92 | 1.16 | 0.33 | -0.22 |
| -13 | 1.79 | 1.53 | 0.53 | 0.51 | 0.52 | 0.13 | 0.97 | 0.24 | 0.51 | -0.55 |
| -14 | -0.59 | -0.26 | 0.26 | -0.02 | -0.15 | -0.38 | 0.29 | -0.73 | -0.21 | -1.06 |
| -15 | 0.32 | 0.32 | -0.28 | -0.28 | -0.24 | -0.24 | -1.02 | -1.02 | -0.85 | -0.85 |

Table 2 shows the percentage AAR and CAAR of the next five major global stock market indices.

*Table 2. AAR and CAAR of the next five major global stock market indices*

| Days | Strait Times Index | | Hang Sang Index | | Shanghai Composite Index | | Nikkei 225 Index | | KOSPI | |
|---|---|---|---|---|---|---|---|---|---|---|
| | % AAR | CAAR | % AAR | CAAR | % AAR | CAAR | % AAR | CAAR | % AAR | CAAR |
| 15 | 0.82 | 0.85 | 1.19 | -2.10 | -0.53 | 0.27 | -0.83 | -1.76 | 1.09 | -0.20 |
| 14 | 0.77 | 0.03 | 0.02 | -3.29 | -0.56 | 0.80 | -1.42 | -0.93 | -1.35 | -1.30 |
| 13 | -0.34 | -0.75 | -1.65 | -3.31 | -0.22 | 1.36 | -0.10 | 0.49 | 0.39 | 0.05 |
| 12 | -0.89 | -0.41 | 3.53 | -1.66 | -2.93 | 1.58 | 0.15 | 0.59 | -0.63 | -0.34 |
| 11 | 0.20 | 0.49 | -1.11 | -5.19 | 1.03 | 4.51 | -0.72 | 0.44 | -0.07 | 0.28 |
| 10 | 0.08 | 0.29 | -0.24 | -4.08 | -0.07 | 3.48 | -1.86 | 1.15 | -0.91 | 0.36 |
| 9 | -0.55 | 0.20 | -3.75 | -3.84 | 2.51 | 3.55 | 0.74 | 3.01 | 0.35 | 1.27 |
| 8 | 0.39 | 0.75 | -0.83 | -0.08 | -2.09 | 1.04 | 0.54 | 2.27 | 0.98 | 0.91 |
| 7 | 0.36 | 0.36 | 2.90 | 0.75 | 2.53 | 3.12 | 0.23 | 1.73 | -0.12 | -0.07 |
| 6 | -0.49 | 0.00 | -1.47 | -2.15 | -1.34 | 0.59 | 0.84 | 1.50 | 0.15 | 0.05 |
| 5 | 0.72 | 0.49 | -9.49 | -0.68 | 6.60 | 1.93 | -1.03 | 0.65 | -0.03 | -0.10 |
| 4 | -0.21 | -0.23 | 1.51 | 8.81 | -4.61 | -4.67 | 1.77 | 1.69 | -0.65 | -0.07 |
| 3 | -0.26 | -0.02 | 2.74 | 7.30 | -0.02 | -0.05 | 0.19 | -0.09 | 1.55 | 0.58 |
| 2 | 0.27 | 0.24 | -1.55 | 4.56 | -0.02 | -0.04 | 1.94 | -0.27 | 0.28 | -0.97 |
| 1 | -0.03 | -0.03 | 6.12 | 6.12 | -0.02 | -0.02 | -2.21 | -2.21 | -1.25 | -1.25 |
| 0 | 0.19 | | -0.08 | | -0.02 | | 1.90 | | -0.03 | |
| -1 | -0.26 | -1.48 | 2.35 | 19.67 | -8.08 | -20.61 | -4.82 | 4.45 | -2.17 | 1.85 |
| -2 | 0.32 | -1.22 | 3.47 | 17.32 | -2.90 | -12.53 | 2.29 | 9.28 | -0.85 | 4.02 |
| -3 | 0.10 | -1.54 | 4.08 | 13.86 | -3.63 | -9.62 | 2.76 | 6.98 | 2.87 | 4.87 |

continued on following page

*Table 2. Continued*

| Days | Strait Times Index | | Hang Sang Index | | Shanghai Composite Index | | Nikkei 225 Index | | KOSPI | |
|---|---|---|---|---|---|---|---|---|---|---|
| | % AAR | CAAR | % AAR | CAAR | % AAR | CAAR | % AAR | CAAR | % AAR | CAAR |
| -4 | 1.16 | -1.64 | 0.59 | 9.78 | -1.18 | -5.99 | -0.21 | 4.23 | -1.38 | 2.00 |
| -5 | 0.50 | -2.79 | 4.05 | 9.19 | -4.17 | -4.82 | 0.54 | 4.44 | 1.11 | 3.38 |
| -6 | -0.31 | -3.30 | -0.15 | 5.14 | -0.46 | -0.64 | -0.03 | 3.90 | 0.30 | 2.27 |
| -7 | 0.30 | -2.99 | 1.28 | 5.29 | -0.05 | -0.18 | 1.50 | 3.93 | 0.45 | 1.97 |
| -8 | -1.06 | -3.29 | 1.92 | 4.01 | -0.71 | -0.14 | 2.10 | 2.42 | 0.18 | 1.52 |
| -9 | 0.10 | -2.22 | -0.08 | 2.09 | -0.51 | 0.57 | 0.46 | 0.32 | -0.03 | 1.34 |
| -10 | -0.57 | -2.32 | 1.28 | 2.18 | -0.02 | 1.08 | -1.06 | -0.14 | -0.03 | 1.37 |
| -11 | -0.15 | -1.75 | 0.22 | 0.89 | -0.02 | 1.10 | -0.03 | 0.93 | -0.03 | 1.41 |
| -12 | -0.10 | -1.60 | 0.66 | 0.67 | 0.46 | 1.11 | -0.71 | 0.96 | 0.10 | 1.44 |
| -13 | -0.65 | -1.50 | 0.69 | 0.01 | 0.15 | 0.65 | 3.38 | 1.67 | 2.30 | 1.35 |
| -14 | -0.46 | -0.85 | -0.81 | -0.68 | 0.80 | 0.50 | -1.52 | -1.71 | -0.43 | -0.96 |
| -15 | -0.39 | -0.39 | 0.13 | 0.13 | -0.30 | -0.30 | -0.19 | -0.19 | -0.53 | -0.53 |

When the CAAR of different global stock market indices are compared, it is lucid that NSE Nifty 50 and Hang Sang Index and Nikkei 225 Index showed greater CAARs, indicating higher adverse impacts on Indian Hong Kong and Japanese stock markets.

## 5.2 Paired Samples Statistics of the Ten Major Global Stock Market Indices:

Table 3 below shows the paired samples statistics of the ten major global stock market indices.

*Table 3. Paired samples statistics*

| | | Mean | N | Std. Deviation | Std. Error Mean |
|---|---|---|---|---|---|
| Pair 1 | Nifty 50 Pre | -4.2747 | 15 | 1.24295 | .32093 |
| | Nifty 50 Post | 1.9227 | 15 | 1.19366 | .30820 |
| Pair 2 | DJIA Pre | .7673 | 15 | .88713 | .22906 |
| | DJIA Post | 1.7907 | 15 | 1.06242 | .27432 |
| Pair 3 | CAC 40 Pre | -.2967 | 15 | .51211 | .13223 |
| | CAC 40 Post | 1.5060 | 15 | 1.60760 | .41508 |

continued on following page

*Table 3. Continued*

| | | Mean | N | Std. Deviation | Std. Error Mean |
|---|---|---|---|---|---|
| Pair 4 | DAX Pre | .1200 | 15 | .84307 | .21768 |
| | DAX Post | 1.6120 | 15 | 1.60072 | .41331 |
| Pair 5 | FTSE 100 Pre | -.3627 | 15 | .52257 | .13493 |
| | FTSE 100 Post | -.5747 | 15 | .43011 | .11105 |
| Pair 6 | Strait times Pre | .1507 | 15 | .42441 | .10958 |
| | Strait times Post | -1.9253 | 15 | .87148 | .22501 |
| Pair 7 | Hang Sang Pre | .0773 | 15 | 4.48802 | 1.15880 |
| | Hang Sang Post | 5.9700 | 15 | 6.57814 | 1.69847 |
| Pair 8 | Shanghai Pre | 1.1633 | 15 | 2.17968 | .56279 |
| | Shanghai Post | -3.3213 | 15 | 6.39821 | 1.65201 |
| Pair 9 | Nikkei Pre | .5507 | 15 | 1.44464 | .37301 |
| | Nikkei Post | 2.7647 | 15 | 2.94916 | .76147 |
| Pair 10 | KOSPI Pre | -.0533 | 15 | .72292 | .18666 |
| | KOSPI Post | 1.8200 | 15 | 1.49144 | .38509 |

The Paired Samples Statistics table analyses the mean, standard deviation, and standard error of major global stock indices before (Pre) and after (Post) the Israel-Iran war, shedding light on its potential impact on global markets. Most indices, including NSE Nifty 50, DJIA, CAC40, DAX, Hang Sang, Nikkei 225, and KOSPI, experienced a decline in mean values, indicating a significant negative effect. For instance, the NSE Nifty 50 mean dropped sharply from 1.9227 to -4.2747, while the Hang Sang index showed a steep decline from 5.9700 to 0.0773, signalling heightened sensitivity in the Indian and Hong Kong markets, respectively. European indices like CAC 40 and DAX also showed substantial decreases, highlighting the broader adverse effects on European markets.

Overall, the findings reveal that the Israel-Iran war had a discernible adverse impact on global stock markets, with regional differences in sensitivity and recovery. Further statistical tests, such as paired t-tests, would confirm the significance of these observed changes.

## 5.3 Paired Samples Correlations of the Ten Major Global Stock Market Indices:

Table 4 below shows the paired samples correlations of the ten major global stock market indices.

*Table 4. Paired sample correlations*

| | | N | Correlation | Sig. |
|---|---|---|---|---|
| **Pair 1** | **Nifty 50 Pre & Nifty 50 Post** | **15** | **-.709** | **.003** |
| Pair 2 | DJIA Pre & DJIA Post | 15 | .733 | .002 |
| Pair 3 | CAC 40 Pre & CAC 40 Post | 15 | .236 | .397 |
| Pair 4 | DAX Pre & DAX Post | 15 | .609 | .016 |
| Pair 5 | FTSE 100 Pre & FTSE 100 Post | 15 | -.304 | .271 |
| Pair 6 | Strait times Pre & Strait times Post | 15 | -.378 | .165 |
| Pair 7 | Hang sang Pre & Hang sang Post | 15 | -.621 | .013 |
| Pair 8 | Shanghai Pre & Shanghai Post | 15 | -.029 | .919 |
| Pair 9 | Nikkei 225 Pre & Nikkei 225 Post | 15 | -.106 | .707 |
| Pair 10 | KOSPI Pre & KOSPI Post | 15 | .211 | .451 |

The Paired Samples Correlations table examines the relationships between Pre-event and post-event values for major global stock indices to assess the impact of the Israel-Iran war. Significant correlations are observed for Nifty50 ($r=-0.709$, $p=0.003$), DJIA ($r=0.733$, $p=0.002$), DAX ($r=0.609$, $p=0.016$), and Hang Sang ($r=-0.621$, $p=0.013$). These results indicate a strong inverse relationship for Nifty50 and Hang Sang, suggesting substantial declines post-event relative to Pre-event levels, whereas DJIA and DAX demonstrate consistent patterns with positive correlations. Other indices, such as CAC40, FTSE100, Shanghai, Nikkei 225, and KOSPI, show weak or negligible correlations, with no statistically significant results, implying limited connections between their Pre-event and post-event values. Notably, Shanghai ($r=-0.029$, $p=0.919$) exhibits virtually no relationship, highlighting its resilience or independence from the event's impact. These findings reveal varied regional responses, with some markets, such as India and Hong Kong, showing marked sensitivity, while others, such as Europe and China, appear less affected. The results underscore the differential impact of geopolitical conflicts on global stock markets.

## 5.4 Paired Samples T Test of the Ten Major Global Stock Market Indices:

Table 5 below shows the results of the paired samples t test of the ten major global stock market indices.

*Table 5. Paired samples t test*

| | Paired Differences | | | | | t | df | Sig (2-tailed) |
|---|---|---|---|---|---|---|---|---|
| | | | | 95% Confidence Interval of the Difference | | | | |
| | Mean | Std. Dev. | Std. Error Mean | Lower | Upper | | | |
| Nifty50<br>DJIA<br>CAC 40<br>DAX<br>FTSE 100<br>Strait times<br>Hang sang<br>Shanghai<br>Nikkei 225<br>KOSPI | -6.19 | 2.25254 | .58160 | -7.44475 | -4.94992 | -10.656 | 14 | .000 |
| | -1.02 | .73089 | .18871 | -1.42808 | -.61858 | -5.423 | 14 | .000 |
| | -1.8 | 1.56775 | .40479 | -2.67086 | -.93447 | -4.453 | 14 | .001 |
| | -1.49 | 1.27661 | .32962 | -2.19896 | -.78504 | -4.526 | 14 | .000 |
| | .21 | .77118 | .19912 | -.21506 | .63906 | 1.065 | 14 | .305 |
| | 2.07 | 1.10413 | .28508 | 1.46455 | 2.68745 | 7.282 | 14 | .000 |
| | -5.89 | 10.00 | 2.58 | -11.43 | -.35 | -2.28 | 14 | .039 |
| | 4.48 | 6.81843 | 1.76051 | .70875 | 8.26059 | 2.547 | 14 | .023 |
| | -2.21 | 3.41868 | .88270 | -4.10720 | -.32080 | -2.508 | 14 | .025 |
| | -1.87 | 1.51409 | .39094 | -2.71181 | -1.03486 | -4.792 | 14 | .000 |

The Paired Samples t test table evaluated the mean differences between Pre-event and post-event values for major global stock indices to determine the statistical significance of changes caused by the Israel-Iran war. The results showed significant changes for most indices, with p-values below 0.05, except for FTSE 100 ($p=0.305$ p = 0.305 $p=0.305$). Nifty 50 experienced the most pronounced decline, with a mean difference of -6.197 ($t=-10.656$, $p=0$), indicating a highly significant impact on the Indian stock market. DJIA ($t=-5.423$, $p=0.000$), CAC40 ($t=-4.453$, $p=0.001$), and DAX ($t=-4.526$, $p=0.000$) also showed significant declines, highlighting the effect on U.S. and European markets. Similarly, Hang Sang ($t=-2.281$, $p=0.039$) experienced a sharp drop, further underscoring the sensitivity of Asian markets. Interestingly, Shanghai exhibited a significant positive mean difference of 4.485 ($t=2.547$, $p=0.023$) suggesting a recovery or resilience in the Chinese market. Strait times ($t=7.282$, $p=0.000$) also showed a substantial positive difference, indicating a unique upward trend post-event. Other indices such as Nikkei 225 ($t=-2.508$, $p=0.025$) and KOSPI ($t=-4.792$, $p=0.000$) reported significant declines, while FTSE 100 displayed no significant change, with its p-value above the threshold.

These results demonstrate that the Israel-Iran war had a significant and varied impact on global stock markets. While most indices showed declines, the magnitude and direction of the changes differed across regions, reflecting diverse market sensitivities to geopolitical events.

## 5.5 Graphical Comparison of AARs of Ten Major Global Stock Indices During the Event Period:

Figure 3 below shows how the Major Global Stock Indices have performed during the Pre event period and Post event period by comparing their AARs.

*Figure 3. AARs of ten major indices during event period*

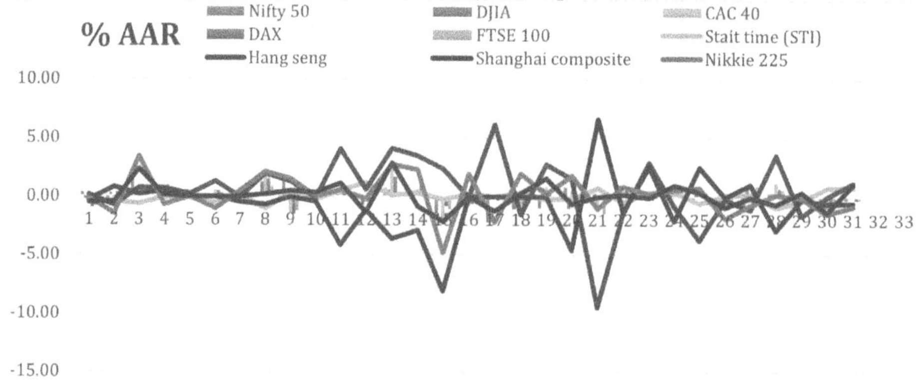


The above chart is a proof for the said results, where Shanghai and hang Sang had volatile effect in Pre-event period especially on -2 and -1 of the event dates, Bothe indexes shown inverse moment. On the other hand, in the Post event period even though the volatility is observed gradually the trend started to become normal. Figure 4 below shows how the Major Global Stock Indices have performed during the Pre event period by comparing their CAARs.

*Figure 4. CAAR of ten major indices during pre-event period*

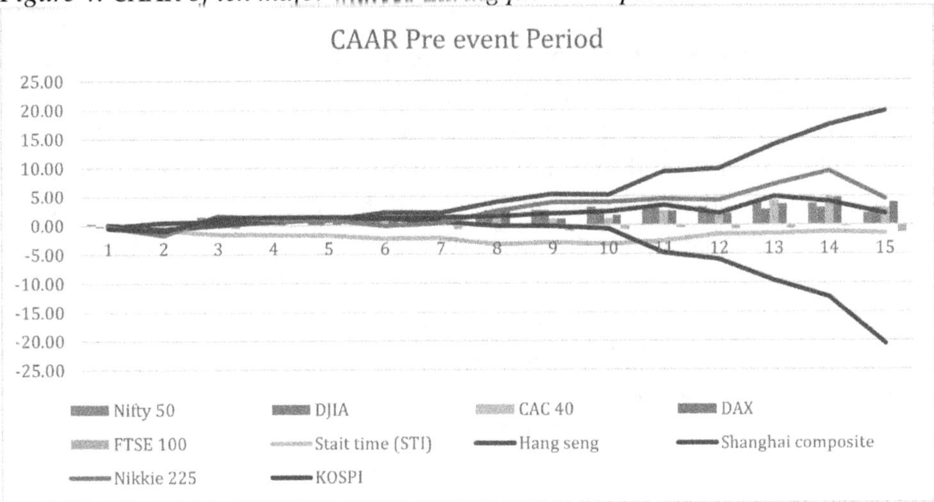


Figure 5 below shows how the Major Global Stock Indices have performed during the Post event period by comparing their CAARs.

*Figure 5. CAAR of ten major indices during post-event period*

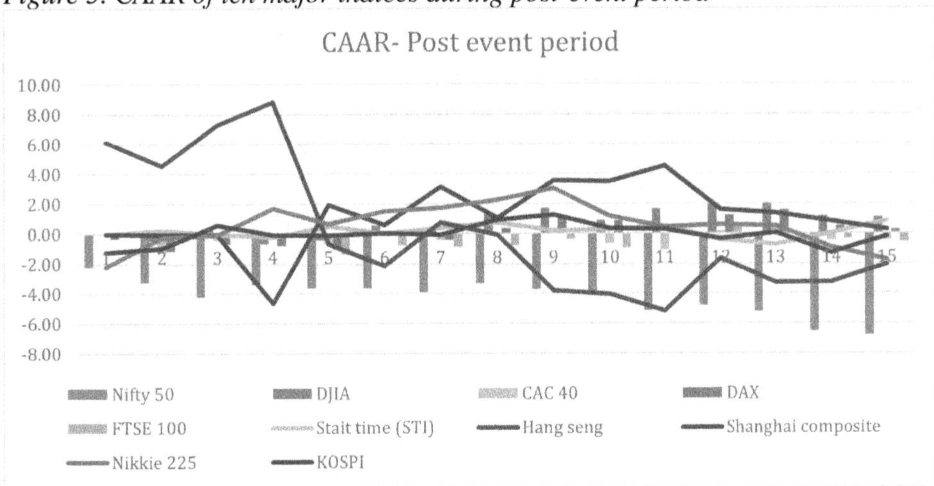

## 5.6 Results of T Test:

As far as the NSE Nifty 50 Index is concerned, the paired samples test for the NSE Nifty 50 index revealed a mean difference of -6.19733 (t=−10.656, p=0.000). The p-value obtained is 0.000 which is well below the significance level of 0.05. This result confirms that there is a significant difference in the AARs of the Nifty 50 index before and after the announcement of the Israel-Iran War. For the DJIA index, the test showed a mean difference of -1.02333 (t=−5.423, p=0.000). The p-value obtained is 0.000 which is well below the significance level of 0.05. Thus, the results indicate a significant difference in the AARs of the DJIA index before and after the event. As far as the CAC 40 Index is concerned, the paired samples test for the CAC 40 index revealed a mean difference of -1.80267 (t=−4.453, p=0.001). The p-value obtained is 0.001 which is well below the significance level of 0.05. This indicates a significant change in the AARs of the CAC 40 index before and after the Israel-Iran war. The analysis for the DAX index indicated a mean difference of -1.49200 (t=−4.526, p=0.000). The p-value obtained is 0.000 which is well below the significance level of 0.05. This confirms that the DAX index experienced a significant difference in AARs before and after the geopolitical event. For the FTSE 100 index, the test showed a mean difference of 0.21200 (t=1.065, p=0.305). The p-value obtained is 0.305 which is well above the significance level of 0.05. This result suggests no significant difference in the AARs of the FTSE 100 index before and after the Israel-Iran war. The paired samples test for the Strait Times index revealed a mean difference of 2.07600 (t=7.282, p=0.000). The p-value obtained is 0.000 which is well below the significance level of 0.05. This indicates a substantial change in the AARs of the Strait Times index due to the event. The test for the Hang Sang index reported a mean difference of -5.89267 (t=−2.281, p=0.039). The p-value obtained is 0.039 which is well the significance level of 0.05. This confirms that there is a significant difference in the AARs of the Hang Sang index before and after the announcement of the Israel-Iran war. For the Shanghai index, the paired samples test revealed a mean difference of 4.48467 (t=2.547, p=0.023). The p-value obtained is 0.023 which is well below the significance level of 0.05. This result indicates a significant difference in the AARs of the Shanghai index before and after the event. The test for the Nikkei 225 index showed a mean difference of -2.21400 (t=−2.508, p=0.025). The p-value obtained is 0.025 which is well below the significance level of 0.05. This confirms that there is a significant difference in the AARs of the Nikkei 225 index before and after the geopolitical event. For the KOSPI index, the analysis reported a mean difference of -1.87333 (t=−4.792, p=0.000). The p-value obtained is 0.000 which is well below the significance level of 0.05. This result demonstrates a significant difference in the AARs of the KOSPI index before and after the Israel-Iran war. Of all the indices, on which paired samples t test was carried out, except the FTSE 100 index, p values were less than the significance level of 0.05%. Hence the alternative hypothesis is being accepted.

## 5.7 Results of Generalised Sign Test:

*Table 6. Sign test*

| | Nifty 50 post – Nifty 50 pre | DJIA post – DJIA pre | CAC 40 post – CAC 40 pre | DAX post – DAX pre | FTSE 100 post – FTSE 100 pre | Strait time post – Strait time pre | Hang sang post – Hang sang pre | Shanghai post – Shanghai pre | Nikkie225 post - Nikkie225 pre | KOSPI post – KOSPI pre |
|---|---|---|---|---|---|---|---|---|---|---|
| Exact Sig (2-tailed) | .000[b] | .001[b] | .001[b] | .007[b] | .607[b] | .000[b] | .118[b] | .118[b] | .118[b] | .000[b] |

In order to make the study more reliable, along with parametric tests, non-parametric tests are also performed. Under the Sign test employed, among majority of the indices, the p value obtained is less than the significance level of 0.05%. This once again proves that the Israel-Iran War had telling impact on the major indices of stock markets around the world.

## 5.7 Results of Rank Test:

*Table 7. Rank test*

| | Nifty 50 post – Nifty 50 pre | DJIA post – DJIA pre | CAC 40 post – CAC 40 pre | DAX post – DAX pre | FTSE 100 post – FTSE 100 pre | Strait time post – Strait time pre | Hang sang post – Hang sang pre | Shanghai post – Shanghai pre | Nikkie225 post - Nikkie225 pre | KOSPI post – KOSPI pre |
|---|---|---|---|---|---|---|---|---|---|---|
| Z | -3.408[b] | -3.237[b] | -3.351[b] | -3.124[b] | -1.022[c] | -3.408[c] | -1.931[b] | -2.329[c] | -2.215[b] | -3.408[b] |
| Asymp. Sig (2-tailed) | .001 | .001 | .001 | .002 | .307 | .001 | .053 | .020 | .027 | .001 |

Under the Rank test performed, among majority of the indices, the p value obtained is less than the significance level of 0.05%. This once again proves that the Israel-Iran War had telling impact on the major indices of stock markets around the world.

## 6. FINDINGS

Most indices, including NSE Nifty 50, DJIA, CAC 40, DAX, Hang Sang, Nikkei 225, and KOSPI, experienced a decline in mean values, indicating a significant negative effect. Overall, the findings reveal that the Israel-Iran war had a discernible adverse impact on global stock markets, with regional differences in sensitivity and recovery. Further statistical tests, namely, paired t-tests, generalised sign test and rank test would confirm the significance of these observed changes. The findings also revealed varied regional responses, with some markets, such as India and Hong Kong, showing marked sensitivity, while others, such as Europe and China, appear less affected. The results underscore the differential impact of geopolitical conflicts on global stock markets. The Israel-Iran war had a significant and varied impact on global stock markets. While most indices showed declines, the magnitude and direction of the changes differed across regions, reflecting diverse market sensitivities to geopolitical events.

## 7. CONCLUSION

The study examining the impact of an Israel-Iran war on global stock markets provides significant insights into how geopolitical conflicts influence major global stock indices. The findings underscore that geopolitical event of this magnitude lead to increased market volatility, risk aversion among investors, and sector-specific shocks, particularly in energy and defence industries (Ranjan et al., 2023). Major global stock indices, including those in developed and emerging markets, exhibit varying degrees of sensitivity to such events, reflecting differences in regional economic dependencies, investor sentiment, and market resilience (A. Mishra, 2025b). Safe-haven assets, such as gold and government bonds, often experience surges in demand, indicating a shift in investor Preferences during times of heightened uncertainty (A. B. Mishra & Gaikwad, 2024). The study highlights the critical role of diversification, risk management, and policy interventions in mitigating adverse market impacts. For investors, the need for robust strategies that incorporate geopolitical risk is evident, while policymakers and financial institutions must prepare for economic stabilization measures to cushion global markets against such shocks.

## REFERENCES

Ahamad, S., Mishra, A. B., Raghuram, K. S., Tiwari, M., & Riyazuddin, Y. Md., & Alanya-Beltran, J. (2024) . Applications of Internet of Things (IoT) in Maintaining Privacy and Security of Smart Cities. In *Computer Science Engineering and Emerging Technologies* (pp. 187–191) . CRC Press. DOI: 10.1201/9781003405580-30

Manoharan, G., Mishra, A. B., Adusumilli, S. B. K., Chavva, M., Damancharla, H., & Sahaya Lenin, D. (2024) . Supervised Learning for Personalized Marketing Strategies. *2024 International Conference on Advances in Computing, Communication and Applied Informatics (ACCAI)*, 1–6. DOI: 10.1109/ACCAI61061.2024.10602307

Mishra, A. (2025a) . Kalyan Jewellers: A Case Study on Brand Perception and Disruptive Innovation in the Jewellery Market. *IGI Global Scientific Publishing*, 261–284.

Mishra, A. (2025b) . *Monitoring the Development of the IoT Concept in Various Application Domains. Taylor & Francis Online*. CRC Press.

Mishra, A. B. (2020) . E- PAYMENT SYSTEM: A RISING TREND OF ECONOMY. *New Paradigm in Business and Education*. https://www.researchgate.net/profile/Anitha-K-2/publication/349605501_E-LEARNING_THROUGH_GAMIFICATION-_AN_ITINERARY_TO_GAIN_IN-DEPTH_KNOWLEDGE/links/6037d566299bf1cc26ef9597/E-LEARNING-THROUGH-GAMIFICATION-AN-ITINERARY-TO-GAIN-IN-DEPTH-KNOWLEDGE.pdf#page=10

Mishra, A. B., Chand, K., & Kaith, K. (2022) . Influencer Marketing as Emerging Promotional Tool in Modern Era and Opportunities to Uprising Sales. *International Journal of Emerging Research in Engineering, Science, and Management, 1*(3) . Advance online publication. DOI: 10.58482/ijeresm.v1i3.3

Mishra, A. B., & Gaikwad, V. (2024) . The Transaction War Between Google Pay and Phonepe. In *IGI Global* (pp. 166–185) . DOI: 10.4018/978-1-6684-7840-0.ch009

Mishra, A. B., Ranjan, N., Sharma, K. M., Padhye, P., & Chand, K. (2023) . Advancement of Digital Transformation to Boost Financial Services Industry. *Journal of Informatics Education and Research, 3*(2), 2435–2440.

Mishra, A. B., & Singh, A. (2024) . The Mumbai Dabbawalas : An Efficient and Sustainable Lunchbox Delivery System. In *IGI Global* (pp. 154–160) . DOI: 10.4018/979-8-3693-1544-6.ch007

Mohseni, M., Othman, B. A., Raturi, P., Mishra, A. B., Priya, S. J., & Saravanan, V. (2022) . The Role of Parallel Computing Towards Implementation of Enhanced and Effective Industrial Internet of Things (IOT) Through Manova Approach. *2022 2nd International Conference on Advance Computing and Innovative Technologies in Engineering (ICACITE)*, 160–164. DOI: 10.1109/ICACITE53722.2022.9823698

Rana, M. S., Cavaliere, L. P. L., Mishra, A. B., Padhye, P., Singh, R. R., & Khanna, R. (2022, April) . Internet of Things (IOT) Based Assessment for Effective Monitoring Data Against Malicious Attacks on Financial Collectors. In 2022 2nd International Conference on Advance Computing and Innovative Technologies in Engineering (ICACITE) (pp. 177-181) . IEEE.

Ranjan, N., Mishra, A. B., & Padhye, P. (2023) . Dynamics of Digital Payments Enable the World's Safest Way to Pay. *Journal of Informatics Education and Research, 3*(2) . Advance online publication. DOI: 10.52783/jier.v3i2.406

Usman, M. S., Sheoliha, N., Prabhakar, P. V., Mishra, A. B., & Dondapati, A. (2023) . Leading Strategies for Organizational Adaptation and Growth in Digital Transformation in Marketing. Journal of Informatics Education and Research.

# Conclusion

As we conclude this journey through the complexities of social entrepreneurship and sustainability, we are reminded that the path ahead is fraught with challenges, but also filled with opportunities. The dedication, resilience, and innovation of social entrepreneurs, innovators, and change-makers inspire us to strive for a better world.

This book, *"Organizational Risks, Challenges, and Barriers in Developing Sustainability Start-Ups"*, has explored the intricate relationships between social entrepreneurship, sustainability, and organizational risk management. We have examined the theoretical foundations, practical applications, and real-world examples that illustrate the power of social entrepreneurship to drive positive change.

Through these pages, we have emphasized the importance of:

1. Embracing sustainability principles to ensure long-term impact
2. Developing effective risk management strategies to navigate uncertainty
3. Fostering collaborative partnerships to amplify social impact
4. Leveraging technology and innovation to scale social entrepreneurship
5. Cultivating leadership and talent to drive social entrepreneurship forward

As we look to the future, we recognize that social entrepreneurship will continue to evolve, adapt, and innovate. The global community of social entrepreneurship practitioners, researchers, and policymakers must work together to:

1. Address the world's most pressing social and environmental challenges
2. Develop evidence-based solutions to inform practice and policy
3. Foster inclusive, equitable, and sustainable ecosystems
4. Support the next generation of social entrepreneurs and innovators

As social entrepreneurship continues to evolve, it's essential to recognize the interconnectedness of global challenges and the imperative for collective action. The future of social entrepreneurship demands:

1. Interdisciplinary collaboration: bridging silos between business, academia, government, and civil society.

2. Contextual understanding: recognizing the nuances of local contexts and adapting solutions accordingly.
3. Inclusive innovation: prioritizing accessibility, equity, and justice in social entrepreneurship.
4. Systems thinking: addressing root causes, not just symptoms, of social and environmental issues.

To achieve this vision, we must:

1. Invest in social entrepreneurship education and training.
2. Foster inclusive ecosystems, providing access to resources and networks.
3. Develop and deploy technology-enabled solutions.
4. Encourage policy frameworks supporting social entrepreneurship.

The next generation of social entrepreneurs will face unprecedented challenges, but also unparalleled opportunities. As we empower them with knowledge, networks, and resources, we must also acknowledge the complexity and uncertainty of the social entrepreneurship landscape.

In this context, resilience becomes a critical factor. Social entrepreneurs must develop coping mechanisms, adaptability, and perseverance to navigate the turbulence of social and environmental change.

Moreover, social entrepreneurship must prioritize well-being – for individuals, communities, and the planet. This requires redefining success beyond financial returns, incorporating social and environmental impact assessments.

Ultimately, social entrepreneurship's transformative potential relies on our collective ability to:

1. Challenge assumptions and disrupt status quos.
2. Embrace uncertainty and experimentation.
3. Foster empathy, compassion, and inclusivity.
4. Cultivate collaborative leadership and shared vision.

As we embark on this journey, we draw inspiration from the countless social entrepreneurs, innovators, and change-makers who have paved the way. Their stories, struggles, and triumphs remind us that social entrepreneurship is:

1. A movement, not a moment.
2. A collective effort, not an individual achievement.
3. A journey, not a destination.

In the face of uncertainty, social entrepreneurship offers a beacon of hope. By working together, we can create a brighter future – one that balances social, environmental, and economic imperatives.

The time for action is now. The future of social entrepreneurship demands our collective commitment, creativity, and resilience.

Let us rise to the challenge.

> In closing, we reiterate the dedication that opened this book:
> To the social entrepreneurs, innovators, and change-makers who dedicate their lives to creating a better world. May this book inspire and empower you to overcome the challenges and achieve your vision.

Together, we can create a brighter, more sustainable future – one that benefits all people, planet, and prosperity.

## FINAL THOUGHTS

As you close this book, we invite you to reflect on your own role in driving positive change. What will you do differently? What will you create? What will you inspire?

The future of social entrepreneurship is in your hands.

We hope that this book has inspired and empowered readers to embrace entrepreneurship. Together, we can create a brighter future. Thank you for joining us on this journey.

In conclusion, *"Organizational Risks, Challenges, and Barriers in Developing Sustainability Start-Ups"* serves as a testament to the power of collaboration and knowledge-sharing in addressing the complexities of entrepreneurship. As we move forward, let us continue to prioritize entrepreneurship, even for economic development and as a society enhancement vehicle, fostering an age that is both innovative and responsible. Last, to retain consulting services, in general, or for your startup or business needs, please contact sales@LadyMirageGlobal.com or visit our website at www.LadyMirageGlobal.com to learn more about our consulting services and how we can support your organization's startup, transformation, or journey.

**Kyla L. Tennin**
*Lady Mirage Global, Inc., USA*

# Compilation of References


Adams, R. B., & Ferreira, D. (2012). Regulatory pressure and bank directors' incentives to attend board

Adams, W. M. (2006). *The future of sustainability: Re-thinking environment and development in the Twenty-first century*. Report of the IUCN Renowned Thinkers Meeting, 29–31 January 2006. Retrieved on: 2024-01-01.

Adams, C., & Adams, M. (2011). Green human capital: The role of human resource management in sustainable development. *Business Strategy and the Environment, 20*(6), 366–381.

Ahamad, S., Mishra, A. B., Raghuram, K. S., Riyazuddin, Y. M., & Alanya-Beltran, J. (2024). *Applications of Internet of Things (IoT) in Maintaining Privacy and Security of Smart Cities*. Taylor & Francis Journal., DOI: 10.1201/9781003405580-30

Ahamad, S., Mishra, A. B., Raghuram, K. S., Tiwari, M., Riyazuddin, Y. M., & Alanya-Beltran, J. (2024). Applications of Internet of Things (IoT) in Maintaining Privacy and Security of Smart Cities. In *Computer Science Engineering and Emerging Technologies* (pp. 187–191). CRC Press.

Ahmad, N., Kummerow, L., & Wilson, C. (2006). A cross-cultural study of entrepreneurial competencies among business owners in SMEs: Evidence from Australia and Malaysia. *51st ICSB World Conference,* Melbourne.

Ahmed, F., Capretz, L. F., Bouktif, S., & Campbell, P. (2013). Soft skills and software development: A reflection from software industry. *International Journal of Information Processing and Management, 4*(3), 171–191. DOI: 10.4156/ijipm.vol4.issue3.17

Ahmed, G., Amponsah, C. T., & Johnson, D. S. (2019). Gender differences in entrepreneurial attitudes and intentions: The case of Brand Dubai. *International Journal of Business and Emerging Markets, 11*(4), 315–334. DOI: 10.1504/IJBEM.2019.105230

Ahmed, M. (2011). Defining and measuring literacy: Facing the reality. *International Review of Education*, *57*(1-2), 179–195. DOI: 10.1007/s11159-011-9188-x

Ahrari, S., Krauss, S. E., Ariffin, Z., & Meng, L. K. (2019). "Making a difference… on my terms": Motivational factors of youth involvement in social entrepreneurship in Malaysia. In *Societal Entrepreneurship and Competitiveness* (pp. 227–246). Emerald Publishing Limited., DOI: 10.1108/978-1-83867-471-720191015

Aigner, D. J. (1973). Regression with a binary independent variable subject to errors of observation. *Journal of Econometrics*, *1*(1), 49–59. DOI: 10.1016/0304-4076(73)90005-5

Aisha, A. N., Siswanto, J., & Sudirman, I. (2016). Competencies model for entrepreneur development in software industries. *IEEE International Conference on Industrial Engineering and Engineering Management, 2016-Decem*, 184–188. DOI: 10.1109/IEEM.2016.7797861

Ajzen, I. (1991). *The theory of planned behavior*. DOI: 10.1016/0749-5978(91)90020-T

Ajzen, I. (2002). *Constructing a TpB questionnaire: Conceptual and methodological Considerations*. http://chuang.epage.au.edu.tw/ezfiles/168/1168/attach/20/pta_41176_7688352_57138.pdf

Akkaya, D. H., & Uzman, E. E. (2010). Hızla Yok Olan BirKültürün Son İzleri: *Eskişehir Sakana Örnekleri. Green Age Symposium, Mimar Sinan Fine ArtUniversity*, 6-8 December 2010, İstanbul.

Alam, M., Gale, A., Brown, M., & Khan, A. I. (2010). The importance of human skills in project management professional development. *International Journal of Managing Projects in Business*, *3*(3), 495–516. DOI: 10.1108/17538371011056101

Alberti, F. G., & Varon Garrido, M. A. (2017). Can profit and sustainability goals co-exist? New business models for hybrid firms. *The Journal of Business Strategy*, *38*(1), 3–13. DOI: 10.1108/JBS-12-2015-0124

Ali, N. M. Farkhanda. (2023, February 27). *India raises $2bn in first Sovereign Green Bond issuances*. Structured Finance In Brief. https://www.structuredfinanceinbrief.com/2023/02/india-raises-2bn-in-first-sovereign-green-bond-issuances/

Ali, I., Ali, M., & Badghish, S. (2019). Symmetric and asymmetric modeling of the entrepreneurial ecosystem in developing entrepreneurial intentions among female university students in Saudi Arabia. *International Journal of Gender and Entrepreneurship*, *11*(4), 435–458. DOI: 10.1108/IJGE-02-2019-0039

Al Mamary, Y. H. S., & Alraja, M. M. (2022). Understanding entrepreneurship intention and behavior in the light of TPB model from the digital entrepreneurship perspective. *International Journal of Information Management Data Insights*, *2*(2), 100106. DOI: 10.1016/j.jjimei.2022.100106

Al-Nuaimi, S. R., & Al-Ghamdi, S. G. (2022). Sustainable consumption and education for sustainability in higher education. *Sustainability (Basel)*, *14*(12), 7255. DOI: 10.3390/su14127255

Alomoto, W., Niñerola, À., & Pié, L. (2021). Social impact assessment: A systematic review of literature. *Social Indicators Research*, *161*(1), 225–250. DOI: 10.1007/s11205-021-02809-1

Aloulou, W. J., & Algarni, E. A. (2022). Determinants of social entrepreneurial intention: Empirical evidence from the Saudi context. *Social Enterprise Journal*, *18*(4), 605–625. DOI: 10.1108/SEJ-11-2021-0086

Alper, K. (2017). *Anadolu'nun İş Yapma Kültürü "İmece" ÖrnekOlmalı*. Retrieved from https://www.hurriyet.com.tr/ekonomi/anadolunun-is-yapma-kulturu-imeceornek-olsun40678579, (Acces date: 02 May 2023).

Alshebami, A. S., Seraj, A. H. A., & Alzain, E. (2022). Lecturers' creativity and students' entrepreneurial intention in Saudi Arabia. *Vision (Basel)*, *09722629221099596*, 09722629221099596. Advance online publication. DOI: 10.1177/09722629221099596

Amofah, K., & Saladrigues, R. (2022). Impact of attitude towards entrepreneurship education and role models on entrepreneurial intention. *Journal of Innovation and Entrepreneurship*, *11*(1), 1–30. DOI: 10.1186/s13731-022-00197-5 PMID: 35036286

Anand, S., & Sen, A. K. (1996). Sustainable human development: Concepts and priorities, Office of Development Studies Discussion Paper, No. 1, UNDP, New York.

Anderson, J., & Smith, B. (2024). *The Immersive Frontier: Unraveling the Potential of AR Commerce in E-commerce Evolution*. EasyChair.

Aparisi-Torrijo, S., & Ribes-Giner, G. (2022). Female entrepreneurial leadership factors. *The International Entrepreneurship and Management Journal*, *18*(4), 1707–1737. DOI: 10.1007/s11365-022-00798-2

Armuña, C., Ramos, S., Juan, J., Feijóo, C., & Arenal, A. (2020). From stand-up to start-up: Exploring entrepreneurship competencies and STEM women's intention. *The International Entrepreneurship and Management Journal*, *16*(1), 69–92. DOI: 10.1007/s11365-019-00627-z

Aron, R. (2010). *Sosyolojik Düşüncenin Evreleri (Çev: K.Alemdar).* Bilgi Yayınevi.

Arshad, A., Parveen, S., & Mir, F. N. (2024). The role of green bonds in reducing $CO_2$ emissions: A case of developing countries. *Journal of Economic and Administrative Sciences.* DOI: 10.1108/JEAS-09-2023-0242

Asmare, A., & Zewdie, S. (2022). Omnichannel retailing strategy: A systematic review. *International Review of Retail, Distribution and Consumer Research, 32*(1), 59–79. DOI: 10.1080/09593969.2021.2024447

Aydemir, A. (2015). Social cooperation and solidarity in divanu lugati't-Türk. *Route Educational and Social Science Journal, 2*(2), 226–240. DOI: 10.17121/ressjournal.237

Ayodeji, A., & Okunade, R. A. (2019). Board independence and financial performance of deposit money banks in Nigeria and Canada. *Asian Journal of Economics. Business and Accounting, 11*(3), 1–9.

Bainbridge, S. M. (2002). Why a board-group decisionmaking in corporate governance. *Vand. L. Rev., 55*, 1. Basmah A, Lakshmi K. Is excess board independence good for firm performance? An empirical investigation of non-financial listed firms in Saudi Arabia. International Journal of Financial Research. 2016;

Baker, S. (2015). *Sustainable development.* Routledge. DOI: 10.4324/9780203121177

Baltaci, A., & Balcı, A. (2017). Complexity leadership: A theorical perspective. *International Journal of Educational Leadership and Management*, 30-58.

Banerjee, A. (2019). Financing the climate change through green (Climate sustainable) bonds. *2019 Advances in Science and Engineering Technology International Conferences (ASET)*, 1–4. DOI: 10.1109/ICASET.2019.8714408

Bartels, M. (2025). *TV advertising research for Facebook.* Tobii.

Bartlett, C. A., & Ghoshal, S. (1997). The myth of the generic manager. *California Management Review, 40*(1), 92–116. DOI: 10.2307/41165924

Basterretxea, I., Cornforth, C., & Heras-Saizarbitoria, I. (2022). Corporate governance as a key aspect in the failure of worker cooperatives. *Economic and Industrial Democracy, 43*(1), 362–387. DOI: 10.1177/0143831X19899474

Baysinger, B. D., & Butler, H. N. (1985). The role of corporate law in the theory of the firm. *The Journal of Law & Economics, 28*(1), 179–191. DOI: 10.1086/467079

Ben Shahar, D., Carmeli, A., Sulganik, E., & Weiss, D. (2024). Regulating diversity and inclusiveness in boards of directors. *The Academy of Management Perspectives*, *38*(3), 434–439. DOI: 10.5465/amp.2023.0474

Bernier, I. (2004). A UNESCO international convention on cultural diversity. *Free trade versus cultural diversity: WTO negotiations in the field of audiovisual services*, 65-76.

Bhagat, S., & Bolton, B. (2008). Corporate governance and firm performance. *Journal of Corporate Finance*, *14*(3), 257–273. DOI: 10.1016/j.jcorpfin.2008.03.006

Bharatan, I., Logan, K., Manning, R. M., & Swan, J. (2023). Values alignment in sustaining healthcare innovation processes. In *Organizational behaviour in health care* (pp. 315–338). DOI: 10.1007/978-3-031-24212-0_14

Bharwani, S., & Mathews, D. (2023). Sustainable luxury: From an oxymoron to a tautology – the case of the Indian luxury hospitality industry. *Worldwide Hospitality and Tourism Themes*, *15*(3), 231–248. DOI: 10.1108/WHATT-01-2023-0013

Bhuiyan, N., & Baghel, A. (2005). An overview of continuous improvement: From the past to the present. *Management Decision*, *43*(5), 761–771. DOI: 10.1108/00251740510597761

Bianchi, M., & Vieta, M. (2020). Co-operatives, territories and social capital: Reconsidering a theoretical framework. *International Journal of Social Economics*, *47*(12), 1599–1617. DOI: 10.1108/IJSE-03-2020-0135

Biggins, J. V. (1999). Making Board Diversity Work. *Corporate Board*, *20*(117), 11–17.

Bilimoria, D., & Piderit, S. K. (1994). Qualifications of corporate board committee members. *Group & Organization Management*, *19*(3), 334–362. DOI: 10.1177/1059601194193007

Bird, B. (1995). Towards a theory of entrepreneurial competency. *Advances in Entrepreneurship, Firm, Emergence, and Growth*, 2(1), 51–72.

Bohra, D. K., Nagansur, S., & Anute, N. (2022). *Comparative Analysis of FMCG Products with Special Reference to HUL and ITC*. OmniScience A Multi-Disciplinary Journal. DOI: 10.37591/omniscience.v12i2.3395

Botha, M., & Taljaard, A. (2021). Exploring the entrepreneurial intention-competency model for Nascent Entrepreneurs: Insights from a developing country context. *Frontiers in Psychology*, *12*, 516120. DOI: 10.3389/fpsyg.2021.516120 PMID: 34393866

Böttcher, T. P., Empelmann, S., Weking, J., Hein, A., & Krcmar, H. (2023). Digital sustainable business models: Using digital technology to integrate ecological sustainability into the core of business models. *Information Systems Journal*. Advance online publication. DOI: 10.1111/isj.12436

Bougie, R., & Sekaran, U. (2019). *Research methods for business: A skill building approach*. John Wiley & Sons.

Bourdieu, P. (1985). The social space and the genesis of groups. *Social Sciences Information. Information Sur les Sciences Sociales*, *24*(2), 195–220. DOI: 10.1177/053901885024002001

Bower, J. L. (2016). Resource allocation theory. In *Palgrave Macmillan UK eBooks* (pp. 1–3). DOI: 10.1057/978-1-349-94848-2_677-1

Brick, I. E., & Chidambaran, N. K. (2007). Board meetings, committee structure, and firm performance. *Committee Structure, and Firm Performance (November 2007)*.

Browne, J., Bullock, A., Poletti, C., & Cserző, D. (2021). Recent research into healthcare professions regulation: A rapid evidence assessment. *BMC Health Services Research*, *21*(1), 934. Advance online publication. DOI: 10.1186/s12913-021-06946-8 PMID: 34493260

Brown, R. (2020). The social identity approach: Appraising the Tajfellian legacy. *British Journal of Social Psychology*, *59*(1), 5–25. DOI: 10.1111/bjso.12349 PMID: 31691319

Brown, R., Alderson, H., Kaner, E., McGovern, R., & Lingam, R. (2019). "There are carers, and then there are carers who actually care"; Conceptualizations of care among looked after children and care leavers, social workers, and carers. *Child Abuse & Neglect*, *92*, 219–229. DOI: 10.1016/j.chiabu.2019.03.018 PMID: 31005828

Brundtland, G. H. (1987). What is sustainable development. *Our Common Future*, *8*(9).

Bureau, A. N. (2024, December 10). *Future of sustainable finance: How green bonds can evolve*. https://news.abplive.com/business/future-of-sustainable-finance-how-green-bonds-can-evolve-1736797

Butler, M. J. R (2008). . Neuromarketing and the perception of knowledge. *Journal of Consumer Behaviour*, *7* (4–5)., 415–419. DOI: 10.1002/cb.260

Byrne, B. M. (2010). *Structural equation modeling with AMOS: Basic concepts, applications, and programming (multivariate applications series)*. Taylor & Francis Group.

Canestrino, R., Ćwiklicki, M., Magliocca, P., & Pawełek, B. (2020). Understanding social entrepreneurship: A cultural perspective in business research. *Journal of Business Research*, *110*, 132–143. DOI: 10.1016/j.jbusres.2020.01.006

Capra, F. (2007). Sustainable living, ecological literacy, and the breath of life. [CJEE]. *Canadian Journal of Environmental Education*, •••, 9–18.

Capretz, L. F., & Ahmed, F. (2010). Making sense of software development and personality types. *IT Professional*, *12*(February), 6–13. DOI: 10.1109/MITP.2010.33

*Carbon credits, how they work, and who buys them*. (n.d.). Investopedia. Retrieved December 12, 2024, from https://www.investopedia.com/terms/c/carbon_credit.asp

*Carbon market | bureau of energy efficiency, government of india, ministry of power*. (n.d.). Retrieved December 11, 2024, from https://beeindia.gov.in/en/programmes/carbon-market

Carrizales, A., Branje, S., & Lannegrand, L. (2021). Disentangling between-and within-person associations between empathy and prosocial behaviors during early adolescence. *Journal of Adolescence*, *93*(1), 114–125. DOI: 10.1016/j.adolescence.2021.10.006 PMID: 34740152

Carter, D., D'Souza, F. P., Simkins, B. J., & Simpson, W. G. (2007). The diversity of corporate board committees and firm financial performance. *Available atSSRN* 972763. DOI: 10.2139/ssrn.972763

Carver, J., & Carver, M. (2006). *Reinventing your board: A step-by-step guide to implementing policy governance* (Vol. 18). John Wiley & Sons.

Cerchia, R. E., & Piccolo, K. (2019). The ethical consumer and codes of ethics in the fashion industry. *Laws*, *8*(4), 23. DOI: 10.3390/laws8040023

Chandler, G. N., & Hanks, S. H. (1993). Measuring the performance of emerging businesses: A validation study. *Journal of Business Venturing*, *8*(5), 391–408. DOI: 10.1016/0883-9026(93)90021-V

Chandler, G. N., & Jansen, E. (1992). The founder's competence and venture performance. *Journal of Business Venturing*, *7*(3), 223–236. DOI: 10.1016/0883-9026(92)90028-P

Chan, J. H., Chen, S. Y., Piterou, A., Khoo, S. L., Lean, H. H., Hashim, I. H. M., & Lane, B. (2021). An innovative social enterprise: Roles of and challenges faced by an arts hub in a World Heritage Site in Malaysia. *City, Culture and Society*, *25*, 100396. DOI: 10.1016/j.ccs.2021.100396

Che Nawi, N. R., Arshad, M. M., Krauss, S. E., & Ismail, I. A. (2022). Challenges faced by youth social entrepreneurs in Malaysia: Career transition to become a social entrepreneur. *European Journal of Training and Development*, *46*(3/4), 317–336. DOI: 10.1108/EJTD-02-2020-0021

Chege, S. M., & Wang, D. (2020). Information technology innovation and its impact on job creation by SMEs in developing countries: An analysis of the literature review. *Technology Analysis and Strategic Management*, *32*(3), 256–271. DOI: 10.1080/09537325.2019.1651263

Chen, P. C., Chan, W. C., Hung, S. W., & Lin, D. Z. (2020). How entrepreneurs recognise entrepreneurial opportunity and its gaps: A cognitive theory perspective. *Technology Analysis and Strategic Management*, *32*(2), 223–238. DOI: 10.1080/09537325.2019.1648790

Chen, W. D. (2023). Crowdfunding for social ventures. *Social Enterprise Journal*, *19*(3), 256–276. DOI: 10.1108/SEJ-05-2022-0051

Chillakuri, B. (2020). Understanding Generation Z expectations for effective onboarding. *Journal of Organizational Change Management*, *33*(7), 1277–1296. DOI: 10.1108/JOCM-02-2020-0058

Ciccullo, F., Pero, M., & Patrucco, A. S. (2023). Designing circular supply chains in startup companies: Evidence from Italian fashion and construction startups. *International Journal of Logistics Management*, *34*(3), 553–581. DOI: 10.1108/IJLM-04-2022-0158

Çıkın, A. (2007). Tarımsal Örgütlenme II. Çiftçiler NasılÖrgütlenmeli. *Ege Tarım Dergisi*, *1*(2).

*Climate finance*. (n.d.). Shakti Sustainable Energy Foundation. Retrieved December 16, 2024, from https://shaktifoundation.in/climate-finance/

Coase, R. H. (1993). The nature of the firm (1937). *WILLIANSON, OE; WINTER, SG.*

Cockburn, A., & Highsmith, J. (2001). Agile software development. *The People Factor.*, (November), 131–133.

Colombo, M. G., & Grilli, L. (2010). On growth drivers of high-tech start-ups: Exploring the role of founders' human capital and venture capital. *Journal of Business Venturing*, *25*(6), 610–626. DOI: 10.1016/j.jbusvent.2009.01.005

Corrêa, V. S., Brito, F. R. D. S., Lima, R. M. D., & Queiroz, M. M. (2022). Female entrepreneurship in emerging and developing countries: A systematic literature review. *International Journal of Gender and Entrepreneurship, 14*(3), 300–322. DOI: 10.1108/IJGE-08-2021-0142

Corsini, L., & Moultrie, J. (2019). Design for social sustainability: Using digital fabrication in the humanitarian and development sector. *Sustainability (Basel), 11*(13), 3562. Advance online publication. DOI: 10.3390/su11133562

Cosic, D. (2016). Neuromarketing in Market Research. *Interdisciplinary Description of Complex Systems, 14*(2), 139–147. DOI: 10.7906/indecs.14.2.3

Coşkun, A. E., & Erturgut, R. (2023). How do uncertainties affect supply-chain resilience? The moderating role of information sharing for sustainable supply-chain management. *Sustainability (Basel), 16*(1), 131. DOI: 10.3390/su16010131

Crowne, M. (2002). Why software product startups fail and what to do about it. Evolution of software product development in startup companies. *IEEE International Engineering Management Conference, 1*, 338–343. DOI: 10.1109/IEMC.2002.1038454

D'amato, A., Henderson, S., & Florence, S. (2009). Corporate social responsibility and sustainable business. *A Guide to Leadership tasks and functions*, 102.

Da Silva Nunes, A. K., Morioka, S. N., & Bolis, I. (2022). Challenges of business models for sustainability in startups. *RAUSP Management Journal, 57*(4), 382–400. DOI: 10.1108/RAUSP-10-2021-0216

Daily, C. M., & Dalton, D. R. (1994). Corporate governance in the small firm: Prescriptions for CEOs and directors. [archive only]. *Journal of Small Business Strategy, 5*(1), 57–68.

Dalton, D. R., Daily, C. M., Ellstrand, A. E., & Johnson, J. L. (1998). Meta-analytic reviews of board composition, leadership structure, and financial performance. *Strategic Management Journal, 19*(3), 269–290. DOI: 10.1002/(SICI)1097-0266(199803)19:3<269::AID-SMJ950>3.0.CO;2-K

Daoud, J. I. (2017, December). Multicollinearity and regression analysis. [). IOP Publishing.]. *Journal of Physics: Conference Series, 949*(1), 012009. DOI: 10.1088/1742-6596/949/1/012009

Daspit, J. J., Fox, C. J., & Findley, S. K. (2023). Entrepreneurial mindset: An integrated definition, a review of current insights, and directions for future research. *Journal of Small Business Management, 61*(1), 12–44. DOI: 10.1080/00472778.2021.1907583

Datta, N. (2018). Impact of corporate governance on financial performance: A study on DSE listed insurance companies in Bangladesh. *Global Journal of Management and Business Research, 18*(2), 32–39.

Davidson, M. (2009). Social sustainability: A potential for politics? *Local Environment, 14*(7), 607–619. DOI: 10.1080/13549830903089291

De Lange, D. E. (2017). Start-up sustainability: An insurmountable cost or a life-giving investment? *Journal of Cleaner Production, 156*, 838–854. DOI: 10.1016/j.jclepro.2017.04.108

De Lange, D., & Dodds, R. (2017). Increasing sustainable tourism through social entrepreneurship. *International Journal of Contemporary Hospitality Management, 29*(7), 1977–2002. DOI: 10.1108/IJCHM-02-2016-0096

Deloitte. (2022). *Sustainability through Human Capital Lens Guide.*

Dempsey, N., Bramley, G., Power, S., & Brown, C. (2011). The social dimension of sustainable development: Defining urban social sustainability. *Sustainable Development (Bradford), 19*(5), 289–300. DOI: 10.1002/sd.417

Department of Statistics of Malaysia (DOSM). (2022). *Key Statistics of Labor Force in Malaysia, November 2022,* available at: https://www.dosm.gov.my/v1/index.php?r=column/cthemeByCat&cat=124&bul_id=dVNkcjZsRkF4amVjSCtxYmhiV2JxUT09&menu_id=Tm8zcnRjdVRNWWlpWjRlbmtlaDk1UT09 [accessed on 2 December 2022].

Diaz Gonzalez, A., & Dentchev, N. A. (2021). Ecosystems in support of social entrepreneurs: A literature review. *Social Enterprise Journal, 17*(3), 329–360. DOI: 10.1108/SEJ-08-2020-0064

Dingliwal, U., & Gupta, D. (n.d.). *Redefining Retail: The Evolving Landscape of Retailing in a Tech-Driven eCommerce Era.*

Donaldson, L., & Davis, J. H. (1991). Stewardship theory or agency theory: CEO governance and shareholder returns. *Australian Journal of Management, 16*(1), 49–64. DOI: 10.1177/031289629101600103

Duncan, R. C. (2003). Governance and growth. Paper presented to the Symposium on Governance held at the University of the South Pacific. *Suva, September.*

Dunphy, D., Turner, D., & Crawford, M. (1997). Organizational learning as the creation of corporate competencies. *Journal of Management Development, 16*(4), 232–244. DOI: 10.1108/02621719710164526

Duong, C. D. (2023). Applying the stimulus-organism-response theory to investigate determinants of students' social entrepreneurship: Moderation role of perceived university support. *Social Enterprise Journal, 19*(2), 167–192. DOI: 10.1108/SEJ-10-2022-0091

Durkheim, E. (2006). *Toplumsal İşbölümü (Çev: Ö.Ozankaya).* Cem Yayınları.

Dweck, C. S. (1986). Motivational processes affecting learning. *The American Psychologist, 41*(10), 1040–1048. DOI: 10.1037/0003-066X.41.10.1040

Earle, H. A. (2003). Building a workplace of choice: Using the work environment to attract and retain top talent. *Journal of Facilities Management, 2*(3), 244–257. DOI: 10.1108/14725960410808230

Edison, H., Smørsgård, N. M., Wang, X., & Abrahamsson, P. (2018). Lean internal startups for software product innovation in large companies: Enablers and inhibitors. *Journal of Systems and Software, 135*, 69–87. DOI: 10.1016/j.jss.2017.09.034

Eisenberg, M. A. (2017). Legal models of management structure in the modern corporation: Officers, directors, and accountants. In *Corporate Governance* (pp. 103–167). Gower. DOI: 10.4324/9781315574288-5

Elliott, C., Mantler, J., & Huggins, J. (2021). Exploring the gendered entrepreneurial identity gap: Implications for entrepreneurship education. *International Journal of Gender and Entrepreneurship, 13*(1), 50–74. DOI: 10.1108/IJGE-04-2020-0048

Ennis, C. A. (2019). The gendered complexities of promoting female entrepreneurship in the Gulf. *New Political Economy, 24*(3), 365–384. DOI: 10.1080/13563467.2018.1457019

Environment, U. N. (2023, October 31). *Carbon markets | unep—Un environment programme.* https://www.unep.org/topics/climate-action/climate-finance/carbon-markets

Esim, S. (2014, September). The cooperative key to sustainable development. In *Conference on Cooperatives and the Sustainable Development Goals: Focus on Africa,* Berlin, Germany (Vol. 2).

Etefa, D. F. (2022). Contributions of cooperatives and encountering challenges in Ethiopia. *American Journal of Research in Business and Social Sciences, 2*(1), 1–14.

European Commission. (2018). *Entrepreneurship competence EntreComp :* DOI: 10.2767/88978

Fairbairn, B. (2016). The Meaning of Ochda.Usaskstudies.coop. Archivedfrom the original on 2012-01-11. Retrieved 2023-12-21.

Fawzy, S., Osman, A. I., Doran, J., & Rooney, D. (2020). Strategies for mitigation of climate change: A review. *Environmental Chemistry Letters*, *18*(6), 2069–2094. DOI: 10.1007/s10311-020-01059-w

Finlayson, E., & Roy, M. J. (2019). Empowering communities? Exploring roles in facilitated social enterprise. *Social Enterprise Journal*, *15*(1), 76–93. DOI: 10.1108/SEJ-04-2018-0035

Florin, J., Lubatkin, M., & Schulze, W. (2003). A social capital model of high-growth ventures. *Academy of Management Journal*, *46*(3), 374–384. DOI: 10.2307/30040630

Francoeur, C., Labelle, R., & Sinclair-Desgagné, B. (2008). Gender diversity in corporate governance and top management. *Journal of Business Ethics*, *81*(1), 83–95. DOI: 10.1007/s10551-007-9482-5

Franken, J. R., & Cook, M. L. (2019). Do corporate governance recommendations apply to US agricultural cooperatives? *Sustainability (Basel)*, *11*(19), 5321. DOI: 10.3390/su11195321

Freeman, R. E., & Phillips, R. A. (2002). Stakeholder theory: A libertarian defense. *Business Ethics Quarterly*, *12*(3), 331–349. DOI: 10.2307/3858020

Freestone, R., & Favaro, P. (2022). The social sustainability of smart cities: A conceptual framework. *City, Culture and Society*, *29*, 100460. DOI: 10.1016/j.ccs.2022.100460

García-González, A., & Ramírez-Montoya, M. S. (2023). Social entrepreneurship competency in higher education: An analysis using mixed methods. *Journal of Social Entrepreneurship*, *14*(1), 91–109. DOI: 10.1080/19420676.2020.1823872

García-Ramos, R., & García-Olalla, M. (2011). Board characteristics and firm performance in public founder- and nonfounder-led family businesses. *Journal of Family Business Strategy*, *2*(4), 220–231. DOI: 10.1016/j.jfbs.2011.09.001

García-Uceda, E., Murillo-Luna, J. L., & Lafuente, J. A. (2022). Determinant factors in entrepreneurial intention among social work degree students: The moderating effect of entrepreneurship education. *Social Enterprise Journal*, *18*(4), 563–584. DOI: 10.1108/SEJ-07-2021-0061

Germann, C. (2023). Methodology and Empirical Research. In *Chairperson Succession: Competences, Moderators, and Disclosure* (pp. 87–98). Springer Fachmedien Wiesbaden. DOI: 10.1007/978-3-658-40817-6_5

Gertler, M. E. (2004). Synergy and strategic advantage: Cooperatives and sustainable development. *Journal of Cooperatives*, *18*, 32–46.

Getnet, K., & Anullo, T. (2012). Agricultural cooperatives and rural livelihoods: Evidence from Ethiopia. *Annals of Public and Cooperative Economics*, *83*(2), 181–198. DOI: 10.1111/j.1467-8292.2012.00460.x

Gheorghe, C. M., Purcărea, V. L., & Gheorghe, I. R. (2023). Using eye-tracking technology in Neuromarketing. *Romanian Journal of Ophthalmology*, *67*(1), 2.

Ghobadi, S., & Mathiassen, L. (2016). Perceived barriers to effective knowledge sharing in agile software teams. *Information Systems Journal*, *26*(2), 95–125. DOI: 10.1111/isj.12053

Gieure, C., del Mar Benavides-Espinosa, M., & Roig-Dobón, S. (2020). The entrepreneurial process: The link between intentions and behavior. *Journal of Business Research*, *112*, 541–548. DOI: 10.1016/j.jbusres.2019.11.088

Golnar-Nik, P., Farashi, S., & Safari, M.-S. (2019). The application of EEG power for the prediction and interpretation of consumer decision-making: A neuromarketing study. *Physiology & Behavior*, *207*, 90–98. DOI: 10.1016/j.physbeh.2019.04.025 PMID: 31047949

González-López, M. J., Pérez-López, M. C., & Rodríguez-Ariza, L. (2021). From potential to early nascent entrepreneurship: The role of entrepreneurial competencies. *The International Entrepreneurship and Management Journal*, *17*(3), 1387–1417. DOI: 10.1007/s11365-020-00658-x

Govindan, K., Kannan, D., & Shankar, R. (2014). Sustainable supply chain performance: A review of the literature and research trends. *Journal of Cleaner Production*, *61*, 55–72.

Grashuis, J., & Hakelius, K. (2023). Pricing strategies of corporations and consumer co-operatives in the food retail sector: Evidence from England, Sweden, and the Netherlands. *Journal of Co-operative Organization and Management*, *11*(1), 100204. DOI: 10.1016/j.jcom.2023.100204

Graziotin, D., Fagerholm, F., Wang, X., & Abrahamsson, P. (2017). On the unhappiness of software developers. *Dl.Acm.Org*, *10*, 324–333. DOI: 10.1145/3084226.3084242

*Green indian financial system initiative*. (n.d.). Shakti Sustainable Energy Foundation. Retrieved December 10, 2024, from https://shaktifoundation.in/green-indian-financial-systems-initiative/ India|authorurl:https://www.ey.com/en_in/people/saunak-saha,

Gupta, P., Chauhan, S., Paul, J., & Jaiswal, M. P. (2020). Social entrepreneurship research: A review and future research agenda. *Journal of Business Research*, *113*, 209–229. DOI: 10.1016/j.jbusres.2020.03.032

Hacıfazlıoğlu, Ç. (2024, Ocak). Fındıklı'da Mandalinalar İhtiyaç Sahipleri İçin Toplanacak. https://www.haberetanik.com/haber/findiklida-mandalinalar-ihtiyac-sahipleri-icin-toplanacak-60001.html (Access date: 12 January 2023).

Hair, J. F. J., Black, W. C., Babin, B. J., & Anderson, R. E. (2010). *Multivariate data analysis. A global perspective* (7th ed.). Prentice Hall.

Halkias, D., Esposito, M., Harkiolakis, T., Diaz, J., & Ikpogu, N. M. (2023). Digital entrepreneurship and disruptive innovation in the greek maritime industry: The case of harbor lab. In *Entrepreneurship Development in the Balkans: Perspective from Diverse Contexts* (pp. 131-150). Emerald Publishing Limited. DOI: 10.1108/978-1-83753-454-820231008

Han, D., Konietzko, J., Dijk, M., & Bocken, N. (2023). How do circular startups achieve scale? *Sustainable Production and Consumption*, *40*, 363–375. Advance online publication. DOI: 10.1016/j.spc.2023.06.007

Han, N., & Um, J. (2024). Risk management strategy for supply chain sustainability and resilience capability. *Risk Management*, *26*(2), 6. Advance online publication. DOI: 10.1057/s41283-023-00138-w

Harwood, J. (2020). *Social identity theory. The international encyclopedia of media psychology*, 1–7. https://doi.org/DOI: 10.1002/9781119011071.iemp0153

Hassan, A., Saleem, I., Anwar, I., & Hussain, S. A. (2020). Entrepreneurial intention of Indian university students: The role of opportunity recognition and entrepreneurship education. *Education + Training*, *62*(7/8), 843–861. DOI: 10.1108/ET-02-2020-0033

Hassan, R., & Marimuthu, M. (2018). Bridging and bonding: Having a Muslim diversity on corporate boards and firm performance. *Journal of Islamic Accounting and Business Research*, *9*(3), 457–478. DOI: 10.1108/JIABR-02-2016-0022

Hawkins, D. (2006). *Corporate social responsibility: Balancing tomorrow's sustainability and today's profitability*. Springer. DOI: 10.1057/9780230625815

Hawkins, T. J. (2022). *Corporate Boardroom Gender and Board Diversity Performance*. Capella University.

Hayes, A. F. (2013). *Introduction to mediation, moderation, and conditional process analysis: A regression-based approach*. Guilford Press.

Henderson, G. R., Iacobucci, D., & Calder, B. J. (1998). Brand diagnostics: Mapping branding effects using consumer associative networks. *European Journal of Operational Research*, *111*(2), 306–327. DOI: 10.1016/S0377-2217(98)00151-9

Hill, J. G. (1998) Deconstructing Sunbeam-Contemporary issues in corporate governance. *U. Cin. L. Rev., 67*, 1099.

Hillman, A. J., Withers, M. C., & Collins, B. J. (2009). Resource dependence theory: A review. *Journal of Management, 35*(6), 1404–1427. DOI: 10.1177/0149206309343469

Hilmer, M. J. (1998). Post-secondary fees and the decision to attend a university or a community college. *Journal of Public Economics, 67*(3), 329–348. DOI: 10.1016/S0047-2727(97)00075-3

Hmieleski, K. M., & Sheppard, L. D. (2019). The Yin and Yang of entrepreneurship: Gender differences in the importance of communal and agentic characteristics for entrepreneurs' subjective well-being and performance. *Journal of Business Venturing, 34*(4), 709–730. DOI: 10.1016/j.jbusvent.2018.06.006

Ho, C. A., & Williams, S. M. (2003). International comparative analysis of the association between board structure and the efficiency of value added by a firm from its physical capital and intellectual capital resources. *The International Journal of Accounting, 38*(4), 465–491. DOI: 10.1016/j.intacc.2003.09.001

Hota, P. K., Subramanian, B., & Narayanamurthy, G. (2020). Mapping the intellectual structure of social entrepreneurship research: A citation/co-citation analysis. *Journal of Business Ethics, 166*(1), 89–114. DOI: 10.1007/s10551-019-04129-4

Hudáková, M., Urbancova, H., & Vnoučková, L. (2019). Key criteria and competences defining the sustainability of start-up teams and projects in the incubation and acceleration phase. *Sustainability (Basel), 11*(23), 6720. DOI: 10.3390/su11236720

Hung, H. (1998). A typology of the theories of the roles of governing boards. *Corporate Governance, 6*(2), 101–111. DOI: 10.1111/1467-8683.00089

Hunt, J. L. (2000). Brown v. Board of Education After Fifty Years: Context and Synopsis. *Mercer L. Rev., 52*, 549.

Hyundai. (n.d.). *The all-new Hyundai i20: emotional design meets advanced technology*. Automobile World.

Iancu, A., Popescu, L., & Popescu, V. (2021). Factors influencing social entrepreneurship intentions in Romania, *Economic Research-. Ekonomska Istrazivanja, 34*(1), 1190–1201. DOI: 10.1080/1331677X.2020.1820358

Iandolo, F., & Cosimato, S. (2019). Are Italian Start-Ups 'Born Sustainable'? *A Systems Approach to Sustainability Challenges,* 103-118.

Iden, J., & Bygstad, B. (2017). The social interaction of developers and IT operations staff in software development projects. *International Journal of Project Management*. Advance online publication. DOI: 10.1016/j.ijproman.2017.12.001

Ingley, C., & Van Der Walt, N. (2002). Board dynamics and the politics of appraisal. *Corporate Governance, 10*(3), 163–174. DOI: 10.1111/1467-8683.00281

International Cooperative Alliance. 2024. Cooperative identity, values and principles. https://2012.coop/en/what-co-op/cooperative-identity-values-principles.[accessed November 1

Itaoka, K. (2012, April). Regression and interpretation low R-squared. In *Proceedings of the presentation at Social Research Network 3rd Meeting,* Noosa. Mizuho Information and Research Institute, Inc.

James, P., & Magee, L. (2016). Domains of sustainability. *Global Encyclopedia of Public administration, public policy, and governance,* 1-17.

Jamwal, D., & Singh, N. (2011). Management Information System Competencies and Strategies. *International Journal of Computer Science and Technology, 1*(2), 109–112.

Javadian, G., Figueroa-Armijos, M., Gupta, V. K., Modarresi, M., & Dobratz, C. (2021). Does it pay to act feminine? A cross-cultural study of gender stereotype endorsement and cognitive legitimacy in the evaluation of new ventures. *International Journal of Gender and Entrepreneurship, 13*(4), 330–352. DOI: 10.1108/IJGE-07-2020-0092

Jehn, K. A., Northcraft, G. B., & Neale, M. A. (1999). Why differences make a difference: A field study of diversity, conflict and performance in workgroups. *Administrative Science Quarterly, 44*(4), 741–763. DOI: 10.2307/2667054

Jensen, M. (2001). Value maximisation, stakeholder theory, and the corporate objective function. *European Financial Management, 7*(3), 297–317. DOI: 10.1111/1468-036X.00158

Jia, J., Chen, Z., & Du, X. (2017). Understanding soft skills requirements for mobile applications developers. *Proceedings - 2017 IEEE International Conference on Computational Science and Engineering and IEEE/IFIP International Conference on Embedded and Ubiquitous Computing, CSE and EUC 2017, 1*, 108–115. DOI: 10.1109/CSE-EUC.2017.29

Johl, S. K., & Salami, O. L. (2014). Impact of board composition on firm performance: A study on listed firms in Malaysia. *Journal of Contemporary Management, 3*(3), 94–102.

John, D. R., Loken, B., Kim, K., & Monga, A. B. (2006). Brand Concept Maps: A Methodology for Identifying Brand Association Networks. *JMR, Journal of Marketing Research, 43*(4), 549–563. DOI: 10.1509/jmkr.43.4.549

Johnson, J. L., Daily, C. M., & Ellstrand, A. E. (1996). Boards of directors: A review and research agenda. *Journal of Management, 22*(3), 409–438. DOI: 10.1177/014920639602200303

Joshi, S., Sharma, M., Ekren, B. Y., Kazancoglu, Y., Luthra, S., & Prasad, M. (2023). Assessing supply chain innovations for building resilient food supply chains: An emerging economy perspective. *Sustainability (Basel), 15*(6), 4924. DOI: 10.3390/su15064924

Kalyanaraman, L., & Altuwaijri, B. (2016). The linkage between excess board independence and capital structure: An exploration in the context of listed companies in Saudi Arabia. *Journal of Applied Finance and Banking, 6*(3), 129.

Kamaludin, M. F. (2023). Social sustainability within social entrepreneurship. *Technological Forecasting and Social Change, 192*, 122541. DOI: 10.1016/j.techfore.2023.122541

Kamaludin, M. F., Xavier, J. A., & Amin, M. (2021). Social entrepreneurship and sustainability: A conceptual framework. *Journal of Social Entrepreneurship*, •••, 1–24.

Kamaludin, M. F., Xavier, J. A., & Amin, M. (2022). Social entrepreneurial sustainability during the COVID-19 pandemic. *Social Enterprise Journal, 18*(2), 344–363. DOI: 10.1108/SEJ-05-2021-0041

Karabatak, B. N. (2018). İmece Kültürü ve İmece KelimesiÜzerine. *Türk & İslam DünyasıSosyal Araştırmalar Dergisi, 5*(18), 490–501.

Karafazlı, G. (2021). MECİ Halkın Bakkalı: Fındıklı'da kadınların el emeği aracısız olarak halkla buluşacak. https://yesilgazete.org/meci-halkin-bakkali/.

Karatas-Ozkan, M., Ibrahim, S., Ozbilgin, M., Fayolle, A., Manville, G., Nicolopoulou, K., Tatli, A., & Tunalioglu, M. (2023). Challenging the assumptions of social entrepreneurship education and repositioning it for the future: Wonders of cultural, social, symbolic, and economic capitals. *Social Enterprise Journal, 19*(2), 98–122. DOI: 10.1108/SEJ-02-2022-0018

Karnani, A. (2007). The mirage of marketing to the bottom of the pyramid: How the private sector can help alleviate poverty. *California Management Review, 49*(4), 90–111. DOI: 10.2307/41166407

Kate, N., Padhye, P., & Mishra, A. B. (2022). Studies on Anti-Virus Software Tools: Strong Weapon to Protect Systems. *2022 2nd International Conference on Innovative Practices in Technology and Management (ICIPTM)*, 49–52. DOI: 10.1109/ICIPTM54933.2022.9753877

Kawai, N., & Kazumi, T. (2021). Female entrepreneurs' cognitive attributes and venture growth in Japan: The moderating role of perceived social legitimacy. *International Journal of Gender and Entrepreneurship, 13*(1), 1–29. DOI: 10.1108/IJGE-05-2020-0063

Kaypak, Ş. (2012). Ekolojik turizm ve sürdürülebilir kırsal kalkınma. *Karamanoğlu Mehmetbey Üniversitesi Sosyal ve Ekonomik Araştırmalar Dergisi, 2012*(1), 11–29.

Keasey, K., Thompson, S., & Wright, M. (Eds.). (1997). *Corporate governance: Economic and financial issues.* DOI: 10.1093/oso/9780198289906.001.0001

Ketokivi, M., & Mahoney, J. T. (2020). Transaction Cost Economics As a Theory of Supply Chain Efficiency. Production and Operations Management, 29(4), 1011-1031. Khanchel El Mehdi, I. (2007). Empirical evidence on corporate governance and corporate performance inDOI: 10.1111/poms.13148

Khan, U. U., Ali, Y., Petrillo, A., & De Felice, F. (2023). Macro-environmental factors and their impact on startups from the perspective of developing countries. *International Journal of Sustainable Engineering, 16*(1), 166–183. DOI: 10.1080/19397038.2023.2238754

Khurshid, A., Muzaffar, A., & Bhutta, M. K. S. (2021). Institutional pressures and supplier involvement: A perspective on sustainability. *Operations Management Research. Operations Management Research : Advancing Practice Through Research, 14*(1–2), 123–137. DOI: 10.1007/s12063-021-00181-4

Kim, J. H. (2019). Multicollinearity and misleading statistical results. *Korean Journal of Anesthesiology*, 72(6), 558–569. DOI: 10.4097/kja.19087 PMID: 31304696

Klapper, L. F., & Love, I. (2002). Corporate governance, investor protection and performance in emerging markets. *Investor Protection and Performance in Emerging Markets (March 2002).*

Klein, P., Shapiro, D., & Young, J. (2005). Corporate governance, family ownership and firm value: The Canadian evidence. *Corporate Governance, 13*(6), 769–784. DOI: 10.1111/j.1467-8683.2005.00469.x

Kline, B. R. (2005). *Principles and practice of structural modeling*. The Guilford Press.

Koning, J. (2001, November). Social sustainability in a globalizing world: context, theory and methodology explored. In *Proceedings of the UNESCO/MOST Meeting*, The Hague, The Netherlands (pp. 22-23).

Korkmaz, C. (2011). İmece Usulü Kalkınmanın 21. YüzyıldakiBoyutu: Köy Bankaları.Uluslararası Mikrokredi Konferansı,Kadir Has Üniversitesi,9 Aralık 2010 Toplantı Raporu.

Korpysa, J., Singh, U. S., & Singh, S. (2023). Validation of decision criteria and determining factors importance in advocating for sustainability of entrepreneurial startups towards social inclusion and capacity building. *Sustainability (Basel), 15*(13), 9938. DOI: 10.3390/su15139938

Kothari, D. P., & Nagrath, I. J. (2003). *Modern power system analysis*. Tata McGraw-Hill Publishing Company. Koul, H., & DeWet, T. (1983). Minimum distance estimation in a linear regression model. *The Annals of*

Krueger, N. F.Jr, Reilly, M. D., & Carsrud, A. L. (2000). Competing models of entrepreneurial intentions. *Journal of Business Venturing, 15*(5–6), 411–432. https://linkinghub.elsevier.com/retrieve/pii/s0883902698000330. DOI: 10.1016/S0883-9026(98)00033-0

Kujala, J., Sachs, S., Leinonen, H., Heikkinen, A., & Laude, D. (2022). Stakeholder engagement: Past, present, and future. *Business & Society, 61*(5), 1136–1196. DOI: 10.1177/00076503211066595

Kumar, P., Taneja, S., & Ozen, E. (2024). Exploring the influence of green bonds on sustainable development through low-carbon financing mobilization. *International Journal of Law and Management*. DOI: 10.1108/IJLMA-01-2024-0030

Kumar, S., & Kundalia, L. (2024). Green Bonds—Role and scope in India's financial and fiscal landscape. *Journal of Indian Institute of Banking & Finance*, 43–56.

Kumari, A. (2024, June 1). Reserve Bank of India cancels 10-year green bond auction for first time. *Business Standard*.

Kümbül, G. B. (2011). Yoksullukla mücadelede sosyal girişimcilik: Ashoka üyelerinden sosyal yenilikçi örnek uygulamalar. *Dokuz Eylül Üniversitesi Sosyal Bilimler Enstitüsü Dergisi, 13*(3), 79–111.

Kyazze, L. M., Nkote, I. N., & Wakaisuka-Isingoma, J. (2017). Cooperative governance and social performance of cooperative societies. *Cogent Business & Management, 4*(1), 1284391. DOI: 10.1080/23311975.2017.1284391

Laguía, A., García-Ael, C., Wach, D., & Moriano, J. A. (2019). "Think entrepreneur-think male": A task and relationship scale to measure gender stereotypes in entrepreneurship. *The International Entrepreneurship and Management Journal, 15*(3), 749–772. DOI: 10.1007/s11365-018-0553-0

Lam, D. P. M., Martín-López, B., Wiek, A., Bennett, E. M., Frantzeskaki, N., Horcea-Milcu, A. I., & Lang, D. J. (2020). Scaling the impact of sustainability initiatives: A typology of amplification processes. *Urban Transformations*, *2*(1), 3. Advance online publication. DOI: 10.1186/s42854-020-00007-9

Lamperti, S., Sammut, S., & Courrent, J. M. (2023). From incubator's knowledge transfer to sustainability startups' impact: A case study in a French support program. *Journal of Knowledge Management*, *27*(9), 2393–2413. Advance online publication. DOI: 10.1108/JKM-09-2022-0690

Lang, R., & Roessl, D. (2011). The role of social capital in the development of community-based co- operatives. *New developments in the theory of networks: Franchising, alliances and cooperatives*, 353-370.

Lans, T., Van Galen, M. A., Verstegen, J. A. A. M., Biemans, H. J. A., & Mulder, M. (2014). Searching for entrepreneurs among small business ownermanagers in agriculture. *NJAS Wageningen Journal of Life Sciences*, *68*(1), 41–51. DOI: 10.1016/j.njas.2013.12.001

Lavery, M. R., Acharya, P., Sivo, S. A., & Xu, L. (2019). Number of predictors and multicollinearity: What are their effects on error and bias in regression? *Communications in Statistics. Simulation and Computation*, *48*(1), 27–38. DOI: 10.1080/03610918.2017.1371750

Lawler, E. E.III. (2010). *Talent: Making people your competitive advantage*. John Wiley & Sons.

Lazar, S., Klimecka-Tatar, D., & Obrecht, M. (2021). Sustainability orientation and focus on logistics and supply chains. *Sustainability (Basel)*, *13*(6), 3280. DOI: 10.3390/su13063280

Lee, N., Broderick, A. J., & Chamberlain, L (2007). . What is 'neuromarketing'? A discussion and agenda for future research. *International Journal of Psychophysiology*, *63* (2)., 199–204. DOI: 10.1016/j.ijpsycho.2006.03.007 PMID: 16769143

Lee, S. H., Kang, H. J., & Lee, S. Y. (2022). The Influence of Board Diversity and Board Conflict on Performance in Consumer Cooperatives in South Korea. *Journal of Entrepreneurial and Organizational Diversity*, *11*(1), 55–81. DOI: 10.5947/jeod.2022.003

Lenberg, P., Feldt, R., & Wallgren, L. G. (2015). Behavioral software engineering: A definition and systematic literature review. *Journal of Systems and Software*, *107*, 15–37. DOI: 10.1016/j.jss.2015.04.084

Levesque, P. (2012). Building resilience and sustainability into the Chinese supply chain. *The Shipping Point: The Rise of China and the Future of Retail Supply Chain Management*, pp. 135–161. DOI: 10.1002/9781119199663.ch9

Lihua, D. (2022). An extended model of the theory of planned behavior: An empirical study of entrepreneurial intention and entrepreneurial behavior in college students. *Frontiers in Psychology*, *12*, 6706. DOI: 10.3389/fpsyg.2022.627818 PMID: 35145443

Li, K. J. (2024). Product and service innovation with customer recognition. *Decision Sciences*, *55*(1), 17–32. DOI: 10.1111/deci.12546

Li, X., Wang, S., Lu, X., & Guo, F. (2023). Quantity or quality? The effect of green finance on enterprise green technology innovation. *European Journal of Innovation Management*. Advance online publication. DOI: 10.1108/EJIM-03-2023-0208

Lubberink, R. (2020). Social entrepreneurship and sustainable development. In *Decent work and economic growth* (pp. 913–923). Springer International Publishing.

Luque-Vílchez, M., Cordazzo, M., Rimmel, G., & Tilt, C. (2023). Key aspects of sustainability reporting quality and the future of GRI. *Sustainability Accounting. Management and Policy Journal*, *14*(4), 637–659. DOI: 10.1108/SAMPJ-03-2023-0127

MacAskill, W. (2019). The definition of effective altruism. In Hilary, G., & Theron, P. (Eds.), *Effective Altruism: Philosophical Issues* (pp. 10–28). Oxford University Press. DOI: 10.1093/oso/9780198841364.003.0001

Maheshwari, G., & Kha, K. L. (2022). Investigating the relationship between educational support and entrepreneurial intention in Vietnam: The mediating role of entrepreneurial self-efficacy in the theory of planned behavior. *International Journal of Management Education*, *20*(2), 100553. DOI: 10.1016/j.ijme.2021.100553

Majeed, A., Ghumman, A. R., Abbas, Q., & Ahmad, Z. (2021). Role of entrepreneurial passion between entrepreneurial attitude, subjective norms, perceived behavioral control, and entrepreneurial intention: Measuring the entrepreneurial behavior of Pakistani students. [PJCSS]. *Pakistan Journal of Commerce and Social Sciences*, *15*(3), 636–662.

Maltais, A., & Nykvist, B. (2020). Understanding the role of green bonds in advancing sustainability. *Journal of Sustainable Finance & Investment*, •••, 1–20. DOI: 10.1080/20430795.2020.1724864

Mamo, Y. A., Haji, J., Legesse, B., & Sassi, M. (2021). Challenges of agricultural cooperatives and their impact on profitability of potato growers in eastern Ethiopia. [RAAE]. *Acta Oeconomica et Informatica, 24*(2), 62–77. DOI: 10.15414/raae.2021.24.02.62-77

Manickam, M. K., Rozan, A., & Zaidi, M. (2022). Explaining the intention of software developers to perform entrepreneurial competencies. *Business Management/Biznes Upravlenie, 4.*

Manickam, M. K., Zaidi, M., & Rozan, A. (2023). Bibliometric analysis of entrepreneurial competencies using scopus data and VOSviewer. *International Journal of Advanced and Applied Sciences, 10*(1), 198–207. DOI: 10.21833/ijaas.2023.01.025

Manish, S. (2024, February 8). *Indian parliamentary panel red-flags PhonePe and Google Pay cornering 83% of India's UPI payments*. Techcrunch. https://techcrunch.com/2024/02/08/indian-parliamentary-panel-red-flags-phonepe-and-google-pay-cornering-83-of-india-upi-payments/

Manoharan, G., Mishra, A. B., Adusumilli, S. B. K., Chavva, M., Damancharla, H., & Sahaya Lenin, D. (2024). Supervised Learning for Personalized Marketing Strategies. *2024 International Conference on Advances in Computing, Communication and Applied Informatics (ACCAI)*, 1–6. DOI: 10.1109/ACCAI61061.2024.10602307

Man, T. W. (2001). *Entrepreneurial competencies and the performance of small and medium enterprises in the Hong Kong services sector*. The Hong Kong Polytechnic University.

Man, T. W. Y., Lau, T., & Chan, K. F. (2002). The competitiveness of small and medium enterprises. *Journal of Business Venturing, 17*(2), 123–142. DOI: 10.1016/S0883-9026(00)00058-6

Manzur, E., & Olavarrieta, S. (2021). The 9-SRA scale: A simplified 9-items version of the SRA scale to assess altruism. *Sustainability (Basel), 13*(13), 6999. DOI: 10.3390/su13136999

Mariani, L., Trivellato, B., Martini, M., & Marafioti, E. (2022). Achieving sustainable development goals through collaborative innovation: Evidence from four European initiatives. *Journal of Business Ethics, 180*(4), 1075–1095. DOI: 10.1007/s10551-022-05193-z PMID: 35855697

Maričić, G., Škorić, S., & Radenković, D. (2018). Application of the principles of corporate governance in agriculture cooperatives. *Economy in harm's way, 65*(2), 827-841.

Martínez-Rodríguez, I., Quintana-Rojo, C., Gento, P., & Callejas-Albinana, F. E. (2022). Public policy recommendations for promoting female entrepreneurship in Europe. *The International Entrepreneurship and Management Journal, 18*(3), 1235–1262. DOI: 10.1007/s11365-021-00751-9

Matturro, G., Raschetti, F., & Fontán, C. (2019). *A systematic mapping study on soft skills in software engineering.*

McClelland, D. C., & Boyatzis, R. E. (1982). Leadership motive pattern and long-term success in management. *The Journal of Applied Psychology, 67*(6), 737–743. DOI: 10.1037/0021-9010.67.6.737

McDonald, R. M., & Eisenhardt, K. M. (2020). Parallel play: Startups, nascent markets, and effective business-model design. *Administrative Science Quarterly, 65*(2), 483–523. DOI: 10.1177/0001839219852349

McKenzie, S. (2004). Social sustainability: Towards some definitions.

Mehta, P., Singla, H., Saha, R., & Tyagi, S (2021). . A pathway to technology integration: Eliciting consumer's behavioural intention to use paytm services. *Paradigm, 25* (1)., 7–24.

Menke, C. (2018). Unravelling entrepreneurial competencies and their relation to entrepreneurial intent. *International Journal of Entrepreneurial Venturing, 10*(6), 663–687. DOI: 10.1504/IJEV.2018.095304

Mersha, D., & Ayenew, Z. (2018). Financing challenges of smallholder farmers: A study on members of agricultural cooperatives in Southwest Oromia Region, Ethiopia. *African Journal of Business Management, 12*(10), 285–293. DOI: 10.5897/AJBM2018.8517

Mettler, A., & Williams, A. D. (2011). The rise of the micro-multinational: How freelancers and technology-savvy start-ups are driving growth, jobs and innovation. *Lisbon Council Policy Brief, 5*(3), 1–28.

Middermann, L. H., Kratzer, J., & Perner, S. (2020). The impact of environmental risk exposure on the determinants of sustainable entrepreneurship. *Sustainability (Basel), 12*(4), 1534. DOI: 10.3390/su12041534

Mikulewicz, M. (2019). Is it thwarting adaptation's potential? A critique of resilience and climate-resilient development. *Geoforum, 104*, 267–282. DOI: 10.1016/j.geoforum.2019.05.010

Mishra, A (2025a). . Kalyan Jewellers: A Case Study on Brand Perception and Disruptive Innovation in the Jewellery Market. *IGI Global Scientific Publishing*, 261–284. https://doi.org/DOI: 10.4018/979-8-3693-9783-1.ch010

Mishra, A (2025b). . Monitoring the Development of the IoT Concept in Various Application Domains. *Taylor & Francis Online, CRC Press*. https://www.taylorfrancis.com/chapters/edit/10.1201/9781003596721-41/monitoring-development-iot-concept-various-application-domains-mishra-sarita-rani-panda-anitha-uma-reddy-gaurav-sethi-purnendu-bikash-acharjee

Mishra, A. (2025). Monitoring the Development of the IoT Concept in Various Application Domains. *Taylor & Francis Online, CRC Press*. https://www.taylorfrancis.com/chapters/edit/10.1201/9781003596721-41/monitoring-development-iot-concept-various-application-domains-mishra-sarita-rani-panda-anitha-uma-reddy-gaurav-sethi-purnendu-bikash-acharjee

Mishra, A. (2025a) . Kalyan Jewellers: A Case Study on Brand Perception and Disruptive Innovation in the Jewellery Market. *IGI Global Scientific Publishing*, 261–284.

Mishra, A. (2025a). Kalyan Jewellers: A Case Study on Brand Perception and Disruptive Innovation in the Jewellery Market. *IGI Global Scientific Publishing*, 261–284.

Mishra, A. (2025b). Monitoring the Development of the IoT Concept in Various Application Domains. *Taylor & Francis Online, CRC Press*. https://www.taylorfrancis.com/chapters/edit/10.1201/9781003596721-41/monitoring-development-iot-concept-various-application-domains-mishra-sarita-rani-panda-anitha-uma-reddy-gaurav-sethi-purnendu-bikash-acharjee

Mishra, A. B (2020). . E- PAYMENT SYSTEM: A RISING TREND OF ECONOMY. *New Paradigm in Business and Education*. https://www.researchgate.net/profile/Anitha-K-2/publication/349605501_E-LEARNING_THROUGH_GAMIFICATION-_AN_ITINERARY_TO_GAIN_IN-DEPTH_KNOWLEDGE/links/6037d566299bf1cc26ef9597/E-LEARNING-THROUGH-GAMIFICATION-AN-ITINERARY-TO-GAIN-IN-DEPTH-KNOWLEDGE.pdf#page=10

Mishra, A. B. (2020) . E- PAYMENT SYSTEM: A RISING TREND OF ECONOMY. *New Paradigm in Business and Education*. https://www.researchgate.net/profile/Anitha-K-2/publication/349605501_E-LEARNING_THROUGH_GAMIFICATION-_AN_ITINERARY_TO_GAIN_IN-DEPTH_KNOWLEDGE/links/6037d566299bf1cc26ef9597/E-LEARNING-THROUGH-GAMIFICATION-AN-ITINERARY-TO-GAIN-IN-DEPTH-KNOWLEDGE.pdf#page=10

Mishra, A. B. (2020). E- PAYMENT SYSTEM: A RISING TREND OF ECONOMY. *New Paradigm in Business and Education.* https://www.researchgate.net/profile/Anitha-K-2/publication/349605501_E-LEARNING_THROUGH_GAMIFICATION-_AN_ITINERARY_TO_GAIN_IN-DEPTH_KNOWLEDGE/links/6037d566299bf1cc26ef9597/E-LEARNING-THROUGH-GAMIFICATION-AN-ITINERARY-TO-GAIN-IN-DEPTH-KNOWLEDGE.pdf#page=10

Mishra, A. B. (2025a). Kalyan Jeweller's Case Study of Transformation, Consumer Engagement, and Effective Marketing Strategies for Brand Building. In *Dynamic Strategies for Entrepreneurial Marketing* (pp. 287–310). DOI: 10.4018/979-8-3693-3936-7.ch014

Mishra, A. B. (2025b). The Paytm Puzzle: Navigating Regulatory Compliance in India's Digital Revolution. In *Cultural Sensitivity, Cross-Border Logistics, and E-Commerce in Global Marketing* (pp. 337–348). IGI Global. DOI: 10.4018/979-8-3373-0528-8.ch015

Mishra, A. B., & Gaikwad, V. (2024). The Transaction War Between Google Pay and Phonepe. In *IGI Global* (pp. 166–185). DOI: 10.4018/978-1-6684-7840-0.ch009

Mishra, A. B., & Singh, A. (2024). The Mumbai Dabbawalas : An Efficient and Sustainable Lunchbox Delivery System. In *IGI Global* (pp. 154–160). DOI: 10.4018/979-8-3693-1544-6.ch007

Mishra, A. B., Allen, M., & Tirkey, P (2024). . *Disruption causes to Micromax by once a Market leader now a Myth.* https://www.iimspune.edu.in/images/pdf/Journal/Vol3I1-Paper11.pdf

Mishra, A. B., Allen, M., & Tirkey, P. (2024). *Disruption causes to Micromax by once a Market leader now a Myth.* https://www.iimspune.edu.in/images/pdf/Journal/Vol3I1-Paper11.pdf

Mishra, A. B., Raikwar, A., & Tiwari, A (2024). . *Britannia: Marketing Initiatives Boost A Fledgling Business's Transformation To One Of The Largest FMCG Brands.* https://www.iimspune.edu.in/images/pdf/Journal/Vol3I1-Paper12.pdf

Mishra, A. B., Raikwar, A., & Tiwari, A. (2024). *Britannia: Marketing Initiatives Boost A Fledgling Business's Transformation To One Of The Largest FMCG Brands.* https://www.iimspune.edu.in/images/pdf/Journal/Vol3I1-Paper12.pdf

Mishra, A. B., Satarkar, M., & Joshi, S (2024). . Capitalizing the Retail Industry by Automation and Artificial Intelligence (AI).: Case Study of IKEA. In *IGI Global* (pp. 239–251). . DOI: 10.4018/979-8-3693-2643-5.ch014

Mishra, A. (2025b). *Monitoring the Development of the IoT Concept in Various Application Domains. Taylor & Francis Online*. CRC Press.

Mishra, A. B (2022). . SAHYADRI FARMS: INDIA'S LARGEST FARMER PRODUCER COMPANY. *International Journal of Advance and Applied Research, 10*, 996–998. https://ijaar.co.in/wp-content/uploads/2022/11/1001175.pdf

Mishra, A. B., & Jaiswal Monika. (2024). Case Study of Kalyan Jewellers - Brand Perception Mapping Towards Disruptive Innovation in Jewellery Segment. *International Journal of Advance and Applied Research, 11*(6), 386–396. DOI: 10.5281/zenodo.13902610

Mishra, A. B., Anil, V., & Nitin, R (2021). . Putsch buyer tendency and climbing sales of mobile trade business. *Manager–The British Journal of Administrative Management, 58* (152)., 54–60.

Mishra, A. B., Chand, K., & Kaith, K. (2022). Influencer Marketing as Emerging Promotional Tool in Modern Era and Opportunities to Uprising Sales. *International Journal of Emerging Research in Engineering, Science, and Management, 1*(3). Advance online publication. DOI: 10.58482/ijeresm.v1i3.3

Mishra, A. B., & Dodke, S. D. (2024). ZARA : Technological Influence on Becoming the Fashion Industry's Market Leader. In *Cases on AI Ethics in Business* (pp. 204–215). IGI Publishing., DOI: 10.4018/979-8-3693-2643-5.ch012

Mishra, A. B., Goel, A., & Jajoo, P (2022). . A Case Study of Amul: Implementation of Extension Strategy to Repositioning Brand During Covid-19 Period. *International Journal of Emerging Research in Engineering, Science, and Management, 1* (4). . Advance online publication. DOI: 10.58482/ijeresm.v1i4.3

Mishra, A. B., & Karjodkar, R. (2022). A Case Study of Air India - Maharajah Back to Home. *International Journal of Emerging Research in Engineering, Science, and Management, 1*(3). Advance online publication. DOI: 10.58482/ijeresm.v1i3.5

Mishra, A. B., & Monika, J. (2024). Case Study of Kalyan Jewellers-Brand Perception Mapping Towards Disruptive Innovation in Jewellery Segment. *International Journal of Advance and Applied Research, 11*(6), 386–396.

Mishra, A. B., Rajagopal, N. K., Yousoof, M., & Padhye, P. (2021). A STUDY ON ORGANISATIONAL PRACTICES THAT INFLUENCE EMPLOYEE ENGAGEMENT. *Manager–. British Journal of Administrative Management, 57*(145), 220–225.

Mishra, A. B., & Ranjan, N (2022). . INTERNET OF THINGS BASED EMERGING SMART TOOLS FOR NEW EDGE EDUCATION. *Mukt Shabd Journal, 11* (10)., 80–87. DOI: 10.0014.MSJ.2022.V11I10.0086781.1135708

Mishra, A. B., Ranjan, N., Sharma, K. M., Padhye, P., & Chand, K. (2023). Advancement of Digital Transformation to Boost Financial Services Industry. *Journal of Informatics Education and Research, 3*(2), 2435–2440. https://scholar.google.com/scholar?cluster=15410723285942667834&hl=en&oi=scholarr

Mishra, A. B., Sahu, T., Ranjan, N., & Varma, A. (2021). Green Marketing Practices Prevailing In Hotel Industry. *Journal of Contemporary Issues in Business and Government, 27*(02). Advance online publication. DOI: 10.47750/cibg.2021.27.02.145

Mishra, A. B., Satarkar, M., & Joshi, S. (2023). IKEA - Phygital Transformation in Furniture Manufacturing Industry. *International Journal of Emerging Research in Engineering, Science, and Management, 2*(3), 6–9. DOI: 10.58482/ijeresm.v2i3.2

Mishra, A. B., & Singh, A. (2023). Brand Positioning in the Indian Smartphone Market: A Case Study of OnePlus. *International Journal of Emerging Research in Engineering, Science, and Management, 2*(3). Advance online publication. DOI: 10.58482/ijeresm.v2i3.1

Mishra, A. B., & Singh, R (2024b). . Phygital Transformation of Nilon's: The Brand Building in Ready-to-eat Segment. *International Journal of Emerging Research in Engineering, Science, and Management, 3* (2). . Advance online publication. DOI: 10.58482/ijeresm.v3i2.3

Moe, N. B., Dingsøyr, T., & Dybå, T. (2010). A teamwork model for understanding an agile team: A case study of a Scrum project. *Information and Software Technology, 52*(5), 480–491. DOI: 10.1016/j.infsof.2009.11.004

Mohammed, N., & Lee, B. W. (2015). Role of cooperatives in rural development, the case of south nations nationalities and people region, Ethiopia. *Science Journal of Business and Management, 3*(4), 102–108. DOI: 10.11648/j.sjbm.20150304.12

Mohseni, M., Othman, B. A., Raturi, P., Mishra, A. B., Priya, S. J., & Saravanan, V. (2022). The Role of Parallel Computing Towards Implementation of Enhanced and Effective Industrial Internet of Things (IOT) Through Manova Approach. *2022 2nd International Conference on Advance Computing and Innovative Technologies in Engineering (ICACITE)*, 160–164. DOI: 10.1109/ICACITE53722.2022.9823698

Momaya, K. S., Bhat, S., & Lalwani, L. (2017). Institutional growth and industrial competitiveness: Exploring the role of strategic flexibility taking the case of select institutesin India. *Global Journal of Flexible Systems Managment, 18*(2), 111–122. DOI: 10.1007/s40171-016-0144-2

Moreno Freites, Z., Escorcia-Caballero, J. P., Ziritt Trejo, G., & Silva-Guerra, H. (2022). Human-affective dimensions, entrepreneurial intentions, and entrepreneurial behaviors in entrepreneurship training programs for vulnerable populations. *IBIMA Business Review*, *2022*, 1–11. DOI: 10.5171/2022.110930

Moriano, J. A., Gorgievski, M., Laguna, M., Stephan, U., & Zarafshani, K. (2012). A cross-cultural approach to understanding entrepreneurial intention. *Journal of Career Development*, *39*(2), 162–185. DOI: 10.1177/0894845310384481

Morioka, S. N., Carvalho, H., & Azevedo, S. F. (2018). Sustainability-oriented business model innovation: A systematic literature review. *Journal of Cleaner Production*, *183*, 699–710.

Morris, M. H., Santos, S. C., & Kuratko, D. F. (2021). The great divides in social entrepreneurship and where they lead us. *Small Business Economics*, *57*(3), 1089–1106. DOI: 10.1007/s11187-020-00318-y

Mukhtar, S., Wardana, L. W., Wibowo, A., & Narmaditya, B. S. (2021). Does entrepreneurship education and culture promote students' entrepreneurial intention? The mediating role of entrepreneurial mindset. *Cogent Education*, *8*(1), 1918849. DOI: 10.1080/2331186X.2021.1918849

Mukul, K., & Saini, G. K. (2021). Talent acquisition in startups in India: The role of social capital. *Journal of Entrepreneurship in Emerging Economies*, *13*(5), 1235–1261. DOI: 10.1108/JEEE-04-2020-0086

Munir, H., Jianfeng, C., & Ramzan, S. (2019). Personality traits and theory of planned behavior comparison of entrepreneurial intentions between an emerging economy and a developing country. *International Journal of Entrepreneurial Behaviour & Research*, *25*(3), 554–580. DOI: 10.1108/IJEBR-05-2018-0336

Musara, M., & Nieuwenhuizen, C. (2020). Informal sector entrepreneurship, individual entrepreneurial orientation, and the emergence of entrepreneurial leadership. *Africa Journal of Management*, *6*(3), 194–213. DOI: 10.1080/23322373.2020.1777817

Muse, T. (2025, March 26). *COCA-COLA'S "TASTE THE FEELING" CAMPAIGN*. History Oasis.

Muth, M. M., & Donaldson, L. (1998). Stewardship theory and board structure: A contingency approach. *Corporate Governance*, *6*(1), 5–28. DOI: 10.1111/1467-8683.00076

Neneh, B. N. (2022). Entrepreneurial passion and entrepreneurial intention: The role of social support and entrepreneurial self-efficacy. *Studies in Higher Education*, *47*(3), 587–603. DOI: 10.1080/03075079.2020.1770716

Nenni, M. E., Di Pasquale, V., & Boyer, J. (2024). The Complicated relationship between innovation and sustainability: Opportunities, threats, challenges, and trends. *Sustainability (Basel), 16*(9), 3524. DOI: 10.3390/su16093524

*Nhai to issue green bonds worth rs. 1,000 crores.* (n.d.). Retrieved December 16, 2024, from https://pib.gov.in/pib.gov.in/Pressreleaseshare.aspx?PRID=2081146

Nilsson, J. (2001). Organisational principles for co-operative firms. *Scandinavian Journal of Management, 17*(3), 329–356. DOI: 10.1016/S0956-5221(01)00010-0

Noor Hazlina, A., Ramayah, T., Wilson, C., & Kummerow, L. (2010). Is entrepreneurial competency and business success relationship contigent upon business environment? A study of Malaysian SMEs. *Is Entrepreneurial Competency and Business Success Relationship Contigent upon Business Environment?A Study of Malaysian SMEs, 16*(3), 25. DOI: 10.1108/09574090910954864

Norman, P., & Hoyle, S. (2004). The theory of planned behavior and breast self-examination: Distinguishing between perceived control and self-efficacy. *Journal of Applied Social Psychology, 34*(4), 694–708. DOI: 10.1111/j.1559-1816.2004.tb02565.x

Ntim, C. G., & Osei, K. A. (2011). The impact of corporate board meetings on corporate performance in South Africa. *African Review of Economics and Finance, 2*(2), 83–103.

O'Gorman, C. (2019). *Entrepreneurial intentions and entrepreneurial behavior. Entrepreneurial Behaviour: Individual.* Contextual and Microfoundational Perspectives., DOI: 10.1007/978-3-030-04402-2_2

Oftedal, E. M., Foss, L., & Iakovleva, T. (2019). Responsible for responsibility? A study of digital e-health startups. *Sustainability (Basel), 11*(19), 5433. DOI: 10.3390/su11195433

Oguda, S. E. R. A. H. (2015). *Relationship between board characteristics and firm performance: Survey of firms listed at the Nairobi Securities Exchange* (Doctoral dissertation, University of Nairobi).

Ortmann, G. F., & King, R. P. (2007). Agricultural cooperatives I: History, theory and problems. *Agrekon, 46*(1), 40–68. DOI: 10.1080/03031853.2007.9523760

Öztürk, M. (2013). *Tüketici Ayartma ya da YoksullaşarakTüketme.Bauman Sosyolojisi (der. Zülküf Kara).* Ayrıntı Yayınları.S.

Pai, R. (2021). Nykaa: A comprehensive analysis of a leading Indian e-commerce cosmetic company. *International Journal of Case Studies in Business* [IJCSBE]. *IT and Education*, *5*(2), 354–365.

Pansuwong, W., Photchanachan, S., & Thechatakerng, P. (2023). Social innovation: Relationships with social and human capital, entrepreneurial competencies, and growth of social enterprises in a developing country context. *Social Enterprise Journal*, *19*(1), 51–79. DOI: 10.1108/SEJ-02-2022-0014

Paternoster, N., Giardino, C., Unterkalmsteiner, M., Gorschek, T., & Abrahamsson, P. (2014). Software development in startup companies: A systematic mapping study. *Information and Software Technology*, *56*(10), 1200–1218. DOI: 10.1016/j.infsof.2014.04.014

Peyton, P. R. (2004). *Dignity at work: Eliminate bullying and create a positive working environment*. Routledge. DOI: 10.4324/9780203420799

Pfattheicher, S., Nielsen, Y. A., & Thielmann, I. (2022). Prosocial behavior and altruism: A review of concepts and definitions. *Current Opinion in Psychology*, *44*, 124–129. DOI: 10.1016/j.copsyc.2021.08.021 PMID: 34627110

Pfeffer, J. (1978). *The external control of organization/Pfeffer J., Salancik G.* Harper&Row.

Pfeffer, J., & Salancik, G. (2015). External control of organizations—Resource dependence perspective. In *Organizational behavior 2* (pp. 355–370). Routledge.

Pizzi, S., Corbo, L., & Caputo, A. (2021). Fintech and SMEs sustainable business models: Reflections and considerations for a circular economy. *Journal of Cleaner Production*, *281*, 125217. DOI: 10.1016/j.jclepro.2020.125217

Polas, M. R. H., & Afshar Jahanshahi, A. (2021). The effects of individual characteristics on women intention to become social entrepreneurs? *Journal of Public Affairs*, *21*(2), e2204. DOI: 10.1002/pa.2204

Pollard, D. (2008). *Finding the sweet spot: the natural entrepreneur's guide to responsible, sustainable, joyful work*. Chelsea Green Publishing.

Ponnu, C. H., & Karthigeyan, R. M. (2010). Board independence and corporate performance: Evidence from Malaysia. *African Journal of Business Management*, *4*(6), 858.

Portes, A. (2000, March). The two meanings of social capital. [). Kluwer Academic Publishers-Plenum Publishers.]. *Sociological Forum*, *15*(1), 1–12. DOI: 10.1023/A:1007537902813

Prahalad, C. K. (2006). *The fortune at the bottom of the pyramid: eradicating poverty through profits*. Wharton SchoolPublishing.

Premadasa, M., Siyambalapitiya, J., Jayawardhana, K., & Fernando, I. (2023). Conceptualizing the role of social entrepreneurial orientation in the triple bottom line in the social enterprise context: Developing country perspective. *Sustainability (Basel), 15*(11), 8759. DOI: 10.3390/su15118759

Prihadyanti, D., Aziz, S. A., & Sari, K. (2023). Diffusion of social innovation: The innovation provider's perspective. *Journal of the Knowledge Economy*, •••, 1–55. https://link.springer.com/article/10.1007/s13132-023-01365-y

Project Management Institute. (2021). *PMBOK guide and standards | project management Institute*. https://www.pmi.org/pmbok-guide-standards

Pulka, B. M., Ramli, A., & Mohamad, A. (2021). Entrepreneurial competencies, entrepreneurial orientation, entrepreneurial network, government business support and SMEs performance. The moderating role of the external environment. *Journal of Small Business and Enterprise Development, 28*(4), 586–618. DOI: 10.1108/JSBED-12-2018-0390

Puri, D. L., & Sujarittanonta, L. (2016). Good Governance in Cooperatives of Nepal-Relationship between Participation and Performance of Cooperatives. *Journal of Education and Vocational Research, 7*(2), 19–26. DOI: 10.22610/jevr.v7i2.1335

Rana, M. S., Cavaliere, L. P. L., Mishra, A. B., Padhye, P., Singh, R. R., & Khanna, R (2022, April). . Internet of Things (IOT). Based Assessment for Effective Monitoring Data Against Malicious Attacks on Financial Collectors. In 2022 2nd International Conference on Advance Computing and Innovative Technologies in Engineering (ICACITE). (pp. 177-181). . IEEE.

Rana, M. S., Cavaliere, L. P. L., Mishra, A. B., Padhye, P., Singh, R. R., & Khanna, R. (2022, April) . Internet of Things (IOT) Based Assessment for Effective Monitoring Data Against Malicious Attacks on Financial Collectors. In 2022 2nd International Conference on Advance Computing and Innovative Technologies in Engineering (ICACITE) (pp. 177-181) . IEEE.

Rana, M. S., Cavaliere, L. P. L., Mishra, A. B., Padhye, P., Singh, R. R., & Khanna, R. (2022, April). Internet of Things (IOT) Based Assessment for Effective Monitoring Data Against Malicious Attacks on Financial Collectors. In 2022 2nd International Conference on Advance Computing and Innovative Technologies in Engineering (ICACITE) (pp. 177-181). IEEE.

Ranjan, N., Mishra, A. B., & Padhye, P. (2023). Dynamics of Digital Payments Enable the World's Safest Way to Pay. *Journal of Informatics Education and Research, 3*(2). Advance online publication. DOI: 10.52783/jier.v3i2.406

Rao, M. S (2016). . Tools and techniques to ensure innovative management education in India. *Industrial and Commercial Training, 48* (5)., 265–268. DOI: 10.1108/ICT-10-2015-0071

Rasmussen, E., Mosey, S., & Wright, M. (2011). The evolution of entrepreneurial competencies: A longitudinal study of University spin-off venture emergence. *Journal of Management Studies, 48*(6), 1314–1345. DOI: 10.1111/j.1467-6486.2010.00995.x

Rasyid, Y., & Bowen, R. (2021). Social Entrepreneurship: Policies and Practice in Malaysia. In Jones, P., Huxtable-Thomas, L., Hamidon, S., Hannon, P., & Mohd Tawil, N. (Eds.), *Entrepreneurial activity in Malaysia*. Palgrave Macmillan. DOI: 10.1007/978-3-030-77753-1_6

Raza, A., Muffatto, M., & Saeed, S. (2020). Cross-country differences in innovative entrepreneurial activity: An entrepreneurial cognitive view. *Management Decision, 58*(7), 1301–1329. DOI: 10.1108/MD-11-2017-1167

Research, K. L. D. (2007). *Environmental*. Social and Governance Rating Criteria.

*Reserve bank of india—Press releases*. (n.d.). Retrieved December 16, 2024, from https://www.rbi.org.in/scripts/BS_PressReleaseDisplay.aspx?prid=55004

Rosário, A. T., Raimundo, R., & Cruz, S. (2022). Sustainable Entrepreneurship: A Literature Review. *Sustainability (Basel), 14*(9), 5556. DOI: 10.3390/su14095556

Rosca, E., Agarwal, N., & Brem, A. (2020). Women entrepreneurs as agents of change: A comparative analysis of social entrepreneurship processes in emerging markets. *Technological Forecasting and Social Change, 157*, 120067. DOI: 10.1016/j.techfore.2020.120067

Roseland, M. (2000). Sustainable community development: Integrating environmental, economic, and social objectives. *Progress in Planning, 54*(2), 73–132. DOI: 10.1016/S0305-9006(00)00003-9

Roslan, M. H. H., Hamid, S., Ijab, M. T., Yusop, F. D., & Norman, A. A. (2022). Social entrepreneurship in higher education: Challenges and opportunities. *Asia Pacific Journal of Education, 42*(3), 588–604. DOI: 10.1080/02188791.2020.1859354

Roy, M. J., Donaldson, C., Baker, R., & Kay, A. (2013). Social enterprise: New pathways to health and well-being? *Journal of Public Health Policy, 34*(1), 55–68. DOI: 10.1057/jphp.2012.61 PMID: 23172049

Ruben, R., & Heras, J. (2012). Social capital, governance and performance of Ethiopian coffee cooperatives.

Ruben, R., & Heras, J. (2012, December). SOCIAL CAPITAL, GOVERNANCE AND PERFORMANCE OF ETHIOPIAN COFFEE COOPERATIVES. *Annals of Public and Cooperative Economics, 83*(4), 463–484. DOI: 10.1111/j.1467-8292.2012.00473.x

Saarijärvi, H., Karjaluoto, H., & Kuusela, H (2013).. Extending customer relationship management: From empowering firms to empowering customers. *Journal of Systems and Information Technology, 15* (2)., 140–158. DOI: 10.1108/13287261311328877

Sabah, S. (2016). Entrepreneurial intention: Theory of planned behavior and the moderation effect of start-up experience. In *Entrepreneurship-practice-oriented perspectives*. IntechOpen. DOI: 10.5772/65640

Sabri, M. S., & Thomas, K. (2019). Psycho-attitudinal features: A study of female entrepreneurs in Saudi Arabia. *International Journal of Gender and Entrepreneurship, 11*(4), 459–480. DOI: 10.1108/IJGE-02-2019-0036

Sánchez-Navarro, J. L., Arcas-Lario, N., Bijman, J., & Hernández-Espallardo, M. (2024). The role of agricultural cooperatives in mitigating opportunism in the context of complying with sustainability requirements: Empirical evidence from Spain. *Agricultural and Food Economics, 12*(1), 40. DOI: 10.1186/s40100-024-00332-8

Sarango-Lalangui, P., Santos, J. L. S., & Hormiga, E. (2018). The development of the sustainable entrepreneurship research field. *Sustainability (Basel), 10*(6), 2005. DOI: 10.3390/su10062005

Sarantakos, S. (1998). Measurement and scaling. In *Social Research* (pp. 72–95). Palgrave. DOI: 10.1007/978-1-349-14884-4_3

Satar, M. S., & Natasha, S. (2019). Individual social entrepreneurship orientation: Towards development of a measurement scale. *Asia Pacific Journal of Innovation and Entrepreneurship, 13*(1), 49–72. DOI: 10.1108/APJIE-09-2018-0052

Sauermann, H. (2018). Fire in the belly? Employee motives and innovative performance in start-ups versus established firms. *Strategic Entrepreneurship Journal, 12*(4), 423–454. DOI: 10.1002/sej.1267

Sayılı, M. (2008). Tarımda Örgütlenme Şekilleri.Yem Bitkilerive Meraya DayalıHayvancılık Eğitimi Kitabı, Erciyes Üniversitesi Yayınları, Yayın No:160, Kayseri.

Saz-Gil, I., Bretos, I., & Díaz-Foncea, M. (2021). Cooperatives and social capital: A narrative literature review and directions for future research. *Sustainability (Basel)*, *13*(2), 534. DOI: 10.3390/su13020534

Schick, H., Marxen, S., & Freimann, J. (2002). Sustainability issues for start-up entrepreneurs. *Greener Management International*, *38*, 59–70.

Schneider, H. (1999). Participatory governance for poverty reduction. *Journal of International Development*, *11*(4), 521–534. DOI: 10.1002/(SICI)1099-1328(199906)11:4<521::AID-JID599>3.0.CO;2-J

Scott, R. W. (1995). *Institutions and organizations: Ideas, interests, and identities*. Sage.

*Sebi | green debt securities*. (n.d.). Retrieved December 10, 2024, from https://www.sebi.gov.in/statistics/greenbonds.html

Sehnem, S., Lara, A. C., Benetti, K., Schneider, K., Marcon, M. L., & da Silva, T. H. H. (2023). Improving startups through excellence initiatives: Addressing circular economy and innovation. *Environment, Development and Sustainability*, *26*(6), 1–47. https://link.springer.com/article/10.1007/s10668-023-03247-4. DOI: 10.1007/s10668-023-03247-4 PMID: 37362985

Sekaran, U., & Bougie, R. (2016). *Research methods for business* (7th ed.). John Wiley & Sons Ltd.

Sen, A. K. (2000). 'The ends and means of sustainability', keynote address at the International Conference on Transition to sustainability, Tokyo, May.

Sen, A. (2013). *A survey of sustainable development: social and economic dimensions* (Vol. 6). Island Press.

Sendawula, K., Turyakira, P., Ikiror, C. M., & Bagire, V. (2021). Regulatory compliance and environmental sustainability practices of manufacturing entrepreneurial ventures in Uganda. *Asia Pacific Journal of Innovation and Entrepreneurship*, *15*(1), 62–74. DOI: 10.1108/APJIE-08-2020-0122

Sethi, I. P. S. (2023). *Digital Payments driving the growth of Digital Economy*. National Informatics Centre.

Seyfi, S., Vo-Thanh, T., & Zaman, M. (2024). Hospitality in the age of Gen Z: A critical reflection on evolving customer and workforce expectations. *International Journal of Contemporary Hospitality Management*, *36*(13), 118–134. DOI: 10.1108/IJCHM-01-2024-0035

Sharifah Syahirah, S. S., Fatimah Bibi, H., & Muhd Bazli, H. (2018, March). Leadership, policy and governance in Malaysia: A study on gen Y perception and expectation. In *International Conference on Kansei Engineering & Emotion Research* (pp. 683-691). Singapore: Springer Singapore. DOI: 10.1007/978-981-10-8612-0_71

Sharma, V., Manohar, S., & Carril, V. P. I. (2024). Exploring challenges for sustainable development among circular startups in India. *Environment, Development and Sustainability*. Advance online publication. DOI: 10.1007/s10668-024-04555-z

Shi, L., Yao, X., & Wu, W. (2019). Perceived university support, entrepreneurial self-efficacy, heterogeneous entrepreneurial intentions in entrepreneurship education: The moderating role of the Chinese sense of face. *Journal of Entrepreneurship in Emerging Economies*, *12*(2), 205–230. DOI: 10.1108/JEEE-04-2019-0040

Singh, T. (2020). *Fintech Adoption: A Critical Appraisal of the Strategies of Paytm in India*.

Singh, A., Rishi, M., & Shukla, R. (2011). Green management and environmental sustainability: A case of ITC Green Center. *Emerald Emerging Markets Case Studies*, *1*(2), 1–13. DOI: 10.1108/20450621111159859

Sivertsen, G. (2018). The norwegian model in Norway. *Journal of Data and Information Science*, *3*(4), 3–19. DOI: 10.2478/jdis-2018-0017

Slaus, I., & Jacobs, D. (2011). Human capital and sustainable development: A critical review. In *Human Capital and Sustainable Development* (pp. 1–10). Springer.

Smith, A. Y. (2015). *Indicators for nurse educators' intention to use critical thinking indicators for nurse educators' intention to use critical thinking teaching strategies: A structural equation model analysis teaching strategies: A structural equation model analysis*. https://digitalcommons.andrews.edu/dissertations/1576

Sobel, P. J., & Reding, K. F. (2004). Aligning corporate governance performance measurement and corporate governance. *Management accounting*.

Soykut, R. H. (1980). İnsanlık Bilimi Ahilik.Ankara: HalkBankası Yayınları. TDK, 2020. Türk Dil Kurumu. https://tr.search.yahoo.com/search?fr=mcafee_uninternational&type=E210TR91105G0&p=tdk (Acces dade:11 October 2023).

Sparviero, S. (2019). The case for a socially oriented business model canvas: The social enterprise model canvas. *Journal of Social Entrepreneurship*, *10*(2), 232–251. DOI: 10.1080/19420676.2018.1541011

Spyropoulos, T. S. (2020). Knowledge management challenges for start-ups: A framework proposal. *International Journal of Entrepreneurship and Business Development*.

Sreejesh, S., Mohapatra, S., & Anusree, M. R. (2014). *Business research methods: An applied orientation.*

Sreenivasan, A., Ma, S., Rehman, A. U., & Muthuswamy, S. (2023). Assessment of factors influencing agility in startups industry 4.0. *Sustainability (Basel), 15*(9), 7564. https://www.mdpi.com/2071-1050/15/9/7564. DOI: 10.3390/su15097564

Sreenivasan, A., & Suresh, M. (2022). Green startups: Startups accelerating sustainability. *International Journal of Global Business and Competitiveness, 18*(1), 80–89. DOI: 10.1007/s42943-022-00068-6

Sreenivasan, A., & Suresh, M. (2023). Startup sustainability: Does blockchain adoption drive sustainability in startups? A systematic literature review. *Management Research Review*. Advance online publication. DOI: 10.1108/MRR-07-2022-0519

Sreenu, N. (2024). Examining the dynamics of risk associated with green investment in India: A study on fintech and green bonds for clean energy production. *Journal of Economic Studies (Glasgow, Scotland)*. Advance online publication. DOI: 10.1108/JES-12-2023-0680

Srivastava, A. K., Jonjua Mehak, & Rana Rajesh. (2019). Status of Communicating CSR to Stakeholders on Social Media : A Case Study on ITC Limited & Nestle India. *Journal of Content. Community & Communication, 9*, 81–92.

Stirzaker, R., Galloway, L., Muhonen, J., & Christopoulos, D. (2021). The drivers of social entrepreneurship: Agency, context, compassion, and opportunism. *International Journal of Entrepreneurial Behaviour & Research, 27*(6), 1381–1402. DOI: 10.1108/IJEBR-07-2020-0461

Stoop, E., Brandsen, T., & Helderman, J. K. (2021). The impact of the cooperative structure on organizational social capital. *Social Enterprise Journal, 17*(4), 548–565. DOI: 10.1108/SEJ-08-2020-0063

Sudirman, I., Siswanto, J., & Aisha, A. N. (2020). Software entrepreneurs' competencies based on business growth. *Journal of Research in Marketing and Entrepreneurship, 22*(1), 111–132. DOI: 10.1108/JRME-12-2017-0055

Sukendia, J., & Harianto, N. (2021). The impact of e-service quality on customer engagement, customer experience and customer loyalty in B2C e-commerce. [TURCOMAT]. *Turkish Journal of Computer and Mathematics Education, 12*(3), 3170–3184.

Sun, J., Shi, J., & Zhang, J. (2023). From entrepreneurship education to entrepreneurial intention: Mindset, motivation, and prior exposure. *Frontiers in Psychology, 14*, 14. DOI: 10.3389/fpsyg.2023.954118 PMID: 36891213

Sunny, J., Undralla, N., & Madhusudanan Pillai, V (2020). . Supply chain transparency through blockchain-based traceability: An overview with demonstration. *Computers & Industrial Engineering*, *150*, 106895. DOI: 10.1016/j.cie.2020.106895

Surroca, J., Tribó, J. A., & Waddock, S. (2010). Corporate responsibility and financialperformance: The role of intangible resources. *Strategic Management Journal*, *31*(5), 463–490. DOI: 10.1002/smj.820

Swingewood, A. (1998). *Sosyolojik Düşüncenin Kısa Tarihi (Çev.Osman Akınhay)*. Bilim ve Sanat Yayınları.

Tajpour, M., Hosseini, E., & Mohiuddin, M. (2023). Effects of innovative climate, knowledge sharing, and communication on the sustainability of digital startups: Does social media matter? *Journal of Open Innovation*, *9*(2), 100053. DOI: 10.1016/j.joitmc.2023.100053

Tang, T. Y., Zhang, S. K., & Peng, J. (2021). The value of marketing innovation: Market-driven versus market-driving. *Journal of Business Research*, *126*, 88–98. DOI: 10.1016/j.jbusres.2020.12.067

Tavanti, M. (2023). Assessing and measuring sustainability impact. In *Sustainable development goals series* (pp. 453–473). DOI: 10.1007/978-3-031-36907-0_17

Tay, R. (2017). Correlation, variance inflation and multicollinearity in regression model. *Journal of the Eastern Asia Society for Transportation Studies*, *12*, 2006–2015.

Tefera, D. A., Bijman, J., & Slingerland, M. A. (2017). Agricultural co-operatives in Ethiopia: Evolution, functions and impact. *Journal of International Development*, *29*(4), 431–453. DOI: 10.1002/jid.3240

Thananusak, T. (2019). Science mapping of the knowledge base on sustainable entrepreneurship, 1996–2019. *Sustainability (Basel)*, *11*(13), 3565. DOI: 10.3390/su11133565

Tien, N. H., Anh, D. B. H., Ngoc, N. M., & Do Thi, Y. N. (2019). Sustainable social entrepreneurship in Vietnam. *International Journal of Entrepreneurship*, *23*(3), 1–12.

Tillmar, M., Sköld, B., Ahl, H., Berglund, K., & Pettersson, K. (2022). Women's rural businesses: For economic viability or gender equality?–A database study from the Swedish context. *International Journal of Gender and Entrepreneurship*, *14*(3), 323–351. DOI: 10.1108/IJGE-06-2021-0091

Tittel, A., & Terzidis, O. (2020). Entrepreneurial competences revised: Developing a consolidated and categorized list of entrepreneurial competences. *Entrepreneurship Education*, *3*(1), 1–35. DOI: 10.1007/s41959-019-00021-4

Toker, K. (2021). From social sustainability to social entrepreneurship: a path for social value creation. In *Creating Social Value Through Social Entrepreneurship* (pp. 1–31). IGI Global. DOI: 10.4018/978-1-7998-4727-4.ch001

Tolety, R. K. (2018). E-Wallets–Their cause, Rise and Relevance. *International. Journal of Research in IT and Management, 8*(7).

Tolfo, C., Wazlawick, R. S., Gitirana, M., Ferreira, G., Fernando, I., & Forcellini, A. (2018). Agile practices and the promotion of entrepreneurial skills in software development. *Journal of Software (Malden, MA), 30*(9), e1945. Advance online publication. DOI: 10.1002/smr.1945

Tönnissen, S., Beinke, J. H., & Teuteberg, F. (2020). Understanding token-based ecosystems–a taxonomy of blockchain-based business models of startups. *Electronic Markets, 30*(2), 307–323. https://link.springer.com/article/10.1007/s12525-020-00396-6. DOI: 10.1007/s12525-020-00396-6

Trautwein, C. (2021). Sustainability impact assessment of start-ups–Key insights on relevant assessment challenges and approaches based on an inclusive, systematic literature review. *Journal of Cleaner Production, 281*, 125330. DOI: 10.1016/j.jclepro.2020.125330

Trejo-Pech, C. O., Servín-Juárez, R., & Reyes-Duarte, Á. (2023). What sets cooperative farmers apart from non-cooperative farmers? A transaction cost economics analysis of coffee farmers in Mexico. *Agricultural and Food Economics, 11*(1), 14. DOI: 10.1186/s40100-023-00256-9

Tsay, W. J. (1998). On the power of Durbin-Watson statistic against fractionally integrated processes. *Econometric Reviews, 17*(4), 361–386. DOI: 10.1080/07474939808800423

Tseng, M., Chang, C., Lin, C., Wu, K., Chen, Q., Xia, L., & Xue, B. (2020). Future trends and guidance for the triple bottom line and sustainability: A data-driven bibliometric analysis. *Environmental Science and Pollution Research International, 27*(27), 33543–33567. DOI: 10.1007/s11356-020-09284-0 PMID: 32572746

Tsordia, C., & Papadimitriou, D. (2015). The role of theory of planned behavior on entrepreneurial intention of greek business students. *International Journal of Synergy and Research*. DOI: 10.17951/ijsr.2015.4.1.23

Turan, N., Kara, M., Gürbüz, M., & Sarıtaş, D. Ö. (2011). Konut Yapı Kooperatifçiliği.Anadolu Üniversitesi Yayın No: 2541, Açıköğretim Fakültesi Yayın No: 1512.http://ds.anadolu.edu.tr/eKitap/EMY201U.pdf

Tura, N., Van Tulder, R., & Muche, M. (2019). Business model innovation for sustainability: Evidence from the circular economy. *Journal of Cleaner Production, 215*, 1241–1249.

Ünal, Ü. A., & Taşçıoğlu, M. (2022). Sustainable, therefore reputable: Linking sustainability, reputation, and consumer behaviour. *Marketing Intelligence & Planning, 40*(4), 497–512. DOI: 10.1108/MIP-03-2022-0102

Urban, B. (2020). Entrepreneurial alertness, self-efficacy, and social entrepreneurship intentions. *Journal of Small Business and Enterprise Development, 27*(3), 489–507. DOI: 10.1108/JSBED-08-2019-0285

Urbano, D., Aparicio, S., & Audretsch, D. (2019). Twenty-five years of research on institutions, entrepreneurship, and economic growth: What has been learned? *Small Business Economics, 53*(1), 21–49. DOI: 10.1007/s11187-018-0038-0

Urdea, A. M., & Constantin, C. P. (2021). Exploring the impact of customer experience on customer loyalty in e-commerce. *InProceedings of the International Conference on Business Excellence, 15*(1), 672–682. DOI: 10.2478/picbe-2021-0063

Usman M, Sheoliha N, Prabhakar P V, Mishra, A. B., & Dondapati. (2023). Leading Strategies for Organizational Adaptation and Growth in Digital Transformation in Marketing. *Journal of Informatics Education and Research.*

Usman, M. S., Sheoliha, N., Prabhakar, P. V., Mishra, A. B., & Dondapati, A (2023). . Leading Strategies for Organizational Adaptation and Growth in Digital Transformation in Marketing. Journal of Informatics Education and Research.

Usman, M. S., Sheoliha, N., Prabhakar, P. V., Mishra, A. B., & Dondapati, A. (2023) . Leading Strategies for Organizational Adaptation and Growth in Digital Transformation in Marketing. Journal of Informatics Education and Research.

Usman, M. S., Sheoliha, N., Prabhakar, P. V., Mishra, A. B., & Dondapati, A. (2023). Leading Strategies for Organizational Adaptation and Growth in Digital Transformation in Marketing. Journal of Informatics Education and Research.

Vafeas, N. (1999). Board meeting frequency and firm performance. *Journal of Financial Economics, 53*(1), 113–142. DOI: 10.1016/S0304-405X(99)00018-5

Valentinov, V., & Iliopoulos, C. (2021). Social capital in cooperatives: An evolutionary Luhmannian perspective. *Journal of Evolutionary Economics, 31*(4), 1317–1331. DOI: 10.1007/s00191-021-00744-5

Vallance, S., Perkins, H. C., & Dixon, J. E. (2011). What is social sustainability? A clarification of concepts. *Geoforum, 42*(3), 342–348. DOI: 10.1016/j.geoforum.2011.01.002

Van der Vegt, G. S., Van de Vliert, E., & Huang, X. (2005). Location-level links between diversity and innovative climate depend on national power distance. *Academy of Management Journal, 48*(6), 1171–1182. DOI: 10.5465/amj.2005.19573116

van Ewijk, A. R., & Belghiti-Mahut, S. (2019). Context, gender, and entrepreneurial intentions: How entrepreneurship education changes the equation. *International Journal of Gender and Entrepreneurship, 11*(1), 75–98. DOI: 10.1108/IJGE-05-2018-0054

Varma, S. R., & Mishra, A. B (2015). . Study of Consumer Buying Behaviour in General Insurance Industry. In *Excellence through creativity, Research, innovation in field of IT and Management.*

Varma, S. R., & Mishra, A. B. (2015). Study of Consumer Buying Behaviour in General Insurance Industry. In *Excellence through creativity, Research, innovation in field of IT and Management.*

Varma, S. R., & Mishra, A. B (2013). . *Distribution Channels of Indian Insurance Business - A Study*. Abhinavan.

Varnum, M. E. W., & Grossmann, I. (2021). The psychology of cultural change: Introduction to the special issue. *American Psychologist/the American Psychologist, 76*(6), 833–837. DOI: 10.1037/amp0000898

Varol, B. (2024, Ocak). Fındıklı Belediyesi'nden Geliri Öğrencilere Burs Verilmesi Üzerine "Fındık Mecisi"... Başkan Çervatoğlu: "Bütün Kötülüklere Karşı İyilik Bulaşıcıdır". 12.08.2023. https://ankahaber.net/haber/detay/findikli_belediyesinden_geliri_ogrencilere_burs_verilmesi_uzerine_findik_mecisi_baskan_cervatoglu_butun_kotuluklere_karsi_iyilik_bulasicidir_150370

Vendrell-Herrero, F., Bustinza, O. F., & Opazo-Basaez, M (2021). . Information technologies and product-service innovation: The moderating role of service R&D team structure. *Journal of Business Research, 128*, 673–687. DOI: 10.1016/j.jbusres.2020.01.047

Vezzoli, C., Ceschin, F., & Diehl, J. C. (2021). Product-service systems development for sustainability. A new understanding. In *Lecture notes in mechanical engineering* (pp. 1–21). DOI: 10.1007/978-3-030-66300-1_1

Vogel, P., & Fischler-Strasak, U. (2013). Fostering sustainable innovation within organizations. In *Sustainable Entrepreneurship: Business Success through Sustainability* (pp. 191–205). Springer Berlin Heidelberg.

Voinea, C. L., Logger, M., Rauf, F., & Roijakkers, N. (2019). Drivers for sustainable business models in start-ups: Multiple case studies. *Sustainability (Basel), 11*(24), 6884. DOI: 10.3390/su11246884

Volery, T., Mueller, S., & von Siemens, B. (2015). Entrepreneur ambidexterity: A study of entrepreneur behaviors and competencies in growth-oriented small and medium-sized enterprises. *International Small Business Journal, 33*(2), 109–129. DOI: 10.1177/0266242613484777

Vrontis, D., Makrides, A., Christofi, M., & Thrassou, A. (2021). Social media influencer marketing: A systematic review, integrative framework and future research agenda. *International Journal of Consumer Studies, 45*(4), 617–644. DOI: 10.1111/ijcs.12647

Wadewitz, C. D. (2023). FOMENT: Promoting technology acceleration and adoption in the Australian and international wine tourism industry. In *Technology Advances and Innovation in Wine Tourism: New Managerial Approaches and Cases* (pp. 153-181). Singapore: Springer Nature Singapore. https://link.springer.com/chapter/10.1007/978-981-19-8277-4_10

Wagner, D. A. (2014). Literacy. In *Handbook of cultural developmental science* (pp. 161–173). Psychology Press.

Walljasper, J. (2015). *Müştereklerimiz*. Metis Yayınları.

Wang, H., Lin, Q. P., & Zhang, H. H. (2011). Entrepreneurial competencies of college students: A qualitative analysis. *Proceedings of the 2011 International Conference on Business Computing and Global Informatization, BCGIn 2011*, 550–553. DOI: 10.1109/BCGIn.2011.145

Wang, X., Cai, L., Zhu, X., & Deng, S. (2020). Female entrepreneurs' gender roles, social capital, and willingness to choose external financing. *Asian Business & Management*, •••, 1–26. DOI: 10.1057/s41291-020-00131-1

Weaver, R. L. (2023). The impact of COVID-19 on the social enterprise sector. *Journal of Social Entrepreneurship, 14*(2), 177–185. DOI: 10.1080/19420676.2020.1861476

Wei, X., Ren, H., Ullah, S., & Bozkurt, C. (2023). Does environmental entrepreneurship play a role in sustainable green development? Evidence from emerging Asian economies. *Ekonomska Istrazivanja, 36*(1), 73–85. DOI: 10.1080/1331677X.2022.2067887

Wells, E. C., Lehigh, G. R., & Vidmar, A. M. (2021). Stakeholder engagement for sustainable communities. In *Springer eBooks* (pp. 1–13). DOI: 10.1007/978-3-030-38948-2_10-1

Wheeler, S. (2013). *Planning for sustainability: creating livable, equitable and ecological communities*. Routledge. DOI: 10.4324/9780203134559

White, K. J. (1992). The Durbin-Watson test for autocorrelation in nonlinear models. *The Review of Economics and Statistics, 74*(2), 370–373. DOI: 10.2307/2109675

Wijayati, D. T., Fazlurrahman, H., Hadi, H. K., & Arifah, I. D. C. (2021). The effect of entrepreneurship education on entrepreneurial intention through planned behavioral control, subjective norm, and entrepreneurial attitude. *Journal of Global Entrepreneurship Research*, •••, 1–14.

Williamson, O. E. (1979). Transaction-cost economics: The governance of contractual relations. *The Journal of Law & Economics, 22*(2), 233–261. DOI: 10.1086/466942

Woodcraft, S. (2015). Understanding and measuring social sustainability. *Journal of Urban Regeneration and Renewal, 8*(2), 133–144. DOI: 10.69554/VRWG6415

Wu, J. (2013). Landscape sustainability science: Ecosystem services and human well-being in changing landscapes. *Landscape Ecology, 28*(6), 999–1023. DOI: 10.1007/s10980-013-9894-9

Wulandhari, N. B. I., Gölgeci, I., Mishra, N., Sivarajah, U., & Gupta, S. (2022). Exploring the role of social capital mechanisms in cooperative resilience. *Journal of Business Research, 143*, 375–386. DOI: 10.1016/j.jbusres.2022.01.026

Wu, Y. J., Wu, T., & Arno Sharpe, J. (2020). Consensus on the definition of social entrepreneurship: A content analysis approach. *Management Decision, 58*(12), 2593–2619. DOI: 10.1108/MD-11-2016-0791

Xi, J., Lee, M. T., Carter, J. R., & Delgado, D. (2022). Gender differences in purpose in life: The mediation effect of altruism. *Journal of Humanistic Psychology, 62*(3), 352–376. DOI: 10.1177/0022167818777658

Xu, P., & Shen, Y. (2015). Leading agile teams: An exploratory study of leadership styles in agile software development. *2015 Americas Conference on Information Systems, AMCIS 2015*, 1–7. https://www.scopus.com/inward/record.uri?eid=2-s2.0-84963575828&partnerID=40&md5=0646ff65636eab9aded104faaee7d02c

Yadav, P., & Mathew, J. (2022). Educational perspective & antecedental outcomes of green HRM for employee's sustainable behaviour. *Journal for ReAttach Therapy and Developmental Diversities, 5*(1s), 95–101.

Yadav, P., & Mathew, J. (2023). Improving organizational environmental performance through green training. In *Implications of Industry 5.0 on Environmental Sustainability* (pp. 116–131). IGI Global. DOI: 10.4018/978-1-6684-6113-6.ch006

Yadav, P., & Mathew, J. (2023). Improving Organizational Sustainable Performance of Organizations Through Green Training. [IJSESD]. *International Journal of Social Ecology and Sustainable Development, 14*(1), 1–11. DOI: 10.4018/IJSESD.321166

Yaghoubi Farani, A., Karimi, S., & Motaghed, M. (2017). The role of entrepreneurial knowledge as a competence in shaping Iranian students' career intentions to start a new digital business. *European Journal of Training and Development, 41*(1), 83–100. DOI: 10.1108/EJTD-07-2016-0054

Yanık, S., & Türker, İ. (2012). Sürdürülebilirlik ve sosyal sorumluluk raporlamasındaki gelişmeler (Tümleşik Raporlama). İstanbul Üniversitesi Siyasal Bilgiler Fakültesi Dergisi, (47).

Yermack, D. (2006). Board members and company value. *Financial Markets and Portfolio Management, 20*(1), 33–47. DOI: 10.1007/s11408-006-0003-9

Yücel, Ş., & Baki, B. (2020). Türklerde "İmece" ve "Kooperatifleşme" Kültürüne Bir Bakış. *Turkish Journal of Agriculture - Food Science and Technology, 8*, 155–159.

Zachow, M., & Bertolini, G. R. F. (2019). Use of Balanced Scorecard in Cooperatives. [IJAERS]. *International Journal of Advanced Engineering Research and Science, 6*(10), 160–166. DOI: 10.22161/ijaers.610.25

Zapkau, F. B., Schwens, C., Steinmetz, H., & Kabst, R. (2015). Disentangling the effect of prior entrepreneurial exposure on entrepreneurial intention. *Journal of Business Research, 68*(3), 639–653. DOI: 10.1016/j.jbusres.2014.08.007

Zencirkıran, M. (2021). *Sosyoloji*. Dora Yayıncılık. Journal of Vocational and Social Sciences of Turkey.

Zhang, L. (2012). Board demographic diversity, independence, and corporate social performance. *Corporate Governance (Bradford), 12*(5), 686–700. DOI: 10.1108/14720701211275604

Zhu, Y., & Wu, Y. (2021). Green bond financing development research in china. *2021 5th Annual International Conference on Data Science and Business Analytics (ICDSBA)*, 463–469. DOI: 10.1109/ICDSBA53075.2021.00095

Zhu, B., Liang, C., Mirza, N., & Umar, M. (2023). What drives gearing in early-stage firms? Evidence from blue economy startups. *Journal of Business Research, 161*, 113840. DOI: 10.1016/j.jbusres.2023.113840

Zubeltzu-Jaka, E., Álvarez-Etxeberria, I., & Ortas, E. (2020). The effect of the size of the board of directors on corporate social performance: A meta-analytic approach. *Corporate Social Responsibility and Environmental Management, 27*(3), 1361–1374. DOI: 10.1002/csr.1889

Zulfiqar, S., Sarwar, B., Aziz, S., Ejaz Chandia, K., & Khan, M. K. (2019). An analysis of influence of business simulation games on business school students' attitude and intention toward entrepreneurial activities. *Journal of Educational Computing Research, 57*(1), 106–130. DOI: 10.1177/0735633117746746

# About the Contributors

**A. B. Mishra** is an Associate Professor and as the Dean (Academics) at the International Institute of Management Studies, Pune, India, with a PhD in Business Management and extensive corporate experience in Sales & Marketing with top multinational companies. Blending industry expertise with academic rigor, he has been instrumental in bridging theory with practical application. An alumnus of the Faculty Development Program at IIM Kozhikode, He has actively participated in high-profile nationally and internationally seminars, conferences, and workshops across renowned educational and corporate settings. His experience extends internationally, with participation in an International Immersion Program that broadened his global perspective. His research contributions are published in respected journals, including Scopus, ABDC, and Web of Science, and he is also an accomplished author and patent holder, showcasing his diverse impact in the field. His research interests span Disruptive Innovations, Phygital, Banking & Insurance, Sales and Marketing, Sustainability, E-business, Artificial Intelligence (AI), Internet of Things (IoT), and Sustainable Consumer perception. Beyond research, he is passionate about developing future business leaders through teach core courses like Marketing Management, Sales and distribution Management, B2B Marketing and so on. His dynamic, holistic approach to teaching motivates students to excel in the fast-evolving world of business and academia.

***

**Mohd Zaidi Abd Rozan**, Associate Professor in Information Systems at Faculty of Management. Previously, he served as the Director of UTM XCITE, a university-level centre for innovation and entrepreneurship building between UTM community and external stakeholders. He has over 27 years of experience in private and public organizations and has been an entrepreneur since 1993. He has BSc, M.IT and D. Eng in Information Science and Control Engineering in 2007 from Japan and a

Diploma in Digital Entrepreneurship in 2020. Dr. Zaidi continues his professional development, having recently been selected as one of 16 worldwide participants of the International Visitors Leadership Program (IVLP) USA focusing on the Science and Technology Entrepreneurship Inter-Regional Project. He also led the Impact Digital Entrepreneurship Apprentice@KPT National Program, and just recently completed a Master's Program in Data Scientist. Since 2013, he has accumulated 1.53 million industry grants and 2.03 million public grants from the Ministry of Higher Education Malaysia on projects relating to entrepreneurship development. Actively involved in coaching and mentoring start-ups, he has assisted many projects or enterprises owned by young entrepreneurs. This applies mainly to technologically driven enterprises within the domain of Computing and Electronics.

**Ajey Kumar** is a passionate researcher and faculty. He is working as an Associate Professor in Symbiosis Centre for Information Technology, SIU, Pune, India.His research work has been published in reputed journal and conferences. Actively associated as a TPC member / reviewer for various international conferences and refereed journals. His research interest includes Wireless/Mobile Computing, Location based Services,Cloud Computing, Internet of Things, Online Social Networks, Software Defined Networks and Big Data Analytics.

**Joseph Varghese Kureethara** is a professor of Mathematics at Christ University. He has over eighteen years of experience in teaching and research at Christ University, Bengaluru. He has published over 170 articles on Graph Theory, Number Theory, History, Religious Studies and Sports in English and Malayalam. Kureethara has co-edited five books, including Recent Trends in Signal and Image Processing, Neuro-Systemic Applications in Learning and Data Science and Security, and authored five books. His blog articles, comments, facts and poems have earned about 1.7 lakh pageviews. He has delivered invited talks at over fifty conferences and workshops. He is a member of the Editorial Board and a reviewer of several journals. He has worked as a member of several institutions' Board of Studies, Board of Examiners and Management Committees. He was the Director, Centre for Research, Christ University and was its Personnel Officer. He has supervised 8 PhDs and 12 MPhils, and is supervising 7 PhD scholars.

**Amirah Mohamad Fuzi** is a Ph.D. candidate in the Faculty of Education, Universiti Malaya, Kuala Lumpur, Malaysia. Her main research activity is organizational studies, leadership, and educational management. She has published widely on these subjects in publications such as An-Nisbah: Jurnal Ekonomi Syariah and the Journal of Entrepreneurship and Public Policy. She can be reached through her email at amirah21@um.edu.my.

**Nurul Hidayana Mohd Noor**, Ph.D. is Senior Lecturer in Faculty of Administrative Science and Policy Studies, Universiti Teknologi MARA (UiTM), Seremban, Negeri Sembilan, Malaysia. Her main research activity is entrepreneurship, environmental, nonprofit, organizational management, and youth studies. She has published widely on these subjects in publications such as the Journal of Entrepreneurship in Emerging Economies, Journal of Entrepreneurship and Public Policy, and Human Service Organizations: Management, Leadership & Governance. She can be reached through her email at hidayana@uitm.edu.my.

**Surjit Singha** is a dedicated researcher interested in UN Sustainable Development Goals, Organizational Climate, Workforce Diversity, Organizational Culture, HRM, Marketing, Finance, IB, Global Business, Business, AI, Women Studies, and Cultural Studies. Currently serving as a faculty member in the Department of Commerce at Kristu Jayanti College (Autonomous), Dr. Surjit holds prestigious positions as Editor, reviewer, and author for renowned Global Publications and Journals. With over 13 years of extensive experience in Administration, Teaching, and Research, both in Industry and Higher Education Institutions (HEIs), Dr. Surjit is committed to imparting knowledge and guiding students in their research pursuits. As a research mentor, Dr. Surjit is vital in nurturing young minds and fostering academic growth. Leading a team of approximately 35 faculty members, Dr. Surjit also heads website management, promotion, and social media publicity efforts. Dedicated to continuous learning, Dr. Surjit boasts certifications as a Life Skill Trainer by RGNYID, a Microsoft Innovative Educator by Microsoft, and a Yoga Volunteer certified by The Yoga Certification Board, Ministry of AYUSH, Gov. of India. A trailblazer in academia, Dr. Surjit has guided and mentored 21 student projects in the academic year 2022-23, resulting in all 21 students publishing papers under Dr. Surjit's astute guidance. As NSS Faculty Mentor, Dr. Surjit has successfully mentored 65 students in the academic year 2022-23, ensuring all students achieve credits and qualifications. Dr. Surjit Singha has made substantial contributions to research with an impressive track record of over 65 publications as articles, including chapters in books, edited books, and various textbooks. Dr. Surjit continues to excel in academia after being granted 2 US Copyrights and receiving two fully funded minor research projects (Completed and Published) from Kristu Jayanti College (Autonomous). With a firm commitment to excellence in education and research, Dr. Surjit Singha elevates the institution's status and fosters an environment of knowledge dissemination and growth.

**Preksha Yadav**, an alumna of IIM-Indore, possesses extensive experience of over fourteen years in academia, research, and administration. Currently serving as an Assistant Professor at JAIN (Deemed-to-be University), she holds a UGC-NET qualification. Additionally, she has served as a corporate trainer, imparting valuable knowledge on stress management, leadership, interpersonal skills, and life skills to employees in both public and private sectors. Prof. Yadav's research interests span multiple disciplines, including Sustainability, Green HRM, Digital Wellbeing, Mental Health, and Online Learning, among others. Her scholarly contributions include more than 15 publications, encompassing research papers, articles, and book chapters. She has actively participated in over 20 national and international conferences held across the country. She has obtained 2 patents and authored 1 book.

# Index

## A



## B



## C



## D



## E



## F



## G

## H



## I



## M



## N



## O



## P



## Q



## R

# Index

## A



## B



## C



## D



## E



## F



## G

## H



## I



## M



## N



## O



## P



## Q



## R

## S



## T



## U



## W



## Y

www.ingramcontent.com/pod-product-compliance
Lightning Source LLC
LaVergne TN
LVHW061550290926
849162LV00004B/965